Chabad - Lubavitch
of Fairfield County
Third Annual Dinner
2 Adar I 5757 - February 9. 1997

With best wishes to the Honoree's

Carl & Dorothy Bennett

TORAH STUDIES

≈≈

Discourses by the
LUBAVITCHER REBBE
Rabbi Menachem M. Schneerson
זצוקללה"ה נבג"מ זי"ע

≈≈

Adapted by
Rabbi Jonathan Sacks
Chief Rabbi of Great Britain

Published by
KEHOT PUBLICATION SOCIETY
770 Eastern Parkway • Brooklyn, N.Y. 11213
5756 • 1996

TORAH STUDIES
NEW REVISED EDITION
Copyright © 1996

First edition 1986 by Lubavitch Foundation, UK
Second printing 1990
Third printing 1992

Kehot Publication Society
770 Eastern Parkway / Brooklyn, New York 11213
(718) 774-4000 / FAX (718) 774-2718

Order Department:
291 Kingston Avenue / Brooklyn, New York 11213
(718) 778-0226 / FAX (718) 778-4148

ISBN 0-8266-0493-5

Printed in the United States of America

TABLE OF CONTENTS

INTRODUCTION VII

FOREWORD TO THE NEW EDITION... XI

BEREISHIT

BEREISHIT: The mystery of Light....................................... 1

NOACH: The fault you see in others is your own........................ 6

LECH LECHA: Descent in order to rise................................. 10

VAYERA: Abraham's decision to be circumcised......................... 16

CHAYEI SARAH: A life of perfection transcends death................. 21

TOLEDOT: Four interpretations, each expressing freedom.............. 28

VAYYETZE: Understanding the "forbidden" marriages of Jacob.......... 36

VAYISHLACH: "Jacob" and "Israel"—two aspects of the Jew 42

VAYESHEV: Joseph's dreams and their meaning......................... 48

CHANUKAH: Illuminating the outer realms of darkness................. 55

MIKKETZ: The distinction between
the sacred and the secular... 60

VAYIGASH: Joseph's heritage to every Jew today 66

VAYECHI: The disclosure of the end of days 71

SHEMOT

SHEMOT: Moses and the Messiah....................................... 77

VAERA: Knowledge, Emotion and Action 84

BO: The uniqueness of the final plague in Egypt.................... 91

BESHALACH: Analysis of a miracle—the division of the Sea 97

YITRO: Two paths—the righteous man,
    and the man of repentance 103

MISHPATIM: Action and intention in the keeping of Torah law... 112

TERUMAH: Building an inner Sanctuary 119

TETZAVEH: The Altars of copper and of gold 124

PURIM: Finding the joy in the hidden face of G-d 128

KI TISSA: Vacillation and idolatry.. 135

VAYAKHEL: The spirit of Shabbat 141

PEKUDEI: The dialogue between G-d and man.............................. 148

V A Y I K R A

VAYIKRA: Animal sacrifice (within the heart) 153

TZAV: The fire of love 159

PESACH: (1) The meaning of liberation 165
            (2) The festival of Spring... 169
            (3) The "fifth son" 171

SHEMINI: Human endeavor and Divine revelation 174

TAZRIA: Man's place in creation 180

METZORA: Leprosy—a spiritual cleansing process 186

ACHAREI MOT: The return from ecstasy 191

KEDOSHIM: Beyond "holiness" is unity
    with G-d in the everyday world.. 197

EMOR: Stages in redemption, in history and in life 202

BEHAR: The inner meaning of the seventh and fiftieth years......... 209

BECHUKOTAI: Engraving the words of Torah on one's being....... 216

B A M I D B A R

BAMIDBAR: The counting of the children of Israel 222

SHAVUOT: (1) Unity in diversity 227
(2) Sinai, King David, and the Baal Shem Tov 231

NASO: Sin—a moment of apparent faithlessness 236

BEHAALOTECHA: Lighting the Menorah,
a spiritual task for today... 241

SHELACH: A Chassidic perspective on the account of the Spies 245

KORACH: The false quest for separatism 252

CHUKAT: Analysis of Rashi's comment on the Red Heifer 258

BALAK: Forbidden union... 263

PINCHAS: The motives of the zealot 270

MATTOT: Betrothal and marriage in relationship with G-d 277

MASSEI: Egypt is a state of mind 281

DEVARIM

DEVARIM: The Ninth of Menachem-Av
and the vision of the final Redemption...................................... 286

VAETCHANAN: The unique significance of the Second Temple... 290

EKEV: The contrast between the first and second
paragraphs of the Shema 297

RE'EH: The power of Repentance 304

SHOFTIM: The Cities of Refuge and their expression
in the Jewish calendar.. 311

KI TETZE: The paradox of divorce 316

KI TAVO: The offering of the first fruits 323

NITZAVIM: The unity of the Jewish people..................... 328

THE TEN DAYS OF TESHUVAH: Teshuvah, Tefillah
and Tzedakah 334

VAYELECH: The Holy of Holies and the world............................. 338

HA-AZINU: Towards heaven, and towards earth—two
stages in the meaning of Rosh Hashanah and Yom Kippur 341

VEZOT HABERACHA: Simchat Torah, the festival cycle,
and the Second Tablets of the Law 349

INDEXES

Index of Scriptural and Rabbinic Quotations 359

General Index 375

INTRODUCTION

Translation is an act fraught with difficulties. Ever since Babel, the multiplicity of languages has stood for more than a variety of ways of saying the same thing. Each language, even each dialect, embodies a culture. To translate is thus of necessity to adapt, and to capture no more than an approximation to the original.

This general reservation is singularly in place when translating a work of Chassidut. The Lubavitcher Rebbe, on whose work the present volume is based, has himself given a classic definition of Chassidut. It is not to be understood as one among many of the branches of Jewish thought. Instead it reaches to the core of Torah and is addressed to the inward essence of the soul, touching upon the very nature of existence. It illuminates the other modes of Jewish expression—*halacha* and *aggadah* alike—and reveals the inner unity behind their diversified forms.

Chassidut belongs, in other words, to uniqueness of Torah, and as such is almost by definition untranslatable. Far from being reproducible in the language and structures of contemporary Western thought, it challenges secularity at every point. It invites us to "see through" the sensory universe of the secular mind, to the mystic reality beneath and beyond. Therein lies its unmistakable challenge and relevance to a century which has witnessed the tragic consequences of a secularity that makes man the measure of all things, and leaves morality without a Divine foundation.

What, then, is a translator to do? Maimonides, almost eight hundred years ago, stated the problem and a route to its solution. In a letter to his own translator, Shmuel ibn Tibbon, he wrote: "One who wishes to translate from one language to another, rendering each word literally and adhering to the original order of words and sentences, will meet with much difficulty and will end up with a translation that is questionable and confusing.

"Instead the translator should first try to grasp the sense of the subject and then explain the theme, according to his understanding, in the other language. But this cannot be done without changing the order of words, sometimes using many words to translate one, or one word to translate many. He will have to add or delete words so that the concept may be clearly expressed in the language into which he is translating."

It was in this spirit that the present translations were undertaken, in an attempt to do no more than sketch the mood and thrust of the original ideas, full as they are of detail, nuance and subtlety that verge on the untranslatable. Certainly if this work serves to whet the reader's appetite for further study, they will have fulfilled their function.

———————

To hear or read a *sicha*, of the Lubavitcher Rebbe is to undertake a journey. We are challenged and forced to move: where we stand at the end is not where we were at the beginning. Time and again a talk will be set in motion by a seemingly microscopic tension—a question on a comment by *Rashi*, perhaps, or a problem in understanding a *halacha*, a practical provision of Jewish law. Once in motion, however, the argument leads us into fresh perspectives, provisional answers and new questions, until we climb rung by rung to the most elevated of vantage points. From here, as we survey the ground beneath us in its widest of contexts, the initial question is not only resolved but also revealed as the starting point of a major spiritual search. The question only existed because we were looking at the surface, not fathoming the depths, of Torah.

Thus a problem in the laws of divorce leads us to consider the concepts of separation and unity and to a radical reinterpretation of the nature of exile. A passage relating to the fruit of trees in their fifth year takes us through the levels of spiritual reality, an examination of the Baal Shem Tov's life, and a reversal of our normal understanding of holiness and sanctification. A meditation on the name of a Sidra passes through the subjects of leprosy, repentance and personal identity. Each talk moves from the specific to the general, the finite to the infinite, and back again. Each invites us to undergo a profound transformation in our way of seeing the world and ourselves, so that when we return at the end of a *sicha* to the question with which we began, everything has changed.

Each, in short, is a Chassidic journey of descent and ascent, climbing and returning, through—Torah, the universe and the soul. Key themes recur: the inseparability of the soul from G-d, the constant demands and possibility of *teshuvah*, the unity of Israel, the error of despair, the insistent light beneath the dark surfaces of history. These are the motifs of Chassidut, and are like a continuing thread through the Rebbe's teachings. The very form of the talks—their intellectual rhythms of question and answer, their reasoning and rigor—mirrors a central feature of Chabad, that through a mental journey we affect both emotion and action. A truth grasped first by the mind then shapes heart and limb, and in perceiving reality we become our real selves.

These talks, then, are addressed with relentless clarity to the contemporary Jewish condition. Their implicit starting-point is the darkness of a post-holocaust world in which spirituality, moral conviction, and the Divine purpose of creation, seem almost beyond reach. Their tacit faith is that step by step we can be led from the present moment of confusion to the timeless lucidity of Torah, beyond the low clouds to the Infinite Light.

———————

In the original work of translating and adapting these talks, I was encouraged and immeasurably helped by Rabbi Fyvish Vogel and Rabbi Shmuel Lew. The credit is theirs; the errors and infelicities my own. To their friendship and inspiration, this book is dedicated.

Jonathan Sacks,
London, 5746 / 1986

FOREWORD
TO THE NEW EDITION

It is with conflicting emotions that I write these words for the new edition of *Torah Studies*. I am delighted that the book has now passed through several editions, but deeply saddened that the great spiritual leader whose thoughts it contains, the Lubavitcher Rebbe of blessed memory, has passed away. I hope that in a small way this volume will help to ensure that his words and teachings live on.

Torah Studies represents only a fragment of the vast body of the Rebbe's teachings. His collected writings and speeches are gathered in more than two hundred volumes in Hebrew and Yiddish, and constitute an immense legacy to future generations. They include Torah expositions, halakhic analysis, Talmudic discourses, explorations of Jewish mysticism and letters of guidance to Jews throughout the world.

The essays collected here are selected from the Rebbe's investigations into the weekly Torah portion. In these studies of our most sacred texts, the Rebbe weaves together the results of many centuries of traditional Jewish scholarship, focusing them through the prism of his intense Chassidic spirituality. Time and again the result is a fresh insight into the great themes of Jewish life, themes no less relevant today than in our long and distinguished past.

The Rebbe wanted us to see the unity that lies behind the apparent diversity of existence. Listening to his expositions, we move beneath the surface of conflict and come to see that disagreement between the great sages is no more and no less than a difference of perspectives on a single Divine reality. The more we travel inward in our understanding of Torah the closer we come to the Oneness that pervades all spiritual truth.

For the Rebbe this was no mere academic exercise. At an individual level it is a journey toward integration of the human personality. At a collective level it is the ultimate path to the unity of the Jewish people. We are one because we are part of the Torah. The Torah is one because it is the word of G-d. That is the truth which our ancestors carried with them from generation to generation, enlarging not only themselves but the moral horizons of mankind. It was the truth to which the Rebbe dedicated his life, inspiring those who came into contact with him or were touched by his message.

Great spiritual teachings do not die. It is my hope that this brief selection taken from the Rebbe's words will serve as a living reminder that the Torah continues to be our Tree of Life.

Chief Rabbi Jonathan Sacks,
Tu b'Shvat 5756

TORAH STUDIES

פרשת בראשית

BEREISHIT

In the chronicling of creation, one detail strikes us with the force of mystery: Why was light created before everything else, when there was nothing to benefit from it? The Rabbinical explanation only adds to the mystery, for we are told that the light was immediately "hidden for the righteous in the world to come." The Rebbe explains the difficulty and elucidates the implications of the creation narrative for the individual and the conduct of his life.

1. THE FIRST CREATION

"And G-d said, Let there be light, and there was light."[1] This was the first of the utterances by which G-d created the world, and light was the first of all creations.

But why was this? For light has no value in itself; its usefulness depends on the existence of other things which are illuminated by it or which benefit from it. So why was light created when nothing else existed?

One cannot say that this was simply a *preparation* for the things which were later to be made (in the way that the Talmud[2] says that man was created last so that all should be in readiness for him). For if so, light should have been created just before the animals (which can distinguish between light and darkness), or at the earliest just before the plants (which grow by the help of light), on the *third* day of creation.

2. THE HIDDEN LIGHT

The Rabbis[3] explain that the light made on the first day was "hidden for the righteous in the world to come." But this is

---

1. *Bereishit* 1:3.
2. *Sanhedrin*, 31a.
3. *Chagigah*, 12a. *Bereishit Rabbah*, 3:6.

paradoxical. Since the whole purpose of light is to *illuminate,* why should it have been hidden immediately after it was created; the very denial of its raison d'etre? And even though the Rabbis explained why the light should have been hidden, we still need to understand why, if G-d foresaw this, He still created it at the outset.

A further comment requiring explanation is that of the Zohar,[4] which points out that the Hebrew words for "light" and "secret" are numerically equivalent.[5] Numerical equivalence is a sign that the two things are related to one another (for since things were created through the permutations of the letters of the Divine utterances, two things whose names are comprised of letters of the same value share a common essential form). But again we have a paradox: Light is, of its essence, a *revealed* thing, and a secret is necessarily *hidden.* How can two opposites share a common form?

3. THE ARCHITECTURE OF THE UNIVERSE

To resolve these difficulties we must consider a remark made by the Midrash:[6] "Just as a king wishing to build a palace does not do so spontaneously but consults architect's plans, so G-d looked into the Torah and created the world."

In other words, by examining the order in which a man sets about making something which requires planning and forethought, we can learn something of G-d's order in bringing the world into being.

First, he fixes in his mind the purpose which he desires his work to achieve. Only then does he begin the labor.

This, as it were, was G-d's procedure. And the purpose of the world that He was to create (a place where the Divine light would be hidden[7] in the heavy shrouds of material existence)

---

4. Part III, 28b.
5. The derivation of associations of meaning by utilizing numerical values of the Hebrew letters is known as "Gematria." Cf. *Tanya*, Part II, ch. 1.
6. *Bereishit Rabbah*, beginning.
7. "World" and "hidden" are semantically related in Hebrew *(olam—he'elam).*

was that it should be purified and the pristine light of G-d restored. He sought, ultimately, a "dwelling place in the lower world,"[8] meaning that His hiddenness (darkness) be transformed into a revealed presence (light).

Since light was thus the purpose of the creation, and the purpose is the first thing to be decided on in the order of a work, light was created on the first day. The intention of all the subsequent creations was captured in that opening phrase, "Let there be light."

4. THE IMPLICIT LIGHT

There is, however, an allusion to light in each of the subsequent days of creation. For each day's work concluded with the pronouncement "And G-d saw that it was good." And the word "good" alludes to light, as it is written "And G-d saw *the light*[9] that it was good." It follows that light was present on *each* day of creation, but how can this be, if light is the *purpose* of creation, and as such explicit only at the outset?

The answer is that purpose manifests itself in two ways:

(i) *explicitly* at the start of a labor; and

(ii) *implicitly* at every stage of the work, guiding each endeavor in a pre-arranged pattern, so that it conforms to the original design.

It follows that there were two aspects to the primeval light: Firstly as it was revealed, as the purpose of creation, on the first day, prior to any other existing thing; and secondly, as it was felt indirectly (and hence only alluded to) on the other days, shaping the remainder of creation towards its function.

5. REVELATION AND FULFILLMENT

Now we can understand why the Zohar points out the connection between "light" and "secret," and why the Rabbis said that it was hidden for the righteous in the world to come.

---

8. Cf. *Tanya*, Part I, ch. 36.
9. *Bereishit* 1:4. Cf. *Sotah*, 12a.

While a building is under construction, its final shape is not apparent, except in the mind of the architect. Its ultimate form is disclosed only when the work is completed.

So with the world: Only when it has been brought to its perfection, by our service during the 6,000 years[10] which precede the Messiah, will its purpose ("light") be revealed.

The light now is hidden, but in the world to come (when our worldly service has been completed) it will once again shine as it did on the first day.

But anything which is hidden, is hidden *somewhere*. Where is the light hidden? The Rabbis say:[11] in the Torah. For just as an architect's drawings guide the builders' hands, so Torah guides us—through learning and the performance of the commandments—in shaping the world to its fulfillment.

6. FROM WORLD TO MAN

Each person is a microcosm of the world, and its destiny is his. So that this order of spiritual history is also an order of individual service.

"Light" is the purpose of each Jew: That he transforms his situation and environment to light. Not merely by driving out the darkness (evil) by refraining from sin, but by changing the darkness itself to light, by positive commitment to good.

And his order must be that of G-d's in the act of creation: First he must formulate his purpose. Immediately, as he awakes from sleep (when he is a "new creation"[12])—indeed at every moment, for the world is continually created anew,[13] he must recognize that his task is "Let there be light."

Then he must let this purpose be implicit in each of his actions—by aligning them with Torah, the blueprint of creation.

---

10. Corresponding to the Six Days of Creation.
11. *Midrash Ruth*, in *Zohar Chadash*, 85a.
12. *Yalkut Shimoni* on *Psalms*.
13. *Tanya*, Part II, beginning.

7. DARKNESS INTO LIGHT

If light is the purpose of every created thing, it follows that it must also be the purpose of *darkness* itself. For darkness has a purpose, not merely that it should *exist to be avoided* (should present man with a choice between good and evil), but that it should be *transformed into light.*

And if a man should sometimes despair, in the oppressive darkness of a wayward world,[14] of making light prevail, let alone of turning the bad itself into good, he is told at the very outset: "In (or, for the sake of) the beginning, G-d created. . . ." And the Rabbis translate it as: "For the sake of Israel, who are called 'the *beginning* of (G-d's) produce', and for the sake of Torah, which is called 'the *beginning* of (G-d's) way.'"[15]

The world was made so that Israel through Torah should turn it into the everlasting light of G-d's revealed presence, in the Messianic fulfillment of Isaiah's words,[16] "The sun shall no more be your light by day, nor for brightness shall the moon give you light: But the L-rd shall be for you a light everlasting."

(Source: Likkutei Sichot, Vol. X pp. 7-12)

---

14. "Waste and void, and darkness was on the face of the murmuring deep." *Bereishit* 1:2.
15. Cf. *Rashi, Bereishit* 1:1.
16. *Isaiah* 60:19.

פרשת נח

NOACH

In this Sicha, the Rebbe brings together two related lessons of this Sidra: The virtue of Shem and Japheth in covering their father's nakedness and averting their eyes from it; and the use of a lengthy euphemism in place of the word "unclean," which teaches the necessity of delicacy in speech. It then solves the paradox that on the one hand we should not notice the faults of others, while on the other, we should seek to correct their errors.

1. PURITY OF SPEECH AND SIGHT

On the verse from this week's Sidra, "of clean beasts and of beasts that are not clean (they came to Noah and into the ark, two by two),"[1] the Talmud[2] comments: "An unrefined word should never pass a man's lips, for the Torah goes out of its way and uses eight extra letters to avoid an unpleasant word." Rashi explains that the word *"tammay"*[3] would have saved eight letters in place of the phrase "that are not clean." And since the Torah is always as concise as possible, the message of this elaborate phrase is that one's speech should be at all times free of improper expressions.

The Sidra also contains, besides the directive about *speech,* a lesson about *sight.* Shem and Japheth were so careful not to look upon their father Noah's nakedness that "they went backwards, and their faces were turned backwards, and they did not see their father's nakedness."[4] And the reward promised emphasizes their virtue: "Blessed be the L-rd, G-d of Shem,

---

1. *Bereishit* 7:8.
2. *Pesachim*, 3a.
3. Hebrew word denoting the positive state of uncleanliness (rather than the negation of cleanliness).
4. *Bereishit* 9:23.

and may Canaan be servant to them. May G-d enlarge Japheth and may he dwell in the tents of Shem."[5]

But the story is slightly puzzling. It is *clear* from the fact that Shem and Japheth walked backwards, that they did not see their father's state. Why then does the Torah add the apparently redundant words: "And they did not see the nakedness of their father?"

2. THE MIRROR WHICH REFLECTS FAULTS

There is a saying of the Baal Shem Tov[6] that if a person sees something wrong with someone else, this is a sign that he himself has a similar fault. He sees himself, as it were, in a mirror—if the face he sees is not clean, it is his own which is dirty.

Now, we can ask: Why should one not be able to see a genuine wrong in someone else without being at fault oneself?

The reason is that Divine Providence is present in every event. If we see bad in someone, this also has its Divine purpose, and that is to show us our own failings which need correcting. And we need to be shown our faults in an indirect way for "love covers all faults,"[7] and self-love is always strong. Man is blind to his own shortcomings. He needs to see them exemplified in someone else, to force him to reflect on himself and see their counterparts in his own life.

But the task of the Jew is not only self-perfection, but also the improvement of others: "You shall surely rebuke your friend, even a hundred times."[8] Surely, then, when he sees his friend's failings, Providence intends him to help to correct them, not only to introspect on his own weaknesses?

To put it more strongly, a Jew is an end in himself, and not merely a means for others to make use of. How then can we be asked to use a friend for our own purposes? And without any

5. Ibid., v. 26-27.
6. *Meor Einayim* on *Parshat Chukat.*
7. *Proverbs* 10:12.
8. *Baba Metzia*, 31a.

palpable benefit to the friend concerned? If so, perhaps the reason one notices the fault is only to benefit his friend, and not that he also has the fault?

3. NOTICING AND CORRECTING

To understand this we must refer to the continuation of the above quotation from the Talmud:[2] "A man must always speak in proper expressions."

The Talmud, after answering a relatively incidental problem, then asks, "But do we not find in the Torah the expression 'tammay'?" (i.e., the very term that we have been asked to avoid).

But this is strange. For the word "tammay" is found in the Torah in more than one hundred places! It is so obvious a problem that it should surely have been raised *immediately,* not after a more minor point. Nor does the surprised tone of the question seem appropriate to such a straightforward objection.

The explanation is, that in legal (halachic) contexts, the requirement of clarity and unambiguousness outweighs the consideration of propriety: And so "tammay" is used. In narrative contexts, however, the concern for delicate expression compensates for the lengthier wording of these euphemisms.

Therefore the Torah's use of words like "tammay" does not contradict the principle that wherever possible we should use the more delicate phrase. And the Talmud raises its objection in the way it does, because "tammay" is used only rarely in the *narrative* sections of the Torah. Indeed, even in the *halachic* sections, when the law does not relate directly to uncleanliness but mentions it only in passing, the Torah still prefers the euphemism.[9]

This applies not only to speech but also to sight. When one sees a Jew doing something wrong, one's first concern must be to seek the "halacha" (i.e., the duty) required of him—namely,

---

9. Cf. *Devarim* 23:11.

that one reproaches him and tries, with tact and grace, to correct his ways.

But when one finds oneself seeing this wrong not as something directed at *himself* (i.e., something that he must correct), but just as a failing in his *fellow* (when one's attitude is critical without being constructive), this is evidence that this is a "mirror," and that one is oneself at fault.

4. THE VIRTUE OF SHEM AND JAPHETH

And this explains why the Torah, after saying that Shem and Japheth turned their faces away from Noah, adds "and they did not see their father's nakedness." It is here emphasizing that not only did they (physically) not see him; they were not even *aware* of his fault as such—they were concerned only with *what must be done* (which was to cover him with a mantle). Ham, the third brother, did however see his father, and thus betrayed his own failings.

The story conveys to us the moral that not only should we not talk about the shortcomings of others (as Ham did in telling his brothers about his father),[10] but we should not even *think* about them except insofar as it lies with us to set them right. And whoever follows this, participates in the reward, "Blessed be the L-rd, G-d of Shem" and "May G-d enlarge Japheth," and contributes to the unity and brotherly love of Israel which will bring the Messiah to the world.

(Source: Likkutei Sichot, Vol. X pp. 24-29)

---

10. *Bereishit* 9:22.

פרשת לך לך
Lech Lecha

There appears to be a contradiction between the name of this Sidra
and its content. For "Lech Lecha," as the Sicha will explain, means
"Go to yourself"—Abraham's movement towards the fulfillment of
his task. But the Sidra describes a series of events which happened
to Abraham, seeming to deflect him from his mission. The Rebbe
resolves the contradiction by going in depth into the meaning of
fulfillment, or "ascent," for the Jew.

1. WHAT'S IN A NAME?

Names are not accidents in Torah. We find in many places
that the name of a person or a thing tells us about its nature.
And the same is true of the *Sidrot*. The names they bear are a
cue to their content, even though on the face of it they are simply taken from the first words of the Sidra and are there, as it
were, by chance. For there is no such thing as pure chance in
events, since everything happens by Divine Providence; certainly in matters of Torah.

We might think that the names of the Sidrot are a relatively
late convention, since we are not *certain* that they are mentioned
in the Talmud,[1] while the names of the *books* of the *Torah*[2] and
of the divisions of the Mishnah[3] are all detailed there. But there
is a law relating to legal documents, that a name mentioned in
one becomes a name recognized by Torah law if it has stood
unchallenged for 30 days.[4] *A fortiori,* since the names of the
Sidrot have stood unchallenged for more than 1,000 years, and

---

1. Cf. *Megillah*, 29b; 31a, *Sotah*, 40b.
2. *Baba Batra*, 14b.
3. In many places.
4. *Baba Batra*, 167b; *Shulchan Aruch, Choshen Mishpat,* 49:3; *Remo* in *Shulchan Aruch,
   Even Hoezer,* 120:3.

are mentioned by the Sages (Rashi,[5] for example), they are recognized as such by Torah.

So we can sum up the inner content of the whole of this week's Sidra by understanding the implications of its name: Lech Lecha.

2. LECH LECHA: GO TO YOURSELF

This is usually translated as *"Get thee out* (from your country and your birthplace and your father's house. . . .)" But it literally means, "Go to yourself." "Going" has the connotation in Torah of moving towards one's ultimate purpose—of service towards one's Creator. And this is strongly hinted at by the phrase, "Go to *yourself*"—meaning, towards your soul's essence[6] and your ultimate purpose, that for which you were created.

This was the command given to Abraham, and the first part of the narrative bears this out. For he was told to leave his heathen background and go to Israel. And within Israel he was "going and journeying to the South," that is, towards Jerusalem. He was moving progressively towards an ever increasing degree of holiness. But then we suddenly find: "And there was a famine in the land, and Abram went down to Egypt." Why this sudden reversal of his spiritual journey, especially as the whole Sidra (as testified by its name) is supposed to contain an account of Abraham's continual *progress* towards his fulfillment?

3. ASCENT OR DESCENT?

That it was a reversal seems clear. To go to Egypt was itself a spiritual descent—as the verse explicitly says, "And Abram went *down* to Egypt." And the *cause* of his journey—"and there was a famine in the land"—also seems like the deliberate concealment of G-d's blessing. The more so as G-d promised Abraham, "And I will make you a great nation, and I will bless you and make your name great." Is it not strange that when he

---

5. *Bereishit* 47:2; *Shemot* 19:11; 25:7, etc.
6. *Alshich*, beginning of our Sidra.

reached the land that G-d had shown him, a famine forced him to leave?

A possible answer is that this was one of the trials which Abraham had to face to prove himself worthy of his mission (and the Midrash[7] tells us when faced with this inexplicable hardship Abraham "was not angry and did not complain").

But this will not suffice. For Abraham's mission was not simply a personal one—it was his task to spread G-d's name and gather adherents to His faith. The Midrash[8] compares his many journeyings to the way a spice box must be shaken about, to spread its aroma to all corners of a room. So an explanation of his descent in terms of a personal pilgrimage will not do justice to the difficulty. Especially since its immediate effect was to endanger Abraham's mission. It could not help the work of spreading G-d's name for the arrival of a man of G-d to be followed by a bad omen of a national famine.

Worse is to follow, for when Abraham entered Egypt, Sarah, his wife, was taken by Pharaoh by force. And even though he did not so much as touch her,[9] it was an evident descent from the spiritual course that seemed to be outlined for them.

And even before this, when they first approached Egypt, Abraham said to Sarah, "Now I know you are a woman of beautiful appearance." Thereby he had already begun to see (though only relative to his own exalted standard) with "Egyptian" eyes; for previously he had not noticed this[10] because of the spirituality of their modest relationship.

So how, in the face of so many contrary indications, can it be that the whole story of Lech Lecha is—as its name would seem to imply—one of Abraham's continual ascent towards his destiny?

---

7. *Bereishit Rabbah*, 40:2.
8. Ibid., 39:2.
9. Cf. *Tanchuma*, 5 (on our Sidra).
10. But he had seen her previously (cf. *Kiddushin*, 41a).

4. HISTORY FORESHADOWED

We can work towards a resolution of these difficulties by understanding the inner meaning of the famous dictum, "The works of the Fathers are a sign for the children." This does not mean simply that the fate of the Fathers is mirrored in the fate of their children. But more strongly, that what they do brings *about* what happens to their children.[11] Their merit gives their children the strength to follow their example. And in Abraham's wanderings, the subsequent history of the children of Israel was rehearsed and made possible.

Abraham's journey down to Egypt foreshadows the future Egyptian Exile. "And Abram went up out of Egypt" presages the Israelites' redemption. And just as Abraham left, "weighed down with cattle, silver and gold," so too did the Israelites leave Egypt "with great wealth."

Even that merit for which the Israelites were saved they owed to Sarah; for just as their women kept themselves from sinning with the Egyptians,[12] so had Sarah protected herself from Pharaoh's advances.

5. THE END IS IMPLICIT IN THE BEGINNING

Understood in this light, we can see the end of Abraham's journey to Egypt foreshadowed in its beginning. For its purpose was his eventual departure "weighed down with cattle, silver and gold," expressing the way in which he was to transform the most secular and heathen things and press them into the service of G-d. This was indeed the purpose of the Israelites' exile into Egypt, that G-d's presence should be felt in this most intransigent of places. The final ascent was implicit in the descent.

There is, in Jewish learning, an image which captures this oblique directedness. The Babylonian Talmud, unlike the Jerusalem Talmud, never reaches its decisions directly but arrives at

---

11. Cf. *Ramban*, 12:6. *Bereishit Rabbah*, 40.
12. *Shir Hashirim Rabbah*, 4:12.

them through digressions and dialectics which shed, in their apparent meandering, more light than a direct path could. Indeed, when the two books are in disagreement, the Babylonian verdict is always followed.[13]

So too do the seeming digressions of Jewish history represent not a wandering from the path of destiny but a way of shedding the light of G-d on untouched corners of the world, as preparation for, and part of, their subsequent redemption.

Abraham's removal to Egypt was not an interruption but an integral part of the command of "Lech Lecha"—to journey towards that self-fulfillment which is the service of G-d.

And as Abraham's destiny was the later destiny of the children of Israel, so it is ours. Our exile, like his, is a preparation for (and therefore *part of*) redemption. And the redemption which follows brings us to a higher state than that which we could have reached without exile. "Greater will be the glory of this latter house (i.e., the Temple of the Messianic Age) than that of the former (the first Temple)."[14]

Exile, then, is an integral part of spiritual progress; it allows us to sanctify the *whole world* by our actions, and not simply a small corner of it.

Perhaps one will say: Where is this progress apparent? The world does not appear to be growing more holy: Precisely the opposite seems to be the case.

But this is a superficial judgment. The world does not move of its own accord. It is fashioned by Divine Providence.

What appears on the surface to be a decline is, however hidden, part of the continuous process of transformation which we work on the world whenever we dedicate our actions to Torah and G-d's will. In other words, the world constantly becomes more elevated and refined. Nothing could illustrate this more clearly than the story of Abraham's journeyings, seen first on the surface, and then in their true perspective.

---

13. Cf. *Yad Malachi*, beginning of Part 2.
14. *Haggai* 2:9, as interpreted in *Zohar*, Part I, 28a, etc.

Whatever a Jew's situation, when he turns towards his true self-fulfillment in the injunction of Lech Lecha, he places his life and his actions in the perspective of Torah, and takes his proper place in the bringing of the future redemption.

(Source: Likkutei Sichot, Vol. V pp. 57-67)

פרשת וירא

VAYERA

In this Sidra, we read of G-d's appearance to Abraham after his circumcision. But why was his circumcision so great an act as to merit
such a reward? This is the question that the Rebbe answers, and explains in depth the special relationship between the Jew and G-d
which is reached by the performance of the commandment.

1. THE STORY OF THE FIFTH LUBAVITCHER REBBE

The previous Lubavitcher Rebbe, Rabbi Yosef Yitzchak,
told a story[1] about something that had happened to his father,
Rabbi Shalom DovBer,[2] when he was a child of four or five.
The Shabbat on which the Sidra Vayera was read was the
Shabbat closest to Rabbi Shalom DovBer's birthday;[3] and to
mark the occasion he was taken by his mother to see his
grandfather, the Tzemach Tzedek (the third Lubavitcher
Rebbe), to receive a birthday blessing. But as soon as he entered the room, the little boy burst into tears. His grandfather
asked why he was crying. He replied that he had learned in
Cheder (class) that G-d had revealed Himself to Abraham, and
he was crying because G-d does not also reveal Himself to him.

His grandfather explained: When a Jew who is ninety-nine
years old decides that he must circumcise himself, then he is
worthy that G-d should reveal Himself to him.

There is, however, another version of this story (Rabbi
Shalom DovBer, being a little boy at the time, did not remember the incident, and knew the story—in two versions—only
from Chassidim who had been present), according to which
his grandfather's reply was: When a *righteous* Jew who is ninety-

---

1. In 5693 (1932); *Hayom Yom,* p. 103.
2. Fifth Lubavitcher Rebbe, (1860-1920).
3. 20 Cheshvan.

16

nine years old decides that he must circumcise himself, then he is worthy that G-d should reveal Himself to him.

2. THE MEANING OF CIRCUMCISION

What was the significance of this act of Abraham? Even when a Jew is ninety-nine, and not merely in calendrical years, but in uninterrupted years of service (for when the Torah describes Abraham as "advanced in days," the Zohar[4] comments that this means that each day was complete in its service), he is still bound to circumcise himself, meaning, spiritually, to remove the "foreskin" of the world, that surface of selfish pleasures which conceals its true nature as the Divine creation. For it is written in Pirkei Avot,[5] "When a man is one hundred, it is as if he were already dead and passed away and removed from the world." In other words, at such a point, in age or in spirit, when the world no longer masks the Divine, a man has achieved the inner meaning of circumcision. But before this, even by one year or one degree of holiness, the task remains unfulfilled.

3. CIRCUMCISION AND ABRAHAM'S PERFECTION

There is a special connection between Abraham and circumcision. For it is said[6] that six commandments were given to Adam; a seventh was given to Noah . . . and in addition to these a new commandment was given to Abraham—that of circumcision. Since the command was first given to Abraham, it must have had a particular relevance to him; from which it follows that his circumcision did not just *add* something to ninety-nine years of complete service, but that until then his life was lacking its central component. This is reinforced by the fact that, in reference to the command of circumcision, G-d says to Abra-

---

4. Part I, 224a.
5. 5:22.
6. *Rambam, Hilchot Melachim,* beginning ch. 9.

ham, "Be thou perfect," implying that hitherto *Abraham* had been marred, his service incomplete.[7]

4. THE WORKS OF THE FATHERS

The circumcision of Abraham has an even deeper significance. On the one hand, it is known that the commandments which we (subsequent to the Giving of the Torah) fulfill are far higher than those which the Fathers fulfilled before the Torah was given, so much so that the Midrash[8] can say: All the commandments which the Fathers kept before You are like the aroma (of fine oil), whereas ours are like "oil poured forth." What the Fathers did was, compared to our own acts, like an aroma compared to its source, like an emanation compared to its essence.

This is because what the Fathers fulfilled, they did from their own strength and inclination (as when Abraham initiated the morning prayer, and Isaac the tithe), rather than in response to the Divine command. For when, after the Giving of the Torah, we keep one of the commandments, we are thereby related to He who commanded. And this is the essence of G-d, for He gave the Torah with the opening words *"I* (in My essence) am the L-rd your G-d." This relation *permanently* changes the world, investing it with a timeless holiness. But the spontaneous righteousness of the Fathers was not a response to a command. It did not relate them to the essence of G-d. And therefore the holiness of their acts was only temporary in its effect on the world.

Nonetheless, we have the maxim, "The works of the Fathers are a sign for the children," meaning that the spiritual resources that we have in being able to keep the commandments are an inheritance from the virtue of the Fathers before the Torah was given. How was this transmitted if, as it seems, there is no connection between the commands before and after Sinai? However, one command bears this connection, and this

---

7. *Rashi, Bereishit* 17:1. Cf. *Nedarim,* 32a.
8. *Shir Hashirim Rabbah,* 1:3.

was circumcision; because it alone was commanded by G-d to Abraham (albeit not prefaced by the disclosure of His essence, "I am the L-rd your G-d"); and therefore its effect on this world persisted through time. This is the connecting link between all the acts of the Fathers and the later capacity of the Children of Israel to do G-d's will: Abraham's circumcision endured in its merit.

5. MAKING GOOD THE PAST

Now we can understand that Abraham's decision to circumcise himself after ninety-nine years of service was not simply to add something which would make all his *subsequent* life complete, but rather *retroactively* to remedy his *previous* defect.

This applies to all who have yet to reach the stage of "one hundred years": Not merely to add to their service but to bring their previous deficiencies to perfection.

6. THE TWO VERSIONS OF THE STORY

Now we can understand the meaning of both versions of the Tzemach Tzedek's reply to Rabbi Shalom DovBer.

The second version teaches us that it is binding even on the *righteous* man to undergo (the spiritual analogue of) circumcision; how much more so is it binding on the ordinary Jew.

But how can the first version stand? Is it not included *a fortiori* in the second? Also—Abraham was a righteous Jew even before his circumcision (he merely lacked the predicate of perfection). How then could he be called an "ordinary Jew"?

The answer is: Abraham's act of circumcision was a response to the Divine command and related to the deepest aspects of G-dliness. So that this summoned forth the deepest powers of the soul, at which level there is no distinction between the righteous and the ordinary, and where the distinguishing characteristics of men are effaced.

In short, the second version takes the surface point of view where the righteous is distinguished from the others, (and therefore emphasizes the duty of a *righteous* man); the first, the deeper one where all Jewish souls are equal in their source.

7. A RELATIONSHIP ABOVE TIME

Underlying the idea of the merit of Abraham's circumcision is that of the eternal worth of every act of service—it unites commander, commanded and commandment in a bond above time.[9] But despite the fact that this bond exists even for the unrighteous, (for "even the sinners of Israel are full of Mitzvot"),[10] Abraham's act reminds us that even the righteous has constantly to renew it, by "removing the foreskin of the world"; and when he does so, his reward will be that granted to Abraham: The prophetic awareness of G-d.

(Source: Likkutei Sichot, Vol. V pp. 86-91)

---

9. *Tanya*, Part I, ch. 25.
10. *Eruvin*, 19a; end of *Chagigah*.

פרשת חיי שרה

CHAYEI SARAH

Although this Sidra is entitled "The Life of Sarah," it really commences with her death and with the sentence, "And the life of Sarah was 100 years and 20 years and 7 years: These were the years of the life of Sarah." This highly repetitious wording exercised the Midrashic commentators, who gave three explanations, each emphasizing that the Torah is here praising Sarah for her perfection. The Rebbe examines these explanations, showing how each subtly stresses a different aspect of this perfection; and how, in general, righteousness lifts a person above the vicissitudes of time.

1. THE FIRST MIDRASH

"And the life of Sarah was 100 years and 20 years and 7 years: These were the years of the life of Sarah."[1] On this verse the Midrash[2] comments:

"G-d knows the days of the perfect and their inheritance shall be for ever;"[3] just as they are perfect so are their years perfect. At 20 she (Sarah) was as beautiful as at seven; at 100 she was as free from sin as at 20."

(Another reading has it that she was as beautiful at 100 as at 20, and as sinless at 20 as at 7.)

The commentators, including Rashi, explain that the Midrash is commenting on the threefold repetition of the word "years," where the phrase "127 years" would have sufficed. And it cites the verse "G-d knows the days of the perfect," making play of the phrase, which could also mean "the perfect days": Suggesting that each day in the life of the righteous is perfect in itself. And this is reinforced by the verse about Sarah, whose

---

1. *Bereishit* 23:1.
2. *Bereishit Rabbah*, loc. cit.
3. *Psalms* 37:18.

21

wording suggests that all her years were equal in their perfection.

But there are difficulties in this explanation:

(i) The expression of the Midrash is "just *as* they are perfect, so their years *are* perfect." But if perfection here means freedom from sin, then the perfection of the person and of his days are *one and the same thing*. But the Midrash in using the language of *comparison* ("just as") suggests they *are* two distinct things.

If, on the other hand, perfection denotes physical beauty, then the Midrash is surely difficult to understand for though Sarah may have been as beautiful at 100 as she was at 20, this was not true of all the intervening period, for there was a time when Sarah was "withered."[4] So at 100 she may have been perfect but her years (i.e., the period until then) were not.

(ii) The very phrase "their years *are* perfect?" is strange, for normally this would be taken to be related to the years themselves. But the Midrash here is unusually taking it to refer to the perfection of *the person* during these years.

(iii) The Midrash seems to make an unwarranted transition from the phrase "the *days* of the perfect" to the phrase "so their *years are* perfect." Although this verse mentioning "days" is quoted in order to explain the word "years" in the verse from our Sidra, surely it would be more consistent to use the word "days" in explaining the verse discussing "the *days* of the perfect."

2. THE SECOND MIDRASH

After its first explanation, the Midrash adds another: "An alternative explanation is: 'G-d knows the days of the perfect'; this refers to Sarah who was perfect in her actions. Rabbi Jochanan said: Like a perfect calf."

At first glance there are two differences between this and the earlier comment:

---

4. *Bereishit* 18:12.

(a) the first reading takes "perfect" to apply to "days" while the second applies it to people;

(b) the first understands perfection as comprising *all* attributes (including the purely physical trait of beauty), but the second relates it to good deeds alone.

But there are problems even in the second Midrash:

(i) Surely the second comment should *add* something to our understanding of the verse "G-d knows the days of the perfect." But what, in effect, does the second comment contain that is not obvious (i.e., that only one who is perfect indeed can be considered perfect)?

(ii) What does Rabbi Jochanan's comment "like a perfect calf" add to our understanding of what preceded it?

(iii) The Midrash, in saying of the verse from the Psalms, "this refers to Sarah" seems to be explaining *that* verse rather than the verse from our Sidra which it set out to elucidate.

3. THE THIRD MIDRASH

After explaining the threefold repetition of the word "years" in our verse, the Midrash then comments on the apparently redundant phrase "these were the years of the life of Sarah," and relates it to the second phrase of the verse from Psalms, "and their inheritance shall be forever."

"Why did the Torah need to add, 'these were the years of the life of Sarah?' To tell us that the lives of the righteous are precious to G-d, both in this world and in the world to come."

But this too requires explanation:

(i) It is obvious that the righteous have a share in the world to come, and even that their future life is *precious to G-d*. Why then did the Midrash need to tell us this, and bring a verse from the Psalms to prove it?

(ii) Granted that the future life is hinted at by the repetition "And the *life* of Sarah was . . .; these were the years of the *life* of Sarah" (suggesting two lives, in this world and the next); but how from this verse do we learn the *additional* point that the lives of the righteous in the world to come are *precious to G-d?*

(iii) What is the *connection* between the two apparently un-related interpretations of the last phrase of the verse: The sim-ple meaning, that it refers to Sarah's life in this world; and the Midrashic explanation, that it speaks of her future life?

4. THE PRESERVATION OF PERFECTION

We will understand all these points if we first consider the following: When a man finds himself in an environment detri-mental to his standards, there are three ways in which he can preserve his integrity:

(i) He can strengthen himself inwardly not to be influ-enced by his surroundings. But this is an incomplete victory, for if he were to relax his self-control he would capitulate, thus implying a lowering of status.

(ii) He can separate himself from those around him. But again his victory is only because he has removed himself from temptation: He has not met it head-on, and is as prone as ever to be lowered.

(iii) Lastly, he can set out to influence his environment and raise it to his own level.[5] This is a complete triumph over one's surroundings—the dangers have not only been avoided, they have been removed entirely.

In the same way a man can preserve himself from change in the face of sin and even physical decay. He can master the ravages of time.

Firstly by strengthening himself *spiritually* he can discoun-tenance the blandishments of the material world. But here the possibility of sin remains, warded off only by constant vigi-lance. This is why the Midrash in speaking of Sarah says that when she was 100 she was *like* she was at 20—at this level there is only a *resemblance,* not an identity, of old age to youth.

Secondly, by living the life fired by the *essence* of the soul rather than by its manifest levels (i.e., by *retreat* from the physi-

---

5. Since man and his environment are affected by each other, it is ultimately impos-sible that one should not influence the other (Cf. *Rambam, Hilchot Deot,* beginning of ch. 6).

cal), one can transcend time and its bodily effects. But this again is an impermanent state, for the body retains its predilection for materialism.

Lastly, when the perceptions of the soul permeate the body and all its actions, one's physical nature is not suppressed but transformed, and the whole being partakes of the timelessness of the spirit in its relations with G-d. The *possibility* of sin does not arise.

5. THE CONSTANCY OF SARAH

This is why the Midrash explains that Sarah was, at 100, like she was at 20, only after it has cited the verse from Psalms and added, "just as they are perfect so their years *are* perfect." Only by *perfection* of a life comes that state of changelessness which characterized Sarah. And the repetition of the word "years" in the Sidra tells us that each total (100, 20 and 7) is compared to the others: At 100 Sarah was as far from the *possibility* of sin as she was at 20 or at 7. In other words, she had attained the highest of the three degrees of integrity.

But how can we reconcile this with the fact that she *did* undergo changes, and that there was a time when she lost her beauty? The word *"shnotam"* which means "their years" also means "their changes."[6] So the Midrash may subtly be telling us also that even "their *changes* were perfect." Even though (and indeed, because) externally the righteous alter and undergo vicissitudes, these ultimately serve only to reveal their underlying constancy, as the light of their souls shines undimmed.

6. THE FINAL PERFECTION

It has often been explained that the righteous "go from strength to strength"[7]—meaning that their life is (not merely progression within one level, but) a progression to infinitely higher levels of faithfulness. How then can it be to Sarah's

---

6. Cf. *Or Hatorah, Mikketz* 338b, that the word *shana*—year is from the same root as *shinui*—change.

7. *Psalms* 84:8.

praise that all her years were *equal* in their excellence? Surely this implies the *absence* of such a degree of progress?

This is the problem that the second Midrash comes to solve. By telling us that at the point of her death Sarah achieved "perfection in her actions," it discloses that she then reached that level of perfection and closeness to G-d that *retroactively* perfects all her previous actions (just as true repentance transforms the sins of the past into merits).[8]

The second Midrash thus goes beyond the first—for the first speaks of an attribute common to *all* the perfectly righteous figures of history; the second refers to Sarah alone ("this refers to Sarah"), that she transcended this level and actually transformed her earlier actions by her final repentance. And this was why Rabbi Jochanan added the analogy of the "perfect calf," for it was by the sacrifice of a calf (the *Eglah Arufah*[9]) that atonement was retroactively made for all the Children of Israel since their exodus from Egypt.[10]

7. THE PREMATURE DEATH

But still a problem remains.

Each life has its allotted span, and that limit defines the work which that life has to seek to achieve. But Sarah died *prematurely,* for, as the Rabbis say, "her soul fainted away"[11] when she heard the news of the binding of Isaac (through grief at the binding[12] or through excessive joy[13]). If she did not live to complete her span and its task, how can we call her life perfect?

To answer this, the Midrash tells us, the Torah adds "these were the years of the life of Sarah," because "the lives of the

---

8. The Hebrew word for repentance, *teshuvah,* means "return," for the act of repentance is a return, in life, of the soul to its Divine Source. The death of the righteous is also the return of the soul to its Source, and retroactively affects *every* action of their life (*Tanya*, Part IV, ch. 28).

9. Cf. *Devarim* 21:1-9.

10. *Horiot,* 6a; *Keritut,* 26a.

11. *Rosh Hashana,* 16b; *Baba Kama,* 93a.

12. *Bereishit Rabbah,* 58:5.

13. Riva's commentary *Sefer Hayashar.*

righteous are precious to G-d both in this world and the next."
In other words, the righteous who die before their time can
complete their work, even in the after-life. Just as the reward
for the creation of spiritual benefits is ascribed to the de-
ceased,[14] and the good acts of one's child helps a departed par-
ent.[15]

8. THE EVERLASTING SPIRIT

One final difficulty persists. Time in this life is granted to
us, not merely to achieve a certain amount of good works, but
also so that *time itself* be sanctified by our actions. A day filled
with Mitzvot is a day which has been made to fulfill its purpose. So even though Sarah could complete her task in other-
worldly domains, this-worldly time remained unsanctified and
imperfect.

This is why the verse, after mentioning the years of Sarah's
life, then continues: "These are the years of the life of Sarah,"
referring, as the Midrash tells us, to her *after-life*. Since the Torah reckons even this as a continuation of her years, it is telling
us that her sanctifying influence persisted in time even after her
death. The perfect life does not end in death: It sanctifies all
that comes after it.

(Source: Likkutei Sichot, Vol. V pp. 92-104)

---

14. *Pirkei Avot*, 5:8.
15. *Sanhedrin*, 104a.

פרשת תולדות
TOLEDOT

The Sidra of Toledot begins with an account of the generation of "Isaac the son of Abraham," and adds, "Abraham begat Isaac." Why the repetition? The Rebbe quotes four explanations, each of a different kind, each representing a different level of Biblical interpretation.

Each is apparently unconnected with any of the others, but the Rebbe explores them in depth and shows their inner relation to one another—demonstrating, by this example, the essential unity of the various ways of understanding the Torah.

1. THE FOUR EXPLANATIONS

Our Sidra begins with the words, "And these were the generations of Isaac the son of Abraham: Abraham begat Isaac."[1] The commentators on the Torah ask the immediate question, why does the verse repeat itself in telling us that Abraham begat Isaac?

Among the various answers given are the following:

(i) The Talmud[2] (and the Midrash[3]) say that the cynics of the time were casting aspersions on Abraham's parentage of Isaac (Sarah had lived childless with Abraham for many years; and yet she bore Isaac only after she had been forcibly taken by Abimelech).[4] Therefore, G-d made Isaac facially identical with Abraham so that everyone should recognize that he was indeed Abraham's son. The double expression of the verse gives testimony to this fact.

---

1. *Bereishit* 25:19.
2. *Baba Metzia*, 87a.
3. *Tanchuma, Toledot*, 1. Quoted by *Rashi*.
4. *Bereishit*, ch. 20.

28

(ii) The Midrash[5] comments: "Isaac was crowned with Abraham and Abraham was crowned with Isaac." Each was the other's pride.

(iii) The Chassidic explanation[6] is that Abraham is a figure, or paradigm, of the service of love and kindness, while Isaac is the exemplar of fear and strictness. Each of these poles of worship has two levels. There is the lower fear, which is adherence for fear of punishment for sin, or for any harm that may befall one as a result of sin, while the higher fear is a sense of awe in the face of the majesty of G-d, and a withdrawal from sin because it is against *G-d's* will.

The lower love is an attachment to G-d for the ulterior motive of reward, whether material or spiritual. But the higher love is independent of any desire for personal benefit, and is simply a cleaving to G-d for its own sake.

The verse, in its apparent repetition, is teaching us something about the relation of these four forms of service. The order of the names (Isaac, Abraham, Abraham, Isaac) tells us that the order of the worship of G-d starts with the lower fear, ascends to the lower love, and then to the higher love, and finally reaches its highest point in the higher fear.[7] The lower begets the higher, for though one starts by worshipping G-d for ulterior motives, one eventually comes to do it for its own sake.[8] And this applies to all Jews (that they must serve G-d with *both* love and fear[9]), for Abraham and Isaac and Jacob are called the "Fathers" of the Jewish people, meaning that *all* their descendants have inherited their capacities and the obligation to use them.

(iv) The Zohar[10] explains that Abraham stands symbolically for the soul (and Sarah, for the body. For the Torah says, "And

---

5. *Tanchuma, Toledot,* 4.
6. *Or Hatorah,* beginning of *Toledot.*
7. Cf. *Tanya,* Part I, ch. 43.
8. *Nazir,* 23b, etc. Rambam, *Hilchot Talmud Torah,* 3:5; *Hilchot Teshuvah,* 10:5. *Tanya,* Part I, ch. 39.
9. *Tanya,* Part I, ch. 41.
10. Part I, 135a.

Sarah died,"[11] meaning the body, which is mortal; while about Abraham it is written "And Abraham arose above the face of his dead,"[12] alluding to the soul, which transcends death). Isaac, whose name means "laughing" or "rejoicing," stands for the pleasures which the soul will have in the world to come. So the verse, thus translated, reads: "Pleasure will be the reward to the soul" ("Isaac, the son of Abraham") in the world to come, if "the soul begets pleasures ("Abraham begat Isaac") by its service in this world.

2. THE INNER UNITY

There is a general principle that when different interpretations are given to one and the same verse in the Torah, they are connected, even though superficially they seem to bear no relation to each other.

A proof of this is that the Rabbis[13] explain that the word "shaatnez" (the forbidden mixture of wool and linen) is a fusion of three words: "shuah" (combed), "tavui" (spun), and "nuz" (woven); and argue[14] that since the Torah combines these into one word it intends that a cloth must have all three properties before the Torah declares it shaatnez (i.e., that the wool and linen must be combed, spun and woven together). If we learn from the fusion of separate letters into one word that all three terms are connected, a fortiori must different explanations be connected if they are attached to the selfsame letters in Torah.

What is the relation between our four explanations?

All the stories of Torah have moral implication directly relevant to the life of each Jew.[15] And we can readily understand the moral of the Chassidic explanation above. It is that a Jew must serve G-d with both poles of his emotional responses: Love and fear. The implication of the Zohar's interpretation is

---

11. *Bereishit* 23:2.
12. Ibid., v. 3.
13. *Mishnah, Kelayim*, 9:8.
14. *Niddah*, 61b.
15. *Zohar*, Part III, 53b.

that by the this-worldly service of the Jew's embodied soul he creates spiritual pleasures which will be revealed to him in the world to come, and by recognizing this, his whole manner of service takes on a new life.

But what of the interpretations of the Talmud and the Midrash—which on the face of it have no immediate relevance to us?

The connection between these two is that both relate events which were out of the ordinary course of nature.

If *nature* had obeyed its physical laws, Abraham could not have had a child: He and his wife were old and barren. This is why when G-d told him he would bear a son, the Torah says: "He brought him outside,"[16] which the Rabbis[17] translate: "Break away from your astrological speculations," in which Abraham had foreseen that he would be childless.

And if the evolution of the spirit had taken its ordinary course (whereby succeeding generations diminish in spiritual stature; as the Rabbis[18] say, "If the earlier Jews were sons of angels, then we are sons of men, etc.") then Abraham would not have been "crowned" in Isaac. For this implied that Isaac completed and complemented his father's service, and supplied an element which Abraham himself lacked.

So both these explanations convey to us the profound fact that a Jew may transcend the constraints of natural law, not only in spiritual matters, but in material matters as well.

Abraham had, as it were, spiritual offspring before Isaac, for "the offspring of the righteous are their good works."[19] But the birth of Isaac proved that even in the physical domain miraculous events attended him.

And this is the real refutation of the "cynics of the generation." For their claim was (in depth) that though they conceded that a Jew might transcend limitations in the spiritual realms, to

---

16. *Bereishit* 15:5.
17. *Shabbat*, 156a; quoted by *Rashi*.
18. *Shabbat*, 112b.
19. *Rashi*, *Bereishit* 6:9.

produce an effect in the physical world required the temporal
power of the secular rulers (the claim that *Abimelech* was the
father of Isaac); i.e., in material affairs he is subject to natural
law.

In making Isaac facially resemble Abraham, G-d made his
true parentage apparent to all, showing that the channel of
physical power was Abraham (the soul, to follow the Zohar's
reading) not Abimelech (the worldly ruler). The soul has no
hindrances, either in itself or when it seeks to translate the devotion into action.

3. THE SOUL'S FREEDOM

This leads us to an understanding of the words of Rabbi
Yosef Yitzchak (sixth Lubavitcher Rebbe):[20]

"All the people on the face of the earth must know this:
That only our bodies have been sent into exile and the servitude of (foreign) rulers. But our souls have not been exiled or
enslaved.

"We must say openly before all, that in all matters relating
to our religion, the Torah, the commandments and the cus-
toms of Israel, we Jews have no-one who can dictate to us, nor
may any pressure be brought to bear against us."

This is, on the face of it, paradoxical, for what advantage is
it if the soul is free so long as the body is in exile, and the soul
must fulfill G-d's will through the body in the physical world?

But in fact, such is the strength of the soul's arousal that it
can remove the body from its servitude to physical constraints.
And this must be done openly so that "all the people on the
face of the earth" (including the "cynics of the generation")
should see that Abimelech (worldly power) has no domain
over the Jew either in body or in soul.

4. SERVICE AND REWARD

The connection between the four interpretations is now
clear.

---

20. 3 Tammuz, 5627. Printed in *Likkutei Dibburim*, p. 692.

The Talmud belongs to the "revealed" part of Torah, so it addresses itself to the skepticism which can arise here in this "revealed" physical world, answering the challenge of the "cynics" by showing that even at a material level a Jew is not subject to the constraints of nature.

The Midrash is an intermediate link between Torah's "revealed" and "inward" aspects,[21] so it treats the subject in the same way as the Talmud, and also gives a deeper explanation, showing that a Jew transcends nature, also the normal ("natural") spiritual order. He stands aside from the progressive decline of the human spirit, so that "the crown of the old is their grandchildren"[22]—the later generations perfect the service of the earlier. (And since the Midrash, in this, its second comment, speaks from a level in which cynicism has no place, it has no cause to answer it in the way that the Talmud does.)

Chassidut—which explains the path of service of G-d—also takes us into the realm of "higher than nature." Its moral was that each Jew must serve G-d with love and fear together. Now, normally these are incompatible emotions—love means drawing *near;* fear is the consciousness of a *distance* separating. But in worship of G-d the Jew transcends the natural movement of his feelings and can fuse these two opposite responses[23] in a unique involvement of his whole being. When he does this, he is set apart by Heaven from the course of nature, both physically (as in the Talmud's interpretation) and spiritually (as in the Midrash).

The Zohar, which expresses the esoteric aspect of Torah, speaks of the world to come, and explains that by a Jew's efforts in this world to let his soul break through the bounds of embodied existence, he is rewarded by the spiritual delights of the future life.

---

21. Cf. *Tanya*, Part IV, ch. 23.
22. *Proverbs* 17:6.
23. *Sifri, Devarim* 6:5.

5. THE REWARD IS THE ACT

To take this further, it is said[24] that "the reward of a Mitzvah (commandment) is a Mitzvah"; that is, the reward lies in the act itself, and not in the *later and additional* pleasure. For, in the world to come, what is granted to the Jew is not an incidental consequence of his good works, but is the good works themselves, revealed in their true character. For now, possessed of a body, he does not perceive the inner spiritual reality of an act of doing G-d's will. In the afterlife he does, and this is his reward.

The first three explanations speak about the act of performing a Mitzvah, while the Zohar directs itself to the reward. But since *the reward is the act,* we can see a closer unity between all four.

6.   THE SERVICE OF THE BODY, THE REWARD OF THE SOUL

Isaac was so called because the name means "rejoice," and Sarah said, when he was born to her in her old age, "G-d had made rejoicing for me."[25] Now the name of G-d used in this verse is Elokim, which is usually taken to refer to G-d's *imminence* in nature ("Elokim" is, in fact, numerically equivalent to the Hebrew word for nature), which serves to conceal the four-lettered name which stands for G-d's *transcendence.* And there is a Chassidic explanation that the verse means "rejoicing has come from my service of sanctifying nature." That is, that in the physical world is hidden the imminent presence of G-d. And by dedicating one's acts in holiness, one draws out this presence into openness and revelation, which is the Divine purpose in creation, causing G-d Himself to rejoice.

Man, who was created in the image of G-d, also has, as it were, both imminent and transcendent aspects[26]—the body and the soul respectively. And as G-d rejoices through our sanctifi-

---

24. *Pirkei Avot,* 4:2.
25. *Bereishit* 21:6. *Torah Or, Toledot.*
26. Cf. *Tanya,* Part II, ch. 6.

cation of the world, so He rejoices in our sanctification of the body, for this is the fulfillment of the Divine purpose.

And while now it is the soul which gives life to the body, in the world to come it will be the body which will be the giver of life to the soul. For the purpose of creation is realized by refinement of the body, and since the *soul is* the force which refines the body, it will therefore share in the pleasure created through its effect on the body.

This, then, is the ultimate connection between the four interpretations. The first three speak of man's service, of how the soul lifts the body out of its natural constraints, and by transforming nature into manifest holiness brings pleasure to G-d ("Abraham begat Isaac," or "the soul *creates* pleasures"). As a result, the soul is rewarded by these very pleasures in the world to come—the concern of the Zohar—when "Isaac is the son of Abraham," or, "the soul *receives* its pleasures" in return.

(Source: Likkutei Sichot, Vol. III pp. 780-7)

פרשת ויצא

VAYYETZE

This Sidra contains an account of Jacob's four marriages, all (according to Rashi) to daughters of Laban. Now this appears to contradict the traditional view that Jacob (together with Abraham and Isaac) kept all the commandments of the Torah despite the fact that G-d had not yet given them to Israel—out of a combination of personal zealousness and a prophetic knowledge of what the law would be—for marriage to two sisters is later prohibited. Rashi seems to offer no explanation of the difficulty and the Rebbe considers a number of possible solutions, eventually reconciling the apparent contradiction, and drawing out the moral implications of the story.

1. JACOB'S WIVES

An important and well-known principle about Rashi's commentary on the Torah, is that his policy is to answer all the difficulties which are apparent in construing a *literal* interpretation[1] of the verses. And when he cannot find an answer on this level, he will note the difficulty and add, "I do not know" how to resolve it.[2] When there is a difficulty which Rashi does not even point out, this is because the answer is obvious, even to a five-year-old (the age when a Jewish child begins to study the Torah[3]).

It is therefore very strange that we find in this week's Sidra a puzzling fact, that has preoccupied many commentators, and which Rashi not only does not explain, but appears to take no notice of at all.

---

1. The *peshat* as opposed to the other kinds of interpretation: the linking of passages by allusion *(remez);* homiletical or allegorical *(drush);* and esoteric or mystical *(sod).*
2. Cf. e.g., in the previous Sidra; *Bereishit* 28:5.
3. *Pirkei Avot,* 5:22.

36

We are told that Jacob married both Rachel and Leah, and later Bilhah and Zilpah, all daughters of Laban.[4] Now since we have a tradition that the forefathers kept the entire Torah, even though it had not yet been given,[5] how can it be that Jacob married four sisters when we are told in Vayikra[6]: "Thou shall not take a woman to her sister"—that is, one may not marry the sister of one's wife.

Perhaps we could say that Rashi does not comment on the problem because when the "five-year-old" learns this Sidra, he does not know that Jacob's act was forbidden (for the law does not appear until Vayikra, and the child has not yet reached that book). However, this will not do, for Rashi does not explain the difficulty even later on.

Alternatively, it is possible that Rashi felt that, amongst the many explanations of the point given in other commentaries, there was one sufficiently obvious that he was not bound to mention it. But this also will not explain his silence, since firstly, there are many disagreements among these other commentators, so the explanation is not obvious; and secondly, they are not explanations of the *literal* meaning of the text—which is therefore still wanting.

2. SOME EXPLANATIONS

Ramban[7] offers the explanation that the forefathers kept the 613 commandments of the Torah only when they lived in Israel, whereas Jacob married the two (four) sisters while he was in Haran. But Rashi could not consistently hold this view, for he says elsewhere of Jacob, "while I stayed with the wicked Laban (i.e., in Haran), I kept the 613 commandments."[8]

---

4. Cf. *Rashi, Bereishit* 31:50.
5. Cf. *Rashi, Bereishit* 32:5 regarding Jacob.
6. *Vayikra* 18:18.
7. On *Parshat Toledot* 26:5.
8. *Rashi, Bereishit* 32:5—a play on the word "stayed" which in Hebrew has the numerical value 613 (*Garti-Taryag*).

Another explanation[9] is that Jacob was in fact obeying a specific command of G-d in order to have the 12 sons who would later become the 12 tribes. But though it is clear that G-d's explicit command would have overridden the prohibition involved, nonetheless we find no indication in the Torah that G-d commanded Jacob to take Rachel, Bilhah or Zilpah in marriage. On the contrary, it is clear from the narrative that he married Rachel because he wanted her, from the very outset, to be his wife; and both Bilhah and Zilpah were given to Jacob as wives, by their mistresses[10] (they were the handmaids of Rachel and Leah): He did not *take* them in obedience to a command from G-d.

3. THE ARGUMENT FROM LENIENCY

There has been intensive speculation as to whether the forefathers, in undertaking to keep the Torah before it has been given, accepted only those rulings which were more *stringent* than the (then binding) Noachide Laws, or also accepted the rulings which were more *lenient.* If we follow the second view, and remember that all four sisters must have converted to Judaism before their marriages, and take into account the lenient ruling that "a convert is like a new-born child"[11]—then it would follow that the wives were no longer considered sisters, since their lineage was affected by their conversion.

However, even this answer is unsatisfactory at the level of literal interpretation.

(a) Before the Giving of the Torah, there is no Biblical evidence that Jews had any other law than the Noachide Code (other than the specifically mentioned obligation of circumcision etc.). So the undertaking of the forefathers was entirely a *self-imposed* thing, and did not involve their children[12] in any obligation. It follows that there was no general legal distinction, before the Giving of the Torah, between Jews as such and the

---

9. *Parashat Derachim.*
10. *Bereishit* 30:4; Ibid., 9.
11. *Yevamot*, 22a.
12. Cf. *Shemot* 6:20 "And Amram married Yocheved his aunt."

other descendants of Noah. Hence, the whole idea of conversion did not arise.

Nor can we support our point by saying that the voluntary undertaking of the 613 commandments was itself a kind of conversion. For this was a *self-imposed stringency* and could not have included the lenient ruling that "a convert is like a new-born child."

(b) Besides which, Rashi, in his commentary on the Torah, never *mentions* this law; and indeed a literal reading of the Torah inclines one to the *contrary* view, for G-d says to Abraham, "You shall come to your fathers in peace."[13] In other words, even after Abraham's conversion, Terach is still regarded as his *father,* to whom he will be joined in death.

(c) Lastly, the prohibition of marrying one's wife's sister is not simply because she belongs to the category of those forbidden for the closeness of their relation to the would-be husband; but for the additional *psychological* reason that it might put enmity and jealousy in place of the natural love between two sisters.[14] So even if the law "a convert is like a new-born child" applied before the Giving of the Torah, it would not be relevant in the present instance, for there is still a natural love between two converted sisters,[15] which would be endangered by their sharing a husband.

4. INDIVIDUAL AND COLLECTIVE UNDERTAKINGS

The explanation is that the manner in which Abraham, Isaac and Jacob kept the Torah was one of *self-imposed stringency* alone (and this is why it was so esteemed by G-d: "Inasmuch as Abraham harkened to My voice, and kept My charge, My commands, ordinances and laws"[16]). If so, then clearly if something which they *had* been commanded conflicted with something they did only from their own zealousness, the former, having *G-d's* authority, would overrule the latter.

---

13. *Bereishit* 15:15.
14. As stated explicitly in *Vayikra* 18:18 "to be a rival to her."
15. Cf. *Rashi, Bereishit* 32:7-12.
16. *Bereishit* 26:5.

This is—at the simple level—why Abraham did not circumcise himself until he was commanded to (when he was 99
years old); for the Noachide Code forbade shedding one's
blood—even when it would not harm one.[17] And though circumcision outweighed this prohibition, it could only do so
when *commanded* by G-d.

Now, besides the Seven Noachide Laws, there were other
restraints that the descendants of Noah *voluntarily* undertook.
As Rashi says,[18] "the non-Jewish nations had restrained themselves from unchastity (i.e., even in relationships which had not
been *expressly* forbidden to them) as a consequence of the flood
(which was a punishment for this sin)." And this explains what
Rashi says elsewhere,[19] that the Torah mentions the death of
Terach, Abraham's father, *before* Abraham left his father's
house, even though he left, in fact, before his father died, "so
that this matter should not become known to all, in case people
should say that Abraham did not show a son's respect for his
father." Even though respecting one's parents had not yet been
commanded by G-d,[20] nonetheless since the nations had of their
own accord undertaken this duty, it had acquired something of
the force of law. To the extent that Jacob was *punished* by G-d[21]
for not respecting his parents—simply because of the status
which this universal voluntary undertaking had acquired.

It follows that if there were a conflict between the *self-
imposed stringencies* of the Forefathers (as *individuals)* and the
voluntary restraints of the descendants of Noah (en masse), the
latter overruled the former.

And one of these restraints that had become universally
adopted was that of taking care not to deceive others, as is evi-
denced by Jacob's accusation against Laban,[22] "Why have you

17. *Bereishit* 9:5. *Rashi.*
18. *Bereishit* 34:7.
19. *Bereishit* 11:32.
20. *Rashi, Shemot* 24:3; *Devarim* 5:16. *Sanhedrin*, 56b.
21. *Rashi, Bereishit* 28:9.
22. *Bereishit* 29:25.

deceived me?" against which Laban takes pains to *justify* himself (showing that he agreed that deception was a sin).

Now we can at last see why Jacob married Rachel. For he had promised her that he would marry her, and even gave her signs to prove her identity on their wedding night.[23] Not to marry her would have involved deception, and this had a force which overruled his *(individual)* undertaking not to marry his wife's sister (in accordance with what G-d would *later* command).

5. THE CONCERN DUE TO OTHERS

One of the morals which this implies is that when a man wishes to take more on himself than G-d has yet demanded of him, he must first completely satisfy himself that he is not doing so at the expense of others. And indeed, in the case of Abraham, we find that his preciousness in the eyes of G-d was not primarily that he undertook to keep the whole Torah before it had been given, but rather,[24] "I know him (which Rashi translates as 'I hold him dear') because he will command his children and his household after him to keep to the way of the L-rd, doing righteousness and justice."

And the *self-imposed* task of personal refinement must not be at another's expense, either materially or spiritually. When a fellow-Jew knows nothing of his religious heritage and needs, as it were, spiritual charity, it is not open to another Jew who is in a position to help him, to say, "Better that I should spend my time perfecting *myself.*" For he must judge himself honestly and answer the question, "Who am I that these *extra* refinements in myself are worth depriving another Jew of the very *fundamentals* of his faith?" And he will then see the truth which underlies Jacob's marriage to Rachel, that care for others overrides the concern for the self-perfection which goes beyond G-d's law.

(Source: Likkutei Sichot, Vol. V pp. 141-8)

---

23. *Rashi, Bereishit* 29:25.
24. *Bereishit* 18:19.

פרשת וישלח

VAYISHLACH

In this week's Sidra Jacob, after his struggle with the angel, is told that his name is now to be Israel. And yet we find him still referred to, on subsequent occasions in the Torah, as Jacob. Yet after Abraham's name was changed from Abram, he is never again called in the Torah by his earlier name. What is the difference between the two cases? The Rebbe explains the meaning of the names of "Jacob" and "Israel," of the two stages in the religious life that they represent, and of their relevance to us today.

1. WHY JACOB REMAINS

Concerning the verse, "And your name shall no longer be Jacob: Instead Israel shall be your name,"[1] the Talmud[2] poses the following problem: Anyone who calls Abraham, Abram transgresses the command, "And your name shall no longer be called Abram."[3] If so, surely the same applies to one who uses the name Jacob to refer to Israel, for it is written, "'And your name shall no longer be Jacob?" The Talmud concludes that the name Jacob is different from the name Abram in this respect, that after G-d gave Abraham his new name, the Torah never thereafter refers to him by any name other than Abraham. Whereas Jacob is so called in the Torah even after he has been given the name of Israel.

Why does the name Jacob remain?

There is a Chassidic explanation[4] that the names "Jacob" and "Israel" denote two stages in the service of G-d, both necessary at different times in the religious life of every Jew.

---

1. *Bereishit* 32:29.
2. *Berachot*, 13a.
3. *Bereishit* 17:5.
4. Cf. *Likkutei Torah* on Balak. *Sefer Hamaamarim-Yiddish*, p. 122.

"Israel" denotes a higher achievement, but it does not supplant
or remove the necessity for the service signified by "Jacob."

2. THE INNER MEANING OF "JACOB" AND "ISRAEL"

The difference between them is this. The name "Jacob"
implies that he acquired the blessings of Isaac "by supplanting
and subtlety"[5] (the name in Hebrew, Ya-akov, means he sup-
planted"). He used cunning to take the blessings which had
been intended for Esau. "Israel," on the other hand, denotes
the receiving of blessings through "noble conduct (Serarah,
which is linguistically related to Yisrael, the Hebrew form of
Israel), and in an open manner."[6]

However the Torah is interpreted, its literal meaning remains true. And the blessings of Isaac referred to the physical
world and its benefits: "G-d give you of the dew of the heaven
and the fatness of the earth."[7] Jacob and Rebecca made great
sacrifices and resorted to deceit to acquire them. Jacob had to
dress himself in the clothes of Nimrod,[8] whose kingdom
turned the whole world to rebellion,[9] in order to take and
transform the elements of the physical world to holiness (to
release their "buried sparks of holiness").

The deeds of the Fathers are a sign to their children.[10] And
the implication for us of Jacob's act is that we have to use cunning in our approach to the acts of our physical nature. The
cunning man does not reveal his intentions. He seems to be
following the path of his *opponent*. But at the crucial point he
does what *he* had all along intended. The Jew in his involvement with the material world *appears* to be preoccupied with it.
He eats, drinks, transacts business. But he does so for the sake
of heaven. His objectives are not material ones. He wears the

---

5. *Rashi*, on *Bereishit* 32:29.
6. Ibid.
7. *Bereishit* 27:28.
8. *Pirkei deRabbi Eliezer*, ch. 24. *Bereishit Rabbah*, 65:16; cited in *Rashi*, on *Bereishit* 27:15.
9. *Eruvin*, 53a. *Rashi, Bereishit* 10:8.
10. Cf. on this theme, supra, p. 13 ff.

"clothes of Esau," but his implicit purpose is to uncover and elevate the "holy sparks."

But the way of "Israel" is to attain the blessings of "the dew of the heaven and the fatness of the earth" by "noble and open conduct." In worldly conduct he has no need to conceal his intention of serving G-d. He experiences no tensions. The world has no hold on him. It does not hide from him its intrinsic G-dliness.

This distinction can be seen in the difference between a Shabbat and a weekday meal. Eating a weekday meal embodies the tension between a physical act and its spiritual motivation for the sake of heaven. This discrepancy between outward appearance and inner intention is a form of cunning. But eating a Shabbat meal in itself fulfills a commandment. The holiness of the physical is manifest.

In the light of this we can understand the meaning of the verse, "Your name shall no longer be Jacob, but Israel, for you have contended with G-d *(Elokim)* and with *men* and you have prevailed."[11] "Elokim" in this context means "angels,"[12] and generally connotes the "seventy heavenly princes" through whom flow the Divine emanations which sustain physical existence, and who thereby act to conceal G-dliness.[13] "Men" signifies a still greater concealment, for men are capable of denigrating the Jew for performing G-d's will, and this is a harder concealment to bear. For this reason, the first paragraph of the entire Shulchan Aruch warns us "not to be ashamed of men who ridicule." And this is the basis of the whole of a Jew's service—to break down the concealment of G-d.

This was the virtue of Israel, to have "contended with Elokim and with men" and to have prevailed over their respective concealments of G-d. They are no longer barriers to him; indeed they assent to his blessings. He not only won his struggle with the angel (the guardian angel of Esau) but the angel

---

11. *Bereishit* 32:29.
12. Cf. *Targum Yonathan*, ad loc. *Chullin*, 92a.
13. Cf. *Tanya*, Part IV, ch. 25.

himself blessed him. This is the achievement of which the Proverbs speak: "He makes even his enemies be at peace with him."[14]

3. THE STRUGGLE

This distinction accords with the explanation given in Likkutei Torah[15] of the verse, "He has not seen sin in Jacob nor toil in Israel."[16] At the level of "Jacob" the Jew has no sin, but he still experiences "toil"—his freedom from sin is achieved only by tension and struggle for he has concealments to overcome. This is why he is called "Jacob, my servant"[17] for "service" (in Hebrew, *avodah*) has the implication of strenuous effort to refine his physical nature (his "animal soul"). He does not sin but he still experiences the inclination to sin, which he must overcome. But "Israel" encounters no "toil," for in his struggle "with Elokim and with men" he broke down the factors which conceal G-dliness and silenced his dissenting inclinations. Israel no longer needs to contend with those forces which oppose the perception of G-dliness. His progress lies entirely within the domain of the holy.

4. PARTIAL AND COMPLETE VICTORY

There is a story told by the previous Lubavitcher Rebbe, Rabbi Yosef Yitzchak, about the Tzemach Tzedek (the third Rebbe): Once in the middle of a Chassidic gathering the Tzemach Tzedek jumped onto a table in great excitement and said: "What is the difference between something which is killed completely and something which is only partially killed? (This refers to a statement in the Talmud:[18] that to have 'partially' killed something *is* to have killed it.) The Tzemach Tzedek giving the halachic point a Chassidic meaning, applies it to the

---

14. *Proverbs* 16:7.
15. *Parshat Balak*, 72b.
16. *Bamidbar* 23:21.
17. *Isaiah* 44:1.
18. *Baba Kama*, 65a.

'killing' of the inclination to sin. Even a 'partial' killing is a killing, but at the very least we must partially kill it." After some time had passed in speaking and dancing, he continued: "At the moment that one has reached the point of 'killing' (the moment of which the Psalms[19] speak in the words, 'My heart is void within me') one's life has taken on a new character."

These two statements of the Tzemach Tzedek refer to the two levels of "Jacob" and "Israel." At the level of "Jacob" there is still a struggle against one's inclinations, a life of tension—a partial killing. But at the level of "Israel" when the killing is "complete," life is transformed into a new serenity and spiritual pleasure.

5.   LEVELS IN THE LIFE OF THE TZADDIK AND THE BENONI

These two stages of service pertain to two levels within the "G-dly soul." "Jacob" can be analyzed into the letter Yud and the work *ekev* (the heel). Here the perception of G-d (symbolized by the letter "Yud") has reached only the *lowest* levels of the soul, creating the possibility of a concealment which has to be broken down. On the other hand "Israel" contains the same letters as "Li Rosh" ("The head is mine"). The whole soul, to its *highest* capacities, has been permeated by the awareness of G-d, and no concealment is possible, no struggle necessary.

In general terms, "Israel" denotes the *Tzaddik* (the stage of complete righteousness) and "Jacob" the *Benoni* (the intermediate level, attainable by every man[20]). And in particular, *within* this intermediate level, that "Jacob" represents the weekday service, and "Israel" the service of Shabbat. Even within the stage of complete righteousness, there are still analogues of both "Jacob" and "Israel." This is clear from the fact that Israel himself was still occasionally called Jacob after his change of

---

19. 109:22. Cf. *Tanya*, Part I, ch. 1.
20. *Tanya*, Part I, ch. 14.

name. Within him, and indeed in every Jew, "Jacob" remains as a necessary element in the service of G-d.

6. THE CONTEMPORARY MEANING OF "JACOB"

From the fact that, as we mentioned before, the level of Jacob is without sin, and yet involves continual effort, it follows that the Jew—though his struggle with contending desires is difficult and fraught with risk—has the power to achieve victory and remain free from sin. For he is "a branch of My planting, the work of My hands,"[21] and "a part of G-d above."[22] As nothing can prevail over G-d, so can nothing prevail over the Jew against his will. And he has been *promised* victory, for we are told, "His banished will not be rejected by Him"[23] and "All Israel has a share in the world to come."[24]

This promise (like all the words of Torah) is relevant to our present spiritual concerns. The assurance of ultimate victory should strengthen our joy in the act of service, and this joy will itself contribute to the victory over our physical natures, and shorten the battle. The previous Rebbe said:[25] though a soldier confronts danger, he goes with a song of joy, and the joy brings him victory.

This is why we say, after the end of Shabbat, "Do not fear, My servant Jacob." For, as we explained above, during Shabbat the Jew stands at the level of Israel; beyond the Shabbat, when we return to the level of "Jacob, My servant," and to the toil of the weekday service, we are told, "Do not fear." This is not merely a command but also a source of strength and of the joy that will shorten the work and hasten its reward—to the point where we are worthy of the time which is "an eternal life of Shabbat and rest."

(Source: Likkutei Sichot, Vol. III pp. 795-9)

---

21. *Isaiah* 60:21.

22. *Job* 31:2 (*Tanya*, Part I, ch. 2).

23. *II Samuel* 14:14. *Shulchan Aruch Harav, Hilchot Talmud Torah*, 4:3; *Tanya*, Part I, end of ch. 39.

24. *Sanhedrin*, 90a.

25. *Sefer Hamaamarim* 5710, p. 191.

פרשת וישב
VAYESHEV

Vayeshev, and the following Sidra of Mikketz, have a common theme: Dreams. In Vayeshev we are told of Joseph's dreams, and in Mikketz, about the dreams of Pharaoh. Both dreamt twice, and in each case the dreams shared a single meaning, conveyed in different symbols. What was the significant difference between Joseph's and Pharaoh's dreams? Why did they dream twice? And what is the implication of their detailed symbolism? The answers are given in terms of the Jew's contemporary search for a path to G-d.

1. TWO DREAMERS AND FOUR DREAMS

In the beginning of this week's Sidra we are told about Joseph's two dreams.[1] Both had the same meaning: That Joseph would rule over his brothers and that they would pay homage to him. The second dream merely added that the "sun and the moon"—Jacob and Bilhah would be included in this homage.

There is a striking parallel between this and next week's Sidra (Mikketz) which relates the two dreams of Pharaoh,[2] which also shared a single meaning. But in Pharaoh's case the Torah states a reason why there should have been two dreams: "Because the thing is established by G-d, and G-d will shortly bring it to pass."[3] Of Joseph's dreams, no explanation is given of their repetition, and indeed the additional information that the second conveys could have been hinted at in the first. We are forced to conclude that Joseph's two dreams, alike though they are in their meaning, are allusions to two different things.

What are these two things? And, since the actions of the Fathers are both a sign and a lesson to their descendants,[4] what

---

1. *Bereishit* 37:5-9.
2. *Bereishit* 41:1-7.
3. *Bereishit* 41:32.
4. Cf., for example, supra p. 13.

48

are their implications for us? For Joseph's actions are included in the works of the Fathers, since he brought Jacob's work into fruition in the world as hinted to in the verse: "These are the generations of Jacob: Joseph. . . ."[5]

2. THE SHEAVES AND THE STARS

Joseph's two dreams have the following difference. The first concerns things of the earth: "And behold, we were binding sheaves in the midst of a field." But the second is about the heavens: "The sun and the moon and eleven stars."

Both of Pharaoh's dreams, however, had an earthly symbolism regressing in fact from the domain of living things (the seven cows) to that of plants (the seven ears of corn). For Pharaoh had no link with the realm of heaven. And whereas his dreams represent a regression, Joseph's display an ascent in holiness.[6]

This distinction between Joseph and Pharaoh exemplifies one of the unique characteristics of the Jew, that he is simultaneously involved in both the material and spiritual, this world and the next. As the previous Lubavitcher Rebbe said[7] when he was arrested in Russia in 1927 and one of his interrogators threatened him with a revolver: "Men who have many gods and one world are frightened by a revolver; a man who has one G-d and two worlds has nothing to fear." These two worlds are not separate in time—a this-worldly present and an other-worldly future. The Jew is instead bound to a higher spiritual reality even in the midst of this world. He stands on a "ladder" set on the earth whose top reaches to heaven"[8] and moves in his service from the mundane ("earth") to the most exalted spirituality ("heaven"), always ascending.

---

5. *Bereishit* 37:2. Cf. *Biurei HaZohar*, 30a. *Or Hatorah*, 386a.
6. For the relation between these notions of "ascent" and "regression" in holiness, and the idea of Chanukah (which always falls at the time of these two Sidrot) cf. *Shabbat*, 21b, and Chassidic writings on Chanukah.
7. Cf. *Rabbi Joseph I. Schneersohn* (biography) p. 13.
8. *Bereishit* 28:12.

3. TWO WORLDS WITHIN ONE WORLD

The Torah is precise, and every detail contains a lesson which has a bearing on the conduct of our life.[9] The implication of the fact that Joseph's dreams were about two worlds (earth and heaven) and yet had a single meaning, is that the Jew must fuse his dual involvement, with the material and the spiritual, into one. Not only must there be no tension between his two worlds, but the material must contribute to his spiritual life until it is itself spiritualized.[10]

The idea that physical acts like eating and drinking are directed towards G-d, is a natural one to every Jew.

There is a story[11] about the Rebbe, Rabbi Shmuel:[12]

Once, when his two sons were children they were discussing the special virtues of the Jew, and to demonstrate his point he asked their servant:

"Bentzion—have you eaten?"

The servant replied: "Yes."

"Did you eat well?"

"I am satisfied, thank G-d."

"Why did you eat?"

"In order to live."

"Why do you live?"

"To be a Jew and to do what G-d wishes."

As he said this, the servant sighed.

Later, the Rebbe told his children:

"You see, a Jew by his nature eats to live, and lives to be a Jew and to do what G-d has told him; and still he sighs that he has not yet reached the ultimate truth."

---

9. Cf. *Zohar*, Part III, 53b.

10. Cf. *Hayom Yom*, 27 Elul. The point is emphasized by *Rambam* (*Hilchot Deot*, beginning of ch. 4) where he says "a healthy and perfect body is part of the path of (serving and knowing) G-d."

11. *Likkutei Dibburim*, p. 421.

12. The fourth Lubavitcher Rebbe (1834-1882).

Since the Jew has a spiritual intention in every physical act, the acts themselves are spiritualized. In the words of the Baal Shem Tov: "Where a man's desires are—there he is."[13]

4. THE MEANING OF THE SHEAVES

This, then, is the significance of the fact that Joseph had two dreams. What is the meaning of the detailed content of each?

The first begins, "We were binding sheaves in the midst of a field." It begins, in other words, with *work,* an activity wholly absent from the dreams of Pharaoh. In the domain of unholiness, work (i.e., *avodah,* the effort involved in the service of G-d) may be absent, as we find it written: "We ate in Egypt free" (i.e., without the effort of the Mitzvot).[14] But the rewards of holiness (the emanations of the Divine) come only through effort. And so the Jew's ascent on the ladder from earth to heaven must—from the very beginning—involve the *work* of dedicating his physical actions to holiness.

The nature of this work—as in Joseph's dream—is *binding sheaves.*[15] We are born into a world of concealment which is like a field, in which things and people, like stalks of corn, grow apart, living separately, in and for themselves. In man we call this orientation towards the self, the "animal soul," which creates diversity and separateness. And the Jew must go beyond it, binding like sheaves the many facets of his being into the unified service of G-d, a service which transcends self and separation.

In the dream, the sheaves, after they were bound, bowed down to Joseph's sheaf. And so, for us, the next stage in service must be "bowing down," the submission to what is higher than us. Jews form a unity, as if they were the limbs of one body.[16] And just as a body is coordinated only when its muscles act in

---

13. Cf. *Sefer Hamaamarim-Kuntresim,* p. 818. *Likkutei Dibburim,* p. 226, and elsewhere.
14. *Bamidbar* 11:5. *Sifri* and *Rashi* there. Cf. also *Zohar,* Part II, 128a.
15. Cf. *Torah Or,* 28a.
16. *Likkutei Torah,* beginning of *Parshat Nitzavim.*

response to the nervous system of the brain, so the spiritual health of the collective body of Jews is dependent on their responsiveness to their "head"—the spiritual leader of the generation.[17] It is he who instructs it so that its individual members act in harmony towards their proper goal.

Indeed, inwardly this submission *precedes* the act of unifying one's existence in the service of G-d. The capacity to effect this "binding together" derives from the inner submission to the spiritual leader of the generation. But the outward manifestation of this service follows the order of Joseph's dream: First the "binding," and then the submission.

5. THE MEANING OF THE STARS

But this is at the level of Joseph's first dream. Service at this level is still confined to the "earth"—the limits of physical existence. And it remains for the Jew to transcend these constraints, in the act of *teshuvah* ("repentance," or more correctly, "return"). The real process of teshuvah comes when "the spirit returns to G-d who gave it";[18] that is, when the soul of the Jew regains its pristine state, as it was prior to its embodiment. This does not mean that soul and body should—G-d forbid—become separate or that bodily existence should be denied, but that the body should cease to conceal the light of the soul. This is the ultimate purpose of the descent of the soul into the body within a physical existence—that without denying or standing aloof from this mode of existence—the soul should retain its unmediated closeness to G-d.

This is the meaning of Joseph's second dream. It speaks of the Jew who has already passed beyond the service which is confined to "earth." He has left the world of "separation"—the state where things are seen to exist in and for themselves—and no longer needs to "bind" together the schismatic elements of his being. His service is now wholly at the level of "heaven," the path of return to the pristine state of the soul.

---

17. Cf. *Tanya*, Part I, ch. 2. *Sefer Hamaamarim* 5710, p. 254.
18. *Ecclesiastes* 12:7. Cf. *Likkutei Torah*, beginning of Parshat Ha-azinu.

But the act of submission to the "head" of the collective body of the Jewish people is repeated in this dream (where the sun, moon and eleven stars bow down). This clearly implies that this inward attitude of reference is not restricted to the Jew who is still working "in the field," but extends to the Jew who has already, as it were, reached the heavens. Certainly he no longer needs guidance to avoid the concealments and distortions that the physical life may bring to one's spiritual sight. But even at this level, he must still act in harmony with other Jews in collective response to their spiritual leader.

6. THE RUNGS OF THE LADDER TO HEAVEN

This, then, is the path mapped out for every Jew by the dreams of Joseph. First there is the "work in the field," the effort (avodah) to unify a world of separate existences and divided selves, within the service of G-d ("binding sheaves"). And though the Jewish people are called "the sons of kings,"[19] or even simply "kings,"[20] this does not imply that this effort can be dispensed with. For the rewards of holiness must be worked for in this world. And they are rewards which it is beyond our power to anticipate: They will be "found"—that is, they will be unexpected.[21] We read: "If a man says to you, I have labored and have not found (a reward), do not believe him. If he says, I have not labored, but still I have found, do not believe him. But if he says, I have labored and I have found—believe him."[22]

Secondly, at all levels of service there must be submission to the "head" of the "body" of the Jewish people.

And then, as we are told in the Pirkei Avot,[23] when "your will is nullified (in the face of His will)" it will follow that "He will nullify the will of others in the face of your will." In other words, the concealments of this world of plurality and disunity

---

19. *Shabbat*, 67a. *Zohar*, Part I, 27b.
20. *Berachot*, 9b.
21. Because they will be far more abundant than our service merits.
22. *Megillah*, 6b.
23. 2:4.

("others") will lose their power, and we will be open to the flow of revelation and spiritual life that is the life of Joseph and of righteousness.

(Source: Likkutei Sichot, Vol. III pp. 805-10)

חנוכה

CHANUKAH

In this Sicha, the Rebbe explains the Mitzvah of the Chanukah
lights, and concentrates on two of their features, that they are to be
placed by the door of one's house that is adjacent to the street, or
the public domain, and that they must be placed on the left-hand
side of the door. These features have a deep symbolism: The "left-
hand side" and the "public domain" both stand for the realm of the
profane, and by placing the lights there, we are, as it were, bringing
the Divine light into the area of existence which is normally most
resistant to it. The Sicha goes on to explain the difference between
the positive and negative commandments in their effect on the
world, and concludes with a comparison between the Chanukah
lights and tefillin.

1. THE CHANUKAH LIGHTS AND THE MEZUZAH

The Mitzvah of the Chanukah lights is similar in two re-
spects to that of the mezuzah: Both have to be placed by the
side of the door of a house or a courtyard, and both must be set
on the *outside*.[1] But there are also two significant differences
between them. The mezuzah must be fixed on the right-hand
side of the door, and the Chanukah lights set on the left.[2] And
though both are placed outside, in the case of the mezuzah, this
is only to signify where the house or the courtyard begin—to
mark the *entrance.* On the other hand the Chanukah lights are
intended specifically to illuminate the outside, the public domain. The mezuzah, as it were, points inward while the
Menorah shines outward.

These two points of difference may be connected. For the
"public domain" *(reshut ha-rabim;* literally, "the domain of the
many") suggests the idea of multiplicity or lack of unity; and

---

1. *Shabbat,* 21b; *Menachot,* 33b.
2. *Shabbat,* 22a.

the "left-hand side" is the name for the source of that life in which there is separation and disunity. "Public domain" and "left-hand side" are therefore related by being symbolic names for the dimension of division and alienation from G-d.[3]

2. THE MEZUZAH AND THE OTHER COMMANDMENTS

The precept of mezuzah is said to be equal in importance to all the other Mitzvot together: It is said to *include* them all within itself.[4] So we would expect to find them all sharing the two features which characterize the mezuzah—the idea of the right hand, and of being directed inward rather than towards the outside.

And almost all of them do.

Most have to be performed with the right hand.[5] Indeed, burnt offerings were vitiated if they were not offered with the right hand.[6] Also, certain commandments must be performed indoors, while those which may be done outside have no integral connection with the idea of the "public domain," since they may *also* be performed indoors—in short, they have no connection with *place* at all.

It follows that the Chanukah lights—which occupy the left-hand side, and are intended for the outside—have a different character to almost every other precept in Judaism.

3. POSITIVE AND NEGATIVE COMMANDS

This difference between the mezuzah (and all other Mitzvot) and the Chanukah lights is analogous to another distinction—between the positive and negative commands.

The positive commands (can only be performed with objects which) belong to the domain of the permitted;[7] the negative to the (non-performance of the) *forbidden*.

---

3. *Torah Or*, 42c. *Ner Chanukah* of 5643 and 5704.
4. *Siddur* (of Rabbi Schneur Zalman), p. 275a.
5. Cf. *Shulchan Aruch, Orach Chayim*, ch. 2.
6. *Rambam, Hilchot Bi'at Hamikdash*, 5:18.
7. Cf. *Shabbat*, 28b.

Every performance of a Mitzvah brings spiritual life to the world—in the form of "Divine light." And the light which is drawn down by the fulfillment of a positive command is of the kind that can be internalized in the act, "clothed" or contained within it. The act "clothes" the light in the same way as the body "clothes" the soul. But a Divine light which can be contained in such a way is finite, taking on the character of that which contains it.[8] It cannot descend to the realm of the impure or forbidden, for the character of the forbidden is that of a negation of G-d's will, and this is a character which a light which emanates from G-d cannot take on.

On the other hand, the light which inhabits this and which is released by the fulfillment of a negative command, is infinite. It cannot be *contained* by the forbidden (or indeed by any) act, nor does it share its character, and so it can be released not by *performing* it, but only by *refraining* from it. Indeed, only an infinite light could descend this far into impurity, being, as it were, undimmed where it shines.

And the Chanukah light is of this infinite kind, because it brings light to the "left-hand side" and the "public domain"— both symbols of impurity and alienation from G-d.

In fact the Chanukah light goes beyond the negative commandment for it is, in itself, a positive command. Refraining from a forbidden act may *negate* it. But the Chanukah lights do not negate but *illuminate* and purify the world of "outside"— just as a positive command purifies the world of "inside" (i.e., the permitted).

And this is the connection between the Chanukah lights and the Torah, which is itself called a "light."[9] For the Torah also concerns itself with (specifying) the acts which are forbidden and the things which are impure. And through studying the Torah, the sparks of holiness embedded in the realm of the forbidden are released and elevated.[10]

---

8. *Torah Or*, 52d. *Likkutei Torah, Pekudei*, 6d.
9. *Proverbs* 6:23.
10. Cf. also *Likkutei Torah, Re'eh*, 30b and 31b.

4. THE CHANUKAH LIGHTS AND TEFILLIN

It is known that the seven commandments which the Rabbis instituted, one of which is the command of the Chanukah lights, derive ultimately from commandments to be found in the Torah.[11] So there must be amongst the Torah commandments one which is an analogue of the lights of Chanukah, one which brings the Divine light into the "left-hand side" and the "public domain." And this is the Mitzvah of tefillin. For the hand-tefillin are worn on the left arm (the weaker arm, i.e., the left if the person is right-handed), and the reason is, as explained in the Zohar,[12] that the "Evil Inclination" (the "left side of the heart"; the voice of emotional dissent to G-d's will) should itself be "bound" into the service of G-d. And the head-tefillin must be worn uncovered and exposed so that "all the people of the earth shall see that the name of the L-rd is called upon you; and they shall be in awe of you."[13] Its purpose, then, is to reveal G-dliness to "all the people of the earth" and to cause them to be "in awe." So it is, that the tefillin, like the Chanukah lights are directed to the "left-hand side" and the "public domain"—towards that which lies "outside" the recognition of G-d.

In the light of this we can understand the Rabbinic saying that "the whole *Torah* is compared to (the commandment of) tefillin."[14] The tefillin have, like Torah, the power to effect a purification even in the realm of the profane.

5. THE MITZVAH OF TEFILLIN

On Chanukah one has to give an extra amount of charity,[15] "both in money and in person,"[16] both material and spiritual

---

11. *Tanya*, Part IV, 29.
12. Part III, 283a.
13. *Devarim* 28:10. *Berachot*, 6a.
14. *Kiddushin*, 35a. Cf. also *Midrash Tehillim* (1:2): "Fulfill the Mitzvah of tefillin, and I will count it as if you had toiled in *Torah* by day and by night."
15. *Magen Avraham*, in *Shulchan Aruch*, beg. *Hilchot Chanukah*.
16. *Peri Megadim*, Ibid.

charity. And since the Mitzvah of tefillin has, as we have seen, a special connection with the lights of Chanukah, Chanukah is itself a particularly appropriate and pressing time to devote to the work of the "tefillin campaign," helping as many other Jews as possible to participate in the Mitzvah.

And when one brings it about that another Jew fulfills the Mitzvah of tefillin, then, as it is recorded in the Mishna, "a Mitzvah draws another Mitzvah in its train."[17] If this is true for any Mitzvah, all the more is it true of tefillin to which are compared all the other Mitzvot.[18] And so from the seed of this single observance will grow, in time, the observance of all the others.

The miracle of Chanukah is apparent not only in the fact that "for Your people Israel You worked a great deliverance and redemption as at this day"[19]—a deliverance from a people who were "impure," "wicked" and "arrogant," and despite their being "strong" and "many"; but also in the result that "afterwards Your children came into Your most holy house, cleansed Your Temple, purified Your Sanctuary, and kindled lights in Your holy courtyards."[19]

And so it is with tefillin. By the observance of this Mitzvah, not only is a "deliverance and redemption" achieved from "all the people of the earth"—for since they will be "in awe of you," they will no longer stand in opposition to Israel, but will be as if "our hearts melted, and there was no courage left in any man because of you."[20] But also, and as a consequence of the Mitzvah, "Your children (will come) into Your most holy house"— into the Third Temple which will be revealed speedily on earth, as a sign of the Messianic Age.

(Source: Likkutei Sichot, Vol. V pp. 223-7)

---

17. *Pirkei Avot*, 4:2.
18. As is the *literal* meaning of the *Talmud* quoted in note 14, above: that the Mitzvot of the Torah are all compared to tefillin.
19. *V'Al Hanissim* prayer.
20. *Joshuah* 2:11.

פרשת מקץ
MIKKETZ

The beginning of our Sidra, which tells in what appears to be excessive detail of the two dreams of Pharaoh, invites a number of questions. Why are these dreams recounted in the Torah at such length? What can we learn from the differences between Pharaoh's dreams and the dreams of Joseph in last week's Sidra? Do they characterize some fundamental contrast between the worlds which Joseph and Pharaoh represent? And if so, what is the implication for us?

1. PHARAOH'S DREAMS

At the beginning of our Sidra, a long account is given of the dreams of Pharaoh—about the cows and the ears of corn—and the interpretation which Joseph gave them, that they were symbols of the years of plenty and of famine.

But why is this narration given at such length and in such detail? The point of the episode is simple: Joseph forecasted the seven years of plenty and the seven years of famine, and as a result became viceroy to Pharaoh in Egypt. What significant difference does it make, whether this came about through dreams and their interpretation, or by some other chain of events?

Even if the Torah wished to emphasize that it was specifically through Pharaoh's *dreams* that Joseph obtained his position, it could have informed us of the fact without narrating every detail of the dreams.

2. THE INFLUENCE OF JOSEPH

The answer is, that Pharaoh's dreams must be understood in the context in which they occurred. Pharaoh dreamed *because* of Joseph. In the previous Sidra we learned that Joseph received Divine communication through dreams. And Joseph

60

was the heir to Jacob's spiritual heritage, bringing to the world all that Jacob represented.[1] He was, in short, a "collective soul," the medium through which Divine emanations to the world must pass, the "righteous man who is the foundation of the world." If to him the Divine revelation came through the medium of dreams, then this was to be the order in the world. So that when a communication was necessary for the world, and for Pharaoh, its ruler,[2] it came to him in a dream.

3. THE JEW AND THE WORLD

This indicates a fundamental lesson about our service to G-d. When a Jew encounters severe challenges, from harmful attitudes and desires, he must realize that their ultimate source lies not in the world but in himself. It is not true that he must follow the world; neither is it true that in order to live a faithful Jewish existence one must make concessions to the world. The reverse is the case. The Jew himself creates the state of the world he inhabits. If his Judaism is tempered by an inner reluctance, this is mirrored in the world. But it is the nature of the world to conceal its spiritual source. So this fact, too, is concealed, and attitudes hostile to Judaism are sensed as coming from the outside, from the world at large, pulling the Jew away from his faith. But the truth is: The Jew is himself the author of these attitudes. Were he to change his own desires, from reluctance to affirmation, he would change the attitude of the world as well.

This is not all. Even where we cannot find the origin of such conflict *within* the Jew, because he is personally wholly free of conflict, then it is still *because* of the Jew that it occurs. For in him lies the purpose of creation. As the Rabbis said: The world was created in the beginning for the sake of Israel who are called the beginning of (G-d's) produce.[3] The conflict oc-

---

1. Cf. *Biurei HaZohar*, 30a. *Or Hatorah*, 386a. Cf. also *Likkutei Sichot*, Vol. III, p. 832.
2. Cf. *Targum Sheni* on *Megillat Esther* at the beginning.
3. *Otiot deRabbi Akiva*—letter Beit. *Seder Rabbah of Bereishit*, 4. *Vayikra Rabbah*, 36:4. *Tanchuma—Buber*—3. Rashi, Ramban, on *Bereishit* 1:1.

curs as a test of the Jew's inner strength. And if he refuses to be overwhelmed by it, it will turn out to have had no reality. Because the state of the world is dependent on the state of the Jew in his Judaism.

4. DIFFERENCES BETWEEN JOSEPH'S AND PHARAOH'S DREAMS

Although Pharaoh's dreams were dependent on the fact of Joseph's dreams, they were radically different in their nature. Joseph's dreams belonged to the realm of holiness; Pharaoh's did not. Thus we find several distinctions between them, in their structure and detail.[4]

Firstly, Joseph's dreams begin with an image of service, of bread by labor: "We were binding sheaves." But this idea is wholly absent from the dreams of Pharaoh, in which food is seen as coming without any effort. Blessings which come from G-d to the Jew are good to the point of perfection.

Thus they must come in response to effort. For that which is received without having been worked for—the "bread of shame"—lacks something, namely, that man has been a partner in its creation. But that which derives from outside the realm of the holy—the food of which Pharaoh dreamt—is not wholly good, and can therefore sometimes come gratuitously, without effort.

Secondly, Joseph's dreams represent a progression from lower to higher forms of perfection. They begin with "ears of corn"—individual ears, each separated from the next. They progress to "sheaves"—where things which were apart have been bound into a unity. And then, in the second dream, we pass to the sun, moon and stars—the things of the Heavens. Even at the physical level, sheaves are more valuable than ears, and jewels (the earthly counterpart of the stars[5]) more precious than sheaves.

---

4. Cf. supra p. 50 ff. (and notes).
5. *Likkutei Torah, Re'eh, Vesamti Kadkod.*

But in Pharaoh's dreams, the order is reversed: From cows we descend to corn, from the animal to the vegetable kingdom. The natural order would in any case have been the opposite, for the condition of the cows, both healthy and lean, would depend on whether they feed from rich or meager corn. Within each dream there is the same notion of descent or decline. First appear the healthy cows and corn, then the lean, to the point that the good is wholly consumed by the bad. And this order is preserved in their interpretation. First came the seven years of plenty, followed by the decline to the seven years of famine, until "all the plenty shall be forgotten, and the famine shall consume the land." (The fact that after the years of hunger, prosperity returned, does not belong to Pharaoh's dreams at all, but to the blessing of Jacob.)

5. THE SACRED AND THE SECULAR: STASIS AND CHANGE

These differences between the dreams of Joseph and of Pharaoh disclose the difference between sanctity and its opposite. Sanctity is eternal and unchanging. In the realm of sanctity, if there are changes, they are always ascents, going "from strength to strength"—which is in truth not a change at all, but a more perfect realization of something which remains the same. And even though the Jewish people suffers vicissitudes, sometimes in the ascendant, sometimes in decline,[6] these are not real changes. For the Jew always carries with him a single mission,[7] and a single faith:[8] to fulfill the Torah and the Mitzvot, and to be elevated in sanctity. And since "where a man's will is, there he is to be found"; since, moreover, the descent of the Jewish people is always for the sake of a subsequent elevation an "everlasting peace," the fluctuations in Jewish history

---

6. Additions to *Torah Or*, 118a.
7. The opposite is by evil, because only in their *source* is the intent for the sake of Heaven (*Likkutei Torah, Chukat,* 62a).
8. *Rambam, Hilchot Gerushin,* end of ch. 2.

are not ultimately changes but "peace," the absence of change.
A single will and intention runs through them all.

Against this, the realm of unsanctity is subject to change,
indeed, to continual decline. For whatever is not holy does not
exist in and for itself. It is at most the means to an end, to test
man and to evoke his highest powers of sanctity. The more
man responds to the test, becomes strong and elevated in his
service, the less he needs to be tested. And automatically, the
existence of unsanctity becomes weaker, more tenuous. "When
this one ascends, the other falls"[9]—as the realm of the holy is
strengthened, the realm of the purely secular declines.

This is also the basic distinction between the Chanukah
lights and the sacrifices of the festival of Succot. On Succot,
seventy bullocks were sacrificed in the course of its seven days,
representing the "seventy nations of the world."[10] And on each
day a successively smaller number was offered up (from thirteen on the first day to seven on the seventh), representing a
continual decrease or decline.[11] But the lights of Chanukah signify sanctity: Thus each day sees an increase in the number of
lights kindled. For holiness is always ascending.

6. EFFORT AND REWARD

From all this we learn a specific lesson. When a person believes that he can receive benefits or blessings without effort,
merely as a result of certain natural causes, he can be sure that
this belief derives from his "animal soul," the unspiritual side
of his nature. For at this level, there can indeed be benefit
without effort. But he must equally be aware that the things of
this realm are continually in a state of decline: He will, in the
end, be left with nothing.[12] Were he, on the other hand, to labor in the service of G-d, he would be assured of the promise,
"You have toiled and you have found." He will "find" from

---

9. *Rashi, Bereishit* 25:23. *Tanya*, Part I, ch. 13.
10. *Sukkah*, 55b, mentioned in *Rashi, Bamidbar* 29:18.
11. *Sukkah*, 47a; *Rashi*, Ibid.
12. Cf. *Kunteres Uma'ayon*, end of seventh discourse.

Heaven more than he has labored for. And always, as he progresses, he will be "ascending in holiness."

(Source: Likkutei Sichot, Vol. III pp. 819-822)

פרשת ויגש

VAYIGASH

Not only did Joseph save the Egyptians from the seven years of famine, by arranging for grain to be stored during the previous years, but he also provided for his family during that time, as Sidra Vayigash tells us, despite the harm that his brothers had earlier sought to do him. Because of this, the entire Jewish nation is called by his name in one of the Psalms. The Rebbe investigates the underlying meaning of this appellation, and of a Midrash which makes three requests to G-d to treat Israel in the way that Joseph treated his brothers.

1. JOSEPH THE PROVIDER

"And Joseph supported his Father and his brothers and all his Father's household, according to their little ones."[1]

Amongst the many things that the Torah tells us about the relations between Joseph and his brothers, it specifically mentions that he sustained them and their families: And there is no detail of the stories of the Torah which does not have a profound meaning for us, waiting to be uncovered.

This particular act of Joseph's is so esteemed that because of it, the entire Jewish nation is called, in perpetuity, by his name, as we find in the Psalms: "He (G-d) leads Joseph like a flock."[2] His act, as it were, is a permanent heritage to us.

2. THE COMMENT OF THE MIDRASH

There is a Midrashic commentary on this verse from the Psalms,[3] to the effect that G-d not only leads His people (who are called "Joseph") but that He does so *in the manner of* Joseph: "Just as he stored food from the years of plenty as provision for

---

1. *Bereishit* 47:12.
2. 80:2, and cf. *Rashi's* commentary.
3. *Yalkut Shimoni*, Ibid.

the period of famine, so may G-d store up blessings for us from this world to enjoy in the world to come.

"Just as Joseph provided for each according to his deeds, so may G-d sustain us according to our deeds.

"Rabbi Menachem said in the name of Rabbi Abin: Just as Joseph's brothers acted badly towards him, but he repaid them with good, so we act badly towards You (G-d)—and may You bestow good on us in return."

Now, this Midrash is puzzling in a number of ways:

(i) When Joseph laid up food from the years of plenty, had he not done so, it would have gone to waste. But what analogy is there with our good deeds in this world? They will not go to waste, so why need they be "stored up" for the future life?

(ii) How can we compare this world to the time of plenty, and the next to the years of famine, when we are told that this world is only a "vestibule" leading to the "hall" of the world to come?[4]

(iii) Joseph's virtue was that he bestowed good on those who had done bad to him. How can the Midrash state, therefore, that he "provided for each according to his *deeds*" (and not "according to his *needs*")?

(iv) Why, in any case, did the Midrash need to *request* that G-d sustain us according to our deeds: For this is no more than the strict requirements of the law, and we did not need to infer it from the conduct of Joseph?

3. THE BLESSINGS OF THIS WORLD AND THE NEXT

We can understand the first request of the Midrash, that G-d stores blessings for us from the "years of plenty" of this world to enjoy in the "years of famine" of the world to come, once we realize that the nature of our reward in the world to come is a revelation of what our acts have achieved in *this* world—an outflowing of G-d's essential presence. The world to come is thus, as it were, a "time of famine"—in it we are

---

4. *Pirkei Avot,* 4:16.

sustained by a flow of spiritual life that we brought about in the "time of plenty," in this world. And though we find it written in the Mishnah that "an hour of blissfulness of spirit in the world to come is better than all the life of this world,"[5] this is only from the point of view of *man,* who finds his reward in the future life. From the point of view of G-d and of the Divine purpose of human existence, "an hour of repentance and good deeds in this world is better than all the life in the world to come."[5] Only here can we fulfill our task, and create the spiritual pleasures that will be revealed to us in the world to come.

Now, if we were to follow the logic of the strict requirements of the law, it could be said that many of the occasions when we obey G-d's will, we do so for ulterior motives. We do not align ourselves with the essence of the commandment, which seeks no other reward than the act itself. Therefore, though "the essential thing is the act,"[6] and though such acts do indeed bring about an outflowing of G-d's essence, surely they should not be rewarded in the world to come by a *revelation* of that essence?

So, when we ask (in the second request of the Midrash): "Sustain us according to our *deeds* (and not according to our *motives*)" we are not merely asking G-d to follow the strict requirement of the law. Instead we are asking that He look only at our outward acts, and not to judge us by the shortcomings of our motives. And in terms of acts, "even the sinners of Israel are as full of good deeds as a pomegranate (with seed)."[7]

And indeed, this is what Joseph himself did, when he said to his brothers:[8] "You *intended* evil against me; but G-d meant it for good, to act, as it is this day, to save many people alive." Although they intended to harm Joseph by selling him into slavery, it transpired that their act brought Joseph to a position where he was able to save many lives by his prudential policy of

---

5. Ibid. 4:17.
6. Ibid. 1:17.
7. *Eruvin,* 19a; end of *Chagigah.*
8. *Bereishit* 50:20.

storing food for the imminent famine. And Joseph judged them on their action (which turned out well), not their intention.

We can take the argument a stage further. The advocate of strict adherence to the law might concede that even though a man does good for ulterior motives, in the subconscious depths of his soul he desires closeness to G-d for its own sake, and should be rewarded for it. But surely when he sins he can have no such holy desires, however subconscious; for the soul in its unfelt depths *dissociates* itself from the sin.[9] How then can G-d allow us retroactively to transform our sins into merits[10] by the act of repentance, when our sins have no saving grace?

This is the *extra* act of mercy for which the Midrash, in the name of Rabbi Menachem, asks as its third request: "Just as Joseph bestowed good on those who had harmed him, so we acted badly toward You: May You bestow good on us in return." May You judge us, in other words, in the light of the *ultimate* good (our act of repentance) as if it had been our *original* intention, at the moment when we sinned, only to bring about good.

4. THE MEANING OF JOSEPH

Why is it on the strength of *Joseph's* conduct that we make these three requests of G-d? The difference between Jacob and Joseph[11] is that while Jacob lived on the highest plane of spiritual existence, Joseph translated this spiritual reality into material terms. In the individual, this is the power that allows the perception of G-d's *essence* to enter the dimensions of the human mind, emotions—and actions even into actions done from ulterior motives.

Because the depths of the Jewish soul can make themselves be felt in this world (the capacity which derives from Joseph), he is able to bring into the world the outflowing of G-d's essence in the world to come.

---

9. Cf. *Rambam, Hilchot Gerushin*, end of ch. 2.
10. *Yoma*, 86b.
11. Cf. *Biurei HaZohar*, 30a ff.

And thus his innermost intentions—which are pure even though his conscious motives are not—have a tangible reality even in this world: So that G-d may bestow good on him even when his acts have been bad.

This is Joseph's heritage to every Jew. In his act of feeding his family in a time of famine, despite all their wrongs towards him, he has given us the power to reach beyond the surface of our fellow Jew, with all its superficial failings, and to penetrate to the core of his being and respond to its fundamental holiness. And when we treat another Jew in this way, we *arouse* that core of holiness in him, and in ourselves as well, so that in time it breaks through its coverings, and the essence of our soul stands revealed.

(Source: Likkutei Sichot, Vol. V pp. 239-50 (adapted))

פרשת ויחי

VAYECHI

We read in our Sidra that Jacob twice called his sons to gather
round him and listen to his blessings and prophecies. The Rabbis
infer that these were two separate events, though they followed each
other closely in time. What he said on the second occasion is nar-
rated in the subsequent verses. But as to what happened on the first,
the Torah is silent. The Rebbe discusses the Rabbinic explanation of
this event, in which Jacob tried to reveal to his sons "the end of
days," and concludes with a searching investigation into the meaning of "the end of days" for our own time.

1. WHAT JACOB DID NOT SAY

"And Jacob called to his sons and said: Gather yourselves
together and I will relate to you what will happen to you in
later days."[1] The Rabbis comment[2] on this verse, that "Jacob
wished to reveal to his sons the end of days, but the Divine
Presence (the *Shechinah*—which gave him his power of prophecy) departed from him."

But what forces the Rabbis to make this interpretation?
The literal reading of the verse on the face of it would be to
understand Jacob as referring to the blessings which he was to
give his sons, and which are mentioned later in the chapter.

Some commentators explain the Rabbis to be concerned
with the phrase, "in later days," which elsewhere[3] in the Torah
has the meaning of "at the end of days."

But this is difficult to accept.

Firstly, because "in later days," does not *always* have this
meaning. For example, when Balaam says to Balak,[4] "I will an-

---

1. *Bereishit* 49:1.
2. *Pesachim*, 56a.
3. *Devarim* 4:30; *Isaiah* 2:2; *Jeremiah* 23:20.
4. *Bamidbar* 24:14.

71

nounce to you what this people will do to your people in later days," Rashi[5] takes this as a reference to the time of King David.

Secondly, even if we accept that Jacob wished to speak about the end of days, why should we say that he wished to "reveal" to his sons *when* this would be? It seems closer to the literal sense of the verse to say he merely wanted to tell them *what* would happen then—as he proceeds to do[6] later in the chapter.

And thirdly, even if we accept the Rabbinic interpretation it surely is not the *literal* reading of the verse. And yet Rashi himself cites it, and Rashi is avowedly concerned only with the literal meaning.

2. THE TWO MEETINGS

The explanation is that there is an apparent repetition in the text of the Torah. First, Jacob says "Gather yourselves together, and I will relate to you. . . ." and then he says,[7] "Assemble yourselves and hear." Since the Torah contains no redundant passages, it follows that there must have been *two* separate occasions when Jacob brought his sons together. The second gathering is continued in the chapter. But the first remains a mystery. Why are we not told what Jacob intended to say, and why he did not say it? This is why the Rabbis explain that he "wished to reveal to his sons the end of days" but he could not, because "the Divine Presence was removed from him." And this is why he gathered them a second time, with a word *(hikabtzu:* "Assemble yourselves") which did not have the implication of preparing to hear words emanating from the Divine Presence (as did *he-asfu:* "Gather yourselves together").

But something is missing from this explanation. Granted that the text of the Torah forces us to realize that Jacob brought his sons together wishing to tell them something which in fact he failed to do; nonetheless, perhaps this was merely some ad-

---

5. *Bamidbar* 24:17.
6. Cf. *Rashi*, ad loc.
7. *Bereishit* 49:2.

ditional information about what would happen to them in the future—and for some reason he was prevented from doing so. Where is the evidence that he wished to reveal "the end of days?"

3. THREE KINDS OF COMMUNICATION

We can go further in our understanding by means of a distinction made in the Zohar[8] between three kinds of speech: "speaking," "saying" and "relating."[9] "Speaking" is a merely verbal act. "Saying" comes from the heart. But "relating" is the voice of the soul.

A difference between them is this: Speaking and saying come from the surface, not from the depth of the soul. The mouth can sometimes speak what the heart does not feel. Even what the *heart* says can be at odds with what the man truly wills in his soul. Sometimes, in his heart, a Jew can desire what the Torah forbids. But in his true inwardness he never seeks to separate himself from G-d's will.[10] The eye sees, the *heart* desires,[11] but the innermost soul never assents to a sin.

But "relating" comes from the depths of a man's being. Aggadah, the inward part of Torah, means, literally, "relating." And the Rabbis said about Aggadah:[12] "You wish to recognize He who spoke and brought the world into existence? Learn Aggadah, for in it you will find G-d." In other words, through the part of Torah called "relating" you encounter the inwardness of G-d.

And what Jacob at first wished to do was to "relate" to his sons, to disclose to them the "end of days" when the inward-

---

8. Part I, 234b.
9. In Hebrew, *dibbur, amirah* and *haggadah* respectively.
10. Cf. *Rambam, Hilchot Gerushin,* 2:20, where he explains why a husband may be legitimately compelled to grant a divorce to his wife. Surely consent given under compulsion is not true consent? *Rambam* comments: forcing a man to do what Torah commands him is not real compulsion. The only compulsion is when the man refuses to grant a divorce, and here it is the evil desires which are compelling him to do what he does not *truly* will.
11. *Rashi, Bamidbar* 15:39. Cf. *Bamidbar Rabbah,* 10:2.
12. *Sifri* on *Devarim* 11:22. *Shulchan Aruch Harav, Hilchot Talmud Torah,* 2:2.

ness of the soul and of G-d would be revealed through the inwardness of Torah.

4. THE DIVINE PRESENCE DEPARTS

But why were the Rabbis insistent that the *Divine Presence (Shechinah)* was removed from Jacob as he was about to "relate?" Why not say, more simply, *"the end of days* was hidden from him?" In particular, since immediately afterwards, in his blessings to his sons, Jacob makes many prophecies, implying that the Divine Presence was still with him.

The reason is that Jacob wished to reveal the "end of days" to his *sons,* thinking that after they had "gathered themselves together" (after they had *united* themselves, in the deepest sense of the word, in preparing to receive this revelation), they would be capable and worthy of such a disclosure. But they could not receive the Divine Presence: It could not become *present*[13] in them. And so it departed. Not from Jacob, who could still see "the end of days" and could still prophesy. But from his attempt to "relate" it to his sons.

Despite this, however, the Rabbis still said that the Divine Presence departed from *him*—from Jacob. Because the fact that his sons could not accommodate the Presence within themselves caused a failing in Jacob himself.[14]

But if so, why did the Presence depart only when Jacob wished to reveal "the end of days?" His sons were then as they had been. If Jacob was at fault because of his sons, then he was so beforehand. There was no sudden change, that the Divine Presence should have been within him until now, and just at this moment depart.

The answer is that even though his sons had been beforehand unworthy of the revelation that Jacob intended to relate, so long as he was uninvolved with them and their situation, he

---

13. *Shechinah* being that aspect of G-dliness which dwells *(shochen)* and is revealed *(Tanya,* Part I, ch. 41).

14. Just as Moses' greatness was affected by the Golden Calf *(Berachot,* 32a. *Rashi, Shemot* 32:7).

was not affected by it. But when he tried to *relate* to them, he was affected, and the Presence departed.[15]

5. TODAY AND THE END OF DAYS

The Torah is eternal. It is addressed to every Jew, and therefore what it relates involves every Jew. And the continuing effect of Jacob's actions is this: In saying, "Gather (unite) yourselves together and I will relate to you" he gave to his children and to their descendants until "the end of days" the power to reach by their service to G-d, a revelation of that end, albeit in a way that they cannot inwardly accommodate in its completeness.

This has an important implication. Someone reflecting on the state of the world might say: How can this age and this orphaned generation be prepared for a revelation of the future redemption, a revelation for which even generations of great stature were unworthy?

Against this, the Torah teaches that through Jacob's act of seeking to grant this revelation to his sons, every Jew has the power at all times—even when the "Divine Presence departs from him," even when it has concealed itself, as now, in double shrouds of darkness—to reach in a single bound the "revelation of the end," the true, complete redemption.

Indeed, the very fact that we feel that our time is unworthy of redemption is itself proof of Messianic nearness. For the Rabbis say:[16] "The Messiah will come when he is not expected" (literally: "When the mind is turned elsewhere"). And an age like ours which cannot find a place for the possibility of redemption, is evidence against its own beliefs, and a sign that redemption is imminent.

This does not mean that we are right to despair, so as to ensure that the Messiah is unexpected. On the contrary, it is a principle of Jewish faith that "each day I wait for him to

---

15. Just as Moses was affected and couldn't bear to hold the Tablets only *after* descending and nearing the camp of Israel (*Shemot* 32:19. Cf. *Jerusalem Talmud, Taanit*, 4:5).
16. *Sanhedrin*, 97a.

come."[17] It means rather that, without regard for the fact that our minds cannot envisage it, we have a faith which goes beyond rational expectation. And this faith itself will speedily bring the redemption of "the end of days."

(Source: Likkutei Sichot, Vol. X pp. 167-172)

---

17. *Rambam*, 12th principle of faith.

פרשת שמות
SHEMOT

In this Sidra, when G-d asks Moses to undertake the mission of re-
deeming the Israelites from Egypt, Moses replies, "Send, I pray You,
by the hand of whom You will send." The Midrash interprets this
to be a plea for the Messiah to be sent in his place. What is the connection between Moses and the Messiah—the past and future re-
deemers? And what is the difference between them, that each was
given a separate mission? The Rebbe answers these questions, and
explains their significance in the life of the individual Jew.

1. THE TWO REDEEMERS

After G-d has repeatedly asked Moses to return to Egypt
and lead the Jewish people out of their captivity, Moses finally
says,[1] "Send, I pray You, by the hand of whom You will send."
The Midrash[2] says on this verse, "(Moses) said before Him,
'Master of the Universe, send, I pray You, by the hand of
whom You will send'—by the hand of the Messiah who will be
the future redeemer." But this request of Moses was not
granted, for it was he, specifically, whom G-d wanted to deliver
Israel from Egypt.

It can be inferred from the Midrash that there is a special
connection between Moses and the Messiah, and it was because of this that Moses wanted the Messiah himself to be sent
to Egypt. Nonetheless, the redemption from Egypt was the task
of Moses; the mission of the Messiah belongs to the final exile.

The similarity which they share (in virtue of which they
have been given similar tasks—redemption from exile) is indicated in the Rabbinic saying:[3] "Moses was the first and he will

---

1. *Shemot* 4:13.
2. *Lekach Tov.*
3. Cf. *Shemot Rabbah*, 2:4. *Zohar*, Part I, 253a.

be the last redeemer." This does not mean that Moses in person will be the Messiah (since he was a Levite, and the Messiah, who will be a descendant of David,[4] will be from the tribe of Judah); but rather that the redemptive power of the Messiah will be drawn from Moses.

The reason is that the first and major virtue of the Messiah will be Torah (according to Rambam,[5] he will be steeped in it); from this, his redemptive strength will be drawn; and the Torah is called "the Torah of Moses."[6] Likewise, the power of Israel to bring the Messiah derives from the service articulated in the Torah.

This inner connection between Moses and the Messiah is alluded to in the verse[7] "And the scepter shall not depart from Judah . . . until Shiloh come *(ad ki-yavo Shilo)*." This is taken to refer to the Messiah, because the words *"yavo* Shiloh" and "Mashiach" ("Shiloh come" and "Messiah") are numerically equivalent.[8] The same equivalence also applies to the words "Shiloh" and "Moses" so that the coming of the Messiah is related to Moses. In addition, *"yavo"* ("come") has the same numerical value as *"echad"* ("one"). Thus we can state the equivalence: "Messiah = Moses + One," and its meaning is that the Messiah will be brought by service which has the attribute of "Oneness"; and the power to achieve this is transmitted through Moses.[9]

2. DESCENT FOR THE SAKE OF ASCENT

How are we to understand this?

The Rabbis said: When the world was created, everything was in a state of perfection.[10] But after the sin of the Tree of

4. *Rambam, Hilchot Melachim*, end of ch. 11.
5. Ibid.
6. *Malachi* 3:22. Cf. *Shabbat*, 89a.
7. *Bereishit* 49:10.
8. *Baal Haturim* on *Bereishit*, Ibid. Cf. supra, p. 2 and note 5.
9. Cf. *Tanya*, Part I, beg. of ch. 42.
10. Cf. *Bereishit Rabbah*, 14:7; 3:3.

Knowledge, when the serpent infected Eve with impurity,[11] man and the world fell from perfection until the Giving of the Torah; for when Israel were at Mt. Sinai the "spirit of impurity" departed.[12] But it returned with the sin of the Golden Calf,[13] and it remains in the world until the Messianic Age when the promise will be fulfilled to remove (utterly destroy) impurity;[14] and the world will be ultimately purified and cleansed.

It is a general principle in Judaism that every fall is for the sake of some ascent;[15] and subsequent ascent is higher than the state before the fall. Hence the state ushered in by the Giving of the Torah was higher than that which preceded Eve's sin. And by implication the Messianic Age will be superior to the time of the Giving of the Torah.

A twofold movement creates this achievement of hitherto unreached heights: A *descent* of light (revelation, spiritual power) from its source in the infinite; and a corresponding *ascent* of Israel and the world.

We find this in the Giving of the Torah. Even though the strength to fulfill Divine commandments preceded it (Adam had 6 commandments, Noah 7, extra ones were given to each of Abraham, Isaac and Jacob,[16] and the Fathers kept the whole Torah before it was given[17]), not only was *greater* strength given at the time of the Giving of the Torah, but a new power, different in kind from all that had existed before, was given to Israel when the relation of *chosenness* between them and G-d began ("and You have chosen us"[18]). This was a revelation of G-d's *essence;* something that had not been disclosed in revelation before.

---

11. *Shabbat*, 146a.
12. Ibid. *Zohar*, Part I, 52b; Part II, 193b.
13. *Zohar*, Ibid. Cf. *Tanya*, Part I, end of ch. 36.
14. *Zechariah* 13:2.
15. Cf. supra, pp. 11 ff.
16. *Rambam, Hilchot Melachim*, 9:1.
17. *Yoma*, 28b; *Kiddushin*, 82a.
18. Cf. *Shulchan Aruch Harav, Orach Chaim*, 60:4.

Likewise, the elevation of Israel and the world was un-precedented—in the inwardness and intensity of their purifica-tion. Hence their subsequent degradation, in committing the sin of the Golden Calf, was not so great. Thus, although its ef-fects (the presence of impurity) remain visible today, still, the effects of the Giving of the Torah are evident.

3. THE MESSIANIC AGE

In a similar way, the elevation that will belong to the Mes-sianic Age—when the Messiah will teach his Torah to all Is-rael[19]—will be correspondingly greater than that of the Giving of the Torah;[20] and this in two ways:

(i) *In the Divine revelation.* For though at Sinai it was so in-tense that they could *see* it with their physical senses, it was only *like* the Messianic revelation[21] (when "the Glory of the L-rd will be revealed")[22] and not equal to it.

(ii) *In the elevation of Israel.* Whereas at Sinai the spirit of im-purity departed, it remained in potential and reappeared with the sin of the Golden Calf. But in the Messianic time it will be destroyed and consumed *forever.* The whole essential nature of the world *itself* will be changed; not temporarily altered by spe-cific Divine intervention from *Above.*

4. THE TASK OF EXILE

Since every elevation must be preceded by a fall, the fall is a necessary preparation for it.[15] It is the service in the time of the fall (while its effects persist) which brings about the elevation. The service of the Fathers, and the catharsis of the "iron fur-nace"[23] of Egypt, brought the Giving of the Torah. And like-wise, the Messiah will be brought by our continual service in exile to purify the whole essence of the world.[24]

---

19. *Likkutei Torah, Tzav,* 17a. *Shaar Hoemunah,* ch. 56.
20. Cf. *Kohelet Rabbah,* end of ch. 11 and beg. of ch. 2.
21. *Tanya,* Part I, ch. 36.
22. *Isaiah* 40:5.
23. *I Kings* 8:51.
24. *Tanya,* Part I, beg. of ch. 37.

5. THE MEANING OF "ONE"

This can be understood by first understanding a well-known difficulty[25] about the Shema. Why does it say, "the L-rd is One" and not "the L-rd is *unique?*" For "one" is an attribute of a countable thing; it is compatible with a second. But "unique" rules out the possibility of another.

The explanation is this: The true Oneness of G-d is not perceived merely by denying at the outset the existence of anything besides Him ("uniqueness"—world-denying attitude); but rather by perceiving in the *midst* of the physical world that it has no existence in itself, by feeling in the context of a worldly existence that it is in *one* with (united with) G-d.

The word "one" itself suggests this. Its letters in Hebrew *(echad: alef, chet, daled)* have the numerical values, 1, 8, 4. 8 symbolizes, as it were, the seven heavens and the earth, and 4, the four directions. All these are emanations from 1 *(alef)* the Source and Master *(aluf)* of the world.[26] In other words, the perception of Oneness must not be a spiritual one alone, but one which permeates one's whole view of the physical world and is realized in it.

6. TORAH AND THE TRANSFORMATION OF THE WORLD

But how can it be that this world whose nature is (and whose name in Hebrew means) the "concealment"[27] of G-dliness, should be receptive to a revelation *within it* of the Aluf (Master, One) of the universe?

For this purpose, to make the world a fit dwelling-place for G-d, Israel was given the Torah and the commandments.

At Sinai, it was not merely that they were given so that *through them* the world should be purified and refined; but also the accompanying revelation transmitted the *power* by which this could be done.

---

25. Cf. *Torah Or*, Vaera, 55b.
26. *Shulchan Aruch, Orach Chaim*, ch. 61. Cf. *Berachot*, 13b.
27. *Olam—he-elam.*

At the moment when the Torah was given, the whole world was entirely nullified in the face of the revelation—even "the birds did not sing and the earth was silent"[28]—but this was a force from *above* rather than from *within* (and hence it was not a permanent state).

But *from* this was derived the world's power to become refined *itself,* and hence become a fitting receptacle for a yet higher revelation.

7. MOSES AND THE MESSIAH

Now we can understand why the Messiah = Moses + One. For the Messiah will be brought by the service which makes the Oneness manifest, and the power to do this was given through the hand of Moses.

Hence the inner *connection* between Moses and the Messiah: The latter will be brought by powers transmitted through the former. And hence also their *difference:* The exile to and liberation from Egypt was for the sake of the Giving of the Torah,[29] and this was to give Israel the *power* to purify themselves and the world. The task of the Messiah is to *complete* this process, and to innovate the subsequent service, when the purity of the world is complete.

8. "ONENESS" AND THE INDIVIDUAL

Man is a microcosm of the world.[30] And this cosmic process finds its echo in every man at all times: When he works and performs his service until evening; and entrusts his soul to G-d at night; and next day is made new again,[31] and begins a new service.

The service of the day begins with prayer and Torah. Through them a man receives the strength to serve (the G-dly spirit is diffused through his whole being by prayer) and to

---

28. *Shemot Rabbah,* end of ch. 29.
29. *Shemot* 3:12.
30. *Tanchuma, Pekudei,* 3.
31. *Yalkut Shimoni,* Remez, 702.

overcome the inclination to evil (through Torah which instructs him in the right course of action). Then he is able to enact this service in the practical world (to the extent that, as Rambam says,[32] "his wisdom is manifest in his eating and drinking"). His worldly existence (the *chet* and *daled* of *echad*) is subordinated to his Divine wisdom *(alef);* a recognition of Oneness permeates his physical actions.

Then, when his day of service is over, he makes a spiritual reckoning of his day's actions and rededicates his task to G-d. He says, "Into Your hands I entrust my soul . . . G-d of Truth," and Truth itself is Oneness. For the Hebrew word for truth is *emet*—the first, middle and last letters of the *alef bet,*[33] reminding us that G-d is He who has said, "I am the First and I am the Last, and besides Me there is no god."[34] There is no reality which does not emanate from Him, for when the *alef* (the One) is removed from *emet,* the word becomes *met,* "death," the absence of life.[35]

Just as the Torah (through the hand of Moses) gives the *world* the power to bring the Messiah, so it gives each and every *individual* the power to refine his own life and environment, and so hasten the Messianic Age.[36]

(Source: Likkutei Sichot, Vol. XI pp. 8-13)

32. *Hilchot Deot,* 5:1.
33. *Jerusalem Talmud, Sanhedrin,* 1:1. Cf. *Devarim Rabbah,* 1:10.
34. *Isaiah* 44:6.
35. *Maharsha, Sanhedrin,* 97a.
36. Cf. *Tanya,* Part IV, 4.

פרשת וארא

VAERA

After G-d had sent Moses to Pharaoh to ask for the release of the Jewish people from Egypt, not only was the request not granted, but the enslavement of the people became more oppressive. Moses therefore asks G-d: "Why have You dealt badly with this people?" The reply he receives, in effect, commends him to follow the example of the Fathers, Abraham, Isaac and Jacob, who did not ask questions of G-d. The Rebbe examines the nature of the virtue of the Fathers, the reason why Moses asked the question, and the contemporary implications of G-d's answer.

1. MOSES' QUESTION

At the end of the previous Sidra, Shemot, we read of Moses' question to G-d: "Why have You dealt badly with this people?" The force of his question was this: How could a mission which had been ordered by G-d, which had been carried out by Moses, and which concerned the redemption from Egypt, have resulted in harm to the Jewish people? The redemption itself was wholly good;[1] Moses, the emissary, was he of whom it was said, "And she saw that he was good";[2] and the initiator of the mission, and the redeemer was G-d Himself (G-d as He transcends nature,[3] for the redemption of a people already sunk to the "49th gate of impurity"[4] could only be a supernatural event), who is certainly wholly good and compassionate. So what could have been the source of the harm?

The answer with which Moses' question was met (in the opening of this week's Sidra) was, "And He said to him: I am the L-rd. And I appeared to Abraham, to Isaac and to Jacob as

1. Cf. *Torah Or, Vaera,* 56d.
2. *Shemot* 2:2. *Sotah,* 13a.
3. Cf. *Likkutei Torah, Tzav,* 12c.
4. *Zohar Chadash,* beg. of *Yitro.*

G-d Almighty *(Kel Sha-dai),* but by My name 'the L-rd' (the Tetragrammaton) I did not make Myself known to them." In other words, Abraham, Isaac and Jacob underwent many trials and deprivations, and yet they asked no questions of Me.

Yet there are several points of difficulty in this story: (1) Moses had attained to greater spiritual heights than the Fathers. He was the seventh generation in descent from Abraham, and the Rabbis say: "The seventh is always (especially) precious."[5] How then, if they had not raised questions about G-d, could Moses have done so? (2) G-d, in His answer to Moses, was underlining the virtue of the Fathers. Why did He not then say, "I appeared . . . to *Israel*" instead of ". . . to *Jacob?*" For "Israel" connotes a higher spiritual state than "Jacob."[6] (3) Every narrative in the Torah has a moral implication for every Jew.[7] And the Torah goes out of its way not to use an impolite expression even of an animal,[8] let alone of a Jew, more still of Moses, the finest of them all. So we must assume that when it gives voice to a criticism of Moses, it must have a pressing reason for doing so, namely to emphasize to every Jew the necessity for emulating the Fathers who raised no questions about G-d's conduct.

But this is hard to understand. For it presupposes that every Jew in every generation has the choice of behaving like Moses or like the Fathers. It is true that, as the Rabbis say,[9] "there is no generation that does not have a man like Abraham, like Isaac, like Jacob . . . and like Moses." But this refers only to isolated individuals. And the Torah was given to *all;* it "speaks of the majority." So how can we say that to *every* Jew it is open to act like Moses or like the Fathers, and that in this respect they should follow the Fathers?

---

5. *Vayikra Rabbah,* 29:11.
6. Cf. supra, p. 44.
7. Cf. *Zohar,* Part III, 53b.
8. Cf. *Pesachim,* 3a. Supra, p. 6.
9. *Bereishit Rabbah,* 56:7.

2. MOSES AND THE FATHERS

The difference between Moses and the Fathers is that Moses embodies the attribute of Knowledge *(chochmah)*—and thus it was through him that the Torah, which is the Divine Knowledge, was given. Relative to him, the Fathers were the embodiments of the Emotions *(middot)*. Abraham served G-d primarily through *love* and compassion. He is called, "Abraham, My loved one";[10] and to men as well as to G-d his relation was one of kindness, both material and spiritual. Isaac exemplified the service of *fear* and austere judgment: The Torah speaks of G-d as the "Fear of Isaac."[11] And as a result he could tolerate no evil in the world. His "eyes became dim" when he knew of the idolatry of Esau's wives.[12] And lastly Jacob represents *mercy*— the perfect synthesis of love and fear, kindness and judgment. "The G-d of my father, the G-d of Abraham and the Fear of Isaac have been with me"[11]—that is, he embraced both their modes of service. Therefore all his acts were perfect, whether in withstanding the trial of wealth (kindness) while he was with Laban and "the man (Jacob) increased exceedingly,"[13] or in the trial of anxiety (judgment) when Esau came to confront him accompanied by four hundred men. In all this, "Jacob came whole"—that is, in a state of perfection.[14]

This is not to say that we do not find the attribute of Knowledge amongst the Fathers, nor of Emotion in Moses. The Fathers learned Torah, as the Rabbis say:[15] "G-d made Abraham's two kidneys like two wise men who instructed and advised him and taught him knowledge," and[16] "From the days of our Fathers the Yeshiva (the academy for learning Torah)

---

10. *Isaiah* 41:8.
11. *Bereishit* 31:42.
12. *Rashi, Bereishit* 27:1.
13. *Bereishit* 30:43.
14. Ibid., 33:18. *Shabbat,* 33a.
15. *Avot deRabbi Nathan,* beg. of ch. 33. Cf. *Bereishit Rabbah,* beg. of ch. 61. *Tanchuma, Vayigash,* ch. 12.
16. *Yoma,* 28b. Cf. *Rambam, Hilchot Akum,* end of ch. 1.

never departed from them (the Jewish people)." And Moses displayed both compassion and austere judgment: Compassion when "he saw their (the Israelites') burdens"[17] and his eyes and heart went out to them; judgment when he admonished the Jew who was fighting with his fellow,[18] "Why did you smite your neighbor?" Nonetheless Moses' *primary* attribute was Knowledge, namely that he gave the Torah to the Jewish people and that it is called by his name: "Remember the Torah of Moses My servant"[19] And the primary mode of service of the Fathers was through the Emotions—a path which through them has become the inheritance of every Jew.[20]

3. THE REASON BEHIND THE QUESTION

We can now understand why Moses, despite his higher spiritual achievements than the Fathers, brought a question against G-d. For Knowledge, or intellect, seeks to *comprehend* everything. And when it encounters something that it cannot understand, this acts as a barrier to going further in the service of G-d. Moses sought an answer—an explanation of what was incomprehensible to him so—that he could continue along his path to G-d through knowledge.

4. THE FAITH WHICH HAS NO QUESTIONS

The answer which he received was, "I am the L-rd. And I appeared to Abraham, to Isaac and to Jacob as G-d Almighty *(Kel Sha-dai)* but by My name 'the L-rd' (the Tetragrammaton) I did not make Myself known to them." Before the Giving of the Torah, G-d was revealed only as Elokim—a finite disclosure, revealing G-d as He is imminent in the world,[21] the world of plurality: Hence the name Elokim which is in the plural. But after Sinai, He was revealed in His four-letter name—as infi-

---

17. *Shemot* 2:11.
18. Ibid., 2:13.
19. *Malachi* 3:22.
20. Cf. *Rambam, Hilchot Aivel*, 14:2.
21. And so the name *Sha-dai* represents G-d as He appears in the finite world—He who said to His creation *dai*—enough! *Bereishit Rabbah*, 46:2.

nite, transcending all divisions, a Unity. At that moment, divisions were dissolved,[22] the division between higher and lower powers, between Knowledge and Emotion.

What G-d therefore said to Moses was: When you stand at the threshold of a redemption which will culminate in the Giving of the Torah, you must surpass the division between Knowledge and Emotion. And even though you are primarily a man of Knowledge, this must be conjoined with the emotional power to have a faith which does not raise questions.

This is why He used the name "Jacob" instead of "Israel" in speaking of the Fathers. "Jacob" refers to a lower level than "Israel" ("Jacob" is related in Hebrew to the word *"ekev"*—the *heel;* while "Israel" is composed of the letters *"li-rosh"*—the *head* is mine).[6] And the implication to Moses was that his Knowledge should embrace and be embraced by his Emotions in *kabbalat ol*—the acceptance of the weight of faith. The higher (knowledge) and the lower (the "heel") should interpenetrate one another.

5. KNOWLEDGE AND ACTION

Not only do the emotions carry the strength to have a faith which goes beyond questions, but they also lead to *action*. Love brings a man to "do good"; fear leads him to "turn from evil."[23] But knowledge, in itself, leads to detachment. The mind becomes engrossed in learning and loses its concern with action. Even though it may thereby gain the knowledge of what to do, it loses the inclination to do it.

This is why the Rabbis warned: "He who says, I have nothing but (my learning of) Torah, does not even have Torah." That is, the learning of Torah in itself could lead naturally to detachment, whereas the Jew must accompany it with actual service towards G-d and acts of compassion towards man. Learning, alone, without acting, is not true learning.

---

22. Cf. *Shemot Rabbah*, 12:3.
23. *Tanya*, Part I, ch. 4.

6. "Father" and Offspring

And this is why Abraham, Isaac and Jacob, whose main path of service was through the Emotions, are called the "Fathers." A father is someone who begets children. And the "generations of righteous men are their good deeds."[24] Being men of Emotion, and since Emotion leads to action, their (principal) achievement was "good deeds."

And in another sense, too, their achievement lay in their offspring. They were not detached; they were concerned with the welfare of others; and therefore they transmitted their values to their children as an everlasting heritage.

This explains the puzzling comment of Rashi on the word (at the beginning of our Sidra) "I appeared." Rashi comments, "to the Fathers." But this seems self-evident and not worthy of mention, since the Torah itself continues, "to Abraham, Isaac and Jacob." The point that Rashi is making, however, is that it is as *"Fathers"* that their primary virtue lies earning them G-d's revelation. This was not for their individual spiritual achievements, but for their being men with offspring (whether understood as "good deeds" or as "children" who inherit their righteousness). G-d loved Abraham because:[25] "I know him, that he will command his children and his household after him, and they shall keep the way of the L-rd."

7. The Meaning of G-d's Answer

The answer which G-d gave to Moses' question was therefore that without foregoing his character as a man of Knowledge, nonetheless he should be animated by the Emotions, as the Fathers were, so that firstly his faith would become unconditional, asking no questions, and secondly he would become a man who translated his knowledge into action. Indeed, we find that Moses eventually went beyond the Fathers in this respect. While they were shepherds, removed from the world,

---

24. *Rashi, Bereishit,* 6:9. *Bereishit Rabbah,* 30:6.
25. *Bereishit* 18:19. *Rashi,* Ibid.

Moses translated the Torah[26] and transmitted it to the world and bore the burden of the Jewish people to the extent that he could say:[27] "You say to me, 'Carry them in your lap. . . ?'"

The two-way process of revelation at Mt. Sinai—when the "high came down low" and the "low became high"[22] thus had its counterpart in the inner life. The high, that is the intellect, descended into the field of action, and the low, that is the "heel" of Jacob (the symbol of *kabbalat ol,* or absolute acceptance of G-d's will) ascended until it shaped the intellect into its own unconditional faith.

And this is the moral for every Jew of G-d's reproof to Moses: That the highest and lowest amongst Jews should work together mutually. The "heads of your tribes" must "descend" to involve themselves with "the hewers of your wood and the drawers of your water,"[28] who must in turn "ascend" by learning Torah (both in its "revealed" and "inward" aspects) and by performing the Mitzvot and "beautifying" them. And each Jew, even the "heads of your tribes," must not be so detached in his studies as to neglect his involvement with the world, and his unconditional acceptance of the will of G-d. This power—to unite "higher" and "lower"—is our inheritance from Moses. And this conduct, which in Moses brought the redemption from Egypt, will, in us, bring that final redemption which transcends all boundaries—the imminent realization of the Messianic Age.

(Source: Likkutei Sichot, Vol. III pp. 854-62)

---

26. *Rashi, Devarim* 1:5. Cf. *Sotah,* 36a.
27. *Bamidbar* 11:12.
28. *Devarim* 29:9-10.

פרשת בא

BO

Two unusual features distinguish the tenth plague—the smiting of the Egyptian firstborn—from the other nine that G-d brought against the Egyptians. Firstly, Moses announced the specific time that it would take place ("about midnight"), and secondly, the Israelites themselves were commanded to take precautions against the plague afflicting them—they were to stay indoors, and set a sign, in blood, on their doorposts. The Rebbe explains why these features were attached only to this plague, and how they indicate to us the path that we must follow to bring about the redemption of the future—the Messianic Age.

1. THE TIME AND THE PRECAUTIONS

When Moses announced to Pharaoh the coming of the final plague, the smiting of the firstborn, he mentioned the *time* that it would occur. G-d had said that it would take place at midnight. Moses said that it would be at *"about* midnight,"[1] fearing that Pharaoh's astrologers might make a mistake in their calculations of the precise fixing of midnight and might accuse him of inaccuracy.[2] Nonetheless, this raises a difficulty. Why was the timing of the plague mentioned at all? The mere warning of its imminence would surely have been sufficient, as it was in the case of the other nine plagues. We are forced to conclude that there is a special and significant connection between the plague of smiting the firstborn and the time of midnight, so that in mentioning one, Moses had to mention the other.

In two further ways, the tenth plague was unique.

---

1. *Shemot* 11:4.
2. *Rashi*, ad loc. *Berachot*, 4a.

Firstly, the Jews had to make a special sign "on the two doorposts and the lintel"[3] of their houses, a sign in the blood of circumcision and of the Paschal lamb,[4] so that the plague would not be visited on them.

Secondly, they had to remain indoors throughout the night: "And none of you shall go out from the entrance of his house until the morning,"[3] because "once the force of destruction is given permission (to unleash itself) it makes no distinction between the righteous and the wicked."[5]

But why should these provisions have been necessary? The previous plagues had been directed solely against the Egyptians, without the Israelites needing to take any special precautions to preserve their immunity. Why was the tenth plague different in this respect? And why were *two* precautions (the sign of the blood, and the confinement to their houses) needed?

2. THE UNIQUENESS OF THE FINAL PLAGUE

We can approach an answer by first understanding that the other nine plagues were not of the kind whereby "the force of destruction is given permission (to unleash itself)." They were *limited* to a specific manner and extent of damage. The hail, for example, destroyed "the flax and the barley . . . but the wheat and the spelt were not smitten because they were not grown up."[6] But the smiting of the firstborn was not limited to any specific manner of destruction; the force which "makes no distinction between the righteous and the wicked" was set loose— and therefore the Israelites had to guard themselves against it.

At a deeper level, the smiting of the firstborn was unique in its *purpose,* not only in its manner. The other plagues were not primarily to destroy, but to create in the Egyptians an awareness of G-d: "In this you shall know that I am the L-rd."[7] And

3. *Shemot* 12:22.
4. *Pirkei deRabbi Eliezer*, ch. 29; *Targum Yonathan, Shemot* 12:13. *Zohar*, Part II, 35b.
5. *Rashi, Shemot* 12:22.
6. *Shemot* 9:31-32.
7. *Shemot* 7:17. Cf. also 8:18; 9:14.

this was not a lesson that needed to be enforced amongst the Israelites, who already acknowledged G-d.[8] It also meant that in the first nine plagues, those who were afflicted were not killed, so that they could benefit from this revelation of G-d's power. But in the tenth plague, since the firstborn were killed, the aim could not have been (as regards the victims) to *educate* them. It was to punish and destroy them. And in this case the voice of strict justice could claim: What is the difference between the Israelites in their idolatry[9] and degeneracy, and the Egyptian firstborn? Surely both deserve punishment? Hence the Israelites' need to safeguard themselves against the force of destruction—the instrument of strict justice.

These safeguards were of two orders. In Egypt generally, the force of destruction was "given permission" to loose itself. Since it is indiscriminate and has no limitations, no "sign" is a protection against it. Therefore the Israelites had to withdraw to their houses. Within them (since they were "passed over" by G-d) the plague was subject to a limitation—and so there was room (and necessity) for a "sign" which would single out Jew from Egyptian.

3. MIDNIGHT AND ESSENCE

But what is still difficult to understand is this: The voice of strict justice raised the question, "What is the difference" between a G-dless Egypt and a sinful Jewish people? How could a "sign" have answered the claim?

The answer is that the tenth plague was executed by "G-d Himself in His glory and His essence," G-d as He transcends characterization, in particular, as He is beyond the attribute of strict justice. At this level, the accusations brought in the name of severity and justice are silent, inoperative.

This is the connection between the tenth plague and midnight. For midnight is the moment when this all-transcending face of G-d is revealed. Midnight binds the two halves of the

---

8. Cf. *Torah Or, Vaera,* 57a.
9. *Yalkut Reuveni, Shemot* 14:27; *Zohar,* Part II, 170b.

night, the first half which leads from light into darkness and is therefore a symbol of severity and holding-back *(gevurah),* and the second which leads from darkness into light, and stands for kindness and giving-forth *(chesed).* And so, momentarily harmonizing these two opposing tendencies and thereby transcending them, midnight is the time at which G-d in His Essence is revealed.[10]

Thus at the time of the tenth plague, G-d displayed his essential love for Israel, a love which in its infinity finds no place for the accusations of the voice of justice. When the voice claims, "Was not Esau Jacob's brother?" (Are they not equal?) G-d answers, "Yet I loved Jacob and I hated Esau."[11] For His love for the Jewish people is as deep and invulnerable as the love of a father for his children: "You are the children of the L-rd your G-d."[12]

This is why Moses told Pharaoh the time of the plague ("about midnight"). In this, he was hinting that it would be brought about by G-d in His transcendence. For otherwise Pharaoh and his court would have been convinced that a plague whose purpose was to destroy and not to educate, would afflict the Israelites as well, since they too were guilty of sins. Only a revelation of G-d's *unconditional* love (i.e., at midnight) would have saved them.

4. SIGN AND LOVE

Why, though, did the Israelites still need a sign?

The answer is that to draw down into the physical world a revelation of G-d, man must perform acts of service, the acts which are specified in the Torah. Even G-d's *unconditional* love, which is always present and constant, requires an active response by the Jew if he is to internalize it and bring it into openness of revelation. But in this case, since the love is un-

10. Cf. *Or Hatorah, Vayeichalek Aleihem* etc., ch. 5. *Bereishit,* p. 75 ff.
11. *Malachi* 1:2-3.
12. *Devarim* 14:1.

conditional, the response, too, must be unconditional—going beyond the limits of rationality.

Both of the signs—the blood of circumcision and of the Paschal lamb—were of this character. The covenant of circumcision is performed on a Jewish child who is only eight days old, at an age when his faculty of reason is as yet undeveloped. It is a union between the Jew and G-d which goes beyond the rational. And the sacrifice of the Paschal lamb was at that time so fraught with danger as to constitute an act of self-sacrifice (mesirat nefesh). The lamb was an Egyptian deity. And not only were the Israelites to kill it, but they also had to keep it for four days beforehand with the full knowledge of the Egyptians. Self-sacrifice is never rational. And so the Paschal lamb was itself a sign of a Jewish response to G-d that surpassed reason.

Therefore these two signs were answered by G-d with an act of supra-rational love—the love of midnight, of G-d's Essence, of the delivery from the tenth plague.

5. FAITH AND REASON

Now we can resolve an apparent contradiction in the statements of the Rabbis as to the virtue in whose merit the Israelites were redeemed from Egypt. In one place, we find that it was their faith:[13] "And the people believed, and when they heard that the L-rd had visited the children of Israel and that He had looked upon their affliction, they bowed their heads and worshipped."[14] In other places,[15] it is stated that it was a reward for their signs of blood: "In your blood: Live."[16]

But the two opinions are one. The signs were of a bond between Jew and G-d surpassing reason. And their faith was one which went beyond reason. Before the redemption, "no slave had been able to escape from Egypt because the land was

---

13. *Mechilta, Shemot* 14:31.
14. *Shemot* 4:31.
15. *Pirkei deRabbi Eliezer,* ch. 29. *Mechilta, Shemot* 12:6, cited by *Rashi,* Ibid.
16. *Ezekiel* 16:6.

closely shut in (on all sides)."[17] How much less reasonable was it to believe that 600,000 could escape, a people broken by the rigors of oppression, and threatened with extinction through Pharaoh's decree that every male child be drowned. The pure faith with which the Israelites believed in Moses' mission and G-d's promised deliverance went far beyond the rational. And this faith aroused the unconditional love in G-d for His people, which constituted their inseparable bond. The signs by which it was then expressed, brought the revelation of G-d's love down to this world.

6. THE FUTURE REDEMPTION

"Like the days of your exodus from the land of Egypt, I will demonstrate wonders."[18] This means the future redemption will parallel the redemption of the past.

The deliverance from Egypt was a reward for the supra-rational faith which was so internalized by the Israelites that it affected even their most extraneous powers (signified by the blood of circumcision) and even the non-human environment (the Paschal lamb).

So, too, will the future redemption be a reward for faith—the faith which disregards the great concealments of G-d that our exile brings, and which still holds firm to the belief in the Messiah; a faith which does not hover at the outer edges of our minds, but which constitutes our most inward certainty and extends to every facet of our being.

(Source: Likkutei Sichot, Vol. III pp. 864-8, 872)

---

17. *Mechilta*, *Shemot* 18:11; cited by *Rashi*, 18:9.
18. *Micah* 7:15.

פרשת בשלח

BESHALACH

This Sidra relates the story of the division of the Red Sea, its waters
parted by a powerful wind sent by G-d. When the wind ceased and
the waters closed on the pursuing Egyptians, we are told that "the
sea returned to its strength." Why did the Torah add this extra
phrase? The Midrash finds an allusion in it to the condition (the
words "strength" and "condition" in Hebrew are composed of the
same letters) which G-d made with the Red Sea when it was first
created, that it should part its waters for Israel when the time came.
The Rebbe explores this theme in depth, analyzing in general the
part which natural objects and forces have to play in G-d's design
for the universe.

1. THE DIVISION OF THE SEA

"And Moses stretched forth his hand over the sea and the
sea returned to its former strength at the turning of the morning; and the Egyptians fled towards it; and the L-rd overthrew
the Egyptians in the midst of the sea."[1]

The Midrash[2] comments on this that G-d made a stipula-
tion at the time when the Red Sea was first created, that it
should divide itself for Israel when they needed to cross it. This
is the meaning of the phrase "the sea returned to its former
strength," namely that it "kept to the terms of the condition
which I stipulated from the beginning" (a play on the words
"condition" and "former strength" which have the same letters
in Hebrew).[3]

But the Midrash is difficult to understand. For the verse
refers, not to the fulfilling, by the sea, of the undertaking to *di-*

---

1. *Shemot* 14:27.
2. *Bereishit Rabbah*, 5:5; *Shemot Rabbah*, 21:6. *Zohar*, Part II, 198b.
3. *L'eitano—Lit'nao.* Cf. *Baal Haturim* on *Shemot* 14:27.

vide; but clearly to its *returning* to its former state, closing its waters over the pursuing Egyptians.

An answer has been suggested.[4] In the Talmud,[5] Rabbi Pinchas ben Yair tells the River Ginnai to divide its waters and when it refused, he told it "If you do not do so, I will decree that no water shall flow in you forever." If the same were true of the Red Sea, then its returning to its former strength would be evidence of its having fulfilled its agreement with G-d.

But the answer itself is incomplete:

(i) It suggests that if the Red Sea had not divided, it would not only not have had its strength returned, it would not have had any waters *at all.* The verse, on the other hand, suggests that only the *full strength* of the Red Sea hung on the agreement, not its very continuance as a sea.

(ii) In any case, the Midrash sought to couple the words "full strength" with the word "condition." But the explanation makes the Sea's strength only a *consequence* of its previously fulfilling the condition and does not link it with the condition itself.

2. THE CONDITION MADE AT THE BEGINNING OF CREATION

We can resolve the first of these difficulties by the explanation given by the Maggid of Mezeritch[6] (which he had heard from the Baal Shem Tov). At the time of the creation of the world all the objects of nature were created on the condition that they obeyed the will of righteous men, even if it ran counter to their normal physical laws.[7] So that if they did not do so, not only would they *cease to exist:* It would be as if they had *never been created.* In other words, had the Red Sea not divided, it would not only never have water again, its *whole previous* existence would be obliterated. So that when the verse

---

4. *Yedei Moshe*, commentary on *Bereishit Rabbah*, loc. cit.
5. *Chullin*, 7a.
6. In his book, *Or Torah.* Quoted in *Hayom Yom*, p. 20.
7. Cf. *Bereishit Rabbah*, 5:5.

tells us "the sea returned to its *former strength,*" it is conveying that in the fulfilling of its agreement with G-d it *both* assured its *future* continuity and at the same time ratified its *past* existence.

This point may be difficult for us to understand: For though we know what it is for something to be obliterated, surely its past existence is an objective fact, which cannot be *retroactively* removed? The mental block we have in comprehending this possibility is because of a two-fold secular conception to which our minds tenaciously cling: Firstly, that objects have a real and independent existence, and secondly that our time-scheme (in which we cannot reach back and change the past) is the only possible one. Both conceptions are false in Judaism. In the first instance objects only exist because G-d continually creates them; in the second instance, time is a *human* conception, one by which G-d is not bound (indeed, one which G-d created and so, obviously, can stand aside from). It follows that if G-d decides to "uncreate" something, He can do so retroactively and by removing its whole (past as well as future) being. The closest analogy in human terms (and one which is germane to the subject in hand) is that of a conditional legal agreement. If the condition is not fulfilled, it is not that the agreement suddenly *terminates,* but rather that this establishes that the agreement never *came* into being.

3. Two Kinds of Miracles

But the second difficulty still remains: That the sea's returning to its strength was a *result* of and not the *same as* its fulfilling its condition.

To resolve this we must understand why the Midrash *needed* to comment on the phrase "the sea returned to its strength." What is problematic about it? The answer is that since the phrase "the sea returned" would have sufficed,[8] there must be some *additional* point made by the phrase "to its strength." Now why should we doubt that the sea's strength

---

8. Cf. e.g., the previous verse—*Shemot* 14:26—"that the waters return."

would return? Is there any ground for thinking that its parting, to leave dry land for the Israelites' crossing, permanently "weakened" it, so that a *second* miracle was needed to restore its force?

Now we can discern *two* distinct *types* of miracles:

(i) The miracle which transforms the whole nature of a thing, so that a second miracle is needed to return it to its original state (for example: When G-d made Moses' hand leprous as a sign of the authenticity of the revelation at Horeb? He performed a second miracle in turning it back).[9]

(ii) The miracle which only changes the *appearance* or form of a thing, leaving its essential character unaltered, so that when the miracle ceases it returns to its earlier state of its own accord (like the rivers which were changed into blood, the first of the ten plagues, which later returned to water without further miracle:[10] For the rivers, were not *essentially* transformed: They still remained as water when the *Israelites* drank from them.)[11]

Therefore, if we were to say, that the division of the Red Sea was of the first kind, it would follow that a *second* miracle would be needed to return it to its former state. This is what the verse negates by informing us that the Sea returned "to its strength," i.e., that the Sea had only changed externally, but not essentially.

But in fact we *cannot* say this, for the Torah already stressed that the Sea was only kept in its divided state by constant vigilance: "And the L-rd caused the sea to go back by a powerful east wind *all the* night."[12] From which it is clear that, had the wind dropped, it would have returned to its flowing of its own accord, so why need the Torah stress in a later verse that the Sea returned "to its strength?"

Therefore the Midrash implies that the extra information conveyed by telling us that the Sea returned to its strength,

---

9. *Shemot* 4:6-7.
10. *Shemot* 7:19-25.
11. *Shemot Rabbah*, 9:10.
12. *Shemot* 14:21.

must be that it had its whole *previous* existence ratified by its fulfillment of G-d's *condition*. And even though it had fulfilled it by *dividing* rather than returning, the *sign* of its fulfillment was evident only when its waters were restored.

4. TEMPORAL AND ETERNAL EXISTENCE

But why did G-d *need* to make an agreement with the Sea, and why particularly at the moment when it was created? For His power over His creations is unlimited and He could have divided the Sea when He wanted and without its "consent."

Rashi's comment that the world was created "for the sake of Israel and the Torah"[13] does not simply mean that it exists to *allow* Israel to perform G-d's will on earth, but more strongly that by Israel's service the world *itself* is sanctified into becoming a "dwelling-place" for G-d and thus brought to its own fulfillment.

Thus by stipulating at the outset that objects should change their nature when it was necessary for the sake of Israel, G-d wrote this miraculous possibility into their very constitution. So that when miracles occurred, this would not be an *interruption* of their normal purpose but a continuation and *fulfillment* of it.

And indeed this makes their existence of an entirely different order. They become not things which exist for a while and then pass away; but rather things whose destiny is (by the very nature of their creation) linked with that of Israel. And Israel is, in the deepest sense, eternal. They are, to G-d "the branch of My planting and the work of My hands."[14] And this makes natural objects far more than the *instruments* of Israel's progress (for they would then be bound to their natural functions only); but instead they are *embodiments of G-d's will* (even when this involves a *change* in their nature).

This is why the Midrash connects the fulfilling of its agreement with G-d with the sea's return to its strength, rather than

---

13. *Bereishit* 1:1; cf. also *Bereishit Rabbah*, loc. cit.
14. *Isaiah* 60:21.

with its division. For while it was divided to reveal dry land, it still did not show the vindication and eternalization of its existence (for it could have been a (change and) *negation* of its nature). Its true fulfillment came only when its waters returned. And when they returned, it was to their "full strength," not simply as they had been before, mere waters of a sea, but as the eternal bearers of G-d's will for the destiny of His people.

(Source: Likkutei Sichot, Vol. VI pp. 86-94)

פרשת יתרו
YITRO

In this elaborate and profound Sicha, two disagreements in interpretation of events connected with the Giving of the Torah are explored. In both cases the disputants are Rabbi Akiva and Rabbi Ishmael; and their opinions reveal a deep underlying difference in their orientation towards the service of G-d. The two problems they confront are, what did the Israelites answer to G-d when they accepted the Ten Commandments, and, when the Torah tells us that they "saw the voices (of the thunder)," did they literally see a sound, or did they only hear it? From these apparently slight beginnings, the Rebbe uncovers fundamental themes; in particular, the difference in perception between the righteous man and the man of repentance.

1. THE ANSWERS OF THE ISRAELITES

As a preliminary to the giving of the Ten Commandments the Torah tells us that "And G-d spoke all these things, saying."[1]

The usual meaning of the Hebrew word of "saying" is "to say to others."[2] For example, the meaning of "And G-d spoke to Moses, saying . . ." is that Moses should transmit the word of G-d to the Children of Israel. But this cannot be the meaning of the present verse, for at the time of the Giving of the Torah, G-d *Himself* spoke to *all* the Israelites. Nor can it mean "for transmission to the later generations," for we have a tradition that *all* Jewish souls, of past and future lives, were gathered at Sinai to witness the revelation.[3]

---

1. *Shemot* 20:1.
2. Cf. e.g., *Rashi, Shemot* 19:12 and *Vayikra* 1:1.
3. *Pirkei deRabbi Eliezer*, ch. 41. *Shemot Rabbah*, 28:6; *Tanchuma, Yitro* 11. *Zohar*, Part I, 91a.

Therefore the Mechilta interprets "saying" as meaning that, for every commandment, the children of Israel *answered* G-d saying that they would do what it demanded to them.

But the Mechilta cites two opinions as to the manner in which the Israelites answered. Rabbi Ishmael says that on the positive commandments they answered "yes" and on the negative, "no" (i.e., that they would do what G-d commanded, and would not do what He forbade). Rabbi Akiva, on the other hand, says that they answered "yes" to both positive and negative commands (i.e., that they would do G-d's will, whatever form it took). But what is the substance of the disagreement between the two opinions? Surely, they both, in essence, say the same thing?

2. THE VOICE OF THE THUNDER

There is another disagreement between Rabbi Akiva and Rabbi Ishmael concerning the Giving of the Torah. We are told that "all the people saw the voices (of the thunder) and the lightning"[4]—a problem, for how can voices be *seen?*

Rabbi Ishmael says: "They saw what is (normally) seen and heard what is (normally) heard," taking the verb "saw" to apply not to the voices of the thunder, but to the lightning. But Rabbi Akiva says, "they saw what is (normally) heard, and heard what is (normally) seen" i.e., that they did indeed see the voices, and did not see, but *heard,* the lightning.

Now there is a general principle that G-d does not perform miracles for no reason. From which we can infer that the miracles that Rabbi Akiva describes were not *extraneous* to the giving of the Torah, but were an essential part of it. So elevated were the Israelites by the revelation of the Ten Commandments that their senses took on miraculous powers. If so, we must understand the verse "they saw the voices (of the thunder) and the lightning" as relating to the ecstatic state of the Israelites. But

---

4. *Shemot* 20:15.

now we cannot understand Rabbi Ishmael's opinion, for he interprets the verse as relating to a purely *natural* phenomenon.

3. RASHI'S QUOTATIONS

Since these two disagreements relate to the same subject and are between the same protagonists, we can assume that their opinions on the answer of the Israelites are connected to their opinions on the seeing of the thunder (that one entails the other).

This would appear to be contradicted by the fact that Rashi, on the word "saying," quotes *Rabbi Ishmael's* opinion (the Israelites answered "yes" to the positive commands and "no" to the negative); while on the phrase "they saw the voices" he cites (part of) *Rabbi Akiva's* explanation (that they saw what is normally heard).

Since Rashi's commentary is consistent, it would seem that the two problems are not related if he can cite one side on one question, and the other on the other. This however does not follow. For Rashi quotes only *half* of Rabbi Akiva's explanation, omitting "the Israelites heard what is normally seen." And it is this *second* half which forces Rabbi Akiva to his opinion that the Israelites answered "yes" to the negative command (i.e., his difference of opinion with Rabbi Ishmael). And the *reason* why Rashi selects Rabbi Ishmael's answer to one question and one half of Rabbi Akiva's to the other, is because these are the most appropriate to a *literal* understanding of the text (which is Rashi's concern). How this is so, will be explained later.

4. SIGHT AND SOUND

As a preliminary, we must understand the difference between "seeing" and "hearing."

Firstly the impression made on a man by seeing something happen is far stronger than that made by just hearing about it. So much so that "an eyewitness to an event cannot be a judge in a case about it"[5]—for no counter-argument could sway his

---

5. *Rosh Hashanah*, 26a.

fixed belief about what he saw. Whereas so long as he has only *heard* about it, he can be open to conflicting testimonies, and judge impartially between them.

Secondly, only a physical thing can be seen; while what can be heard is always less tangible (sounds, words, opinions).

These two points are connected. For man is a physical being, and it is natural that the physical should make the most indelible impression on him; while the spiritual is accessible only by "hearing" and understanding, hence its impression is weaker.

This explains the nature of the elevation that the Giving of the Torah worked on the Israelites. They saw what was normally heard—i.e., the spiritual became as tangible and certain as the familiar world of physical objects. Indeed, the *Essence* of G-d *was revealed* to their eyes, when they heard the words, "I (the Essence) the L-rd (who transcends the world) am thy G-d (who is imminent in the world)."

At a time of such revelations, the world is known for what it truly is—not an independently existent thing, but something entirely nullified before G-d. If so, how do we know that there is a world and not simply an *illusion* of one? One by *inference*, from the verse "In the beginning, G-d created heaven and earth." In other words, the Israelites "heard what was normally seen"—they had only an *intellectual* conviction (and not the testimony of the senses) that there was a physical world.

5. RABBI ISHMAEL'S INTERPRETATION

But if this was so, what elevation was there in the Israelites according to Rabbi Ishmael, who holds that they only heard and saw what was normally heard and seen? How could this be, when the revelation was the greatest in all history?

The explanation is that the main revelation at the Giving of the Torah was that "the L-rd *came down* upon Mt. Sinai"[6]—the high came low; and the miracle was that G-d Himself should

---

6. *Shemot* 19:20.

be revealed *within* the limits of nature. This is why it was so extraordinary that the Israelites should, *without any change* in their senses, perceive G-d in His Essence and so abdicate themselves that "they trembled and stood far off."[7]

6. THE PRIEST AND THE REPENTANT

Why do Rabbi Ishmael and Rabbi Akiva hold opposing views as to the nature of the elevation brought about in the Israelites at Sinai?

Rabbi Ishmael was a High Priest (a *Kohen Gadol*)[8] and the nature of a priest is to be "sanctified to his G-d."[9] His service is that of the righteous, to transmit holiness to this world (to take the high and bring it low). This is why he saw the greatest miracle as being that G-d Himself came down to this world, so far as to be perceived by the *normal* senses ("they saw what is normally seen").

But Rabbi Akiva was a man of repentance (a *Ba'al Teshuvah*), whose descent was from converts[10] and who only started to learn Torah at the age of 40.[11] Repentance colors his whole manner of service: The desire to ascend higher than this world (and, as is known,[12] he longed *throughout his life* to be able to martyr himself in the cause of G-d). So that for him the greatest miracle was the transcending of all physical limitations ("they saw what is normally heard").

7. TWO FACES OF COMMANDMENT

There are two aspects to every commandment:

(i) the element which is *common* to them all that—they are commands from G-d; and

---

7. *Shemot* 20:15.
8. *Chullin*, 49a, *Rashi* loc. cit.
9. *Vayikra* 21:7.
10. Cf. *Seder Hadorot. Rashi, Yoma*, 22b.
11. *Avot deRabbi Nathan*, 6:2. Cf. *Pesachim*, 49b; *Ketubot*, 62b.
12. *Berachot*, 61b.

(ii) the characteristics which are *individual* to each, each in-volving different human activities and sanctifying a different aspect of the world.

Rabbi Akiva and Rabbi Ishmael each attend to a different aspect. Rabbi Ishmael, who sees the ultimate achievement in translating G-dliness into this world, with all its limitations, sees principally the *details* of the commandments, (how each sanctifies a different part of this world). And thus he holds that the Israelites answered "yes" to the positive ones and "no" to the negative—that they attended to what *distinguished* one kind of command from another.

But to Rabbi Akiva, what was important was the transcend-ing of the world and its limitations, and hence in a command-ment the essential element was what was *common to each*, that it embodies the will of G-d which has no limitations. Therefore he says that the Israelites responded primarily to this common element, they said "yes" to positive and negative alike.

8. THE POSITIVE IN THE NEGATIVE: THE CHARACTER OF RABBI AKIVA

We can in fact go deeper in our understanding of Rabbi Akiva's statement. When he says that the Israelites said "yes" to the negative commandments, this was not simply that they sensed in them the element common to all expressions of G-d's will; but more strongly, that they only saw what was *positive* even in a negative thing—the holiness that an act of re-straint brings about.

And this follows from the second clause of his second ex-planation (which Rashi omits in his commentary) that the Isra-elites "heard what was normally seen." For since the physical world's existence was for them only an *intellectual* perception and the only sensed reality was the existence of G-d, they could not sense the existence of things which opposed holiness ("the other gods") but saw only the act of affirmation involved in *"thou shall have no* other gods."

We can see this orientation of Rabbi Akiva very clearly in the story related in the Talmud,[13] that Rabban Gamliel, Rabbi Elazar ben Azariah, Rabbi Joshua and Rabbi Akiva were on a journey and decided to return to Jerusalem (after the destruction of the second Temple). When they reached Mt. Scopus they rent their garments. When they reached the Temple Mount, they saw a fox emerging from the Holy of Holies and they began to weep—but Rabbi Akiva *laughed*. They asked him, "Why are you laughing?" and he replied, "Why are you weeping?" They said, it is written, "the common man who goes near (to the Holy of Holies) shall die,"[14] and now *foxes* enter it—should we not cry?

He said, "this is why I laugh. For it is written 'And I will take to Me faithful witnesses, Uriah the priest and Zechariah the son of Jeberechiah.'[15] Now what connection has Uriah with Zechariah? Uriah lived during the times of the First Temple, while Zechariah prophesied at the time of the second. But the Torah links the prophecies of both men. Uriah wrote, 'therefore shall Zion, because of you, be plowed like a field.' And Zechariah wrote 'Yet shall old men and women sit in the broad places of Jerusalem.' So long as Uriah's prophecy had not been fulfilled, I was afraid that Zechariah's would not be. Now that it has, it is certain that Zechariah's will come true."

Even in the darkest moment of Jewish history—when foxes ran freely in the Holy of Holies Rabbi Akiva saw only the good: That this was proof that the serene and hopeful vision of Zechariah would be vindicated.

9. THE MEANING OF RASHI

The two kinds of service which Rabbi Akiva and Rabbi Ishmael exemplify (the service of the righteous and the repentant) are relevant only to one who is already some way along the

---

13. At the conclusion of *Makkot*.
14. *Bamidbar* 1:51.
15. *Isaiah* 8:2.

path to perfection. But to the "five-year old"[16] (whether in years, or more generally to those at the beginning of the way) to whom Rashi addresses his commentary, he need only quote *part* of Rabbi Akiva's explanation, that "they saw what is normally heard." For the beginning of worship, stated in the *first* chapter of the Shulchan Aruch, is "I have set the L-rd before me continually." In other words, it is to strive to make G-dliness (normally only an intellectual notion, something "heard") as real for oneself as if one had literally seen Him with one's own eyes.

But Rashi does not quote the rest of the sentence, "they heard what was normally seen," for however real G-d may become for one; at the *beginning* of one's life of service, the world still seems like a tangible reality. And physical acts like eating and drinking are still prompted by physical desires, and are not unequivocally for the sake of Heaven.

And thus, since the physical world still has an independent reality for him, and he can still perceive the bad, Rashi gives Rabbi Ishmael's comment, that the Israelites answered "no" to the negative commandments.

Indeed, though Rashi cites Rabbi Akiva, that the Israelites "saw what was normally heard," this is consistent even with the opinion of Rabbi Ishmael. For his comment speaks to a man already at the level of righteousness when he can perceive G-dliness even within the constraints of the lowest of this world, symbolized by the expression that he "hears what is normally heard" (i.e., where G-dliness is so concealed that it is only affirmed as a result of intellectual proofs). But at the beginning of the path, one must relate to G-d only at a level, when he "sees what is normally heard" (i.e., where G-dliness is readily perceived).

The implication of Rashi for the conduct of the individual Jew, is that when the world still exercises its pull on him, he must strive to make his sense of the presence of G-d as clear as

---

16. The age when a child begins to learn Chumash (*Pirkei Avot* end of ch. 5).

his sense of sight. But this is only a preliminary stage, from which he must take one of the two paths to perfection—Rabbi Ishmael's way of righteousness (bringing G-d into the lowest levels of this world) or Rabbi Akiva's way of repentance (bringing the world up to the highest level of perceiving G-d, so that this world is seen only as an expression of G-dliness). And since both are paths of Torah—both of them are true; therefore, one must combine aspects of both in his spiritual life.

(Source: Likkutei Sichot, Vol. VI pp. 119-129)

פרשת משפטים
MISHPATIM

Our Sidra begins with the words, "And these are the judgments which you shall set before them," and the last phrase of this sentence has troubled many commentators. What is the precise meaning of the expression "set before them?" Several different answers have traditionally been given, and the Rebbe explores the relationship between them. The word "judgments" *(mishpatim)* also requires comment, for this is a technical term in Torah, referring in general to social legislation of the kind which, had it not been given by G-d, man could have devised for himself on rational grounds. It is to be contrasted with "testimonies" *(edut)* such as the Shabbat and the festivals, which though they are rationally comprehensible, could not have been invented by man; and with "statutes" *(chukim)* which are laws whose purpose lies altogether beyond our understanding. Why are only "judgments" singled out to be "set before" the people? In answering this, the Rebbe explores the difficult and much misunderstood relationship between our obedience to and our understanding of G-d's law.

1. THE MEANING OF "BEFORE THEM"

"And these are the judgments which you shall set before them."[1] The Rabbis have given several explanations of the phrase "before them."

The first[2] is that every legal dispute amongst Jews should be tried "before them," before a *Jewish* court of law, which tries cases according to the Torah. They should not take the case before non-Jewish judges, even if their law in this instance coincides with that of the Torah.

The second[3] is that when one is teaching the Torah to a pupil, he should "show the face"; in other words, he should

---

1. *Shemot* 21:1.
2. *Gittin*, 88b. Cited by *Rashi, Shemot* 21:1.
3. *Eruvin*, 54b.

explain the reasons for the law,[4] so that the pupil understands it rather than receiving it as a dogma.

The third, given by the Alter Rebbe,[5] is that "before them" means "to their innermost selves."[6] The verse therefore means that the knowledge of G-d should enter the most inward reaches of the Jewish soul. There is an allusion to this in the Jerusalem Talmud,[7] which relates the phrase "You shall set" *(tasim)* to the word "treasure-house" *(simah)*. The treasure-house of the Torah should thus awaken the treasure-house of the soul, that is, its innermost core.[8]

2. THREE KINDS OF LAW

It is a general principle that different interpretations of the same words of Torah bear an inner relationship to one another.[9] What, then, is the connection between these three explanations?

Also, why should the words "before them," however they are interpreted, be attached specifically to "judgments?" There are three kinds of commandments contained in the Torah: Judgments, testimonies and statutes.[10] *Statutes* are laws which transcend our understanding and which we obey simply because they are the word of G-d. *Testimonies* can be rationally explained, but they are not *necessitated* by rational considerations: Had G-d not decreed them, man would not have invented them. *Judgments,* however, are laws which reason would have compelled man to devise even if they had not been Divinely revealed. As the Rabbis say, "If the Torah had not been given, we would have learned modesty from the cat and hon-

---

4. Based on the word *lifneihem* (before them) which literally means "before their faces."
5. *Torah Or, Mishpatim.*
6. Based on the verbal similarity between *lifneihem* (before them) and *lipnimiusam* (to their innermost selves).
7. *Avodah Zarah*, 2:7.
8. *Zohar*, Part III, 73a. *Likkutei Torah, Vayikra*, 5c.
9. Cf. supra, p. 30.
10. Cf. commentaries, *Devarim* 6:20.

esty from the ant. . . ."[11] Why, then, is it judgments that the Torah singles out to be set "before them?"

If we take the first interpretation of "before them," this is easy to understand. It is only in the sphere of judgments that Jewish and non-Jewish law are likely to coincide. Hence the necessity to urge, specifically of judgments, that disputes concerning them to be taken to a Jewish court. In the case of testimonies and statutes, which can be derived only from Divine revelation, there would be no possibility of taking disputes to a non-Jewish court which based its laws on human reason.

In the second interpretation, however, we run up against a difficulty. If "set before them" means to teach them with explanations, then this is surely more applicable to testimonies and statutes, which are difficult to understand, than to judgments. It is *obvious* that judgments should be explained. Whereas it would be a significant point to demand that testimonies (which can be comprehended, even if they are not necessitated, by reason) and statutes (which reason cannot grasp) should also be taught as far as possible through explanation and rational acceptance.

The same difficulty arises with the third explanation. It surely is not necessary to awaken the innermost reaches of the soul to be able to obey judgments, when reason is sufficient to compel adherence to them. But obedience to testimonies and statutes is not demanded by reason, and so it requires the arousal and assent of the inward self if it is to be done with a feeling of involvement rather than simply in blank response to coercion. Again, the connection between judgments and the phrase "before them" seems misplaced.

3. ACTION AND INTENTION

An important truth about the Divine command is that "the principal thing is the act." If, for example, a person has made all the appropriate mental preparations for putting on Tefillin but

---

11. *Eruvin*, 100b.

stops short of actually putting them on, he has not fulfilled the commandment. And if on the other hand he has put them on, but without the proper intentions, he has nonetheless performed the Mitzvah, and must make a blessing over it.

Despite this, it is also G-d's will that every facet of man be involved in the Mitzvah; not only his power of action and speech, but also his emotion, intellect, will and delight. This applies not only to the commandments which obviously involve feeling and understanding—like the Mitzvot of loving and fearing, believing in and knowing G-d—but to every command, including those which require a specific action. Each Mitzvah must be affirmed by the deepest reaches of man's being, especially by his delight, so that he performs it with joy[12] and a willing heart. This is true, furthermore, even of statutes, which by nature lie beyond his understanding. It is not enough to obey them in action only, as if he had no choice but to submit to G-d's will without sense or comprehension. Nor is it enough to say: I do not understand them, but G-d must certainly have a reason for decreeing them, and that is sufficient for me. For this attitude is not one of unconditional obedience. It is as if to say: I will obey only what is reasonable, but I will allow a mind greater than mine to decide what is reasonable and what is not. Instead, the true acceptance of statutes is one which goes beyond reason, and which makes no conditions. It is one in which the desire to serve G-d for His own sake is so strong that even the intellect positively assents to the call of He who is beyond it.

In the light of this we can understand the Rabbinical saying about the word "statute": "It is a decree before Me: You have no right to speculate about it."[13] This is strange because, since "the principal thing is the act" it would have been more natural to say, "you have no right to *disobey* it." However, the saying implies that the physical act is not enough: It must be accompanied by the assent of the mind. And this means more than

---

12. Cf. *Rambam*, end of *Hilchot Lulav*.
13. *Rashi, Bamidbar* 19:2.

the silencing of doubt, more than the prudential acquiescence
in G-d's wisdom. It means that simple faith floods his mind,
leaving no room for second thoughts.

This is why statutes need the awakening of a Jew's innermost soul. Without it, there would still be room for
"speculation" or doubt even if outwardly he continued to obey.
With it, his thoughts and feelings are fired by an inner enthusiasm. And this is the connection between the second and third
interpretations of "before them": "Inwardness" leads to
"understanding," to an acceptance of the law by mind and
heart.

But a question remains. Why are these insights attached by
the Torah to judgments instead of statutes, where they would
seem more appropriate? There is no difficulty in understanding
judgments, and reason—without inwardness—is sufficient to
lead a man to obey willingly.

4. FAITH AND REASON

The answer is to be found in another Rabbinic commentary to our verse. Noticing that the Sidra begins with the word
"and" ("And these are the judgments. . . .") they said, "'And
these' indicates a continuation of the previous subject."[14] In
other words, the judgments of which our Sidra speaks, are a
continuation of the Ten Commandments, and were, like them,
given at Sinai.

The Ten Commandments fall into two categories. The
first commands concern the highest principles of the unity of
G-d. But the others state simple, social laws like "Thou shalt
not murder" and "Thou shalt not steal," judgments whose purpose is immediately intelligible. By fusing these extremes, the
principles of faith and the judgments of reason, the Torah
teaches that even commands such as "Thou shalt not steal"
should be obeyed not simply because they are *reasonable* but be-

---

14. *Shemot Rabbah*; *Tanchuma* and *Mechilta*, ad loc.

cause they are the will of He who said, "I am the L-rd thy G-d."

Thus, when the Rabbis said that the words "And these are the judgments. . . ." were a continuation of the Ten Commandments, they meant that these judgments should be obeyed not because they are understood, but because they were commanded by G-d at Sinai.

This explains the first interpretation, that one should not bring a Jewish dispute before a non-Jewish court. Even if the laws coincide in practice, a law which has its source in reason is not the same as one which is based on the words, "I am the L-rd thy G-d," and its verdicts do not emanate from Torah.

The third interpretation also becomes clear. Even judgments, which can be obeyed for the sake of reason, must be obeyed from the inwardness of the soul. Judgments must be obeyed like testimonies and statutes: Not from reason alone but from an inward response which animates every facet of one's being.

And this explains the force and subtlety of the second interpretation: That the judgments should be taught so that the pupil understands them. The point is that on the one hand they should not be regarded as the mere dictates of reason; on the other, they should not be thought of as irrational. They are to be obeyed *with* but not *because of* the mind's assent. The mind is to be shaped by what lies beyond it.

Why is human reason not sufficient in itself? Firstly because it has no absolute commitment: "Today it (one's evil inclination) says to him, Do this; tomorrow it tells him, Do that; until it bids him, Go and serve idols."[15] This description of the gradual erosion of spiritual standards is interpreted by the previous Lubavitcher Rebbe, Rabbi Yosef Yitzchak, thus: The Jew's evil impulse cannot begin with enticement to a forbidden act. Rather, it bids him "Do this," "Do that," i.e., a *Mitzvah,* but do it because your intellect and ego concur. Thus, gradually the

---

15. *Shabbat,* 105b.

framework is developed in one, whereby even a forbidden act is not excluded.

Secondly, because even though it might lead a man to obey judgments, it would not bring him to closeness with G-d. This is the difference between an act which is reasonable and an act which is a Mitzvah. "Mitzvah" means "connection": It is the link between man and G-d. Speaking of G-d's statutes and judgments, the Torah tells the Jew: "He shall live by them." If he brings the *whole* of his life—action, emotion, reason and inwardness—into the performance of a Mitzvah because it was given at Sinai, he recreates Sinai: The meeting of man and G-d.

(Source: Likkutei Sichot, Vol. III pp. 895-901)

פרשת תרומה

TERUMAH

The Jew faces a paradox when he considers himself: In the *eyes of* G-d all Jews are equal: They each have a soul whose source is from G-d ("And he breathed into his nostrils the breath of life; and the man became a living soul"); but the Jew is an *embodied* soul and in his attributes—intelligence, temperament and strength of will—each is different. Clearly the Jew is called to exercise his individuality to the full; and yet he is supposed constantly to be animated by the life of the soul through which he comes into relation with G-d and in which he stands as no more and no less than any other Jew. How are we to reconcile these two aspects? Where do man's sameness and his distinctness fit into the life of Torah? These are the questions explored in this Sicha.

1. THE THREE KINDS OF TERUMAH

Terumah means a contribution for sacred purposes, something which the Israelites gave for the building and maintenance of the Sanctuary; and our Sidra, in detailing the plans for its construction, describes the form that these contributions should take. There were three kinds of Terumah:[1]

(i) *Shekalim:* The annual contribution of half-a-shekel that was to pay for the sacrifices;

(ii) The once-only payment of a half-a-shekel to provide for the sockets *(Adanim)* of the sanctuary;

(iii) The provision of the materials and the coverings of the Sanctuary, which again was a once-only contribution, ceasing once it was built.

The first, in other words, was a perpetual offering, persisting all the while the Sanctuary and the Temple existed,[2] and still commemorated today, in the donation of half of the com-

---

1. *Jerusalem Talmud, Shekalim,* 1:1.
2. *Rambam,* beg. *Hilchot Shekalim.*

mon unit of currency, before Purim.[3] The second and third, however, were limited in time to the actual period of construction.

What interest, then, can they have for us today? The answer is that the Torah is eternal, meaning that its every detail has some relevant implication for all Jews at all times. And especially so for the details of the Sanctuary, for we read of it, "And they shall make Me a Sanctuary, and I shall dwell in them,"[4] whose meaning is that G-d's presence will rest not only in the Sanctuary itself but also in the heart of each Jew. So that even if the physical building is destroyed, a Jew can construct his own sanctuary of the soul, as an inward correlate of the once-external place. And each detail of its construction will mirror the precise practical directives contained in this and the subsequent Sidrot.

2. THE FOUNDATION AND THE BUILDING OF THE SANCTUARY

The *terumat ha-adanim* (the offering for the sockets) was obligatory, everyone had to give an equal amount (half-a-shekel), and was for the *foundation* of the sanctuary. The *terumat ha-mishkan* (provision of materials) was voluntary, of diverse kinds, and was for the structure itself, and its coverings.

If we are to find their analogues in the inner life of the Jew, the *adanim* must be the original act of *kabalat ol*—the gesture of submission to G-d's will, when one foregoes one's independent existence and becomes a vehicle through which the Torah flows. For this act is one in which all men are equal—it does not depend on the particularized capacities of intellect or emotion; it is not the exercise of a power but a state of receptivity. And it is the foundation of all true service, for without it a man is always distant from G-d. If his thoughts and desires form a closed circle, there is no gap through which revelation can enter.

---

3. *Shulchan Aruch, Orach Chaim*, ch. 694.
4. *Shemot* 25:8.

The Mishkan, on the other hand, is that which is built on the foundation. It is the articulation of one's faith and its suffusion through one's mind and heart. In this each man is different, because intellectual powers and temperament are not evenly distributed, and the extent to which he can grasp in thought, or allow his emotions to be refashioned by, the awareness of G-d which he has achieved through *kabbalat ol,* will depend on his particular capacities.

3. INWARD FORMS

What are the forms in which these inner activities are expressed? The *adanim* correspond to prayer, for prayer is the foundation and initiation of a man's daily service. The Mishkan, however, belongs to the realm of learning and action. Through learning, the molten energies aroused in prayer are shaped into thought and action, to be finally enacted in the practical world. Learning and action are the structure and outer covering of which prayer is the support and the animating spirit.

4. A PARADOX

But in both the *adanim* and the Mishkan we can unearth a paradox, one that finds its way correspondingly into prayer on the one hand and learning and action on the other.

The fact that the *terumat ha-adanim* had to be brought in equal amounts by everyone suggests at a deeper level that the inner powers which it summoned forth were equal amongst men, and this is what was suggested by relating it to *kabbalat ol,* the gesture of submission which each man can make in the same way. If so, why was it that it was commanded only of men;[5] why did it exclude women and children who were no less able to make the gesture? Similarly why is regular prayer commanded only to men,[6] while in prayer all are equal, for each reads the same words?

---

5. Ibid., 38:26-7.
6. *Berachot,* 20a; *Rambam, Hilchot Kriat Shema,* 4:1; *Shulchan Aruch, Orach Chaim,* ch. 70.

On the other hand the provision for the Mishkan could be offered by anyone,[7] women and children included. Yet the Mishkan stands for learning and action, precisely those areas where individual differences count and where, if anywhere, we would expect to find discrimination as to who may or may not participate. And similarly, we find that learning and action themselves are demanded of all, albeit suited to the particular individual: Some men are required to spend more time learning, some less, according to their situation;[8] women learn those laws which are applicable to their situation;[9] men must perform all of the Mitzvot; while women are released from positive commands which are bound up with a specific time.

5. THE FOUNDATION OF PRAYER AND ACTION

The answer is that *kabbalat ol* lies even deeper than prayer. Its place is in the simple words of recognition and thanks that every Jew must say when he wakes in the morning, the Modeh Ani ("I make acknowledgment before You, living and enduring King, who has restored to me my soul in mercy great is Your faithfulness"). We say this even before washing our hands, which is necessary before all other prayer, because it comes from so deeply-embedded a recognition that however unprepared we may be for prayer in general, we are always in a position to utter these words.

When we turn later to prayer, we are transmitting this nascent awareness into something we can understand and feel. And because our intellectual and emotional capacities are finite, we must put it into a form of words. But because we pray in the aftermath of the act of *kabbalat ol,* we still stand as equals in submission, so each must use the same words. We are now using our particular powers, but in the light of the equality of souls.

---

7. Cf. *Shemot* 35:22.
8. *Shulchan Aruch Harav, Hilchot Talmud Torah,* 3:5.
9. Ibid., end ch. 1.

So likewise does the paradox resolve itself in the case of the Mishkan, which is for us the symbol of learning and action. In action, unlike prayer, there is no limitation of finitude: We must seek to enact G-d's will *everywhere*. Hence it must devolve on all. But each in his own way. The scope of any individual's involvement in the world is bounded by his capacities and his situation. So neither the offering for the Mishkan nor the parallel acts of learning and Mitzvot, have set limits, even though they are asked of everyone.

6. BUILDING AN INNER SANCTUARY

So we can see that an apparent anachronism—the *terumot* of the *adanim* and the Mishkan—which has no physical application today, in fact describes the precise manner in which a man must seek to build his own sanctuary within himself, and thus create a space for G-d's presence.

First, he must lay the foundation by the act of accepting G-d's will as his own, which he does in the Modeh Ani with his first waking words;

Second, he must articulate this foundation into thought and feeling, in the fixed forms of prayer (the *adanim*);

Third, he must realize its implication for his actions, by learning, which is the discrimination between acts which are in accord with G-d's will and those which are not;

Lastly, he must emerge into the world of action and embody there what has been transmitted to him in the prior stages of service (Mishkan).

These are the foundations, the walls and the coverings, of his personal sanctuary, ever recreated day by day, evolving as they do from what is most universal to what is most particular in his nature; and in this way he is able to admit G-d into the very depths of his being.

(Source: Likkutei Sichot, Vol. XI pp. 109-122 (adapted))

TETZAVEH

The Sidra of Tetzaveh concludes with the instructions for making the altar of gold on which incense was to be burned in the Sanctuary. The Torah is relevant to all Jews and all times, but what is the contemporary application of this passage? We have no Temple and no altar. Seemingly these laws have nothing to tell us in the present. The is, however, not so. For there are two kinds of Temple; and one kind cannot be destroyed. This is the Temple within each Jew, where he still performs his service in an inward reflection of the service of the Sanctuary. The Rebbe explains in detail how one of the laws about the altar can be translated into an important principle about the Jewish soul.

1. ALTARS IN SPACE AND IN THE SOUL

In the Mishnah, the volume of Moed (tractate Chagigah) ends[1] with the law that the altar of gold[2] and the altar of copper[3] did not require ritual immersion because they could not become impure. According to Rabbi Eliezer, this was because they were considered like the earth (which can not become ritually unclean). The other Sages, on the other hand, held that it was because they were plated with metal. The metal covering was considered subsidiary to the inner structure (which was made of shittim wood), and this could not become unclean.

Since the Torah is the word of G-d, who is infinite, it is itself infinite. Infinite in time, because it is eternally binding. Infinite in meaning, because every verse has innumerable layers of interpretation and significance. At the literal level *(peshat)* it contains laws and narratives; at the level of allusion *(remez)* it points obliquely to the deeper principles of Judaism; homileti-

---

1. Ch. 3 para. 8.
2. *Shemot* 30:1 ff.
3. Ibid. 27:1 ff.

cally *(drush)* it outlines the religious ethic of the Jew; and eso-
terically *(sod)* it contains the clues to the mysteries of the experience of G-d.

Thus the law about the altars of gold and copper has more
than just a literal significance. It has a moral that is relevant to
the Jew even when there is no Temple and no altar.

When G-d told Moses to erect a Sanctuary, He said: "And
they shall make Me a Sanctuary, and I will dwell in *them,*"
meaning, in the soul of every Jew. Thus, even though the
physical Temple is destroyed, the inward Temple which each
Jew makes within himself survives, indestructible. And the
service which he conducts in the reaches of his soul mirrors in
every respect the service of the Temple and Sanctuary. So their
laws, which appeared at first sight to have no contemporary application, are in fact precise instructions for the inner life of the
Jew.

2. PURIFICATION

In the Sanctuary, there were many vessels, of different
kinds, each with their own function. The analogy of this in the
Jewish soul is its many facets and capacities: Intellect, emotion,
will and delight. It may be that in the course of serving G-d,
some ulterior motive, some unholy desire, intrudes—perhaps
secular, perhaps even contrary to G-d's will.

This is the equivalent of one of the vessels of the Sanctuary
becoming impure. His thoughts have become impure, and he
must seek ways of removing the impurity so that they become
again worthy of taking part in the service of the inner Sanctuary. For within the Sanctuary, no impurity was allowed.

3. FIRE AND SACRIFICE

There are amongst Jews, men of copper[4] and men of gold.[5]
Those who are rich in spiritual worth are like gold: Their every
act is like a precious coin. The poor in spirit are the copper

---

4. Cf. *Baba Metzia*, 46a
5. Cf. *Baba Batra*, 25b.

coins of the religious life. But *every* Jew, however he behaves inwardly or outwardly, preserves intact at the heart of his being an essential desire to do G-d's will—a spark of faith, sometimes hidden, sometimes fanned into flame. Rabbi Yosef Yitzchak of Lubavitch said: "A Jew does not want, nor is he able, to be torn away from G-dliness." This spark is where the altar of the Jew's inner Temple is to be found.

On the altar, burnt offerings were brought. They were animals, consumed by a fire from G-d. And this happens within the Jew. The sacrifice is of himself. The animal is his "animal soul," his egocentric desires. And the fire which consumes them is the fire of the love of G-d Whose undying source is the spark of holiness at the essential core of his soul.

4. RABBI ELIEZER AND THE SAGES

The point of the law quoted from the Mishnah is this: Whether a Jew belongs to the "altars of gold" or is one of the "altars of copper," as long as he reminds himself that essentially he is an altar where the fire of G-dly love consumes the "animal soul" of his self-centered passions, he cannot become impure. For then he is like the earth. Just as the earth which we tread on is a symbol of humility, so our soul becomes void of any will except the will of G-d, as expressed in the Torah. Thus we say in prayer: "Let my soul be unto all as the dust."

This is the reasoning of Rabbi Eliezer, who was himself the personification of humility. His greatness was such that it was said that, "if all the sages of Israel were in one scale of the balance, and Eliezer the son of Hyrcanos in the other, he would outweigh them all."[6] Yet he would never concede that he had any merit himself, and the Talmud tells us that "he never said anything which he had not heard from his teachers."[7] Living so inward a life, he naturally saw only the inwardness of other Jews. He saw beyond their superficial differences to the point where each is equal in their essential attachment to G-d and

---

6. *Pirkei Avot*, 2:9.
7. *Sukkah*, 27b.

Torah. He saw that the life lived in Torah is the only Jewish reality. And he taught his students, by his self-effacement, that the true exercise of intellect comes only with humility and complete openness to G-d.

The other Sages reasoned differently. They held that this is too difficult for all. Not many can sustain it all the time. They paid attention to the superficial differences amongst Jews. They knew that one occasionally stumbles on the path. Men of gold can become hypnotized by gold. Men of copper can also become over-enamored, by their own, hard-earned, resources. But still—they maintained—the altar of the Jew can never become impure, because it is always covered. The differences between Jews, and their occasional failings, are mere surface coverings. What lies behind is always pure, and so powerful that eventually the covering must become subsidiary to it. The spark will prevail, and the Jew will return to the truth which—inwardly—he never really lost. The truth is that Jewish existence is and can only be a life of Torah and fulfilling the commandments.

The vessels of the inward sanctuary are—as their name implies—receptacles. When they are pure and their service is pure, they are the receptacles of the Divine blessings, physical as well as spiritual, as the Torah tells us:

"If you go according to My statutes and keep My commandments . . . the earth will give forth its produce and the trees of the field its fruit."[8]

(Source: Likkutei Sichot, Vol. III pp. 910-912)

---

8. *Vayikra* 26:3-4.

פורים

PURIM

There is something strange in the name of Purim. Firstly, it is a
Persian word (meaning "lots"—the lots that Haman cast in deciding
when to issue his decree against the Jews). And secondly, its reference is to the danger with which the Jews were confronted, rather
than to their ultimate deliverance. Added to this, the Megillah, the
Book of Esther, is unique amongst the books of the Torah in not
containing a single mention of the name of G-d. All this suggests
that Purim is a symbol of "concealment," of the "hiding" of the face
of G-d. The name "Esther" itself is related to the Hebrew word for
"I will hide," which occurs in Devarim where G-d says "I will
surely hide My face." And yet Purim celebrates a miracle, a revelation of Divine providence. The Rebbe, in resolving this apparent
contradiction, investigates the idea of a miracle, and of whether it is
a natural or a supernatural event. The underlying question is one
which the modern mind finds particularly urgent: Does the disap-
pearance of supernatural revelations mean that the age of miracles is
past?

1. PURIM AND THE PRESENT

"If one reads the Megillah in the wrong order (literally,
'backwards'), he has not fulfilled his obligation."[1]

The Baal Shem Tov[2] explained that this refers to a person
who reads the Megillah believing that the story it tells occurred
only *in the past* (that is, he reads it "backwards," as a retrospec-
tive account) and that the miracle of Purim does not endure
into the present. Such a man has not fulfilled his obligation, for
the purpose of the reading of the Megillah is to learn how a Jew
should behave *in the present.*

If this applies to every verse of the Megillah, and more so
to the Megillah as a whole, it applies still more to the verse

---

1. *Megillah*, 17a.
2. Quoted in *Divrei Shalom, Parshat Bo*.

which explains how the festival of Purim acquired its name. For the name of a thing is a sign of its essential character.[3] And to read the verse which tells us of the inner meaning of Purim as if it applies only to the past is to miss its eternal message to Israel and the Jew.

2. THE NAME OF PURIM

The verse[4] says: "Therefore they called the days Purim ('lots') because of the lot" which Haman had cast to determine when the Jews should be destroyed.

The word *"pur"* is not Hebrew but Persian.[5] Thus the Torah, when mentioning it, translates into Hebrew: "Pur: That is, the *goral* (lot)."[6] Why, then, is the festival called by a Persian name, Purim, instead of the Hebrew equivalent, *goralot?* All other festivals, including Chanukah (the other one to be instituted in Rabbinic times) have Hebrew names.

There is another enigma. The other festivals commemorating miracles of deliverance recall the fact by their names. Purim, instead of being named after the deliverance from Haman's decree, is, on the contrary, named after the danger itself: The lottery which Haman cast to fix the day when he intended "to consume and destroy them," G-d forbid.

3. THE NAME OF G-D

Another feature is peculiar to the Megillah, the Book of Esther: The name of G-d is not once mentioned. All other books of the Torah contain G-d's name many times. This remarkable omission is suggestive of an extreme concealment. Every Jew, even when he is speaking about secular concerns, should have "the name of G-d familiar on his lips." Certainly when he writes, even on secular business, it is a universal custom (and Jewish custom is part of Torah) to preface a letter

---

3. Cf. supra, p. 10.
4. *Esther* 9:26.
5. *Ibn Ezra, Esther* 3:7.
6. *Esther* 9:24.

with the words ('With G-d's blessing," "With the help of Heaven," or the like. It is striking, then, that one of the books of the Torah should be entirely devoid of G-d's name!

4. CONCEALMENT AND REVELATION

As said above, the inner meaning of a thing is signified by its name. And the name Esther suggests the concealment that we find in the Megillah. "Esther" comes from the same root as "hester," or hiding. Indeed it alludes to a double-hiding, as we find in the Talmud:[7] "Where is the name Esther indicated in the Torah? (In the verse)[8] 'I will hide, yes hide My face.'" But revelation is also implicit in the name Megillat Esther, for Megillah means "revelation."[9]

Just as, in the title of the book, we can distinguish two opposites, concealment (Esther) and revelation (Megillah), so too in the festival itself. On the one hand, the idea of concealment lies behind the name of Purim, a Persian word, and one connected with the decree against the Jews. On the other hand, it is a festival which in its celebration and rejoicing surpasses all others, going so far as to enjoin drinking "until one does not know the difference between 'Blessed be Mordechai' and 'Cursed be Haman'"[10]—a celebration without limit.

5. THE ACTIONS OF ESTHER AND MORDECHAI

To understand these apparent contradictions, we must first consider one feature of the story of Esther.

At the time of Haman's decree, the Jewish people had highly honored representatives in the royal court. Mordechai used to "sit at the gate of the King,"[11] and, our Sages tell us, was consulted by Ahasuerus for advice.[12] Besides, he had saved the

---

7. *Chullin*, 139b.
8. *Devarim* 31:18.
9. *Torah Or*, 119a (quoting *Pri Etz Chayim*).
10. *Megillah*, 7b.
11. *Esther* 2:19.
12. *Megillah*, 13a.

King's life.[13] Esther was queen and "found grace and favor in his sight,"[14] On the face of it, when the Jews heard of the decree, they should in the first instance have used these representatives to try and sway Ahasuerus to abrogate it.

But we find in the Megillah that Mordechai's first action was that he "clothed himself in sackcloth and ashes and went out into the midst of the City."[15] He turned to repentance, and urged the rest of the Jews to do likewise.[16] Only then did he send Esther "to come to the King and entreat him and plead with him for her people."[17]

Esther herself behaved in the same way. When it became necessary for her to go to the King, the first thing she did was to charge Mordechai to "Go and gather all the Jews . . . and they should fast for me, and neither eat nor drink for three days and nights."[18] In addition, Esther included herself: "I also . . . will fast likewise."

At first glance it would seem essential for her to have found favor in Ahasuerus' eyes. Her entry into the King's inner court was "not according to the law."[18] It involved the risk of death: "Whoever . . . shall come to the King into the inner court, who is not called, there is one law of his to put to death."[19] Esther could not be sure of royal favor: "I have not been summoned . . . these thirty days."[19] If so, how could she contemplate fasting for three successive days, an act which in the normal course of events would have detracted from her beauty?

6. CAUSE AND CURE

The reason is this. Mordechai and Esther knew for certain that Haman's decree was not an accident of history, but a con-

---

13. *Esther* 2:21-23.
14. Ibid., 2:17.
15. Ibid., 4:1.
16. Ibid., 4:3 and cf. *Targum Sheni*, 4:1.
17. Ibid., 4:8.
18. Ibid., 4:16.
19. Ibid., 4:11.

sequence of failings within the Jewish people.[20] Since one cannot completely remove an effect (the decree) without destroying the cause, their first action was to call the Jewish people to
repentance and fasting. It was not an undefined call: It articulated the specific sin which had to be rectified. The Midrash,[21]
commenting on Esther's words, "and they shall fast for me and
neither eat nor drink," explains them thus: "You are fasting because you have eaten and drunk at Ahasuerus' feast."

They then went to Ahasuerus, to seek his annulment of the
decree, because G-d desires to bless man "through all that you
do"[22]—through natural means. Going to Ahasuerus was (and
was no more than) a way of allowing a Divine deliverance to be
achieved through natural channels. The real cause of the deliverance lay not in the King's decision, but in the fasting and repentance of the Jews. And so, though Mordechai and Esther
used natural means, the emphasis of their concern lay in the
underlying spiritual causes.

7. NATURAL AND SUPERNATURAL BLESSINGS

The moral is plain. In a time of adversity there are those
who believe that the first and crucial step must be to try by all
natural means to combat it. The Megillah teaches otherwise:
That the initial act must be to strengthen one's bond with G-d,
through learning Torah and keeping the commandments. Only
then must one seek some physical channel through which the
deliverance may flow. If one acts in this way, one's deliverance
will be supernatural—whatever natural guise it is revealed in.

This is for both the individual and the community. The
Jew is committed to the knowledge that he is linked to G-d,
and that G-d is not bounded by the laws of nature, even though
He sends His blessings in the form of natural events. Man
must prepare this channel, "through all that you do." But since
this is no more than a channel, his main aim must be to prepare

---

20. Cf. *Rambam, Hilchot Taanit*, 1:2-3.
21. *Yalkut Shimoni, Esther*, beg. of ch. 5.
22. *Devarim* 15:18.

to receive the Divine blessing through learning and fulfilling the Torah.

The effort by natural means is analogous to writing a check, which is of no use if the check is not covered by funds in the bank. The "funds" are the spiritual acts.

Perhaps one might think that this applies only to an age when G-d's presence was manifest; that now, in exile, when instead of revelation there is a "doubled and redoubled darkness," G-d had intrusted His Providence to the domain of natural law.

Purim comes as the refutation of this doubt. For the miracle of Purim occurred when the Jews were in exile, "scattered and dispersed amongst the peoples."[23] Nor did exile cease afterwards. But the deliverance came not—through natural causes, but because of the three day fast of the Jews.

This explains why Purim suggests concealment, in its Persian name, in its being called after the decree of Haman, and in the Megillah being devoid of the name of G-d. It is to bring home the truth that the Jew is not bounded by natural law, not only in his spiritual life, not only in his dealings with fellow Jews, but even in his relation to the secular world: When he is forced to speak another language, when decrees are issued against him, when he is afraid to write G-d's name in case it is defiled.[24]

In the deepest concealment, revelation is found. In the name Megillat Esther, alongside the Esther (concealment) is Megillah (revelation). In the lottery (Purim) is found a symbol for the unpredictable, the supernatural.[25] When G-d says, "I will hide, yes hide My face," He is saying: "Even when My face is hidden, you can still reach the "I"—I as I am beyond all names."[26] And as past redemption gives strength for future re-

---

23. *Esther* 3:8.
24. *Shulchan Aruch, Orach Chaim*, ch. 156.
25. Cf. *Torah Or*, 120d; 123c.
26. Cf. *Likkutei Torah, Pinchas*, 80b.

demption,[27] from Purim the Messianic Age will flow, when concealment will be turned into revelation, and "night will shine like day."[28]

(Source: Likkutei Sichot, Vol. VI pp. 189-195)

---

27. Cf. *Megillah*, 6b.
28. *Psalms* 139:12.

פרשת כי תשא

KI TISSA

The Haftorah for Ki Tissa (I Kings 18, 1-39) records the famous confrontation between Elijah and the prophets of Baal. But Elijah's accusation lay more heavily against the Jewish people for its indecisiveness, than against the "prophets" for their idolatry. The challenge with which he faced them lay in his question, "How long will you vacillate between two opinions?" Why, though, did he direct himself against men of divided loyalties more than against those who were positively antagonistic to Judaism? The Rebbe examines the two sins of vacillation and idolatry, and shows the extent to which vacillation involves betrayal of religious values, and the forms which it takes in modern societies.

1. THE CHALLENGE

The Haftorah to this Ki Tissa contains an account of the prophet Elijah's response to a troubled period in Jewish history, a situation engendered as always by mental confusion and ideological vagueness. His action was to gather together the prophets of Baal, and the Jewish people, and to ask them, "How long will you vacillate between two opinions?"[1]

Why, though, did he put *this* challenge to them? He should, on the face of it, have said, "How long will you worship Baal? The time has come to stop and say, 'The L-rd, He is G-d.'"[2]

To understand Elijah's intention, we must begin by seeing the difference between idolatry and vacillation.

2. THE ROOTS OF IDOLATRY

In fact, it is hard to understand how a Jew could ever turn to idolatry. Jews are called "believers, the children of believers."

---

1. *I Kings* 18:21.
2. Ibid. v. 39.

135

Their nature precludes the possibility of a genuine denial of G-d.

Rambam[3] attributes the origin of idolatry to the fact that the creative energy by which G-d sustains the universe is channeled through natural forces—the stars and the planets. Idolatry begins when these intermediaries are worshipped in themselves, as the rulers of human destiny; whereas in actuality they are only the instruments of G-d, of no power in themselves. They are like "an ax in the hand of the hewer."

Chassidut[4] explains the difference between a father and mother, and the planetary influences. Both seem to be causes of our existence. And yet one is commanded to honor one's parents, and forbidden to worship the stars. The reason is that a mother and father have freewill. In bringing up children, they are responsible and they are to be honored. But the planets and their movements are determined. They have no choice. Our gratitude belongs not to them but to He who created them.

Idolatry, then, is mistaking the intermediary for the source. It is one of the most serious of sins, so much so that the Talmud states: "Idolatry is so grave a sin that to reject it is as if one were committed to the whole Torah."[5] The impulse to idolatry is that, according to this mistaken conception, one receives material benefits by propitiating natural forces. That is: Idolatry always has ulterior motives. And this is why a Jew can be led to it. He is not committed to idolatry as such. He is using it as a means to his own ends. Whereas when he serves G-d he is doing so "not on condition of receiving a reward"[6] but for His own sake and with an undivided heart. The desire for material reward lay at the heart of Baal-worship, and we find the idolaters saying to Jeremiah: "Since we stopped burning incense (to

---

3. *Hilchot Akum*, 1:1.
4. Cf. *Maamar Mayim Rabim*, 5717. Cf. also *Derech Mitzvotecha, Mitzvat Milah*.
5. *Nedarim*, 25a.
6. *Pirkei Avot*, 1:3.

idols) . . . we have lacked all things and have been consumed by the sword and by the famine."[7]

3. THE NATURE OF VACILLATION

Despite this general characterization of idolatry as the attempt to influence nature by worshipping natural forces, there is a difference between idolatry proper and "vacillating between two opinions."

Idolatry involves the genuine belief that the objects of worship, the stars and the planets, are the sources of material welfare. But the person who vacillates is in doubt. At times an uneasy feeling possesses him that idolatry is built on an illusion. Or it may be that he believes that G-d and the forces of nature are in partnership. He believes in both, and that both must be worshipped. However, idolatry even in this muted form, and even if it is in word or act only, without any inward commitment, is so great a sin that it is in the nature of a Jew to be prepared to sacrifice his life rather than participate in it.[8]

4. LEVELS OF BETRAYAL

In a number of ways, vacillation is even worse than real idolatry. In general terms, idolatry is the graver act. It involves the absolute denial of G-d, the complete opposition to Judaism. But it is harder for the vacillating mind ever to return to Judaism or make his turning sincere and complete.

There are two reasons.

Firstly, when the genuine believer in idolatry comes to see that "the L-rd, He is G-d," he realizes the extent to which his previous life had been constructed on error. He feels the full measure of his sin. His repentance is profound. "He returns and he is healed."

But the vacillator cannot see it so. He justifies himself. He says: "I did not deny, I only doubted. And my doubt was only superficial. In reality I was, like all Jews, a believer." His ex-

---

7. *Jeremiah* 44:18.
8. *Tanya*, Part I, ch. 19.

cuses protect him from remorse, and his return to faith is incomplete.[9]

Secondly, although the believing idolater is guilty of a massive error of judgment in substituting Baal for G-d, and thus severing his relation with G-d, he is nonetheless open to a form of spirituality. But the person who hovers between two opinions has removed himself from the spiritual altogether. Although he knows that "the L-rd, He is G-d," he is willing to forsake Him for the sake of material reward. He is ready to trade the "fountain of living waters" for "broken cisterns that can hold no water."[10]

Thus, when they realize their mistake, their response will be different. The idolater, still capable of spirituality, will make his return a spiritual act. But the man of vacillation will return for the wrong reason. He wanted material benefit. He miscalculated in thinking that the natural forces could, of themselves, provide it. So he does turn to G-d, but still seeking only the material reward.

5. THE SELF AND OTHERS

So far, we have spoken only about the individual. In another respect, vacillation is worse than idolatry—in its effect on others.

The complete idolater will not influence the believing Jew, because his antagonism to true faith is obvious, and isolates him. But the person who hovers between two opinions is, in part, still a believer. He is capable of leading others astray, and the act of "causing the many to sin" is the worst sin of all.

6. DIVIDED LOYALTIES AND THE PRESENT

The Talmud[11] says that the impetus of the "Evil Inclination" towards idolatry has been removed. But the tendency to-

9. Cf. *Rabbenu Yonah*, beg. of *Berachot*. *Shulchan Aruch, Orach Chaim*, ch. 603. *Kuntres Uma'ayon*, ch. 14, para. 2.
10. *Jeremiah* 2:13.
11. *Yoma*, 69b; *Chidushei Agadot* (Maharsha), ad loc.

wards vacillation, whether in overt or subtle forms, is today stronger than it is towards idolatry.

There are those who temporarily detach themselves from Torah and the commandments for the sake of material reward: Money, honor or social status. They set aside G-d and the law for a time, shelve them so as not to be thought out of touch with today. They follow the contemporary maxim of the Western world, that rules are to be stretched, traditions forsaken, for the sake of the elusive "spirit of the age." And they are prepared temporarily to sell G-d and their souls for ephemeral status, or for money, which (because it does not come as a Divine blessing) flows from them again in doctors' or psychoanalysts' fees.

This vacillation, this double-mindedness, is worse than idolatry, as we have seen.

First: It is harder to turn from it with a true returning, because the divided mind hides from itself the fact that it has sinned. Such a person can rationalize. He can convince himself that for the most part, he is a good Jew. What is so bad—he tells himself—in bending a few rules once in a while for the sake of making a living?

Second: His integrity is destroyed. He has sold the spirit for the material world. He has traded eternity for the passing moment. He has exchanged the World To Come for the glitter of money and the shadow of honor.

Third: He draws others into his sin. If he were openly to deny Judaism he would sever his contact with the Jewish milieu. But he hides his opposition behind a mask of loyalty. He even cites Torah in his defense. He infiltrates the community and leads others astray.

7. THE PATH OF RETURN

This is the meaning of the Haftorah. The primary challenge to the Jew is, "How long will you vacillate between two opinions?" Sitting on the fence is worse than crossing to the other side.

At the end of the Haftorah, we read that the Jews turned in repentance and said, twice: "The L-rd, He is G-d. The L-rd, He is G-d." This went beyond even the moment of revelation on Sinai, when it was said only once, "I am the L-rd, your G-d."[12] For repentance takes the Jew higher in spirit than he was before he sinned.

This is the clear implication for today. The need is to return, and to reach back to the heights of the spirit.

All Jews are interlinked.[13] And the light of those who return will reach those whom they brought to sin. They will be answered by a Divine response of compassion and mercy. And the leaders and the led will be caught up together in a collective movement of return, in a unified voice which proclaims: "The L-rd, He is G-d. The L-rd, He is G-d."

(Source: Likkutei Sichot, Vol. I pp. 183-187)

---

12. Cf. *Likkutei Torah, Devarim*, 65c; *Derech Mitzvotecha, Mitzvat Vidui Uteshuvah*, para. 2.
13. *Sanhedrin*, 27b; *Shavuot*, 39a.

פרשת ויקהל
VAYAKHEL

Vayakhel begins with Moses assembling the Israelites on the day after Yom Kippur, to repeat to them the commandment of Shabbat. The passage raises several questions, especially in its use of the passive in the phrase, "Six days shall work be done." In its explanations, the Sicha touches on one of the greatest paradoxes of the life of faith. If G-d is the source of all blessings, why work in order to live? And if we do work, how can we avoid the thought that it is our labor alone that produces material results? We seem torn between absolute passivity and the denial of G-d's involvement in the world. The Rebbe develops the important concept of "passive labor" in which this contradiction is resolved, and a new understanding of the inner meaning of Shabbat emerges.

1. THE ASSEMBLY

The Sidra of Vayakhel begins in the following way: "And Moses assembled all the congregation of the children of Israel, and said unto them: 'These are the words which the L-rd has commanded, that you should do them. Six days shall work be done, but on the seventh day there shall be to you a holy day, a sabbath of solemn rest to the L-rd. . . .'"

This raises several questions and points of detail, some of which are mentioned by the commentators.

Firstly, why is the word "assembled" (*Vayakhel)* used? The more usual expression would be, "And Moses *spoke* to all the congregation," as indeed we find several verses later, in the context of the donations for the Sanctuary.

Secondly, the passage says, "These are the words which the L-rd has commanded," but it does not specify what they are. Most commentators take it as referring to the offerings for the building of the Sanctuary, but this is difficult to maintain. For before these offerings are spoken of, the Torah repeats, "And Moses spoke to all the congregation," suggesting that this was the subject of a separate discourse. The implication would seem to be that the "words which the L-rd has commanded" refer to what immediately follows, namely the prohibition of work on the Shabbat. But this raises the further difficulty that the observance of the Shabbat had already been included amongst the Ten Commandments.

Thirdly, what is the significance of the repetitive phrase, *shabbat shabbaton,* translated in English as "a sabbath of solemn rest?"

Fourthly, Rashi, the Talmud, the Midrash[1] and the Zohar[2] all make the comment that this assembly took place on the morrow of Yom Kippur, when Moses came down from Mt. Sinai (with the second tablets of stone). This suggests that there is a connection between the assembly and Yom Kippur, whose essence is, as its name implies, *kippur,* or atonement. This was the day when G-d said to Moses, "I have forgiven according to your word," which was the atonement for the sin of the Golden Calf. What, then, is the connection?

2. PASSIVE LABOR

As a first step towards answering these questions, we must consider the remarks of the commentators about the passive form of the verb in the phrase, "Six days shall work be done." Had it been in the active, "Six days shall you work," it would suggest an *involvement* or preoccupation with the work. The passive suggests that the work will be done, as it were, by itself. The Mechilta comments on this verse: "When Israel performs the will of the Al-mighty, their work is done for them by others." Literally, this refers to a blessing conferred by Heaven, but the comment can also be taken to indicate an attitude that the Jew should adopt in the course of his service towards G-d. It means that during the six days of his work, he should be occupied, but not *preoccupied* by the secular.

---

1. *Mechilta, Yitro,* 2.
2. Part II, 195a.

In the Psalms[3] it is written: "If you will eat the labor of your hands, you will be happy and it will be well with you." The Chassidic interpretation[4] is that the labor in which man engages for his material needs (so that "you will eat") should be only "of your *hands*," an activity of the outer man, not an inward involvement. His thoughts and feelings must remain bound up with Torah and its commandments. Only then "will you be happy and it will be well with you." As the Sages say,[5] "You will be happy—in this world—and it will be well for you—in the World to Come."

This interpretation can also be applied to the phrase, "Six days shall work be done." The passive form of the verb indicates that heart and mind are elsewhere—involved in the Torah—and only man's practical faculties are engaged in the work. And even they are concerned only to make the work a "vessel" for the blessings of G-d. This is what the Torah means when it says; "And the L-rd your G-d will bless you in all that you do." Man is not sustained by his own efforts, but through G-d's blessing. His work merely provides a natural channel for this blessing, and he must remember that it is no more than a channel. Though his hands prepare it, his eyes must remain focused on the source of the blessing.

Man should really not be allowed to work. For of G-d it is said, "I fill the heavens and the earth" and "The whole earth is full of His glory." The proper response to the ever-present nature of G-d would be to stand in absolute passivity. To do otherwise would be to be guilty of what the Rabbis called[6] "making signs before the King," of the presumption of making one's presence felt. It is only because the Torah itself permits, indeed commands, us to work that it becomes legitimate; when it says, "Six days shall you work" and "The L-rd your G-d will bless you *in all that you do*." The Torah permits that which is neces-

---

3. 128:2.
4. *Likkutei Torah, Shelach*, 42d.
5. *Pirkei Avot*, 4:1. *Berachot*, 8a.
6. *Chagigah*, 5b.

sary work. To go beyond that would be, in the first place, to show a lack of faith that human sustenance comes from G-d. And secondly, it would be to make one's presence felt in the face of G-d an act of rebellion.

3. THE MEANING OF "LABOR"

In the light of this, it becomes difficult to understand the expression of the Psalms, "the *labor* of your hands." For the work of the Jew in the secular world is only as a preparation for G-d's blessing, and lacks an inner involvement. There is, however, a psychological principle[7] that work which one enjoys is not tiring, whereas even a small effort towards what one does not enjoy is exhausting. The Jew, therefore, whose pleasures are spiritual, and whose engagement in the material world is forced upon him, finds it an exhaustion. Even though it is a positive command[8] that "Six days you shall labor," the labor itself, however detached he is from it, distracts him from the spiritual, and is therefore felt to be a tiring labor.

4. THE DOUBLE SHABBAT

This, then, is the inner meaning of "Six days shall work be done, but on the seventh there shall be to you a holy day, a sabbath of solemn rest,"—the six days are a necessary preface to the seventh. For the Shabbat to be a day of solemn rest, it must be preceded by work, and the work itself must be passive, with the true focus of one's attention elsewhere. It is written,[9] "On the Shabbat, a man should regard himself as if all his work were complete." If, during the six days, he had been preoccupied with material concerns, on the seventh day anxieties will invade him and he will not be able to clear his mind to "gaze at the glory of the King" in Torah and prayer. He has opened the door to distractions, and they will intrude upon his will. But if he has given his work its proper place during the week, the

7. Cf. *Maamar Karov Hashem*, 5690 (*Sefer Hamaamarim-Kuntreisim*, p. 210).
8. *Mechilta Yitro*, 2.
9. *Shulchan Aruch* Harav, *Orach Chaim*, 306:21.

light of Shabbat will illuminate him, and it will be *shabbat shab-baton*—a Shabbat twice over. For Shabbat will then permeate his whole week,[10] and when the day itself arrives it will have a double sanctity.

Our third question is therefore answered. And the second is also solved: Even though the observance of Shabbat as such had been previously commanded, the opening verses of Vayak-hel explain *how* the spirit of Shabbat is achieved.

5. THE ORIGIN OF IDOLATRY

The connection between the assembly of the Israelites, and the day it took place, on the morrow of Yom Kippur, can also now be understood. The commandment about the Shabbat was in itself the rectification of the sin of the Golden Calf. Ram-bam[11] traces the origins of idolatry to the fact that Divine providence is channeled through natural forces and objects: "Precious fruits (are) brought forth by the sun, and . . . precious things . . . by the moon."[12] Although their worshippers recognized them as merely intermediaries, they attached divine significance to them. Their error was to regard them as objects of worship, whereas they are no more than the instruments of G-d, like "an ax in the hands of the hewer." At another level, the excessive preoccupation with business and the material world is also a form of idolatry.[13] In the same way, it involves the error of attaching significance to what is no more than an intermediary or the channel of Divine blessing. His mental preoccupation is a form of bowing the head, of misplaced worship. Only when he sees his work for what it is, a way of creating a natural channel for the blessings of G-d, will his work take the passive form and the focus of his thoughts be on G-d alone.

---

10. Cf. *Shabbat*, 119a. *Zohar*, Part III, 29a. *Tikkunei Zohar, Tikkun* 21 (46a).

11. *Hilchot Akum*, 1:1. Cf. supra, p. 136.

12. *Devarim* 33:14.

13. Cf. *Likkutei Torah, Acharei*, 27c. *Maamar Mayim Rabbim, 5717.*

This is how idolatry—whether in its overt or its more subtle forms—is atoned. Six days of passive work, in the sense of mental detachment and the realization that human work is only an instrument of G-d, are the corrective for and the denial of the instincts of idolatry.

6. PASSIVITY IN THE SPIRIT

This error and its correction exist on the spiritual as well as the material plane. In Pirkei Avot[14] it is stated: "Do not be like servants who minister to their master on the condition of receiving a reward." It is possible to study and fulfill the Torah for the sake of the attendant spiritual pleasures. But this is to be motivated by reward. The highest service is to perform G-d's will for its own sake, unconditionally. And this is like the passive labor described above. It is labor because it is not done for the sake of pleasure. It is passive because such a man does not regard his spiritual achievements as the result of his own talents, but of the helping hand of Heaven. If he opens himself to G-d, however slightly, G-d responds and helps him along the way. This assistance comes even prior to the fulfillment of a command. Commenting on the verse in Job,[15] "Who has come before Me that I should pay him?" the Rabbis say,[16] "Who made Me a parapet without My making him the roof, who made Me a Mezuzah without My making him the house, who made Me Tzitzit without My making him the garment?" Passivity in the spiritual life means making oneself no more than a channel for the Divine response.

7. ASSEMBLY AND UNITY

Finally, we can now understand why our passage uses the verb "And Moses *assembled*" instead of "And Moses *spoke*." It was the day after Yom Kippur, when the sin of the Golden Calf, which had brought back into the world the spirit of im-

---

14. 1:3.
15. 41:3.
16. *Vayikra Rabbah,* 27:2.

purity,[17] was atoned for. The world was to be restored to its original state, as it was before the first sin. There was to be "one nation in the land," and the world was once again to become a private domain *(reshut hayachid,* literally, the "domain of the One")* for the Unity of G-d. Therefore there had to be an "assembly" in which the people were gathered into a unity.

(Source: Likkutei Sichot, Vol. I pp. 187-192)

---

17. *Shabbat,* 146a. *Zohar,* Part I, 52b.

פרשת פקודי
PEKUDEI

Four of the last five Sidrot have dealt with the construction of the Sanctuary and its vessels by the Israelites. What is the difference between them that justifies their division into four separate Sidrot? There is a clear difference between the first two (Terumah and Tetzaveh) which concern the command itself, and the second two (Vayakhel and Pekudei) which concern its transmission and execution. But what distinguishes Vayakhel and Pekudei? And what links them so that they are often read together in the same week? This is the ground covered next, and its investigation results in an analysis of the stages in the Divine-human encounter.

1. VAYAKHEL AND PEKUDEI

Nothing in the Torah is coincidental. Being the word of G-d, its every detail is precise and intended. This applies to the division of the Torah into Sidrot. This was not necessary simply because it is too large a mass of material to remain without divisions, but because every Sidra contains its own distinct subject and point. And the same is true of the names of the Sidrot. These are not just taken randomly from their first words. Instead, they are precise indicators of their subject-matter; and it is because of this that their names occur within the first few words of their opening passage.

This is the meaning of the comment in the Zohar[1] that there are fifty-three Sidrot in the Torah, a fixed and permanent number, even in those years when two Sidrot are read together to fit the reading of the Torah into the calendrical year. Every Sidra has its individual point, and the occasional joining of two Sidrot means no more than that sometimes two points are read on the same day.

---

1. Part I, 104b. *Tikkunei Zohar, Tikkun*, 13 (29b).

In the light of this it is clear that the Sidrot of Vayakhel and Pekudei are distinct in their message, even though they are in some years read together. Both concern the building of the Sanctuary and its vessels, just as the previous Sidrot of Terumah and Tetzaveh concerned the command and the instructions for its building. But Terumah and Tetzaveh, though they share a subject-matter, tell us different things about it, as we can see by the fact that they are *never* read together. Likewise Vayakhel and Pekudei, though they are both about the building of the Sanctuary, have two quite separate implications.

2. PREPARATION AND REVELATION

The difference between them is this. In Vayakhel we read about how Moses gathered the Israelites together to communicate to them G-d's command to build a Sanctuary and make its vessels, and how they set about fulfilling their instructions. The Sidra of Pekudei tells us about the accounts that Moses made of the voluntary offerings of materials for the Sanctuary, in gold, silver, copper and so on; to what ends they were used; how the Sanctuary and its vessels were anointed with oil; how offerings were made; and how this brought about the drawing down of the presence of G-d—"And the cloud covered the tent of meeting, and the glory of the L-rd filled the Sanctuary."[2]

The essential point of Vayakhel is the service of created beings, namely, how the Israelites built a Sanctuary with their property, their bodies and their souls. From their property, they gave the thirteen (or some say, fifteen) kinds of voluntary offerings of material for the Sanctuary. With their bodies, they gave the labor with which it was constructed. And with their souls they gave the "uplifted heart," the "wisdom" and the "willingness of spirit" which the Torah mentions as accompanying the work. But this was entirely the service of created beings. What Pekudei adds is the Divine response, "And the glory of the L-rd filled the Sanctuary."

---

2. *Shemot* 40:34.

Although the work which is described in Vayakhel brought
about a revelation of G-d, for every act done as part of the Divine service results in an emanation of G-dliness, it was infini-
tesimal in comparison with the glory of G-d filling the Sanctuary, the state that was achieved through the anointing of the
Sanctuary and the bringing of offerings.

There are cases where we say that the preparation for a
Mitzvah is also a holy act.[3] But in its effect of bringing about a
drawing down of G-d into the world, the preparation for an act
cannot be compared with the act itself.[4] And this applies more
strongly to the preparation of the Sanctuary and its vessels—the
theme of Vayakhel. For they do not become holy until they are
anointed with oil or used for actual worship[5]—the point of
Pekudei. Therefore the revelation which was brought about by
the sanctification of the Sanctuary, infinitely exceeded that of
its preparation.

These then are the essential themes of the four Sidrot
which are concerned with the Sanctuary and its vessels:[6]

Terumah and Tetzaveh relate the command of G-d to
construct a Sanctuary, with this distinction, that Terumah concerns the Sanctuary itself and its vessels, and Tetzaveh the special garments of the priests.

Vayakhel tells of Moses communicating this command, and
of the Israelites fulfilling it.

Finally, Pekudei reports the response of G-d in filling the
Sanctuary with His glory.

We have here the three stages in the dialogue between G-d
and man, the three phases through which their relationship
progresses.[7] First there comes the Divine initiative, the
"awakening from above," the command which opens up a path
for man to unite himself with G-d's will. Then there is the

---

3. Cf. *Melo Haroim* and *Encyclopedia Talmudit*, under *Hazmanah*.
4. *Shaarei Orah, Maamar Yaveeu Levush Malchut*, ch. 7.
5. *Shavuot*, 15a.
6. Cf. *Ramban, Shemot* 36:8.
7. *Likkutei Torah, Shir Hashirim*, 24a.

human response, the "awakening from below" in which he rises to the challenge of obedience and creates within himself and his world a hallowed space, hollowed out, as it were, from his delusions of self-sufficiency, for G-d to enter and make His habitation. Finally there comes the Divine response, the revelation of G-d *within* the human sphere. The command, which was the opening voice of G-d, came like a voice from outside, inviting man to break through his shell of self and separation. But the concluding response of G-d is a voice from within, flooding the human sanctuary with "the glory of the L-rd." This is the voice of Pekudei.

3. TWO WEEKS IN ONE

Even though this revelation of Pekudei is wholly beyond that of Vayakhel, (the stage of human response and preparation) still the two Sidrot are often read together in the same week. Because sometimes when time is short, we must achieve in "one week" what normally takes "two."

This does not mean that we must forsake the discipline of time. The Sanctuary was essentially a "dwelling-place in the lower world," within the human dimension, within time and space. It means rather that *within* time, we must not be bound by time.

There is a connection here with the month of Adar, in which these Sidrot are usually read. Adar, is, of course, the month of Purim. And although Purim always falls on a weekday, when we are permitted to work, the essence of Purim lies in the command that on it "a man should be merry until he does not know the difference between 'Blessed be Mordechai' and 'Cursed be Haman.'" This stands for going beyond rationality, beyond knowledge and the limits it implies. So that Purim represents the importation into the weekday working world of "going beyond all limits." It is the infinite in the heart of the finite.

Thus the linking of Vayakhel with Pekudei, of the human preparation with the Divine response, symbolizes the meeting of timelessness with time, the joining of G-d and man. This is both a preface to and a preparation for the future revelation, when in Isaiah's words,[8] "I will make your windows of agate *(kadkod)*" on which the Talmud[9] comments: "The Holy One, blessed be He, said . . . —'Let it be as this one and as that one' *(kedain ukedain)* "when man and G-d are one."

4. COMMAND AND FULFILLMENT

Another implication of the joining of the two Sidrot is this: Between G-d's command to Moses (contained in Terumah and Tetzaveh) and Moses' command to the Israelites and their response (the content of Vayakhel and Pekudei) the events of Ki Tissa and the Golden Calf can intervene. But once the command has entered the world through Moses (in Vayakhel) nothing can prevent its immediate fulfillment (in Pekudei).

Even when they are not read together, even when the evil inclination interposes a gap between command and completion, there is no substance to the interruption, nothing new to serve as a distraction. When Moses, or his successors in every generation,[10] have revealed the command, its fulfillment is assured. The command itself is a promise of achievement, and assurance that "the glory of the L-rd will fill the Sanctuary."

(Source: Likkutei Sichot, Vol. III pp. 933-936)

---

8. *Isaiah* 54:12.
9. *Baba Batra,* 75a. Explained at length in *Likkutei Torah, Re'eh.*
10. *Tikkunei Zohar, Tikkun,* 69 (114a). Cf. *Bereishit Rabbah,* 56:7.

פרשת ויקרא

VAYIKRA

The Sidra of Vayikra is about sacrifice: The offerings that were
made in the Sanctuary, and the procedure that surrounded them.
What does it mean to us today, when there is no Temple? Two
Temples were destroyed. But many millions were not, and could
not be. These are the temples which every Jew possesses within
himself, the holy place of the soul where his worship of G-d takes
place. Judaism is invulnerable, because it has as many Sanctuaries as
there are Jews. But what is the service of this inner sanctum? The
answer lies in this week's Sidra, where every instruction has a double significance: Firstly, to guide the priests in their service, and
secondly, to guide us in ours. The private Sanctuary of the present
is a precise counterpart of the public Sanctuary of the past. The
Rebbe takes us through the act of sacrifice, translating the priestly
procedure into terms of immediate bearing on our spiritual life. It is
a classic example of the power of Chassidut to transform our understanding of neglected parts of the Torah into exact and striking
pictures of the path of religious experience.

1. "AN OFFERING OF YOU"

At the beginning of the Sidra of Vayikra (the Sidra about
the sacrifices), the Torah says, "If any man brings an offering of
you to the L-rd." At first glance we would suppose that the
phrase "of you" refers to "any man," thus: "If any man of you
brings an offering. . . ." But the order of words in the Torah
rules this out. The Torah is precise in every detail. An apparently misplaced word has great significance. The sentence must
read, "If any man brings an offering of you . . . ," and the implication is that the sacrifice must be of yourself. What does this
mean?

This well-known Chassidic interpretation understands the
phrase to be a commentary on the whole nature of sacrifice.
When G-d commanded the Israelites to build Him a Sanctuary.

153

He said: "And they shall make Me a Sanctuary and I will dwell *in them.*" It was not simply in *it* that He would dwell, but in every Jew. Each Jew had, as it were, a Sanctuary within himself. And every act, every facet of the physical Sanctuary, had its counterpart in the sanctuary of the soul.

So there is an inward act of sacrifice in the life of the Jew that precisely mirrors the outward act that took place in the Sanctuary. Even that outward act—though it involved the sacrifice of a physical animal—was essentially a spiritual one. This is why it needed the participation of the priests *(kohanim)* and the accompaniment of the songs of the Levites. The Zohar[1] says that "the Cohanim in their silent service and their desire drew (G-d's presence) downwards and the Levites in their songs and praises drew (man's soul and his sacrifice) upwards." The physical sacrifice was thus a spiritual encounter.

So, indeed more so, is the inward act of sacrifice. And this is the meaning of "If any man brings an offering of you. . . ." "Offering" in Hebrew means "drawing near."[2] And when a Jew wishes to draw near to G-d he must make a sacrifice to G-d of his very self. The offering must be "of you." It is the "you" that is the sacrifice.

2. THE ANIMAL

The sentence continues: ". . . You shall bring your offering from the cattle, the herd and the flock."

Thus there are two sacrifices in the sanctuary of the soul. The first is "of you," of yourself, your "G-dly soul." The second is "from the cattle," from the "animal soul" which constitutes all physical desires, all instincts which a man has in virtue of having a body and being part of the natural world. It is this second offering which is the ultimate aim of sacrifice: The sanctification and redirection of the "animal" in man.

That this is the aim is suggested in the verse itself, and what follows. The offering "of you" is described as being made *"to*

---

1. Part III, 39a.
2. *Korban* and *Kiruv* respectively, which have the same root.

the L-rd." But in the next verse it says that the offering "of the herd" shall be *"before* the L-rd," meaning that it will reach a higher level than "the L-rd,"[3] the four-lettered name of G-d. It is written,[4] "There is much increase by the strength of the ox." When the animal in man is harnessed in the service of G-d it has the power to take him closer to G-d than his G-dly soul alone could reach.

Bringing the "you," the G-dly soul, as a sacrifice brings man only "to the L-rd," to the level signified by the four-lettered name. This is in itself a supernatural experience, but not yet an experience of G-d as He is in Himself, beyond time and change. Whereas the sanctification of the "animal soul" brings an experience of G-d in His absolute transcendence: "When the 'other side' (the natural instincts) is subdued, the glory of the Holy One, blessed be He, is revealed throughout all worlds."[5]

3. THE SEARCH

When an animal was to be sacrificed on the altar, the first thing that had to be done was to see that it was whole, perfect, without blemish. Only then could it be offered. So it is in the "drawing near" of man. The "animal" within himself must be without blemish before it can be sacrificed. The first step is self-examination. He must search the recesses of his soul for faults—rifts in the unity of his being. And having found them, he must set them right.

The search must be sincere, not done out of a mechanical sense of duty. For his whole spiritual integrity depends on it. Once he realizes what is at stake, he will not cover his faults in self-deception, or leave them to fester, uncured.

---

3. *Likkutei Torah, Maamar Leva'er... Adam Ki Yakriv.*
4. *Proverbs* 14:4.
5. Cf. *Tanya*, Part I, ch. 27.

4. THE PRESSURE OF THE PAST

When a man begins this process of self-searching in earnest, it can often happen that even though he is not currently guilty of any sin, there rise to the surface of his memory all the failings and indiscretions of his past, even of his childhood,[6] until he can say, "My sin is continually before me."[7] They persist because they have not been completely set right.

Had they been rectified by his subsequent service they would have been effaced, and replaced by great enthusiasm in Divine Service. For when a man has been through the "dry land of the shadow of death" which comes upon him in the moment of separation from G-d through sin, his desire to be reunited with G-d flares into the fervor of "repentance through great love" which turns "intentional sins into merits."[8]

But this self-examination tells him that it is not so with him. His sins remain as sins in his memory. He has not passed through the transforming fire of love. Sin breeds sin in its chain,[9] and even now he sometimes feels the pressure of wayward desires.

It is not as if his repentance for the past needs only a final touch to complete it, but rather as if it never succeeded in breaking down the barrier between himself and G-d[10] that his past acts had created.

But this may give him pause. He is coming in front of G-d in an act of sacrifice, of "drawing near" with all his being, to be drawn into the Divine fire which is to carry him upwards to the essence of G-d.[11] And he may say: What am I to be worthy of the act? I am imperfect. I am full of faults. The thing is beyond me!

---

6. *Poke'ach Ivrim*, ch. 21-22. Cf. *Shulchan Aruch, Orach Chaim*, end of ch. 343. *Sanhedrin*, 55b.
7. *Psalms* 51:5.
8. Cf. *Tanya*, Part I, ch. 7.
9. *Pirkei Avot*, 4:2.
10. Cf. *Tanya*, Part I, ch. 17.
11. Cf. *Zohar*, Part II, 239a; Part III, 26b.

Rabbi Yosef Yitzchak of Lubavitch answered:[12] the sacrifice is not only *of* "you"; it *depends* on "you." It is within the scope of every Jew, whatever his present and whatever his past. So that every Jew has the right to ask himself,[13] "When will my acts be like the acts of my fathers, Abraham, Isaac and Jacob?"

5. THE FIRE

Once the animal has been examined, and found to be without blemish, it must be killed. That is, one does not destroy its body, merely takes away its life. Then it is offered on the altar, where it is consumed (in some cases, only the fat, in others the whole animal) by fire sent from above by G-d.

This is the procedure for physical sacrifices in the Sanctuary, and it applies also to the inward sacrifice within the Jewish personality.

After one has set right the faults or blemishes in one's way of life, the "animal" must be killed. The life must be taken from one's instinctual, physical drives. Their energy must be redirected. The "body," that is, the physical acts, remain. But their motive is now wholly spiritual, to give strength to the life of Divine Service. Thus in the Talmud,[14] Rava said: "Wine and odorous spices made me wise." To do this is to arrive at the stage of "In all your ways, know Him,"[15] where every act is for the sake of holiness, until every act becomes itself holy. This is the case, for example, on Shabbat when eating and drinking are not simply a means to the sanctification of the day, but are themselves commanded as part of that sanctity; physical wool in Tzitzit; physical leather in Tefillin; and so can every act be sanctified to this degree.

Then comes the moment of "drawing near." The body, the "animal soul" are drawn into the fire of the soul, the fire that is the love of G-d: "Its flames are flames of fire, the flame of

---

12. *Maamar Bati Leganni 5710*, ch. 2.
13. *Tana Deve Eliyahu Rabbah*, ch. 25.
14. *Yoma*, 76b.
15. Cf. *Rambam, Hilchot Deot*, ch. 3. *Shulchan Aruch, Orach Chaim*, ch. 231.

G-d."[16] The love that the Rabbis say[17] is like "the fire of heaven" turns the animal force into molten energy that is reshaped as love of G-d.

"And you shall love the L-rd your G-d with all your heart." The Rabbis asked,[18] what is "with all your heart?" And they answered, "with your two inclinations." When the power and passion of natural man is harnessed to the love of G-d of spiritual man, the fire within the Jew merges with the answering fire of heaven, and man and G-d "draw near."

(Source: Likkutei Sichot, Vol. I pp. 205-208)

---

16. *Song of Songs* 8:6.
17. *Yalkut,* ad loc.
18. *Berachot,* 54a.

פרשת צו

TZAV

Continuing the theme of Vayikra, the Rebbe traces further parallels
between the Sanctuary that was built by the Israelites in the wilderness, and the Sanctuary which every Jew has within himself. This
Sidra mentions the continual fire that was to be kept burning on the
outer altar. What is its importance? What is it a defense against?

1. CONTINUAL FIRE

"Fire shall be kept burning upon the altar continually; it
shall not go out."[1] On this verse the Jerusalem Talmud comments, "continually—even on Shabbat; continually—even in a
state of impurity."[2]

As has been mentioned before,[3] every aspect of the physical
Sanctuary has its counterpart in the inward Sanctuary within
the soul of the Jew.

His heart is the altar. And corresponding to the two altars
of the Sanctuary, the outer and the inner, are the outer and inner levels of the heart, its surface personality and its essential
core.[4]

The altar on which the continual fire was to be set was the
outer one. And for the Jew this means that the fire of his love
for G-d must be outward, open and revealed. It is not a private
possession, to be cherished subconsciously. It must show in the
face he sets towards the world.

---

1. *Vayikra* 6:6.
2. *Yoma,* 4:6.
3. Cf. supra, pp. 151-2.
4. *Likkutei Torah, Devarim,* 78d.

159

2. THE WITHDRAWN AND THE SEPARATED

The concept of Shabbat is that of rest and withdrawal from the weekday world. Everyday acts are forbidden. But Shabbat is not only a day of the week. It is a state of mind. It is, in the dimensions of the soul, the state of contemplation and understanding. Its connection with Shabbat lies in the verse,[5] "And you shall call the Shabbat a delight." On Shabbat, the perception of G-d is more intense, more open. And this leads the mind to a withdrawal from the secular and the mundane.

But to reach this level is to become prone to a temptation. One might think that to have reached so far in perceiving the presence of G-d is to have passed beyond passion to the realm of impassive contemplation. The mind asserts its superiority over the emotions. He has, he tells himself, no need for the fire of love. This is the man to whom the Talmud says, the fire "shall not go out—even on Shabbat."

There is an opposite extreme: The man who has traveled so far on the path of separation that he feels he has now no link with G-d. To him the Talmud says, "it shall not go out—even in a state of impurity." For the fire does not go out. A spark always burns in the recesses of the heart. It can be fanned into flame. And if it is fed with the fuel of love, it will burn continually. The Maggid of Mezeritch said[6] that instead of reading the phrase, "It shall not be put out," we can read it, "It will put out the 'not.'" The fire of love extinguishes the negative. It takes the Jew past the threshold of commitment where he stands in hesitation and says "No."

3. COLDNESS

The remark of the Maggid stresses the fact that to put out the "No," the fire must be *continual*. It must be fed by a constant attachment to Torah and to Mitzvot. "Once" or "occasionally" or "not long ago" are not enough. The fire dies

---

5. *Isaiah* 58:13.
6. Quoted in *Hayom Yom*, 20-21 Adar Sheni.

down, coldness supersedes, and the "No" is given its dominion.

This explains the commandment:[7] "Remember what Amalek did to you by the way as you came out of Egypt: How he met you *(korcha)* on the way. . . ."[8] Amalek is the symbol of coldness in the religious life. *"Korcha,"* as well as meaning "he met you" also means "he made you cold." The historical Amalek "smote the hindmost of you, all those who were enfeebled in your rear, when you were faint and weary: And he did not fear G-d."[8] The Amalek within the Jew attempts to do the same. It is the voice which says "No" when the love of G-d grows faint and weary. It is the voice which does not fear G-d. And we are commanded every day to remember Amalek. That is, never to let coldness enter and take hold of the heart. And that means that the fire of love must never be allowed to die down.

4. FIRE FROM BELOW AND FIRE FROM ABOVE

The continual fire, which was man-made, was the preparation in the Sanctuary for the fire which descended from Heaven. On this the Talmud[9] says: "Although fire comes down from Heaven, it is a commandment also for man to bring fire." It was the awakening from below that brought an answering response from G-d. But it brought this response only when the fire was perfect, without defect.

This is made clear in this and next week's Sidrot. During the days when the Sanctuary was consecrated, it and its vessels were ready, Moses and Aaron were present, and sacrifices were being offered. But the Divine presence did not descend on it. A lingering trace of the sin of the Golden Calf remained. Only on the eighth day, when the continual fire was perfected, was the sin effaced, the "No" extinguished, "fire came forth from be-

---

7. *Shulchan Aruch Harav, Orach Chaim,* 60:4.
8. *Devarim* 25:17-18.
9. *Yoma,* 21b.

fore the L-rd"[10] and "the glory of the L-rd appeared to all the people."[11]

What was this fire from Heaven? Why did it require the perfection of the earthly fire?

Man is a created being. He is finite. And there are limits to what he can achieve on his own. His acts are bounded by time. To become eternal, something Divine must intervene.

This is why, during the seven days of consecration, the Sanctuary was continually being constructed and taken apart. As the work of man, it could not be lasting. But on the eighth day the Divine presence descended, and only then did it become permanent.

The seven days were a week, the measure of earthly time. The eighth was the day beyond human time, the number which signifies eternity. And hence it was the day of the heavenly fire, which was the response of an infinite G-d.[12]

5. LIMITS

Although man cannot aspire to infinity himself, the fire of infinity descends upon him. But only when he has perfected his own fire, and gone to the limits of his spiritual possibilities. Man is answered by G-d, not when he resigns himself to passivity or despair, but when he has reached the frontier of his own capabilities.

This is suggested by the word "continual" in the description of the fire. What is continual is infinite, for it has no end in time. Time, though, is composed of finite parts, seconds, minutes, hours. And even an infinite succession of them is still limited to a single dimension.[13] But by the perfection of our timebounded lives we join ourselves to the timelessness of G-d, so that time itself becomes eternal. And nature itself becomes supernatural. Because the reward of our service to G-d

10. *Vayikra* 9:24.
11. Ibid. v. 23 and cf. *Rashi*, ad loc.
12. Responsa, *Rashba*, pt. 1, ch. 9. Also, *Maamar Vayehi Bayom Hashemini, 5704*.
13. *Derech Mitzvotecha, Mitzvat Haamanat Elokut*, ch. 11.

is the blessing of a success within the natural world which goes beyond the natural order.

6. FIRE IN THE SERVICE OF MAN

The essential implication of this is that every Jew constitutes a Sanctuary to G-d. And even if he learns Torah and fulfills the commandments, if the continual fire is missing, the Divine presence will not dwell within him. For his service is without life. And a trace of that distant sin of the Golden Calf may remain: The "No" which is the voice of coldness.

The Jew must bring life, involvement, fire, to the three aspects of his religious existence: Torah, service and the practice of charity.[14]

Learning should not be something done merely to discharge an obligation, and kept to the minimum required. Words of Torah should never leave the mouth of a Jew. And they should be words spoken with fire. It is told in the Talmud[15] that "Beruriah once discovered a student who was learning in an undertone. Rebuking him she said: Is it not written, 'Ordered in all things and sure.' If it (the Torah) is 'ordered' in your two hundred and forty-eight limbs, it will be 'sure.' Otherwise it will not." In other words, Torah should penetrate every facet of his being until he can say: "All my bones shall say, L-rd, who is like You?"[16]

Service means prayer and of this Pirkei Avot says, "Do not regard your prayer as a fixed mechanical task, but as an appeal for mercy and grace before the All-Present."[17]

The *practice of charity* includes the fulfillment of the commandments. And these again are not to be performed merely out of conscientiousness, but with an inner warmth that manifests itself outwardly in a desire to fulfill them with as much beauty as possible.

---

14. *Pirkei Avot*, 1:2.
15. *Eruvin,* 54a.
16. *Psalms* 35:10. Cf. also *Tanya*, Part I, beg. of ch. 37.
17. 2:13.

These are the places where the fire is lit. And this human fire brings down the fire from heaven. It brings G-d into the world, and draws infinity into the dimensions of the finite.

(Source: Likkutei Sichot, Vol. I pp. 217-219)

פסח

PESACH

Pesach is the festival of liberation, it celebrates a historical event: The exodus of the Israelites from Egypt. But one of the tasks that the event lays upon us is that "in every generation, and every day, a Jew must see himself as if he had that day been liberated from Egypt." The implication is that freedom was not won once and for all. It needs constant guarding. And that every day and every environment carries its own equivalent of "Egypt"—a power to undermine the freedom of the Jew. Perhaps the most potent threat comes from within the individual himself. It is the conviction that certain achievements are beyond him: The strong and comfortable belief that he was not born to reach the heights of the religious life. To believe this is to set bars around oneself, to imprison oneself in an illusion. Pesach is thus an ongoing process of self-liberation. And the festival and its practices are symbols of a struggle that is constantly renewed within the Jew, to create the freedom in which to live out his eternal vocation.

The following extracts are adapted from Pesach letters of the Lubavitcher Rebbe.

1. THE MEANING OF LIBERATION

. . . The days of the Festival of our Freedom are approaching, when we will again recall that great event at the dawn of our history, when our people were liberated from Egyptian bondage in order to receive the Torah as free men.

Memory and imagination are the ability to associate oneself with an event in the past, and in so doing to live again through the emotions that were felt at the time of the event. Only physically are we bound by time and space. In our minds we can travel without limits, and the more spiritual we become, the closer we can approach the past, the more intensely we can experience its message and inspiration.

Remembering is a spiritual achievement. Commenting on the verse, "And these days shall be remembered and done" (Esther 9:28), the Rabbis say that as soon as those days are re-membered, they are re-enacted in Heaven. The Divine be-nevolence that brought the miracles in the past is wakened again by our act of recollection.

This is one of the reasons why we have been enjoined to remember the liberation from Egypt in every generation and every day. And why every Jew must see himself as if he had been freed from Egypt on that day. For every day he must personally "go out from Egypt," that is, he must escape from the limits, temptations and obstructions that his physical exist-ence places in the way of his spiritual life.

The counterpart of the liberation from Egypt is the libera-tion of the Divine Soul from the constraints of its physical en-vironment. And this must be experienced every day if true freedom is to be reached.

And when it is achieved, as it must be, with the help of G-d who freed our people from Egypt, and through a life of Torah and Mitzvot, a great spiritual anguish is ended. The inner con-flict between what is physical and what is Divine in the Jew's nature, is transcended. And then, only then, can he enjoy real freedom, the sense of serenity and harmony which is the prel-ude to freedom and peace in the world at large. . . .

(Source: Letter, 11th Nissan, 5713;
Igrot Kodesh, Vol. 7 pp. 205-6)

. . . One of the most significant lessons of the festival of Pesach is that the Jew has the capacity, even within a short space of time, to transform himself from one extreme to an-other.

The Torah and the Rabbis graphically describe the extent of the enslavement of the Israelites in Egypt, and the spiritual depths to which they had sunk. They were slaves in a country from which none could escape. They were under the power of a Pharaoh who had bathed in the blood of Jewish children.

They were destitute, broken in body and spirit by the lowest kind of forced labor. And then, suddenly, Pharaoh's power was broken, the whole people liberated, and a nation who not long ago were slaves, left the land "with an outstretched arm" and "with great wealth."

And their spiritual liberation was equally dramatic. They had reached the "forty-ninth stage of impurity," to the point of idolatry. And then—they saw G-d revealed in the fullness of His glory. A few weeks later they stood at the foot of Mount Sinai, at the apex of holiness and prophecy and heard G-d saying to each of them, without any intermediary: "I am the L-rd, *thy* G-d."

From this it follows that no matter where a Jew stands, or a Jewish community stands, on the ladder to perfection, the call comes every day to remember the liberation from Egypt, to strive after freedom, boldly ("with an outstretched arm") and with a total commitment ("with great wealth") to become "a kingdom of priests and a holy nation" by accepting the life of Torah "as in the days of your liberation from Egypt." Despair belongs to those who see with human eyes, not to those who see with the eye of faith.

There must be no pause nor hesitation on this road; no resting satisfied with what has already been accomplished. One must press on unrelenting until one experiences the call: "I am the L-rd, thy G-d. . . ."

(Source: Letter, 11th Nissan, 5719;
Igrot Kodesh, Vol. 18 pp. 318-19)

. . . One of the most striking features of the exodus of the Israelites from Egypt was their demonstration of *faith* in the Providence of G-d.

Consider the circumstances: An entire nation, men, women and children, numbering several million, willingly left a well-settled and prosperous country, a country whose pagan values had already left their impression on them, to venture on a long and dangerous journey, without provisions, but with absolute reliance on the word of G-d as spoken by Moses.

What is more, they did not follow the familiar and shorter route through the land of Philistines, which although it involved the risk of war, was far more attractive than the prospect of crossing a vast and desolate desert. In war there is the chance of victory; in defeat there is the chance of escape; but in a desert, without food or water, nature allows no chance of survival. Yet they followed this route, disregarding rationality, and trusting in the word of G-d.

The facts are more remarkable still. The Israelites had spent 210 years in Egypt, a highly agricultural country, where the nomadic life was mistrusted, where the soil was fertile and irrigated by the Nile whatever the caprices of the climate. They forsook all the security of the natural order. . . .

Why did they do so? This question is echoed in every generation. The secular world, and the Jew who has strayed from Jewish truth, asks the practicing Jew: You live like us in a materialistic world. You belong to a competitive society. You too face the struggle for economic survival. How can you exempt yourself from its values? How can you adhere to a code of precepts that burden your life and restrict your actions at every turn?

The answer lies in the exodus from Egypt.

Then, when Jews responded to the call of G-d, disregarding what seemed reasonable at the time, breaking with the values of their Egyptian environment, it transpired that the path they took was the path of true happiness, *spiritually* in receiving the Torah and becoming G-d's chosen people, *materially* in reaching the Promised Land, flowing with milk and honey.

It is so today and always. Through the Torah (the *Torat Chayim,* the "law of life") and the Mitzvot a Jew attaches himself to the Creator of the World, and frees himself from all "natural" limitations. This is the way of happiness, in the spirit and the material world. . . .

(Source: Letter, 11th Nissan, 5721;
Igrot Kodesh, Vol. 20 pp. 204-5)

2. THE FESTIVAL OF SPRING

> Pesach is the festival of Spring. "Observe the month of Spring and keep the Passover unto the L-rd your G-d, for in the month of Spring the L-rd your G-d brought you out of Egypt by night" (Devarim 16:1). This commandment has dictated the form of the Jewish calendar, for although it is primarily based on the lunar month, the seasons are determined by the sun. As a result, every two or three years an extra month must be added to the year, to keep the solar and lunar dates in harmony, so that Pesach will indeed fall during the Spring. Is there a deeper significance in the fact that Pesach is always a Spring festival? True, that was the time of year when, historically, the exodus took place. But why did G-d choose just that season? And what is the lesson that is implied?

... For hundreds of years the Jews had been enslaved by a powerful nation, which had imposed its dominion on all surrounding nations, not merely by brute force (its "chariots and horsemen") but by its overwhelming preponderance in science and technology, in everything which we now call "culture" and "civilization."

The civilization of the Egyptians was based on the forces of nature and natural phenomena, especially the Nile river. Rain is scarce in Egypt; but human ingenuity had devised an elaborate irrigation system which had turned Egypt into a flourishing oasis, surrounded by desert.

This circumstance produced an idolatrous culture, which was characterized by two main features: The deification of the forces of nature, and the deification of the powers of man who was able to use natural forces for his own ends. From here it was only a short step to the deification of Pharaoh, who personified the Egyptian ideal of the god-man.

This system, which viewed the world as an aggregate of natural forces (of which the human element was one), combined as it was with the philosophy expressed in the verse, *"My* power and the strength of *my* hand have made me this wealth" (Devarim 8:17) led to extreme forms of paganism and was the "justification" of the enslavement of, and atrocities towards, the weak and the minority in society.

The cultic activities of the Egyptians reached their climax at the time of annual reawakening of the forces of nature, in the month of Spring, for which the zodiacal sign was the Ram (Aries), a sacred symbol of Egyptian paganism.

Moses' intervention was dramatic. Suddenly he arrived with the announcement from G-d: "I have surely remembered you" (Shemot 3:16). Now was the time when the G-d of Abraham, Isaac and Jacob had willed the liberation of the Jews from Pharaoh's oppression and Egyptian exile. But there was one condition: "Withdraw and take for yourselves a lamb for your families and offer the Pesach (sacrifice)" (Shemot 12:21).

This was the command. "Withdraw"—withdraw from the idolatry of the land. "Take for yourselves a lamb"—take the symbol of the Egyptian deity and offer it as a sacrifice to G-d. It was not enough to deny idolatry inwardly, in their hearts. They had to do it openly, without fear, in accordance with all the details they had been commanded.

If it were done, Moses assured in the name of G-d, not only would they be freed from Egypt, but Pharaoh himself would urge them to leave; and not when the forces of nature were dormant and concealed, but in *the month of Spring,* when they were at the height of their powers.

In this way the Israelites acknowledged that the world was not simply an aggregate of natural forces, nor even a dualism of naturalism and supernaturalism in which nature and the spirit struggle for supremacy. Their action declared that there is One and only One G-d, who is the Master of the world, and in Whom all is a Unity.

This received its highest expression in the Giving of the Torah, which was the culmination and the ultimate purpose of the liberation from Egypt. It lay in the words: "I am the L-rd thy G-d, who brought you out of the land of Egypt, from the house of bondage. You shall have no other gods. . . ."

The gods of Egypt have their descendants. There are those today who base their lives on the deification of the forces of nature, and who still say *"my* power and the strength of *my* hand have made me this wealth." And there are those who leave room for G-d in their homes, while forsaking Him outside for the sake of social norms.

But Pesach intervenes with the reminder: "Withdraw" from the idolatry of the land, in whatever form it is disguised. Do so openly, without fear and with dignity. "Take unto yourselves" all your powers and dedicate them to G-d. Do so "in the month of Spring" at the moment when prosperity, technology and the deification of human achievement is at its height. And remember that every achievement is a Divine blessing, every form of prosperity a facet of G-d's benevolence.

(Source: Letter, 11th Nissan, 5725;
Igrot Kodesh, Vol. 23 pp. 361-5)

3. THE FIFTH SON

> The Seder service, and the reciting of the Haggadah, have always been considered to be directed particularly towards the children: "And you shall relate to your son on that day" (Shemot 13:8). Many of our customs at the Seder table were intended specifically to capture the attention of the child. And the different kinds of education which are needed by different personalities are illustrated in the passage in the Haggadah which tells of the four kinds of son, the wise, the wicked, the simple and the one who does not know how to ask. But there is a fifth, and far more problematic, son. There is a good reason why he is not mentioned explicitly in the Haggadah. For he is the absent son.

. . . While the "four sons" differ from one another in their reaction to the Seder service, they have one thing in common. They are all present. Even the so-called "wicked" son is there, taking an active, if dissenting, interest in what is going on in Jewish life around him. This, at least, justifies the hope that one day he will become "wise," and that all Jewish children attending the Seder will become conscientious and committed Jews.

Unfortunately there is, in our time, another kind of Jewish child: The child who is conspicuous by his absence, who has no interest whatever in Torah and Mitzvot, who is not even aware of the Seder and the miracles it recalls.

This is a grave challenge, which should command our attention long before Pesach and the Seder-night. For no Jewish child should be forgotten and given up. We must make every effort to save the lost child, and bring him to the Seder table. Determined to do so, and driven by a deep sense of compassion and responsibility, we need have no fear of failure.

To remedy any situation, we must discover its origins.

In this case, they lie in a mistaken analysis of their situation on the part of some immigrants arriving in a new and strange environment. Finding themselves a small minority, and encountering the inevitable difficulties of resettlement, some parents had the idea, which they communicated to their children, that assimilation was the solution. But in their efforts to abandon the Jewish way of life, they created a spiritual conflict within themselves. They were determined that their children should be spared the tension of divided loyalties; and to rationalize their desertion of their Jewish heritage they convinced themselves and their children that the life of Torah and Mitzvot did not fit their new surroundings. They looked for, and therefore "found," faults with the Jewish way of life, while everything in the non-Jewish environment seemed attractive and good.

By this attitude, the parents hoped to ensure their children's survival in the new environment. But what kind of survival was it to be, if the soul was sacrificed for the material benefits of the world?

And what they thought was an "escape into freedom" turned out, in the final analysis, to be an escape into slavish imitation, which tended to be so marked by caricature and a sense of insecurity as to command little respect from that younger generation that it was intended for. . . .

The festival of Pesach and the deliverance that it commemorates, are timely reminders that Jewish survival does not rest in imitation of the non-Jewish environment, but in fidelity to our traditions and our religious vocation.

Our ancestors in Egypt were a small minority, and they lived in the most difficult circumstances. But, as the Rabbis tell us, they retained their identity as Jews, preserved their uniqueness, and kept up their traditions without anxiety or shame. It was this that made their survival certain, and assured their liberation from all forms of tyranny, physical and spiritual. . . .

There is no room for hopelessness in Jewish life, and no Jew should ever be given up as a lost cause. Through compassion and fellow-love *(Ahavat Yisroel)* even a "lost" generation can be brought back to the love of G-d *(Ahavat HaShem)* and love of the Torah *(Ahavat HaTorah);* not only to be included in the community of the "four sons" but to belong in time to the rank of the "wise" son. . . .

May the gathering of these "lost tribes of Israel" to the Seder table hasten the true and complete redemption of our people, through the coming of the Messiah speedily in our time.

(Source: Letter, 11th Nissan, 5717; Vol. 15 pp. 33-37)

פרשת שמיני

SHEMINI

The name of our Sidra, Shemini, ("the eighth") refers to the day on which Aaron and his sons were inducted as the priests of the Sanctuary. It was also the day on which the presence of G-d was revealed. But why was it called the *eighth* day? It followed the seven days during which the Sanctuary was consecrated. But it hardly seemed a continuation of them. For they were the days which represented man's effort to draw near to G-d by consecrating himself and his world; whereas the eighth day was the moment when G-d answered his efforts by revealing Himself. And surely there is no comparison between man's efforts and G-d's response. The one is finite, the other infinite. So how can we talk of the eighth day as if it were a mere continuation of the previous seven? Starting from this problem, the Rebbe explores the relation between human endeavor and Divine revelation, as exemplified in the Sanctuary, the Shabbat, circumcision, and the counting of the Omer.

1. ON THE EIGHTH DAY

Our Sidra begins with the words, "And it came to pass on the eighth day. . . ." The Kli Yakar, in his commentary to the Torah, asks why this day, which followed the seven days of consecration of the Sanctuary, was called the "eighth day." For this implies that it was a natural continuation of the previous days. But in fact the consecration was limited to seven days: "And you shall not go out from the door of the tent of meeting for seven days, until the days of your consecration be fulfilled; for He shall consecrate you seven days."[1] During that time the altar was dedicated. And the following day was quite separate: It was set aside for the induction of Aaron and his sons to the priesthood.

---

1. *Vayikra* 8:33.

The answer which the Kli Yakar gives is that it is called the eighth day to emphasize its extraordinary character. For it is written shortly afterwards, "Today the L-rd appears to you." And to explain why it was then that the L-rd appeared, and not during the actual days of consecration, the Torah tells us that it was because it was the *eighth* day. Seven is the number of the days of the week, the measure of earthly time, a symbol of the human dimension. Eight signifies the more-than-human; it is the symbol of holiness.

This is why a circumcision can be performed on Shabbat. For circumcision takes place on the *eighth* day from birth, and Shabbat is the *seventh* day. In other words, Shabbat belongs to human time, but circumcision belongs to the realm of the Holy, the supernatural. And the claims of the spiritual override those of the physical.

2. DEGREES OF HOLINESS

To say that seven is the span of the week does not mean that it is the symbol of the weekday world, the secular. Because Shabbat is itself one of those seven days, and it is a day of holiness. But nonetheless it is reckoned as one of the seven days of creation, and thus belongs to the created order. Whereas the number eight expresses the idea of being beyond the normal confines of time, and thus of being wholly united with G-d as He is in Himself, rather than as He is related to the world.

The Kli Yakar cites an example of this significance of the number eight, namely that the harp which will be used in the Temple of the Messianic Era will have eight strings.[2] The harp which was played in the Sanctuary had only seven. It was holy. But less so than the harp of Messianic times.

The Torah itself is holy. But compared to the way in which it will be learned and revealed in the Messianic Age, our own response to it is called, in the Midrash,[3] "a vanity."

---

2. *Erchin*, 13b.
3. *Kohelet Rabbah*, 11:8.

There are, in other words, degrees of holiness. There is the holiness of this world, which is symbolized by the number seven, which is confined to the limits of human capabilities. And there is the holiness which goes beyond the world, beyond the idea that G-d and the world are two distinct entities, which is expressed in the number eight.

3. GIFTS AND REWARD

Curiously, the answer which the Kli Yakar gives to his own question does not appear to answer it. Instead it seems to make the question more forceful.

If the eighth day stands for the state of absolute unity with G-d, then it signifies something *supernatural*. If so, then it surely has *no* connection with the previous seven days of consecration, which represented *human* activity, the sanctification of the *natural* order, and *earthly* time. Whereas the clear implication of the phrase "the eighth day" is that it was a *continuation* of the previous seven.

The answer is that supernatural revelation depends on our human efforts. The Messianic Age will be brought about by our acts of worship and of service of G-d. Our efforts to consecrate the world during the seven days of human time are the gestures of faithfulness which will produce the Divine response of the eighth day—the day of the Messiah. So that although the Messianic Age will be of an altogether higher level of holiness than we can evoke with our Divine Service in the present, it will not be a sudden break in the history of Jewish consciousness. It will be the outcome of what we do now. It will be the "eighth day" in the sense that it continues and completes the perfection after which we now strive, after we have done all of which we *are* capable.[4]

To draw an analogy: Shabbat, which is the seventh day, has two aspects. Firstly it is one of the days of the week, holier than the other six, but still a part of human time. There is a signifi-

---

4. Cf. supra, *Tzav,* ch. 4 and 5.

cant phrase in the command:[5] "And the children of Israel shall keep the Shabbat, to *make* (usually translated, 'to observe') the Shabbat throughout their generations." Shabbat is something we make. It is a Sanctuary within the week which *we* construct by our own service. But secondly the Shabbat is "a semblance of the World to Come," a glimpse of the Messianic Age. This aspect of the Shabbat is not something we can achieve ourselves. It is something we receive as a gift from G-d. It is this of which the Talmud[6] says, "The Holy One, blessed be He, said to Moses, I have a precious gift in My treasure house, and it is called the Shabbat."

There is a difference between a gift and a reward: A reward is something which the recipient has earned, a gift is something he receives only through the grace of his benefactor. And this facet of Shabbat, this glimpse of the future revelation, belongs entirely to the grace of G-d. It has a holiness which goes beyond human limitations.

Yet, even though it is a gift, we must work for it. The Rabbis say,[7] "If the recipient had not given some pleasure (to the donor of the gift) he would not have given it to him." That is, if we do not give pleasure to G-d by our actions, we will not receive His gift. Whereas "he who labors on the eve of Shabbat will eat on Shabbat."[8] Because of our labors we are given a Divine gift which far outweighs the worth of our work.

The same is true about the revelation within the Sanctuary on the eighth day. Although it was not *earned* by the human activity of consecration on the previous seven days, it was only when this consecration was completed that the Divine response came. G-d gives His gift to man only after man has done all within his power to consecrate himself to G-d. This is why it is called the "eighth day"—the day of Divine grace which answers the seven days of man's own initiative in drawing close to G-d.

---

5. *Shemot* 31:16.
6. *Shabbat*, 10b.
7. *Megillah*, 26b; *Gittin*, 50b; *Baba Batra*, 156a.
8. *Avodah Zarah*, 3a and cf. *Likkutei Torah, Shir Hashirim*, 24b.

4. THE COUNTING OF THE OMER

In many years, the Sidra of Shemini is read immediately after Pesach, near the beginning of the seven week period of the counting of the Omer. What is the connection between the two?

The Torah says about the Omer,[9] "You shall count for fifty days." And yet in fact we count only forty-nine days. Why? In the seven weeks we remove ourselves step by step from the forty-nine "gates of impurity" and pass through the forty-nine "gates of understanding." The fiftieth, the ultimate level of understanding, is beyond us. But it is only when we have reached by our efforts the forty-ninth, that the fiftieth comes to us as a gift of G-d.

The seven weeks of the Omer are like the seven days of consecration. They represent the spiritual achievement of man. The fiftieth day of the Omer is like the eighth day of the Sanctuary: It is the revelation which breaks in on us from the outside, the answer of G-d to our endeavors. The fiftieth day is Shavuot, the day when the Torah was revealed on Mt. Sinai. And that day was a foretaste of the revelation of the Messianic Age.[10]

5. PAST AND FUTURE REDEMPTION

The counting of the Omer was not only a preparation for the Giving of the Torah. It is also a preparation for the Messianic revelation itself.

In Michah[11] it is written, "As on the *days* of your coming out of Egypt, I will show him wonders." But the Exodus from Egypt took place on *one* day, the 15th of Nissan. The previous Lubavitcher Rebbe, Rabbi Yosef Yitzchak, explained:[12] the redemption from Egypt will only be complete when the future redemption has come. Until then we are still captives in a

9. *Vayikra* 23:16.
10. *Tanya*, Part I, ch. 36.
11. 7:15.
12. *Maamar Kimay Tzaytcha* 5708.

metaphorical Egypt, namely the limitations and constraints of our human situation, from which we must liberate ourselves. The historical exodus, in the year 2448, was only the beginning of a continuous process of self-liberation. This will only be complete in the Messianic Age, when we will finally reach the stage where no spiritual heights are beyond the scope of man. If there seem to be dark ages where this process is halted or even reversed, where we seem to be regressing spiritually, this is only because new achievements need sometimes to be preceded by a time of darkness, in which new reserves of strength are discovered. They are not true regressions, for they serve to bring man to new heights of religious understanding. They are part of the Divine plan, stages in the continual ascent of man.[13]

(Source: Likkutei Sichot, Vol. III pp. 973-977)

---

13. Cf. supra, *Lech Lecha*.

פרשת תזריע

TAZRIA

The previous Sidra, Shemini, contained the laws of ritual cleanliness and purity as applied to animals. This week's Sidra applies the same concepts to men and women. In the Midrash, Rav Simlai draws an analogy between the fact that animals were *created* before man, and that they were *legislated about* before him. What is the substance of this analogy? Was man created last because he was higher or lower than the animals? In answering the question, the Rebbe traces the connection between Rav Simlai's opinion and his character, and examines an important distinction between innate and acquired virtue, or between the excellence which is inherited and that which is earned. It is a question that has perplexed many thinkers: Who is better, the man who is born righteous or the man who has made himself righteous? The Rebbe considers in depth the role of *effort* in the religious life.

1. THE NAME "TAZRIA"

The names of the Sidrot, as has been mentioned before,[1] are not merely labels to differentiate one from the next. Every name in Hebrew, the holy language, is an indication of the nature of that which is named. The names of the Sidrot tell us of their essential content. Thus we find that a number of Sidrot are *not* called by their opening words, as is usually the case, but by some later word which more perfectly expresses their theme.

An example of this occurs with this week's Sidra. After the general introduction ("And the L-rd spoke to Moses saying. . . ")[2] the first word is "woman" *(ishah):* "If a woman be delivered and bear a male child." And yet we do not nowadays call the Sidra Ishah but Tazria ("be delivered").

---

1. Cf. supra, pp. 10-11.
2 *Vayikra* 12:1.

180

What, then, is the concept implicit in the word *Tazria* that sums up the content of the entire Sidra?

There is also a difficulty posed by Rashi's comment on the words "If a woman be delivered." Quoting the Midrash,[3] he says, "Rav Simlai said: Just as the formation of man took place after that of the cattle, beast and fowl, when the world was created, so the law regarding him is set forth after the law regarding cattle, beast and fowl (contained in the previous Sidra)." Thus the new theme that our Sidra takes up, by contrast with the previous chapters, is law relating to *humans,* as opposed to the laws relating to animals. Thus the word *ishah* ("woman") is not only the first individuating word in the Sidra: It also seems highly appropriate to its subject-matter—legislation relating to humans. How is it that "Tazria" embodies more completely this idea of "the law of man?"

2. MAN'S PLACE IN CREATION

Rav Simlai, in his comment quoted above, uses the phrase "just as" rather than "because." In other words, the law of man follows that of the animals, not *because* he was created last, but *for the same reason that* he was created last.

What was this reason? Various answers are given in the Midrash[2] and the Talmud.[4] One is: So that if a man's mind becomes too proud he may be reminded that even the gnats preceded him in the order of creation. Alternatively, so that heretics should not be able to say that the Holy One, blessed be He, had a partner (namely, Adam) in creation. Again, man was created last so that he might immediately enter upon the fulfillment of a precept. He was created on Friday so that he could immediately sanctify the Shabbat. Lastly, it was so that he might go "into the banquet" straight away; that is, all nature was ready for his use.

But the commentators have noticed that all these reasons, while they apply to man being last in creation, do not explain

---

3. *Vayikra Rabbah,* ad loc.
4. *Sanhedrin,* 38a.

his being last in legislation. What is the meaning of Rav Simlai's analogy, "just as?"

The Alter Rebbe, in his book Tanya,[5] explained that in one sense man is lower than all other creatures, even beasts which are unclean; lower even than the gnat. For not only does he sin, whereas they do not. But he *can* sin, whereas they cannot. In potentiality as well as in actuality, sin is a reality for man but not for animal.

3. THE ORDER OF LEARNING

The usual order to take in learning Torah is to progress from the simple to the complex, from the light to the weighty. This applies to *what is* learned: A child of five begins with the Chumash, moves to the Mishnah at the age of ten,[6] and so on. It applies also to the *depth* of learning: First comes acquaintance with the text and only afterwards come the questions, the dialectics, the in-depth study.[7] And it applies to the *manner* of learning. We do not reach at once the highest level of Torah study for its own sake, like David who[8] "elevated the Source of the Torah on High, and united it with the Essence of G-d." Instead, "when a man does it (studies), in the first place he does so with himself in mind."[9]

On the other hand, when the Torah was *given,* the order was reversed. Its devolution from the spirituality of G-d to the physical situation of man was, as it were, a descent from higher to lower. In the passage in Proverbs[10] which describes the wisdom of the Torah, it first says: "Then I was by Him, as one brought up with Him, and I was daily His delight." Only subsequently were "my delights with the sons of men." The Torah reached down from the heights of G-d to become the posses-

---

5. Part I, ch. 29; cf. Ibid., Part I, ch. 24.
6. *Pirkei Avot*, end of ch. 5.
7. *Avodah Zarah,* 19a, *Rashi*, ad loc.
8. *Sefer Habahir.*
9. *Pesachim,* 68b.
10. 8:30-31. Cf. *Tanya*, Part V, *David Zemirot.*

sion of man.[11] And we in our learning retrace its path, ascending from our physical situation to spiritual closeness with G-d.

This order of learning is mirrored in the structure of the Torah itself. This is why the laws concerning animals are placed first. To sanctify the animal world, by distinguishing the impure from the pure, is relatively simple. The problem of sin does not arise in their case. But for man to sanctify himself, given his capacity for wrongdoing, is far harder. Thus the laws of human conduct come last. Not because of man's innate *superiority* to the animals, but because of his *deficiencies*. This, too, is Rav Simlai's opinion as to why he was created last: "So that if he becomes too proud, he may be reminded that the gnats preceded him in the order of creation."

4. RAV SIMLAI—THE MAN AND HIS OPINIONS

We can now see the connection between Rav Simlai's comment, that just as man was created last so his legislation comes last in the Torah, and the character of Rav Simlai himself.

A virtue can be possessed in two ways. It can be won by effort, or it can be innate or fortuitous. Each has its advantages. An innate or unworked-for virtue has no natural limits. It is like the difference between talent and expertise. An inborn talent may be unlimited; expertise, painfully acquired, can never quite match it. But in its inwardness, the virtue reached by effort surpasses the virtue which is innate. One is always more closely involved with what one has earned than with what one has been given.

This distinction underlies the two contrasting explanations of man's place as the last of the works of creation: The first that he is the highest, the second that he is the lowest, of creatures.

In innate capacities, he is the highest. From birth, before he has begun to serve G-d, he is nonetheless possessed of a soul which is literally a part of G-d.[12] This he retains, together with

---

11. Cf. *Tanya*, Part I, ch. 4.
12. *Tanya*, Part I, beg. of ch. 2.

an underlying faith, even if he turns away from the Divine will.[13] But in those virtues which he acquires through the effort of service, at the outset he is no better than the rest of creation. In fact, what is most readily apparent is his physical nature, his lack of restraint, his capacity for sin. The powers of the soul are as yet undisclosed. They need to be brought to the surface by effort in the service of G-d. Hence the second opinion, that man was created last to be reminded that even the gnat is in this one respect prior to him.

The connection between this view and its author is this: Rav Simlai did not have an illustrious ancestry. The story is told in the Talmud[14] that he came to Rabbi Jochanan and asked him to teach him the Book of Genealogies. But Rabbi Jochanan refused, because (according to Rashi) his lineage was undistinguished. Therefore Rav Simlai, unable to lay claim to *inherited* virtue, appreciated the value and importance of effort and *acquired* virtue. This explains his reading of the order of creation. When man is created, he has no acquired distinctions except the disposition to sin. He was made last because at that stage he is the lowest of beings.

This also explains why human law should be called *Tazria* ("be delivered"). For the process from conception to birth is a symbol of effort, of bringing to fruition, in other words of "labor" in both its senses. There is an additional symbolism in the phrase "if a *woman* be delivered." The male and female elements in procreation represent respectively the "spiritual awakening from above" (i.e., the Divine initiative) and "from below" (the human initiative).[15] And service, effort, struggle are the forms which the human initiative takes.

5. THE TWO FACES OF MAN

There is a principle expressed in the Lecha Dodi prayer that "last in action, first in thought." Thus man, who was cre-

---

13. Ibid., Part I, end of ch. 24.
14. *Pesachim,* 62'b and cf. *Rashi,* ad loc.
15. *Likkutei Torah, Tazria, Maamar Soss Tassiss.*

ated last, was the original intention behind the whole enterprise of creation.

Both opinions agree with this, that man is the apex of created life. But one side of the argument sees his stature in terms of his *innate essence*: His Divine soul. The other sees it in terms of his *potential achievement* through the effort of serving G-d, while viewing man *in himself* as the lowest of beings. This view, which is Rav Simlai's, sees the two faces of man *("Adam"* in Hebrew). On the one hand he is formed from the dust of the earth *("Adamah")*; on the other, he is capable of becoming Divine *("Adameh* la-Elyon"—"I will resemble G-d"). This is his essential capacity—to transform himself completely, from a natural to a spiritual being.

6. SERVICE AND CREATIVITY

The name "Tazria" therefore symbolizes *"avodah,"* man's *service* of G-d. It also suggests the importance of that service. For when a woman conceives a child and it grows in the womb, an entirely new being is brought into existence. The birth of the child merely *reveals* this creation, which was wrought at the moment of conception. And when man enters on the life of service, he too creates a new being: Natural man becomes spiritual man, *Adamah* (the dust of "the earth") becomes *Adameh la-Elyon* (a semblance of G-d). And his Divine soul, which was innate, becomes also inward, because it has changed from being a gift to being something earned.

(Source: Likkutei Sichot, Vol. VII pp. 74-79)

פרשת מצורע

METZORA

Metzora begins with the laws concerning the purification of the leper. The Rebbe begins with the question, why should we call this Sidra *Metzora,* "the leper," a name with unpleasant connotations? Especially when an earlier generation of Rabbis called it, neutrally, *Zot Tihyeh ("This shall be . . ."* the law of the leper).

To understand the significance of leprosy as discussed in the Sicha, we must remember that it is considered, by the Torah and the Rabbis, not only as a disease but as a punishment specifically for the sin of slander. It was the punishment that Miriam was given for the tale-bearing against Moses (Bamidbar, ch. 12). A leper was isolated from the rest of the people once his illness had been diagnosed, and made to live outside the camp. Since the disease had a spiritual as well as a physical dimension, this was not simply a hygienic precaution, but had a moral purpose. Likewise his purification was a recovery of spiritual as well as physical health. It is the spiritual dimension of this cleansing procedure that the Rebbe analyzes.

1. TWO NAMES

The Sidra Metzora has not always been so-called. Earlier Rabbis, like Rabbi Saadia Gaon,[1] Rashi[2] and Rambam,[3] called it by the preceding words of the verse, Zot Tihyeh ("This shall be"). Only in more recent generations has it become the custom to call it Metzora.[4]

But Metzora means "the leper": A name with unpleasant associations. Indeed, to avoid this, it is referred to in many places as Tahara, "Purification."[5] Why then is it called by this seemingly inappropriate name, especially when there existed

---

1. *Siddur Rabbi Saadiah Gaon—Keriat Hatorah.*
2. *Vayikra* 13:8.
3. *Seder Tefillot of Rambam.*
4. *Tur* and *Shulchan Aruch, Orach Chaim,* ch. 428.
5. Cf. *Likkutei Sichot,* Vol. I, p. 239.

beforehand a name for the Sidra with none of these associations?

2. "HE SHALL BE BROUGHT"

Before we can solve the problem, we must notice two further difficulties in its opening passage, "This shall be the law of the leper in the day of his cleansing: He shall be brought to the priest. And the priest shall go forth out of the camp. . . ."

Firstly there seems to be a contradiction here. On the one hand, the leper is to be "brought to the priest." On the other, the priest is to "go forth out of the camp" and come to him. Who is to go to whom? In fact, it is the priest who comes to the leper, for the leper was not allowed to come within the three camps. What then is the meaning of, "he shall be brought to the priest?"

Secondly, why was the leper to be "brought?" Why does the Torah not say "he shall *come?*" The use of the passive verb "brought" suggests that his meeting with the priest was *against his will.*

In answering the first question, the commentators[6] explain that although the leper was indeed to stay outside the camp, he was to be brought to the edge of it, so as to avoid burdening the priest with a long journey. But this explanation is not easy to understand. Although the leper was, because of his affliction, commanded to remain outside the camp, there was no obligation on him to go far away from it. He could stay near its boundaries. And since the instruction about the cleansing procedure was directed to all lepers, including those who were situated near to the camp, the explanation of the commentators does not remove our puzzlement.

3. REPENTANCE: THE FIRST STAGE

To arrive at an inward understanding of the question, we must consider what Rashi says on the phrase,[7] "All the days

---

6. *Sforno, Chezkuni, on Metzora.*
7. *Vayikra* 13:46.

wherein the plague is in him . . . he shall dwell alone." Rashi comments, "(Even) people who are unclean (for reasons other than leprosy) shall not abide with him . . . because he, by slanderous statements, parted man and wife, or a man from his friend, (therefore) he must be parted (from everybody)." We can say, then, that he is excluded from the three camps because of his association with strife and dissension. His slander causes men to be distant from one another, whereas the idea of holiness is *unity*.[8] He has no place, therefore, in the holy congregation. But what is more, he is to be separated even from the other categories of unclean people, because, as Rambam says,[9] his slander is progressive. At first it is turned against ordinary people, then against the righteous, then against the prophets, and finally against G-d himself, and he ends by denying the fundamentals of faith. This is worse even than idolatry, for the idolater does not deny G-d, he merely denies His uniqueness.

Nonetheless as the Alter Rebbe wrote as a point of Halachic law[10] as well as an inward Chassidic truth,[11] "It is certain (that *every* Jew) will in the end return in repentance."

This explains the phrase "he *shall be brought* to the priest." The form of the verb carries with it an assurance for the future that even he who stands outside the three camps, who is isolated by his sin, will in the end turn to the "priest" in repentance. And this was the man whose very nature was to resist this return to oppose holiness, and join forces with the heathen world "outside the camp." This is why he "shall be brought"— in the passive—for his return is contrary to his will.[12]

4. THE SECOND STAGE

The initiating cause in the awakening of the desire to return is not to be found in the man *himself,* but in the promise of

---

8. Cf. *Tanya*, Part I, ch. 32.
9. End of *Hilchot Tum'at Tzaraat.*
10. *Hilchot Talmud Torah*, 4:3.
11. *Tanya*, Part I, end of ch. 39.
12. Cf. *Ezekiel* 20:32-33.

G-d that even if it requires "a mighty hand . . . I will rule over you."[13]

But if at first the impetus to return breaks in on him from the outside, it is the Divine will that ultimately it should became part of his deepest nature. Thus there is the further assurance that not only will he repent, but he will experience repentance as the truest expression of his own personality in all its facets: Will, intellect and feeling.

In the light of this we can see why, after the Torah stated that the leper "shall be brought to the priest," it continues, "And the priest shall go forth out of the camp."

The first stage of repentance, of "cleansing," is the sudden revelation of G-d coming in, as it were, from the outside. Because it has not yet become part of his own personality, this revelation is unrelated to the personal situation of the man. He is "brought" out of himself and his environment. But afterwards the priest comes to him: That is, his situation becomes important again, as he strives to translate his revelation into a cleansing of the whole circumstances of his life. And since the "cleansing" extends even to his environment, he achieves something that even the perfectly righteous could not: He sanctifies what lies "outside the camp," where the righteous man has never been. Thus we say that repentance done from great love turns even willful sins into merits:[14] it sanctifies even what lies outside the will of G-d.

5. THE EARLIER GENERATIONS AND THE PRESENT

Now, finally, we can see why an earlier age called this week's Sidra Zot Tihyeh, "This shall be . . ." rather than, as we now call it, Metzora, "the law of *the leper*."

Only in the Time to Come will we witness the ultimate transformation of darkness into light, of evil into goodness.

Thus the earlier generations, when this Time was as yet distant, they sensed more readily the idea that evil is conquered

---

13. Ibid., v. 33.
14. Cf. *Rambam, Hilchot Teshuvah*, 7:4.

by something outside itself than that it should transform itself from within. They belonged to the stage where the leper is "brought," against his will, to be cleansed, rather than to the second stage where the cleansing comes from within his own situation "outside the camp." So they did not call the Sidra, "the leper," because in their eyes he was not cleansed *as* himself but rather *despite* himself. Nonetheless, they knew the promise of the Future, and thus they called the Sidra "This shall be." In other words, the "law of the leper"—the time when the leper of his own accord becomes part of G-d's law—was something that *would* be, in the World to Come.

But we, standing already in the shadow cast by the approaching Messianic Age, can make of "the leper" a name for a section of the Torah. We can already sense the time of the revelation of the good within the bad, the righteousness within those who stand "outside the camp." The light is breaking through the wall that separates us from the Time to Come: The light of the age when "night will shine as day."[15]

(Source: Likkutei Sichot, Vol. VII pp. 100-104)

---

15. *Psalms* 139:12. Cf. *Maamar Bati Leganni,* 5710, ch. 5.

ACHAREI MOT

Acharei Mot begins by mentioning the death of Nadab and Abihu, the sons of Aaron. Their death, related in the Sidra of Shemini, is something of a mystery, for on the one hand they seemed to be punished for their faults, while on the other, a Midrashic comment suggests that their merits were extraordinary, excelling even those of Moses and Aaron. Can we reconcile these two analyses of their character? A Chassidic explanation does so by saying that they died because of a religious ecstasy so intense that their souls literally left their bodies. Was there anything wrong in this? There was. What was mistaken was the pursuit of ecstasy at the price of life in the world. They ran towards the higher realms without thought of returning. And yet the Jew must always return, for his task lies within the world, sanctifying, not forsaking, his earthly situation. The rhythm of withdrawal and return, of experience and action, is fundamental to Judaism.

1. THE DEATH OF NADAB AND ABIHU

Our Sidra begins with the verse: "And the L-rd spoke to Moses, after the death of the two sons of Aaron, when they drew near to the L-rd and they died." The final words, however present a difficulty. Why does the Torah add "and they died" when it has already said, "after the death of the two sons of Aaron?"

The Midrash, in giving an explanation of their death, cites the following explanations: They entered the Holy of Holies;[1] they did not wear the priestly garments necessary for their service;[2] they did not have children;[2] and they did not marry.[2] Our second question now arises: What is the source of the

---

1. *Torat Kohanim,* beg. *Acharei; Vayikra Rabbah,* 20:8; *Bamidbar Rabbah,* 2:23; *Tanchuma, Acharei,* ch. 6.
2. *Vayikra Rabbah,* Ibid., 9; *Tanchuma,* Ibid.

Midrashic account? Where, in the Torah, are these four faults alluded to?

Further: How can we suppose that Aaron's two sons, Nadab and Abihu, were guilty of a sin? The Rabbis say[3] that Moses said to Aaron, "Aaron, my brother, I knew that the Sanctuary would be sanctified by those who were beloved and close to G-d. Now I see that they—Nadab and Abihu—are greater than both of us." If this was so, how could they have sinned?

2. A FATAL ECSTASY

There is a Chassidic explanation[4] that Aaron's two sons did not "sin" literally. Their "sin" was to allow their desire to cleave to G-d to mount to such an intensity that they died. Their bodies could no longer contain their souls. Thus the Torah says "when they drew near to the L-rd (with such passion that) they died." And this was counted as a sin! For although a Jew must divest himself of material concerns,[5] at the moment when he stands poised at the ultimate ecstasy of the soul, he must turn again to the work that the soul must do within a physical existence.

It is written in the Pirkei Avot,[6] "Against your will you live." Set against the desire of the soul to rise *beyond* the world, is its task of creating a dwelling-place for G-d *within* the world.[7] Nadab and Abihu achieved the ecstasy but not the return. This was their sin and the reason for their death. They "drew near to the L-rd and they died." They let their spiritual passion override their this-worldly task. They went beyond the world and beyond life itself.

This act lies at the heart of each of the four faults which the Midrash ascribes to them.

---

3. *Torat Kohanim, Shemini; Zevachim,* 115b; *Rashi, Vayikra* 10:3.
4. Cf. *Maamar Acharei Mot,* 5649 (and 5722), at length.
5. Cf. *Shulchan Aruch Harav, Orach Chaim,* beg. ch. 98; *Hilchot* Talmud Torah, 4:5.
6. End of ch. 4. Cf. *Tanya,* Part I, end of ch. 50.
7. Cf. *Tanchuma, Nasso,* ch. 16. *Tanya,* Part I, ch. 36.

They "entered the Holy of Holies," the innermost reaches of the spirit, without thinking of their return to the outer world.

They "did not wear the (priestly) garments." Their concern was to divest themselves of the world and to become purely spiritual. They forsook the necessary "garments" in which the word of G-d is clothed,[8] the *Mitzvot*, the physical actions that sanctify a physical environment.

They "had no children" and "did not marry." That is, they did not fulfill G-d's command to "be fruitful and multiply" and to bring new souls into the world. They did the opposite. They *withdrew* their own souls from the world.

All their faults stemmed from a single misconception, that the Jew draws close to G-d by withdrawal instead of involvement. In fact, both are necessary. And that is why, at the point of the year when we are most powerfully taken out of the world—Yom Kippur—we begin the reading of the Torah from these verses, as a reminder of our ultimate task.

3. ENTRANCE AND EXIT

Rashi explains that the command, "that he (Aaron) come not at all times into the holy place . . . (but) with this shall Aaron come into the holy place," comes immediately after the statement of the death of his sons, to warn that his (and our) service should not be like that of Nadab and Abihu.

A question arises here. Can we really demand of a person at the point of ecstasy, that he return to his mundane role? If his experience is genuine, if he has reached the love of G-d "with all your might" and has broken through all barriers of separation between man and G-d, can he hold himself back at the very point of union, and reimmerse himself in all the constraints of the human situation? Is there not an emotional incompatibility between the absolute abandonment of a person to G-d and a constant vigilance not to go too far?

---

8. Cf. *Tanya*, Part I, ch. 5; Part IV, ch. 29.

The answer lies in how a person begins his spiritual journey. If he sets out with the intention of satisfying his *own* desires, however exalted they are, he will not wish to turn back from his private ecstasy to the needs of the world. But if he sets out in obedience to G-d's command, knowing that though "You shall love the L-rd your G-d . . . with all your might," nonetheless "He created (the world) not to be empty, he formed it to be inhabited,"⁹ then within his ecstatic approach to G-d, the desire ultimately to return and sanctify the world will always be implicit.

There is a famous story in the Talmud.¹⁰ Four men entered the "Grove" (the mystical secrets of the Torah): Ben Azzai, Ben Zoma, Acher and Rabbi Akiva. Ben Azzai looked and died. Ben Zoma looked and was stricken (with madness). Acher mutilated the shoots (i.e., became an apostate). Rabbi Akiva "entered in peace and came out in peace."

On the face of it, the important difference between Rabbi Akiva and the other three was in how he came *out* of the "Grove." Why does the Talmud emphasize that he *"entered* in peace?"

But the truth is that how each of the four entered, determined how they emerged. Ben Azzai entered seeking ecstasy, not return; therefore he "looked and died." (It is interesting to note that his Divine service was generally characterized by aspects of withdrawal.)¹¹

But Rabbi Akiva entered "in peace," in obedience to the Divine will and seeking to unite the higher and lower worlds. That is why he came out in peace. His intention of returning was implicit at the outset of his path to religious ecstasy.

This, too, was how Aaron was to enter the Holy of Holies, in fear, obedience and self-abnegation. And in this way he was

---

9. *Isaiah* 45:18.
10. *Chagigah,* 14b.
11. *Yevamot,* 63b; *Sotah,* 4b. Cf. *Shulchan Aruch Harav, Hilchot Talmud Torah,* beg. ch. 3, in *Kuntres Acharon.*

able to "make atonement for himself and for his house"[12] and to say a prayer for the sustenance of Israel,[13] each of them acts of concern for the world.

4. EXPERIENCE INTO ACTION

All the Torah's narratives have a teaching which is applicable to every Jew,[14] not simply to the outstanding few. What, then, is the universal significance of the story of Nadab and Abihu? Surely not everyone can reach a level of ecstasy where one's life is in danger. A few need the warning; but what of the many?

But every Jew is sometimes awakened to an intense religious experience, especially on Shabbat and the Festivals, more particularly during the Ten Days of Repentance,[15] and above all on Yom Kippur. He is for a while taken out of his daily routine, his normal anxieties, and inwardly rises beyond his usual mental confines. It is at these times that he must remember that whatever he experiences when he enters this holy domain must be carried with him when he returns to his everyday world. He must not seek ecstasy for its own sake, but for the sake of the subsequent return. A religious experience must not be left as a memory; it must remain active in animating the whole of his life. Like Rabbi Akiva, he must enter and come out "in peace," that is, bringing G-d and the world closer together in harmony.

5. THE BLESSING OF G-D

This connection between the manner of entering and of leaving the realm of holiness, applies not only to the service of the Jew, but also to the material world itself. For all the Jew's needs, material as well as spiritual, come to him directly from G-d: "If you walk in My statutes and keep My commandments and do them, then *I* will give you rain in due season, and the

---

12. *Vayikra* 16:6. Cf. beg. *Yoma.*
13. *Yoma,* 53b.
14. *Zohar,* Part III, 53b.
15. Cf. *Rosh Hashanah,* 18a.

land shall yield her produce. . . ."[16] Only through his bond with
G-d does the Jew receive his material needs. He who says "It
will be well with me for I will walk in the stubbornness of my
heart" is always in the last analysis proved mistaken.[17]

And this is intimated in our Sidra, describing the procedure
of the High Priest's service. It was only after he had entered the
Holy of Holies that he was able to pray for and secure the sustenance of the people.

So it is that the public world that the Jew inhabits, and the
private world of his religious experience, are intrinsically related. For if he draws his experience into the world, the world
is thereby sanctified by man and blessed by G-d.

(Source: Likkutei Sichot, Vol. III pp. 987-993)

---

16. *Vayikra* 26:3-4.
17. *Cf. Kuntres Uma'ayon, Maamar* 10.

פרשת קדושים

KEDOSHIM

In the famous 19th chapter of Vayikra, which is a summary of many essential principles of the Torah, the laws about fruit-trees are stated. The produce of the first three years of the tree's life *(orlah) is* forbidden. The fourth year produce *(neta revai) is* set aside as holy, and is to be eaten in Jerusalem or redeemed. But the fruit of the fifth year may be eaten ordinarily, and the Torah tells us that it will be particularly prolific, as a reward for observing the law for the previous four years. The Sicha begins with a problem: If the fifth year's fruit is the reward and purpose of the laws, why is it the *fourth* year fruit which is called "holy, for giving praise to the L-rd?" It resolves this by drawing an analogy between the five years of fruit and the five levels of spirituality, and by showing that there is a level beyond even that of holiness. This is a fundamental emphasis of Chassidut: That beyond holiness, which implies withdrawal from the world, is a domain of unity with G-d in the very midst of a world-affirming life.

1. THE FRUIT OF THE FIFTH YEAR

"And in the fifth year you may eat its fruit, that it may yield more richly to you its increase: I am the L-rd your G-d."[1]

This verse refers to the reward for not eating the produce of fruit-trees for the first three years, and for bringing fourth-year fruit to be eaten in Jerusalem. The phrase which the Torah uses, "that it may yield more richly to you its increase," indicates that the *purpose* of the commandments about the first four years' fruit is so that the fifth year should see a particularly prolific crop.

Rashi offers a straightforward explanation, quoting the Midrash: "Rabbi Akiva used to say, the Torah says this because it has man's evil inclination in mind: That one should not say,

---

1. *Vayikra* 19:25.

197

'Behold, for four years I must take trouble with it for nothing.' The Torah therefore states that (because of your obedience) the land will give you produce in larger quantities."

We can, however, understand the passage at a deeper level. The five years of fruit correspond to the five "universes" or dimensions of spirituality.[2] The first three, which are forbidden for consumption, stand for the three lower levels (asiyah, yetzirah and beriah, or the dimensions of "action," "formation" and "Creation"), where there is a sufficient concealment of G-d for the possibility of sin, division and forbidden action to exist. The fourth year stands for the dimension of atzilut ("emanation") where everything is in a state of holiness, and nothing is separated from G-d.[3] Therefore its fruit is called "holy, for giving praise to the L-rd." But the fifth is the highest level, called keter, the "Crown." The fruit of the fifth year is correspondingly the most precious, as we saw when we understood that the whole purpose of the commandments of the first four years was for the sake of the fifth.

Why then do we find the fruit of the *fourth* year called "holy?" Why is it to be eaten only in Jerusalem, and only by a person who is not ritually unclean? Why do none of these things apply to the fifth-year produce, which may be eaten anywhere by anyone?

2. THE BAAL SHEM TOV AND THE SAGE

To understand this, we must begin with a story told about the Baal Shem Tov.[4]

It was at a time when he had not yet emerged publicly as the leader of the Chassidic movement. He still wore the cloak of anonymity as he traveled through the towns and villages of the Carpathians. It was one of his holy practices to ask every Jew he met—man and woman, the aged and the children—how they were, how business was, and so on. One of his great-

---

2. *Likkutei Torah, Kedoshim,* 30d.
3. Cf. *Philosophy of Chabad,* p. 82, and footnote 30.
4. *Sefer Hamaamarim-Yiddish,* p. 138 ff.

est pleasures was to listen to the answers that each of them would give—answers that came from the heart. For they would reply with words of praise and thanks to G-d. Every answer would contain a "Thank G-d" or a "The L-rd be blessed."

Once he reached a small township and began in his normal way to inquire after the welfare of the Jews he met, to get them to say words of praise and gratitude to G-d, to demonstrate their faith and merit. In the town there was a very old man, a great scholar, who lived in isolation from the affairs of the world. For more than fifty years he had sat and studied Torah day and night, detached and holy. He would sit and learn every day, wrapped in his Tallit and Tefillin until the afternoon service, and would not eat anything all day, until he had said the evening prayers, when he would have a little bread and water.

When the Baal Shem Tov entered his study, a room in one of the corners of the synagogue, he asked the old man about his health and his welfare, but the man did not look up at the Baal Shem Tov, who was dressed in the clothes of a peasant. He repeated his question several times, until the sage became angry and gestured that he should leave the room. The Baal Shem Tov said: "Rabbi, why (as it were) do you not give G-d his livelihood?"[5] When he heard this, the old man was completely confused. A peasant was standing in front of him and talking about G-d and the need to provide Him with a living!

The Baal Shem Tov read his thoughts and said: The Jewish people is sustained by the livelihood which G-d provides for them. But what sustains G-d, that he may continue, as it were, to "inhabit" the world? This is what King David meant when he wrote in Psalm 22, "You are Holy, who inhabits the praises of Israel." "You"—that is, the Master of the Universe, "are Holy"—that is, You are apart from the world. What then is Your livelihood, that you are able to "inhabit" it? It is "the praises of Israel." He is sustained by the praise and the gratitude

---

5. Cf. Ibid., ch. 2, explaining *Shir Hashirim Rabbah*, 1:9.

to which the Jews give voice, for their health and their sustenance with which He provides them. And because of these
praises, He gives them children, health and food, in plenty.

3. THE DWELLING-PLACE

The Baal Shem Tov's remark is not easy to understand. It
is true that the G-d of whom we say "You are Holy" (that is
transcending the world) is brought to "inhabit" the world only
by the service of the Jewish people. But surely learning Torah
is part of that service? Surely it brings the presence of G-d into
the world? And, the old sage had studied Torah day and night
for more than fifty years. Even at the very moment when the
Baal Shem Tov spoke to him, he was preoccupied with study!
How, then, could he have said: "Why (as it were) do you not
give G-d His livelihood?" And even if it is the "praises of Israel" and not the sound of their studies that causes G-d to
"inhabit" the world, the Baal Shem Tov could surely have tried
to elicit words of thanksgiving from the sage for being allowed
by G-d to study in serenity and seclusion. Why did he need to
ask him about matters of physical concern, like his health?

The answer is that the whole purpose of creation was to
make for G-d a "dwelling-place in the lower world."[6] *This*
world was to be transformed into a habitation for G-d.

How is this dwelling-place built? Not, primarily, through
learning or through thanks to G-d for the opportunity to learn.
Study involves the "G-dly soul" of the Jew, the highest part of
his nature. But thanksgiving for food, for money, for health—
these involve a sanctification of the body, of natural desires and
physical needs. When a Jew recognizes even these as the gift of
G-d then he has truly admitted G-d into the "lower world."[7]

That is why when the Baal Shem Tov saw the sage, sitting
in seclusion, disengaged from the world, unconcerned with the
state of his body, eating only to survive, not to sanctify the
physical, he said: "Why (as it were) do you not give G-d His

---

6. *Tanchuma, Nasso*, ch. 16.
7. Cf. *Tanya*, Part I, ch. 37.

livelihood?" For the Divine intention was to have a dwelling-place precisely in the *lower* world that the sage had forsaken. And this is why he said that G-d is made to "inhabit" the world "by the praise and the gratitude to which the Jews give voice, *for their health and their sustenance* with which He provides them." This justified his interrupting him even in the middle of learning, which is the greatest of the commandments.[8] For without this praise, his learning was defective. For, "Anyone who says, I have nothing but (the study of) Torah, even Torah is denied to him."[9]

4. FRUIT AND THANKSGIVING

In the light of this story we can see why the most precious fruit is not that of the fourth year—even though it is called "holy" (that is, set aside, withdrawn) and it is to be eaten only within the walls of Jerusalem; and why it is the fifth year fruit, which could be eaten anywhere by anyone.

When a Jew recognizes that even fruit which is not "holy" depends on the blessing of G-d; when he sees with his own eyes that the land "yields more richly its increase" because of G-d; and when he offers praises for these things, then he brings the "You," the essence of G-d, which is "holy" and beyond all finitude, to "inhabit" the world as His dwelling-place, thus bringing the entire creation to its true fulfillment.

(Source: Likkutei Sichot, Vol. VII pp. 134-138)

---

8. *Shulchan Aruch Harav, Hilchot Talmud Torah,* 4:3.

9. *Yevamot,* 109b.

פרשת אמור

EMOR

An historic controversy arose between the Rabbis and sectarians as to the meaning of the command of counting the Omer: "And you shall count unto you from the morrow after the Shabbat." The Rabbis understood Shabbat to mean Pesach (i.e., "the day of rest"). The sectarians took it to mean, literally, the seventh day, and so they always began their counting on a Sunday. Although the Rabbis proved their case, why did the Torah use a word so open to misinterpretation? In answering this question, the Sicha branches out into a detailed study of the three stages from the Exodus from Egypt to the Giving of the Torah on Sinai, both as they occurred historically and as they recur daily in the life of the individual.

1. THE DAY AFTER

In Emor, the commandment of counting the Omer is stated:[1] "And you shall count unto you from the morrow after the day of rest *('Shabbat'),* from the day that you brought the sheaf *('Omer')* of the waving; there shall be seven complete weeks." The Talmud[2] tells us that the sect of the Boethusians interpreted the word Shabbat to mean the seventh day, rather than the "day of rest" of Pesach. As a consequence they held that the counting of the Omer always begins on a Sunday. There was considerable debate, during which the Rabbis brought many scriptural proofs to establish that the Boethusian interpretation was false. But a persistent question remains: Why did the Torah leave room for this error, instead of stating explicitly, "on the day after the Pesach?"

---

1. *Vayikra* 23:15.
2. *Menachot,* 65a.

2. THREE MONTHS

In the Sidra of Shemot,[3] G-d tells Moses, "When you have brought the people out of Egypt, you shall serve G-d upon this mountain." In other words, the purpose of the Exodus from Egypt lay in the Giving of the Torah. Between these two events, the Exodus and the Revelation on Sinai came the seven weeks of the Omer. These seven weeks were the necessary transition between the start and the completion of redemption.

Three months were involved in this process:

Nissan, in which the Exodus took place; Iyar, which is wholly taken up with the counting of the Omer; and Sivan, in which the Torah was given. Only these three are explicitly mentioned in the context of the redemption. Of Nissan it is written:[4] "the month of Spring,... in it you came out of Egypt." Of Iyar we find,[5] "the second month ... after they had come out of the land of Egypt." And of Sivan,[6] "In the third month after the Children of Israel were gone forth out of the land of Egypt." All three are mentioned because each was an integral part of the redemption.

3. THREE KINDS OF FOOD

Of these three, Pesach is linked to the eating of Matzah. The Omer was a measure of barley.[7] And Shavuot has a special offering of two loaves, of fine flour baked with leaven.[8]

This presents a number of difficulties.

Only two meal offerings did not consist of wheat: The Omer, and the offering of a wife suspected of infidelity. Both of these were of barley. In the latter case the Talmud[9] gives a

---

3. 3:12.
4. *Shemot* 23:15.
5. *Bamidbar* 1:1; and cf. *Zohar*, Part III, 117b.
6. *Shemot* 19:1.
7. *Sotah,* 14a.
8. *Vayikra* 23:17; *Menachot,* 54b.
9. *Sotah,* Ibid.

reason: Her offering was to be of animal food as a humiliation for her immorality. But why was the Omer of animal food?

On Pesach we are forbidden to eat leaven, because leaven symbolizes man's inclination to pride and self-esteem. As leaven raises the dough, so pride inflates a man to arrogance. But why, in that case, are we allowed to eat *leaven* the rest of the year, and indeed *obliged* (in the Temple) to do so on Shavuot.

4. "DRAW ME; WE WILL RUN AFTER YOU"

In the Song of Songs, there is a verse,[10] "Draw me, we will run after you; the king has brought me into his chambers." Each of these three phrases refers to one of the three stages of the departure from Egypt. "Draw me" is the Exodus. "We will run after you" is the counting of the Omer. "The king has brought me into his chambers" is the Giving of the Torah.

"Draw me" is passive—it refers to the Israelites being taken out by G-d. Also it is singular. Whereas "We will run after you" is both active and plural.

By the end of their enslavement, the Israelites were assimilated into the heathen ways of their captors. They were not deserving of redemption. They had to be seized and drawn out of their captivity by the initiative of G-d. Since they were not inwardly prepared for it, this unexpected revelation did not alter them inwardly.[11] They were taken hold of by G-d rather than by the promptings of their heart. And although their "G-dly soul" responded, their "animal soul" was unchanged. One part of their being received the revelation, but the other, the capacity for evil, remained. Indeed, this is why, as the Alter Rebbe explains,[12] the Israelites *fled* from Egypt. What they were running from was the evil within themselves.

So we can understand the phrase "Draw me." Firstly, when we take possession of an object by seizing hold of it, nothing is changed in the subject itself; it merely changes hands: In this

10. 1:4.
11. Cf. supra, p. 189.
12. *Tanya*, Part I, ch. 31.

case, from Israel's being in the hand of Pharaoh to their being in the hand of G-d. Israel in itself was unchanged.

Secondly, it was passive. The drawing out of Egypt was achieved by the hand of Heaven, not by any spontaneous act on the part of the Israelites.

Thirdly, it was singular. The revelation of this sudden intervention of G-d affected only one side of their being. Their spirit responded; their physical passions did not.

5. INTELLECT AND PASSION

For all this, the purpose of a revelation is that the spirit should change the physical nature of man as well. If man were meant to be pure spirit, he would not have needed a body.[13] The point of a religious life within the world is to bring *every* side of human nature into G-d's work: "'And you shall love the L-rd your G-d with all your heart'—this means, with *both* your inclinations."[14] This interplay not only elevates the physical side of man, but also his spiritual life, by adding to it the drive and energy of physical passion.[15] Man as an intellectual being is dispassionate: His emotions and desires are mitigated by the rational control he exercises over them. But animal energy, be it literally in an animal or in the instinctual drives of man, is unchecked, powerful. "There is much increase by the strength of an ox."[16] When the animal in man is no longer at war with his spirit, but is sublimated to it, all its passionate intensity is transferred to the life of holiness.

This is why the Omer was of barley, animal food. Because this was the labor of that period, to transform the "animal soul" of the Israelites, which had remained unaffected by the initial revelation in Egypt.

How is this done? By meditation. Meditation on the nature of G-d awakens love and fear. At first, when one knows that

---

13. *Tanya*, Part I, ch. 37.
14. *Devarim* 6:5; *Berachot,* 54a.
15. Cf. supra, pp. 155-6.
16. *Proverbs* 14:4.

rebellion, pride, animal obstinacy, is still a power within one-self, one must "flee" from it. This is the time of *suppression*. But once one has left the "Egypt" of temptation, there comes a time of meditation and *sublimation,* when the two sides of man no longer battle for possession, and when the spirit rules, and physical nature transfers its energy.

Thus Solomon wrote, "We will run after you." We will *run,* because our service is quickened by this new source of energy. We will run, because it is we, not G-d, who take the religious initiative. And "We," in the plural, because both sides of our nature are caught up in this effort of reaching out towards G-d, and each gives impetus to the other.

6. THE FINAL STAGE

There is still a further stage. At the Exodus, there was the Divine call. During the Omer, there was man's response. But at the Giving of the Torah, there was the final abnegation of man in the face of G-d. While, for forty-nine days, he was transforming himself, he was still a self, still using his powers and relying on himself. But at Sinai, in the face of G-d, "with every single word that went forth from the mouth of the Holy One, blessed be He, the souls of Israel departed."[17] They were empty: The only reality was G-d.

Thus it is that on Pesach we may not eat leaven. At the outset, when pride and fulfillness preserve their power, they must be suppressed, set aside. They cannot be combated rationally, for they can subvert the mind: "They are wise to do evil."[18]

At the stage of the Omer, we use our understanding to redirect our emotions. We use the leaven in ourselves to change ourselves.

And when, at the point of Shavuot, we reach the final openness of all our being to G-d, then we are *obliged* to use the

---

17. *Shabbat,* 88b.
18. *Jeremiah* 4:22.

leaven, making every part of our nature into a channel for the light of G-d.

7. EVERY DAY

The Rabbis said, "In every generation, and every day, a man is obliged to see himself as if he had gone out of Egypt that very day."[19] So each of the three stages of the exodus are components of the task of every day.

In the beginning of our prayers we say, "I give acknowledgment before you . . ." (the Modeh Ani prayer). This is the acknowledgment, the surrender to G-d, that precedes understanding. It is the Nissan of the day, the individual exodus.

There then follow the Psalms of Praise *(Pesukei Dezimrah)* and the *Shema* and its benedictions. These are the prayers of meditation, and understanding. "*Hear,* O Israel," the first phrase of the *Shema,* means "understand." And through this meditation, the emotions are awakened, and the love of G-d is aroused with "all your heart and all your soul and all your might." This is the daily equivalent of the month of Iyar and the counting of the Omer.

But, so far, this represents only the battle against half, the "animal" half, of one's nature *(bittul ha-yesh).* There still awaits the final extinction of self-consciousness *(bittul bi-metziut)* which comes during the *Amidah* prayer, when "like a slave before his master"[20] we have no self with which to speak. We are empty of words. We say, "O L-rd, open my lips." And this is the Sivan of the day, the moment when we confront—like the Israelites at Sinai—the all-possessing presence of G-d.

8. AFTER THE SHABBAT

Now, finally, we realize why the Torah, in the verse quoted at the outset, says, "On the morrow after the Shabbat" instead of ". . . after the Pesach."

---

19. *Pesachim,* 116b; *Tanya,* Part I, ch. 47.
20. *Shabbat,* 10a.

To achieve the transformation of the "animal soul" demands the deepest reserves of spiritual energy. To have brought the Israelites out of their entrenched impurity needed more than an "angel"—an emissary—it needed G-d himself in His Glory and Essence. If this was true of the escape from evil, it is more so for the *transformation* of evil into good. It would need a spiritual source able to enter into the heart of evil without being affected.

Shabbat is a source of intense spirituality. It is the apex of the week. But it still belongs to the week, and thus to time and the finite.[21] "The morrow after the Shabbat" refers to the step beyond Shabbat, beyond time itself: A revelation higher than the world.

To count the forty-nine days of Omer, that is, to transform into holiness every emotion that we feed, we must rest our efforts on the "morrow after the Shabbat"—the light of G-d from beyond the world.

(Source: Likkutei Sichot, Vol. I pp. 265-270)

---

21. Cf. Supra, p. 175.

פרשת בהר

BEHAR

In the Sidra of Behar, instructions are given about the observance of two special kinds of sanctified year—the seventh year (Shemittah or "release") when the land was rested and lay fallow; and the fiftieth year *(Yovel* or "Jubilee"*)* when the Hebrew slaves were emancipated and most property reverted to its original owner. The two institutions were connected, the Jubilee being the completion of seven seven-year cycles. It was not, itself, counted as a year in the seven-yearly reckoning. The Jubilee lapsed as a practical institution when some of the Tribes went into exile. But we can distinguish three periods in its history: (i) a time when the Jubilee was observed, (ii) a time during the second Temple when it was not observed but was still counted for the purpose of fixing the seven-year cycle, and (iii) a time (like the present) when neither Temple stood, and the seven-year cycle was counted without reference to the Jubilee. The Rebbe explores the spiritual meaning of the seventh and fiftieth years, and thus gives an inward interpretation to the three periods, and the religious consciousness they represent.

1. THE JUBILEE

"And you shall sanctify the fiftieth year and proclaim liberty throughout the land unto all the inhabitants thereof; it shall be a Jubilee unto you; and you shall return every man unto his possession, and you shall return every man unto his family."[1]

In this connection, the Talmud states: "When the tribes of Reuben and Gad and the half-tribe of Menasseh went into exile, the Jubilees were abolished, as it is said, 'And you shall proclaim liberty throughout the land unto *all* the inhabitants thereof,—that is (only) at the time when all its inhabitants

---

1. *Vayikra* 25:10.

209

dwell upon it, but not at the time when some of them are exiled."[2]

Despite the fact that the Jubilee—as a time of emancipation of slaves and restitution of property—lapsed, the (Babylonian) Talmud notes that even during the period of the second Temple, "They counted the *Jubilees* to keep the years of *release* holy."[3] Every seventh year was a year of release *("Shemittah")*, a sabbatical year for the land when it was "released" from cultivation and lay fallow. In this cycle, according to the Rabbis,[4] the fiftieth year was not counted, so that they had to continue counting the Jubilees in order to be able to observe the Shemittah years of release in their proper time: To ensure that release was observed in the seventh year after the Jubilee rather than after the forty-ninth year.

Tosefot[5] raises an objection: The Jerusalem Talmud states, "At a time when the Jubilee is not observed as a year of release, neither do you observe the seventh year as a release."[6] If so, during the second Temple period, when the Jubilee was not observed, merely counted, it should follow that the seven-year release of Shemittah should also have lapsed.

Rashi's opinion[7] is that the seventh year was observed during the Second Temple, only as a Rabbinic law. In other words, the Jerusalem and Babylonian Talmuds are not in disagreement, the Jerusalem Talmud asserting that the sabbatical year was not (while the Jubilee was in abeyance) a requirement of *Torah* law, the Babylonian Talmud mentioning that it was nonetheless continued, by *Rabbinic* decree.

But according to Tosefot, the two Talmuds conflict, the Babylonian asserting that the seventh year was obligatory *under*

2. *Arachin,* 32b; *Rambam, Hilchot Shemittah Veyovel,* 10:8.
3. *Arachin, ibid; Rambam,* Ibid. 3.
4. *Arachin,* 33a.
5. *Arachin,* Ibid.
6. *Sheviit,* 1:2; *Gittin,* 4:3.
7. *Gittin,* 36a.

Torah law, independently of the Jubilee, in disagreement with the Jerusalem Talmud.

2. THE SPIRIT AND THE LAW

The legal decisions of the early Rabbis, the *Tannaim* and the *Amoraim,* were not made merely as a result of a this-worldly reasoning.[8] They were men of great spiritual insight, who saw matters in a spiritual light and then translated their vision into intellectual and legal terms. Since their souls differed in the visionary heights they were able to reach, so also their practical decisions differed, and this was the source of their legal disagreements.[9]

Seen in this way, we might say that the disagreement (according to Tosefot) between the Jerusalem and Babylonian Talmuds as to whether the Shemittah year of release was required by Torah law during the second Temple period, has its origin in the different levels of spirituality these two works represent.

The Babylonian is the lower level. " 'He hath made me to dwell in dark places'—this, said Rabbi Jeremiah, refers to the Babylonian Talmud."[10]

At the higher level of the Jerusalem Talmud, it required the sanctity of the Jubilee to complete the sanctity of the Shemittah year. At the lower, Babylonian, level, the seventh year was complete in itself even without the Jubilee.

3. THE LAPSING OF THE JUBILEE

When the Second Temple was destroyed, the year of release was counted in a new way.

While the Temple stood, the fiftieth year was not counted as part of the seven-year cycle. But "during those seventy years between the destruction of the First Temple and the building of the Second, and also after the destruction of the Second,

---

8. Cf. *Biurei HaZohar, Vayishlach,* 20b.
9. Cf. Introduction to , Part I. *Zohar,* Part III, 245a.
10. *Sanhedrin,* 24a.

they did not count the Jubilee year, but only (unbroken) seven-year cycles."[11]

Why, then, is there a difference between the way we count the year of release now, and in the Second Temple, when the Jubilee had ceased to be observed?

Using our previous concept, we might say that while the Temple existed, the level of spirituality was so high that the Shemittah year of release needed the higher sanctity of the Jubilee for its completion—at one period, the actual *observance* of the Jubilee at another, at least the *counting* of it. But when the Temple was destroyed, spiritual achievement sank to the point where the year of release no longer had any connection with the Jubilee.

4. THE INNER MEANING OF THE SEVENTH AND FIFTIETH YEARS

To understand all this, we must discover the equivalents of the seventh and fiftieth years in the religious life of man.

The seventh year, the time of release, represents the "acceptance of the yoke of the kingdom of heaven."[12] This is when man suppresses his ego in obedience to G-d *(bittul ha-yesh).*[13] His ego still exists, and continually needs to be silenced. That is why, as every seventh year approached, its claim would be heard: "What shall we eat on the seventh year? Behold, we may not sow, nor gather in our increase."[14] Even though on each previous occasion it had seen for itself the fulfillment of G-d's promise, "I will command My blessing upon you in the sixth year, and it shall bring forth produce for the three years,"[15] it always renewed its anxieties.

The Jubilee, on the other hand, represents the complete abnegation of one's being to G-d *(bittul bi-metziut).* There is no

---

11. *Rambam*, Ibid., 5.
12. Cf. *Taamei Hamitzvot Lehaarizal, Behar;* quoted in *Derech Mitzvotecha,* 35b.
13. Cf. *Likkutei Torah,* Behar, 42d.
14. *Vayikra* 25:20.
15. Ibid., 21.

longer a contending ego. Instead of serving G-d through an effort of willpower, one serves through understanding, an understanding so complete that it breaks through the curtain of self-deception that separates man from G-d. It is the "year of freedom," meaning, freedom from concealment and from the ego that holds man in its chains.

5. TWO KINDS OF OBEDIENCE

Each of these levels has a certain merit vis-à-vis the other.[16] *Bittul bi-metziut,* or the obedience that comes from understanding, has the advantage of being *extensive.* It encompasses the whole man in its orientation towards G-d.

Bittul ha-yesh, or the obedience that comes from an effort of will, has the advantage of being *intensive.* It is an intense spiritual struggle within the soul of man.

To give an analogy: There are two kinds of relationship between a servant and his master. There is the "simple" servant, whose real desire is to be free, but who serves because he accepts the burden of his situation. And there is the "faithful" servant, who serves his master out of love and a genuine desire to obey. Whereas the obedience of the latter is more complete, since his whole nature affirms his service, the obedience of the former is more intense because it is a result of a deliberate subjugation of part of his character. It cost him more in terms of inward effort.

6. THE THREE AGES

We can now see the full significance of the three periods in Jewish history with respect to the Jubilee and the year of release.

When the first Temple stood, both were observed, that is, Jewish spirituality combined obedience through love and understanding with obedience through effort and subjugation. Love lay even in their *subjugation;* their effort was also with un-

---

16. Cf., for more extensive treatment of the theme, *Likkutei Sichot,* Vol. IX, pp. 72 ff.

derstanding. The love which transcends the self returned to fill the self.

At the time of the Second Temple, the Jubilee was no longer observed but it was still counted. Love and understanding still counted, still left their traces, in the service of effort and will.

But when the Second Temple was destroyed, all that was left was the year of release, the intense struggle to conquer the ego, and obey for obedience's sake. No trace of the Jubilee, of inward unanimity, remained.

7. A DISAGREEMENT EXPLAINED

So now we no longer see the things of the spirit with the clear light of understanding. We are forced to act against our reason, in a gesture of reluctant obedience. True inwardness is beyond us. And yet, the ultimate inwardness never departs. The essence of the soul is always present. In the current spiritual darkness of exile, it still works its subconscious, subliminal influence.

And this is the ultimate source of the disagreement between the Jerusalem and Babylonian Talmuds as to whether the year of release is a matter of Torah or of Rabbinic Law in our time; that is to say, whether it still exists in its own right, or merely as a Rabbinic remembrance of times past,[17] when the Jubilee was celebrated.

To the Babylonian Talmud, the product of exile, the observance of the seventh year and its corresponding service of "acceptance of the yoke of the kingdom of Heaven" seemed like an act in itself, with no connection to that higher state of the Jubilee and the service which came through love and understanding.

The Jerusalem Talmud, with its higher spiritual awareness, still felt the Jubilee and its service as a continuing, if subliminal, presence. So they saw the year of release as still connected with,

---

17. *Gittin*, 36b.

and observed in remembrance of, the time when it belonged together with the Jubilee, when the first Temple stood.

Similarly, it is also a preparation for the time when that former state will return, with the building of the third Temple, when the Messiah comes.

(Source: Likkutei Sichot, Vol. VII pp. 170-174)

פרשת בחוקותי

BECHUKOTAI

The Sidra of Bechukotai begins with the words, "If you walk in My statutes," and the Sicha is in effect a profound commentary—almost a meditation—on this single phrase. It explores two central themes: The nature of Torah learning, and the relationship between faith and understanding.

1. "MY STATUTES"

Our Sidra begins with the phrase, "If you walk in My statutes,"[1] and the Sifra comments, "One might think that this denotes the fulfillment of the commandments; but when the Torah goes on to state, 'and you shall keep My commandments and do them' it is plain that in *this* passage the fulfillment of the commandments is mentioned. How then must I explain 'If you walk in My statutes?' (It means) that you should labor in the study of the Torah."

If "you walk in My statutes" referred to the commandments, we could understand why only statutes *(chukim)* were mentioned, without referring to the other kinds of command, testimonies *(edut)* and judgments *(mishpatim)*. The reason would then be that these other commands, which have a rational explanation, should be performed with the same unconditional acceptance as statutes, which are beyond our understanding.[2]

But since we must understand the phrase as referring to the study of the Torah, why is the word "statutes" used at all? The study of Torah is, for the most part, an act of intellect and understanding. The *labor* involved is not merely to learn, by rote,

---

1. *Vayikra* 26:3.
2. Cf. supra, p.117.

the details of the law, but also to understand their reasons, as explained in the Written and Oral Torah.

But, although statutes are beyond our understanding—as Rashi says,[3] "It is an enactment from before Me; you have no right to speculate about it"—they form only a small part of Torah, the majority of which is susceptible to explanation.

The Written Torah itself is small in comparison with the vast mass of oral tradition. And with the Written Torah, understanding is not crucial, so that a man must make the blessing of studying or being called to the reading of the Torah even if he does not understand what is being read. Whereas the Oral Torah does require comprehension if one is to make a blessing over it.[4]

The quantitative difference between the Written and Oral Torah is further emphasized by the fact that the Written Torah consists of a specified number of words and verses. There can be no additions. But the Oral Torah is open-ended. A finite quantity has already been revealed. But new discoveries are always possible—"whatever a worthy pupil will come in the future to discover."[5] To it, there are no limits.

Similarly, within the Written Torah itself, the "statutes"— laws for which no reason has been communicated to us—form a minority of the commandments.

So the question becomes more forcible: Why in the context of the study of the Torah, are only statutes mentioned? Why cite a minority instance to cover the whole of the Torah? And why, in an activity of understanding, cite precisely those cases which cannot be understood?

---

3. *Bamidbar* 19:2.
4. *Shulchan Aruch Harav, Hilchot Talmud Torah,* end ch. 2; *Likkutei Torah, Vayikra, Biur Velo Tashbit.*
5. Cf. *Jerusalem Talmud, Pe'ah,* 2:4; *Shemot Rabbah,* beg. ch. 47; *Vayikra Rabbah,* beg. ch. 22; *Tanya,* Part V, *Ulehavin Peratei...*

2. LEARNING AND ENGRAVING

In Likkutei Torah, the Alter Rebbe explains that the word "statute" *(chok)* is related to the word "engrave" or "carve out" *(chakikah)*. Thus the phrase in question uses the word "statute" to suggest that study must be an act of "carving out," engraving the words of Torah on the soul.

What is special about engraving as a means of writing?

Firstly, the words are not added, as something extraneous, to the material on which they are written. Rather, they become an integral part of the material itself.

Secondly, and more importantly, the letters have no substance of their own. Their whole existence is in virtue of the material out of which they are carved.

So, when we are told by our verse that our learning should be "engraved" in us, we are not simply being taught that a Jew must become united with the Torah (unlike the superficial learning exemplified by Doeg, of which the Rabbis comment[6] that it "was only from the surface outward"). For unity can sometimes come about by the joining of two separate things (as ordinary writing brings together ink and paper). And this, in learning, is not enough. Instead it must be "engraved," meaning that the person learning should have no substance, his ego should have no voice whatsoever. His whole being must be the Torah.

The great example is Moses, the first recipient of the Torah. So complete was his selflessness that he could say, *"I will give grass in your field."*[7] "The Divine Presence spoke through his throat."[8] He was a void filled by G-d.

The same is true of Rabbi Shimon ben Yochai, who said: "I have seen superior men and they are but few. If there be a thousand, I and my son are among them. If there be a hundred, I and my son are among them. If only two, they are I and my

---

6. *Sanhedrin,* 106b.

7. *Devarim* 11:15; *Likkutei Torah, Bechukotai,* 50a.

8. Cf. *Zohar,* Part III, 232a; Ibid., 7a; 265a; *Shemot Rabbah,* 3:15; *Vayikra Rabbah,* 2:3; *Mechilta, Shemot* 18:19.

son. If only one, it is I."[9] These are words of self-praise; and self-praise is not the way of the righteous. He could say them only because he was so selfless, so filled with G-d, that it was as if he were speaking about someone else.

3. THE EXPLANATIONS RELATED

All explanations in the Torah have an inner unity.[10] And the interpretation of "statutes" as "engraving" complements, rather than conflicts with, its literal sense, as laws which are beyond our understanding.

To learn Torah as if it were composed entirely of statutes is to study in a state of unconditional commitment. This does not rule out the pursuit of understanding. Indeed, the point is to understand. But only if this is accompanied by commitment. Not "I will do when I understand"; nor "I will understand because I enjoy the search for knowledge"; but "I will do, and because I am commanded, I will try to understand." This is true "labor," meaning an effort undertaken beyond the promptings of pleasure.

When learning is of this order, then it becomes "engraved." The person learning, and the Torah which is learned, become literally one thing.

4. "GOING"

This explains one part of the phrase "If you walk in My statutes." But what of the word "walk?" "Walking" or "going" (halicha) suggests a number of levels, and a progression from one level to the next. For example, in the emotional life, one "goes" or ascends from the lower to the higher form of love. But surely in absolute commitment, there are no levels. It seems like a state, rather than a process.

The Alter Rebbe writes that "going" relates not to a man's task but to his reward. If one's service is, in both senses, "in My

---

9. *Sukkah*, 45b; *Sanhedrin*, 97b.
10. Cf. supra, p. 30.

statutes," then the reward is "you shall go"—always higher. And true "going" is without limits.

5. FAITH AND UNDERSTANDING

However, the simple reading of the verse takes the whole phrase "if you walk in My statutes" as man's task, and understands the reward as beginning in the next verse, "Then I will give your rains in their seasons."

It is written in Likkutei Torah[11] that the principal element in faith lies in those levels of G-dliness which are beyond the scope of comprehension. What can be, must be understood. Faith begins where understanding ends.

This is the distinctive quality of Jewish faith. It is a faith beyond, not because of, understanding.

Now, intellect has its levels: "Days shall speak, and the multitude of years shall teach wisdom."[12] And as one comprehends more, so one raises the threshold of faith. Yesterday's faith becomes today's understanding.

This is why "statutes," too, have their levels. What was incomprehensible yesterday—a statute—is understood today and ceases to be a statute. So, for example, G-d said to Moses, "I will reveal to you the reason behind the Red Heifer."[13] The Red Heifer is for us a statute. For Moses it was not, from that point onwards. It was not that Moses lacked the notion of "statute," but that for him the threshold of incomprehensibility lay higher than for us.

This is the meaning of "If you walk in My statutes." By "laboring" in the Torah, by straining to the limit, one daily raises one's understanding, and thus one raises the stage at which a law is a "statute." This is the "going": The progression to an ever-higher faith through ever-higher understanding.

And the reward is then, "I will give your rains in their season . . . *and make you go upright*" which is the unlimited "going,

---

11. *Vaetchanan,* 4a ff; *Derech Mitzvotecha,* 45a ff.
12. *Job* 32:7.
13. *Bamidbar Rabbah,* 19:6.

from strength to strength" of the future revelation, and which leads, in turn, to what lies beyond the "going"—"to the day which is wholly Shabbat and rest for life everlasting."[14]

(Source: Likkutei Sichot, Vol. III pp. 1012-1015)

14. *Talmud,* end of *Tamid.*

פרשת במדבר

BAMIDBAR

Our Sidra opens with G-d's command that a census be taken of the Israelites. In fact there were three such counts taken in the first thirteen months following the Exodus from Egypt. What is the spiritual significance of the counting ordained by G-d? Why were there three censuses in such close proximity and what was the difference between them? And what is the connection between this and Shavuot, which always falls close to the reading of Bamidbar? These questions form the theme of the Sicha.

1. BAMIDBAR AND SHAVUOT

The Sidra of Bamidbar has a particular relevance to the festival of Shavuot. In general, every Sidra has a connection with the time of the year when it is read,[1] and Bamidbar is usually read on the Shabbat before Shavuot.[2] And in particular, Shavuot, which commemorates G-d's giving of the Torah to Israel, is called the *wedding* of Israel to G-d;[3] and on the Shabbat before a wedding, the bridegroom is called to the Torah as a preparation for the wedding. So Bamidbar is, as it were, a preparation for that special union between G-d and his people which came upon their receiving the Torah.

We can find this connection in the opening words of the Sidra, where G-d commands, "Count the number of all the congregation of the Children of Israel." The connection is hidden until we understand the true nature of the act of counting.

2. COUNTING

Rashi makes the following comment on the command: "Because they (the Children of Israel) are dear to Him, He

---

1. *Shaloh, Torah Shebiktav,* beg. of *Vayeshev.*
2. *Tosefot, Megillah,* 31b, *Kellalot.*
3. *Taanit,* 26b.

counts them all the time: When they went forth from Egypt He counted them; when they fell because of (the sin of) the Golden Calf, He counted them; when He was about to make His Presence dwell amongst them (i.e., in the Tabernacle) He counted them. For on the first of Nissan the Tabernacle was erected, and on the first of Iyar (the next month) He counted them."

At first sight, this comment raises three problems:

(1) when one has things that are dear to one, one often takes them out to count them, to become, as it were, re-acquainted with them. But G-d knows the number of the Children of Israel without having to order a census. Why, then, did He command this public counting?

(2) why was there a *delay* of one month between the third census and the event with which it was connected (the erection of the Tabernacle)?

(3) why was there a difference between these three countings? Torah does not tell us by whom the first (on the departure from Egypt) was undertaken. The second was done by Moses.[4] But the third was commanded to both Moses and Aaron.[5] Why was Aaron involved in this and not the others?

3. COUNTING AS A GESTURE OF LOVE

Let us try and understand what was involved in the census. When things are counted, they stand in a relation of *equality;* the greatest man and the least are each counted once; no more, no less. And since, as Rashi tells us, the census was a token of G-d's *love,* it must have been a gesture towards that which in every Jew is equal. Not his intellect, not his moral standing, but his *essence*: His Jewish soul. Now this is something which we can not usually observe. So the *point* of the census was to bring the soul of each Jew into prominence, at the surface of awareness.

---

4. *Shemot* 30:11 ff. (cf. *Rashi*, ad loc. 16).
5. *Bamidbar* 1:3.

Now we can solve one of the difficulties in Rashi: He writes that G-d counts his people *all the time;* and yet, as Rashi himself points out, they were counted only three times in the first year and one month after leaving Egypt; and then only once more (38 years later) during their wanderings in the wilderness; and subsequently only at very infrequent intervals (according to a Midrash,[6] only a total of nine times until today, and the tenth time will be when the Messiah comes). One could interpret Rashi to mean, "at *special* times"; and yet he uses the emphatic phrase "all the time," the implication of which cannot be escaped. But now we are in a position to understand, that if the point of the counting was to reveal the essence of each Jewish soul, then this revelation has a depth which places it beyond the erosions of time—it is operative, literally, *all the time.*

4. TIME AND THE JEW

When, in times of religious persecution, a Jew is coerced into idolatry, (and similarly with any transgression, which results from the coercion of one's evil inclination,[7]) there is a line of thought open to him. He might think, since repentance erases all sins ("Nothing stands in the face of repentance"); and since his betrayal of Judaism is only for a short time; and since the path of repentance will always be open to him; why worry about this one act?

And yet we find in all ages, and amongst all manner of men, Jews have been willing to sacrifice their lives rather than betray their faith, *even for one moment,* without stopping to make this kind of calculation. Why? Because the relation between G-d and the Jewish soul is *beyond time:*[8] to disrupt it for one moment is no less grave than to disrupt it for an age.

This is the meaning of "He counts them all the time": The love which expressed itself in counting is deeper than the vi-

---

6. *Tanchuma, Ki Tissa,* 9; *Bamidbar Rabbah,* 2:11; *Pesikta de Rav Kahana, Parshat Shekalim.*
7. Cf. *Rambam, Hilchot Gerushin,* end of ch. 2.
8. *Tanya,* Part I, ch. 25.

cissitudes of time and calculation. It reveals that innermost point of the spirit of the Jew, which *at every moment* is ready for self-sacrifice. And this consequence, this heritage of the act of counting defines the Jew "all the time."

5. THE THREE COUNTINGS

Now we can understand the difference between the three countings which Rashi mentions: They were evolutionary stages in a process of revelation. In the first, the Jewish soul was awakened by the love of G-d; in the second, it began to work its influence on the outward life of the Israelites; and in the third, it finally suffused all their actions.

The first census was on the Israelites' departure from Egypt, and it aroused their spirit of self-sacrifice to the extent that they were willing to follow G-d into an unsown and barren wilderness.[9] But it left their emotions untouched.[10]

The second was prior to the building of the Tabernacle. It reached further outward to the intellect and emotions of the Israelites, because they were preparing themselves for the work that was to bring the Shechinah—G-d's Presence—into their very midst ("And they shall build Me a Sanctuary, and I will dwell *in them*"). But still the impetus came from outside: It was G-d's command that set them to their work, not any inner compunction.

But with the third census came the actual service of the Tabernacle, when the Israelites, by their *own* actions, brought G-d into their midst. Then all their actions were a testimony to the union of the Jewish soul with G-d.

It now becomes clear why there had to be a delay of one month between the completion of the Tabernacle (in Nissan) and the third census (in Iyar). For Nissan is the month of Pesach, the time when we acknowledge the revelation that comes from above—it was not the merit of the Israelites that caused G-d to take them out of Egypt, but G-d's mercy and kindness

---

9. *Jeremiah* 2:2.
10. Cf. *Tanya*, Part I, ch. 31.

alone.[11] But Iyar is the month of the Omer, the time of special sacrifices; and by sacrifice we bring about the "revelation that comes from below," that answers to our merit and not merely to G-d's grace.

A parallel explanation leads us to understand why Aaron was involved in this and only this census. For Moses was the communicator of G-d's revelation—a channel from above to below. But Aaron the priest was he who elevated the people of Israel from below to above.[12]

And at this third census Israel finally reached the state where their *own* actions were permeated with the soul's awareness. Now and only now could they bring about the "revelation that comes from below."

In this way, the connection between Bamidbar and Shavuot becomes clear. When the Torah was given, Israel and G-d were united in such a way that G-d sent down His revelation from above; and the Children of Israel were themselves elevated. And we read, in preparation for our annual re-creation of the event, the Sidra which tells us of the third census; where the two modes of revelation, symbolized by Moses and Aaron, or by the month of Nissan (which occasioned the census) and the month of Iyar (when it was actually taken), are brought together. So that, by taking to heart the meaning of counting as a gesture of G-d's love for Israel, we can bring about that union which held at the Giving of the Torah, when G-d took His people Israel in marriage; so that through Torah[13] Israel becomes united with G-d.[14]

(Source: *Likkutei Sichot, Vol. VIII pp. 1-7*)

---

11. Cf. supra, p. 203; *Likkutei Torah, Bamidbar*, 3a.
12. *Zohar*, Part III, 20a; 53b.
13. *Likkutei Torah, Vayikra*, 5c (quoting *Zohar*, Part III, 73a).
14. *Zohar*, Part III, 93b.

שבועות

SHAVUOT

Shavuot is the day on which we recall the giving of the Torah on Sinai. The Torah itself does not explicitly mention the connection. It merely says, "You shall count fifty days (from the second day of Pesach) . . . and you shall proclaim on that selfsame day: It shall be a holy convocation unto you." Now although we know that the Torah was given on the 6th of Sivan, during the time when the calendar was fixed by eyewitnesses to the new moon, the fiftieth day—Shavuot—could fall on the 5th, 6th, or 7th of Sivan. Nonetheless, now that the calendar is no longer variable, Shavuot always coincides with the 6th. And there is also a Biblical allusion to the significance of Shavuot in the fact that unlike the other festivals, the word "sin" is not mentioned in connection with the special sacrifices for Shavuot, and this is related to the Israelites' acceptance of the Torah, which gave them the special merit of being forgiven their sins.

These two Sichot are therefore meditations on the significance of the event at Sinai. What revolution in man's spiritual possibilities was brought about by the Torah? What did that first Shavuot usher into the world that had never existed before?

The first Sicha takes as its starting-point the fact that Sivan was the *third* month of the Israelites' journey from Egypt to the Promised Land. Why was the Torah not given immediately? Is there any significance to the number three? Its theme is the different kinds of unity that a Jew can reach in his relationship with G-d.

1. THE THIRD MONTH

The giving of the Torah took place in the month of Sivan—the third month. Since this was clearly part of the Divine plan, there must be a significant connection between the event and the date, between Torah and the third month. The point is made explicitly in the Talmud:[1] "Blessed be the Merciful One who gave a threefold Torah to a threefold people

---

1. *Shabbat*, 88a.

227

through a third-born on the third day in the third month." The figure three is the constant motif. The Torah is in three parts: Pentateuch, Prophets and Hagiographa (Torah, Neviim, Ketubim). Israel consists of three kinds of Jew: Kohen, Levite and Israelite. Moses was born third, after Miriam and Aaron. The Torah was given in the third month, on the third day of the Israelites' separation from their wives.

Why, then, the figure three? Surely the Torah was intended to be unique and to reveal the oneness of G-d. The number one is what we would have expected.

To take the point further. The principal event of the third month was the giving of the *Torah* in itself. The command-ments, as such, were not an entirely new disclosure. There had been commandments before: The seven Noachide Laws, cir-cumcision, and the things that were commanded at Marah. Si-nai certainly changed the nature of a Mitzvah,[2] but the idea of a Mitzvah was not new. But the Torah was. And the difference between Torah and the commandments is this:[3] through a Mitzvah one becomes nullified in the face of G-d's will, as a "chariot to its rider." But through Torah we become *one* with G-d. The two things are not the same. A chariot has no will other than that of its rider, but chariot and rider are not one. The innovation at Sinai was radical—now the Jew could be-come at one with G-d. And if so we must ask again: Why is three, not one, its symbol?

2. TWO KINDS OF UNITY

The purpose of the giving of the Torah was indeed unity. But what is a true unity? When a person recognizes the One in the many, then he perceives unity in the midst of diversity. If he knows only one kind of existence, we do not know what his response will be when he discovers another kind. Perhaps he will then say: There are two realities, G-d and the world. It is only when he has encountered more than one form of exist-

---

2. Cf. *Rambam*, commentary on *Mishnah, Chullin*, end of ch. 7.
3. *Tanya*, Part I, ch. 23.

ence and still maintains that G-d is the only reality that he has seen the true Oneness of G-d.

There is a traditional analogy. If we want to know how close is the bond between a prince and his father, the king, we will not discover it in the palace but only by taking him from it and setting him amongst ordinary men. If he still behaves like a prince, he is a true son of his father.

So with a Jew, it is not within the Sanctuary but within the diversity of the world that his sense of G-d's unity is proved. And he can preserve it in two ways. He can suppress his awareness of other things besides G-d. Or he can be fully aware of other things of the world and *in them* discover G-d. It is the latter which is the deeper response. The person who suppresses his senses and closes his eyes to the ways of the world, believes that they form something apart from and in opposition to G-d, and must be kept at a distance. The unity of his religious life is neither deep nor secure.

3. THREE STAGES

There are, as we can see, three phases in the growth towards the sense of the unity of G-d. And they correspond to the three months from Pesach to Shavuot.[4]

Nissan is the month of the Exodus itself, when G-d was revealed to the Israelites. They "fled" from Egypt, both literally and metaphorically—fled from the knowledge of the world and were filled only with the revelation from above. Their unity was of the world-denying kind. G-d was One because they knew only one thing, because the world had ceased to have being in their eyes.

Iyar, the second month, is the month wholly taken up with the Counting of the Omer, and preparing ourselves for the coming events at Sinai. We are aware of ourselves and our world as something apart from G-d which had to be sup-

---

4. Cf. supra, p. 203.

pressed. Like the chariot and its rider, G-d and the world were one will but two things.

Sivan, the third month, was the time when the Torah was given, when G-d and the world became *one thing*. This was the moment of genuine unity, when what had seemed two things became a third, including and going beyond both.

4. THE HIGH AND THE LOW

This is why the Torah was given on the third month. For, through fulfilling a commandment we efface our own exist-ence, but we are not yet at one with G-d. The ultimate unity comes only through (learning) Torah, when the mind of man and the will of G-d interfuse.[5] The two become a third thing, a complete unity.

This is why Moses received the Torah at Sinai. The Rabbis said that Sinai was chosen because it was the lowest (i.e., the humblest) of the mountains. But if lowness was the sought-for virtue, why was the Torah not revealed on a plane or a valley? Because Sinai represented the fusion of two opposites, the high and the low, G-d and man. And this is the significance of the Torah.

(Source: Likkutei Sichot, Vol. II pp. 301-303)

---

5. *Tanya*, Part I, ch. 5.

Besides the revelation in the wilderness, there are two other events which occurred on Shavuot, at widely separated intervals of time, namely the deaths of two of the greatest figures in history. This serves as a reminder to us that revelation was not just a moment but a continuing process; that new faces of the infinitely meaningful Torah have always been revealed at the critical moments of our religious development; and that Sinai posed an immense challenge to the Jewish people to which we continue to try to rise. These two figures stand at key points in the development of this response, and thus have a special relationship to Shavuot.

1. THREE EVENTS

The main event which Shavuot commemorates is, as we say in the prayers and the Kiddush of the day, "the time of the giving of our Torah." It is the day of the revelation at Sinai.

Many generations later another event occurred on the same date: The death of King David.[6]

And within the span of more recent history a third memory was added to Shavuot: The death of the Baal Shem Tov, the founder of Chassidut.

Seen in the light of Divine Providence, the occurrence of these three events on the same date is no coincidence. It is a sign of an inner connection between them, namely that the initial disclosure of the voice of G-d at Sinai was brought into greater openness by King David and subsequently by the Baal Shem Tov. They represent three peaks in the continual unfolding of the Divine revelation.

2. THE MEETING OF HEAVEN AND EARTH

In the Midrash[7] we are told, about the new state of affairs brought into being by the giving of the Torah, that "David said, Even though the Holy One, blessed be He, decreed that 'The heavens are the heavens of the L-rd, but the earth He has given to the sons of men . . .' when He wished to give the Torah He annulled the initial decree and said, the lower (worlds) shall as-

---

6. *Jerusalem Talmud, Chagigah,* 2:3.
7. *Shemot Rabbah,* 12:3.

cend to the higher, and the higher descend to the low. And I shall take the initiative, as it is said,[8] 'And the L-rd *descended* upon Mt. Sinai' and (subsequently) it is written, 'And to Moses He said, *come up* unto the L-rd.'"[9]

It is significant that though the Midrash quotes G-d as saying "I shall take the initiative," and though the descent of G-d in fact preceded Moses' going up, it still mentions the ascent of the lower worlds *before* the descent of the higher. This is because the ascent of the low was the ultimate purpose of the giving of the Torah, and the ultimate purpose is the *last* to be realized. Though Moses' ascent came after G-d's descent, it was nonetheless of greater importance. But G-d's initiating step was needed beforehand, before man could rise to meet Him.

3. THE DESCENT OF G-D

What was new at Sinai was the descent of G-d to the (lower) world. Although there had been Divine revelations beforehand, especially to the Patriarchs, they were purely spiritual events which did not enter and affect the fabric of the material world. But when "G-d descended on Mt. Sinai," the effect was felt *within* the world. At that moment, says the Midrash,[10] "No bird called, no bird flew" and "the voice which came from G-d had no echo" because it was absorbed into the very texture of the world.[11] The Torah was no longer "in heaven."[12] The word of G-d had descended to earth.

Only afterwards did the work begin of refining, sanctifying and raising the world in spiritual ascent. This was the worship of the Jewish people, to turn the world into a "vessel" receptive of G-d. The *possibility* of this achievement was created at Sinai; the *actuality* began later.

---

8. *Shemot* 19:20.
9. Ibid., 24:1.
10. *Shemot Rabbah*, end of ch. 29.
11. Cf. *Likkutei Sichot*, vol. IV, p. 1095, at length.
12. Cf. *Shabbat*, 89a.

Just as the descent of G-d to the world began with Abraham and culminated in Moses, so the ascent of the world to G-d began after the giving of the Torah and reached its climax in David and Solomon, his son, who in building the Temple took the Jewish people to a new apex in their upward climb to G-d.

4. THE ASCENT OF MAN

With the advent of David came two new developments. Firstly, he was the first king to rule over the whole of Israel (unlike Saul, who according to the Midrash[13] did not rule over the tribe of Judah), and the dynasty was entrusted to him in perpetuity: "The kingship shall never be removed from the seed of David."[14]

Secondly, although the Temple was built by Solomon, it was planned and prepared by David,[15] and it was even called by his name.[16]

Both the kingship and the Temple are symptoms of the real nature of David's achievement: The elevation of the world and the ascent of man.

5. KINGSHIP

The bond between a king and his subjects is different to and deeper than that between a teacher and his pupils. A pupil owes much of what he is to his teacher; but he has a life outside the classroom. The king, however, holds sway over every aspect of his subject's being. Thus the penalty for an Israelite disobeying a king of Israel is death[17]—even if the command in question has, on the face of it, no connection with the king's proper field of authority; if, for example, he says, "Go to such and such a place," or, "Do not leave your house." The reason is

---

13. *Bamidbar Rabbah*, ch. 4.
14. *Rambam, Hilchot Melachim*, 1:7.
15. *I Chronicles* 29:2 ff.
16. *Tanchuma, Naso*, 13; *Rashi* on *Bamidbar* 7:1; cf. *Shabbat,* 30a.
17. *Rambam, Hilchot Melachim*, 3:8.

that kingship is absolute, its domain unlimited and the whole of the subject's life is bound up in it.

This, of course, is a special kind of monarchy. For the absolute obedience of the people to their king rests in turn on the king's absolute obedience to G-d, the King of Kings.[18] And thus it is that through the intermediary of kingship, Israel has an obedience to G-d which is both total and extending to every aspect of their being.

Thus we can see the difference between the acceptance of the Torah at Sinai and the obedience to G-d involved in the idea of Kingship, which David initiated. The revelation at Sinai was an act of G-d: "I shall take the initiative." It did not come from within the hearts of the people. And so it did not affect their whole being absolutely. But kingship does come from the people—their obedience is the source of the king's authority. David's reign signifies a new phenomenon: The voluntary, inward acceptance by the people of an absolute authority over them.

6. THE TEMPLE

The same idea of the elevation of man and the world can be found in the Temple, David's other monument. There was a difference between the Temple, and the Tabernacle (Mishkan) which the Israelites carried with them in the wilderness. The places where the Mishkan rested did not become permanently holy. When the Mishkan departed, so did their sanctity. But the Temple site remains holy ground even after the destruction of the Temples. In both Tabernacle and Temple was the indwelling presence of G-d; but only in the latter did this presence permanently sanctify and elevate the earth on which it stood.

7. THE BAAL SHEM TOV

These two movements, of G-d reaching out towards man and man aspiring towards G-d will ultimately become one in

---

18. *Derech Mitzvotecha, Mitzvat Minui Melech.*

the Messianic Age, when unity will prevail. Indeed, ever since the Torah was given, this unity has become possible, because the "decree" separating heaven and earth was annulled.

But the great impetus to bringing about this unity and the Messianic Age has been the teaching of the Baal Shem Tov. He and the Chassidut which flowed from his inspiration have taught us to see the world as filled with the light of G-d, and to understand that it is the indwelling word of G-d that sustains all things. Through him we have learned to *see* G-d in the world.[19] And this elevation of the world, the Baal Shem Tov revealed through Torah, which represents a revelation from above.

And so the Messianic Age will be brought by the spreading of the teachings of the Baal Shem Tov; and Messiah will be versed and steeped in *Torah* like his ancestor *David*.[20]

(Source: Likkutei Sichot, Vol. VIII pp. 21-8)

---

19. Cf. *Tanya*, Part II, ch. 1.
20. *Rambam, Hilchot Melachim,* end of ch. 11.

פרשת נשא

NASO

Our Sidra includes the details of the procedure through which a *Sotah* had to pass: That is, a woman suspected by her husband of adultery in a case where there were no witnesses. A phrase used in this context, "if any man's wife goes aside," is quoted by the Talmud to support the statement that "a person does not commit a transgression unless the spirit of folly enters him." The connection between them, superficially, lies in a play of words, the similarity in Hebrew between the words for "folly" and for "goes aside." But the Rebbe searches out a deeper parallel, resting on the traditional image which sees the relationship between the Jewish people and G-d as one of marriage, and hence sees sin as a kind of infidelity. Its theme is the implication of this image for the Jew.

1. SIN AND THE SPIRIT OF FOLLY

There is a statement in the Talmud[1] that "a person does not commit a transgression unless the spirit of folly enters him," and the text which is cited in support is a phrase from our Sidra, "If any man's wife goes aside."[2] The previous Lubavitcher Rebbe, Rabbi Yosef Yitzchak, in explaining the nature of folly,[3] also makes use of the same phrase.

What is the connection between them? Why is adultery, of all the many transgressions, the one that most conclusively shows that sin is always irrational? Neither in the Talmud nor in Chassidut are texts quoted for their own sake or to make a show of learning. They are chosen with precision, to make the most comprehensive case.

In this instance, there is a superficial reason. There is a verbal similarity between "goes aside" *(tisteh)* and "folly" *(shetut)*.

---

1. *Sotah*, 3a.
2. *Bamidbar* 5:12.
3. *Maamar Bati Legani*, 5710, ch. 3.

But this does not entirely remove our puzzlement. Why quote a text at all? Many Rabbinic aphorisms are not "derived" from a Biblical text in this way. There must be some deeper connection, not apparent at first sight, between adultery and sin in general.

There is an added difficulty. Adultery is a very grave sin, carrying the death penalty. For someone to commit it is obviously irrational. There could be no grounds for choosing to do an act with such consequences. But the Talmudic saying was intended to apply to *all* sins, to the most minute detail of Rabbinic law, and even to a *permitted* act which was not done for the sake of Heaven.[4] In however slight a way a man turns his back on G-d, the saying applies: It is an act of folly. So how can we prove the folly of a minor sin from the obvious folly of a major one?

2. SIN AS INFIDELITY

The answer is that adultery is the prototype of all sins, and this is so in two ways.

Firstly, the sin of adultery in Jewish law applies only if the woman concerned is married. A single woman cannot be guilty of it. Hence the phrase, "If any man's *wife* goes astray." But the Jewish people as a whole are regarded as the "wife" of G-d. The bond forged between them at Sinai was like a marriage. And so every time a Jew commits a sin, however slight, he is betraying the covenant, the "marriage contract" between himself and G-d. He is guilty of spiritual adultery, unfaithfulness to his Divine partner.

The Zohar[5] relates: A philosopher once asked Rabbi Eliezer: If the Jews are the chosen people, how is it that they are the weakest of the nations? Rabbi Eliezer replied: Such is their fate. *Because* they are chosen, they cannot tolerate any faults, either spiritual or material. Because of their special spiritual vocation, what is pardonable in others is a sin in them.

---

4. Cf. *Tanya*, Part I, ch. 24.
5. Part III, 221a.

And like the heart—the most sensitive and vital of the body's organs—the slightest tremor or faltering is of life and death significance.[6]

This, then, is the connection between our verse about a wife's unfaithfulness and the maxim about the spirit of folly.

Between the Jewish people and G-d is a bond of eternal mutual loyalty, a marriage of which G-d is the male, the initiating partner, and we the female, the keepers of the faith. Even exile is not a separation, a divorce. It is recorded in the Talmud[7] that the prophet Isaiah told ten men to "Return and repent." They answered, "If a master sells his slave or a husband divorces his wife, does one have a claim on the other?" (In other words they argued that with the Babylonian exile G-d had effectively divorced Himself from His people and had no further claim to their obedience.) The Holy One, blessed be He, then said to the prophet: "Thus saith the L-rd, Where is the bill of your mother's divorcement, whom I have put away, or which of My creditors is it to whom I have sold you? Behold, for your iniquities you have sold yourselves, and for your transgressions is your mother put away." In this way, it is certain that even in the temporary separation of exile, G-d will not take another people for His chosen.[8]

If so, then since the faithfulness of a wife lies in her compliance to her husband's desires,[9] when a Jew commits even a slight transgression or even a permitted but self-centered act, it is a gesture of unfaithfulness and betrayal of the Holy Wedding at Sinai.

This is why the statement of the folly of sin—every sin—is followed by the phrase from our Sidra, less as a proof than an explanation. How is it that even a trivial sin is folly? Because it brings about a severing of the link between man and G-d. Why

---

6. Ibid., 221b; *Kuzari, Maamar* 2:36; *Tanya*, Part IV, ch. 31.
7. *Sanhedrin*, 105a.
8. *Kiddushin*, 36a; *Rashba*, Responsa, ch. 194.
9. *Tana Deve Eliyahu Rabbah*, ch. 9.

does it do so? Because it is an act of infidelity intervening in the marriage between G-d and the Jew.

3. SIN AS A PASSING MOMENT

The second connection between the two statements is this: The phrase "if any man's wife goes aside" does not apply to the certain, but merely to the *suspected,* adulterer; where there were no witnesses to the supposed act, and it was "hidden from the eyes of her husband." This suspicion by itself makes her liable to bring an offering of barley, which was an animal food,[10] a humiliation in keeping with the nature of her supposed offense.

The whole procedure is difficult to understand. If the charge against her is only based on suspicion, not proven fact, can we not rely on the presumption that most Jewish wives are faithful, and dismiss the charge? The answer is that so high are the standards of fidelity which the Torah sets for Jewish wives, that it is culpable even to lay oneself open to suspicion.

However, this stigma is short-lived. If, after the procedure for deciding whether the suspicion was well-founded, she is deemed innocent, she returns to her husband untainted; "she shall be cleared and shall conceive seed."[11]

And this, too, is the case with the Jew who, in a spirit of folly, commits a sin. The breach he opens up between himself and G-d is only a temporary one, and in the last analysis, "My glory (that is, the G-dly spark within every Jew) I will not give to another."[12] No Jew is ever so distant from G-d that he cannot return, untainted and pure.

This is the second connection: Just as a wife suspected by her husband is only temporarily displaced from her marital closeness, so is the separation from G-d which a sin creates, only a passing moment.

---

10. *Sotah,* 15b.
11. *Bamidbar* 5:28.
12. *Isaiah* 42:8.

4. THE FRUITFULNESS OF RETURN

Even though it is true that someone who attaches significance to things independently of G-d denies G-d's unity, and
while contemplating his sins he may fall into the despair of
thinking "the L-rd has forsaken me and my L-rd has forgotten
me,"[13] he must remember that he can always recover his closeness to G-d.

More than this, he must remember a third resemblance
between the woman suspected of adultery, and the sinner in
general.

If she is declared innocent, not only is she cleared of any
stain on her character; she shall return to her husband "and
shall conceive seed." This means[14] that if she has previously
given birth with difficulty, now she will do so with ease; if she
has borne girls, she will have sons as well; one authority maintains that she will bear children even if beforehand she was
barren.

This hope lies before the person who has sinned. He must
not fall prey to melancholy or despair. For G-d has said, "My
glory I will not give to another." And when he returns to G-d
he too will be fruitful. He will rise to the love and fear of G-d.
He will work towards true closeness, until "husband and wife
are united," and the presence of the Divine is revealed in his
soul. This is his personal redemption:[15] a preface to the collective redemption which is the Messianic Age.

(Source: Likkutei Sichot, Vol. II pp. 311-314)

---

13. Ibid., 49:14.
14. *Sotah*, 26a; *Rambam, Hilchot Sotah*, 2:10; 3:22.
15. *Tanya*, Part IV, ch. 4.

BEHAALOTECHA

This Sidra opens with the command to Aaron to light the lamps of the Menorah, the seven-branched candelabrum that stood in the Sanctuary. The symbolism of the Menorah and the act of lighting, is the theme of the Sicha, together with the example which Aaron's service represents.

1. AARON'S LOVE

Aaron, whose duties as the High Priest are described in this week's Sidra, was known for his love towards every creature. Hillel said of him, in Pirkei Avot,[1] "Be of the disciples of Aaron, loving peace and pursuing peace, loving your fellow-creatures and drawing them near to the Torah."

What was the feature of his way of life that stands as a supreme example of spreading the spiritual light of Torah? It was that he did not wait for those who stood in darkness to come within the circle of light, but that he went out to them. He went, in Hillel's words, to his "fellow creatures," a word including those who had no other merit than that they too, were G-d's creations.[2] But nonetheless he "drew them near to the Torah" rather than drawing the Torah near to them. He did not simplify or compromise its demands to bring it down to their level. He did not lower the Torah; he raised men.

2. LIGHTING THE LAMPS

This facet of Aaron's life is suggested in this Sidra, which opens with the command, "When you light (literally, 'raise up')

---

1. 1:12.
2. *Tanya*, Part I, ch. 32.

the lamps, the seven lamps shall give light in front of the candlestick."[3]

The lamps of the Menorah of the Sanctuary are a symbol of the Jewish soul—"The lamp of the L-rd is the soul of man."[4] And the seven lamps, the branches of the Menorah, are the seven kinds of Jewish soul.[5] Aaron's task was to raise up every soul, to bring out the Divine within the Jew from its concealment in the subconscious.

The Rabbis sought an explanation for the fact that the word "raise up" *(behaalotecha)* is used, instead of the more obvious "light" or "kindle." And they concluded that the verse meant that Aaron was to kindle them "until the flame rises up by itself."[6]

Aaron's spiritual achievement was therefore not only to light the flame in the souls of the Jewish people, but to take them to the stage where they would give light of their own accord. He did not simply create disciples, people who were dependent on his inspiration. He engendered in them a love of G-d that they could sustain without his help.

3. THREE RULES

There are three rules which applied to the Menorah in the Sanctuary and the Temple.[7]

Firstly, even a person who was not a priest could light the lamps.

But, secondly, only a priest could prepare the lamps, setting the wicks and the oil.

And, thirdly, the Menorah could only be lit in the Temple Sanctuary.

These rules are similarly the conditions in which spiritual awakening can take place, lighting the lamp of the soul.

---

3. *Bamidbar* 8:2.
4. *Proverbs* 20:27.
5. Cf. *Likkutei Torah*, beg. of *Behaalotecha.*
6. *Sifra* to *Vayikra* 24:2; *Shabbat*, 21a; cf. *Rashi* to *Bamidbar* 8:2.
7. Cf. *Yoma*, 24b; *Rambam, Hilchot Bi'at Hamikdash*, ch. 9.

Firstly, it is not the prerogative of the priest alone, or of the chosen few, to spread the light of Torah. The task belongs to every Jew, both as a privilege and as an obligation. Hillel's words, "Be of the disciples of Aaron" were addressed to every individual.

But only the priest can do the preparation. We may be tempted to think that in pursuit of our aim of drawing Jews to the life of Torah, the end justifies the means; that concessions can be made on our own initiative for the sake of winning commitment. But against this is the warning that not everyone is capable of deciding which interpretations, which lines of influence are valid. This belongs to the priest.

What is a priest? In the time of the Temple, when Jews first possessed their land, the priests had no share of its territory. "G-d is his inheritance," his only possession. This was his sanctity. In Rambam's words,[8] "Not only the tribe of Levi, but any man of any place whose spirit is willing . . . to separate himself and to stand before G-d and to minister to and serve Him," he and only he is the mentor in whose footsteps we must follow.

And the place where the lamps are to be lit is in the Sanctuary. There are shades and levels of holiness. The Sanctuary is not the only holy place. But this specific task of lighting the flame could not be done in any place of a lesser degree of holiness. We must awaken the spirit of ourselves and others, to the highest degree of sanctity possible.

4. SEVEN BRANCHES

The Menorah in the Sanctuary had seven branches and these represent the seven kinds of Jewish soul.[5] There are some whose vocation is to serve G-d with love and kindness (chesed), some with fear and strictness (gevurah) and some who synthesize the two (tiferet). In all, there are seven general paths to the service of G-d and each Jew has one which is his own personal

---

8. *Hilchot Shemittah Veyovel*, 13:13.

direction. But common to them all is the fact that they are alight with the flame of Torah: They burn with love and they shed the light of truth within the Sanctuary and from there to the whole world.

There was a peculiarity of the Temple, that its windows were "broad and narrow,"[9] on which the Rabbis comment,[10] "they were broad on the outside and narrow within, for I (G-d) am not in need of light." Unlike other buildings whose windows are designed to admit light, the Temple was constructed to *send* light out to the world.

The source of this light was the lamps, the souls of the Israelites. And although each of them was unique, with his own special talents to bring to his work, they shared the fact that they were all sources of light.

This is the common goal of the efforts of every Jew, to bring the light of Torah to the world. Their means may differ—some approaching through strictness, some through love. But for those who choose the path of love, the ends and the means are the same: The goal is light and the way is light. This was Aaron's path, "loving peace and pursuing peace, loving his fellow creatures and drawing them near to Torah." And so has been the path of the great leaders of Chabad, lighting the dormant flame in the souls of Jews wherever they were to be found, preferring to be close than to be aloof, to be kind rather than severe, in bringing all our people near to Torah.

(Source: Likkutei Sichot, Vol. II pp. 314-318 (adapted))

---

9. *I Kings* 6:4.
10. *Menachot*, 86b; *Vayikra Rabbah*, 31:7.

פרשת שלח

SHELACH

The Sidra of Shelach contains the episode of the spies whom Moses sent to gather intelligence about the land of Canaan. Ten of the twelve spies returned with disparaging reports, that although the land was fertile, its inhabitants were too strong and their cities too well guarded to be defeated by the Israelites. The whole story is shot through with difficulties. How could the spies, so soon after the miraculous deliverance from Egypt, doubt that G-d would give them victory? How could the morale of the Israelites be so easily broken? Why did Caleb and Joshua, the only faithful voices amongst the spies, not dispel the anxiety by mentioning the great catalogue of miracles in which the people had witnessed the power of G-d? It is clear that some unease lay beneath the surface of the spies' behavior. What this was, and how it is capable of affecting us, is the subject of this Sicha.

1. THE SPIES' DESPAIR

In our Sidra we read of the report of the spies who were sent by Moses to discover the nature of the promised land of Canaan and its inhabitants. Ten of the twelve returned with a counsel of despair. They broke the morale of the Israelites by suggesting that they would not be able to conquer it because "the people that dwell in the land are fierce and the cities are fortified and very great." They argued that "We are not able to go up against the people; for they are stronger than we."

Indeed, the Rabbis in the Talmud[1] understood them to have made an even stronger claim. The Hebrew word for "than we" can also be translated as "than Him." The spies said "they are stronger than Him," that is, that the Canaanite nations were—as it were—too powerful even for G-d. The Rabbis pungently expressed this audacious proposition as saying, as it

---

1. *Sotah*, 35a.

were, that "even the master of the house cannot remove his furniture from it."

2. MYSTERIES

What is the meaning of this remarkable episode?

It is part of our spiritual task to remove the cry of despair which the Israelites first gave when they heard the ominous news and which has had its echoes throughout our history. As the Talmud[1] says: That day was the ninth of Av and the Holy One blessed be He said, "They are now weeping for nothing, but I will fix (this day) as an occasion for weeping for generations." So our many chapters of national mourning have written through them a trace of that moment when faith was lacking in the saving power of G-d. And we have, by faith, to compensate that moment of faithlessness.

But what was the specific meaning of the event? Why did the spies argue as they did? What was the answer to their challenge? And how were they able to reduce the people to despair, a people who had witnessed the great miracles of deliverance—the plagues and the division of the Red Sea—the miracles of protection against the snakes and scorpions of the desert,[2] and the miracles of providence, the Manna and the Well? These were not events that made demands on their *faith*. They had *seen* them happen with their own eyes. How could the report of ten men suddenly outweigh the natural conviction that what G-d had done to Egypt He would do to Canaan in its turn?

More remarkable still: Why, when Caleb replied to their arguments, did he not mention these recent miracles? They were surely the most convincing proof of his case. And yet we find instead that he says only, "We shall go up, indeed go up, and inherit it (the land) for we are well able to overcome it." Was it, perhaps, that the Canaanites were a stronger force[3] than the Egyptians, so that G-d's victory in Egypt did not assure

---

2. *Yalkut Shimoni*, Remez 729; *Mechilta, Beshalach*, 13:21; *Sifri, Behaalotecha*, 10:34; *Bamidbar Rabbah*, 1:2; *Tanchuma, Beshalach*, 3.
3. Cf. *Rashi, Bamidbar* 14:16.

victory in Canaan? But this could not have been Caleb's reason, for at the crossing of the Red Sea the Israelites had sung,[4]
"All the inhabitants of Canaan are melted away. Terror and
dread fall upon them. By the greatness of Your arm they are as
silent as stone." Forty years later, when Joshua began the conquest of the land, evidence of this terror still remained. His two
spies were told in Jericho:[5] "For we have heard how the L-rd
dried up the water of the Red Sea for you when you came out
of Egypt . . . and as soon as we had heard, our hearts melted,
and there was no spirit left in any man because of you." So the
Israelites could not have felt that Canaan represented a more
formidable obstacle than Egypt, which was the dominant
power at that time.[6]

3. FEAR OF INVOLVEMENT

The explanation, given in Chassidut,[7] is this. The spies
were not animated by fear of physical defeat. Instead they
feared a kind of spiritual defeat.

In the wilderness, each of the Israelites' needs was met by a
direct gift from G-d. They did not work for their food. Their
bread was the Manna which fell from the heavens; their water
came from Miriam's Well; their clothes did not need repair.[8]

The possession of the land of Israel meant a new kind of
responsibility. The Manna was to cease. Bread would come
only through toil. The providential miracles would be replaced
by labor; and with labor came the danger of a new preoccupation.

The spies were no ordinary men. They were princes of
their tribes, especially selected by Moses for the mission. And
their anxiety was a spiritual one. Their fear was, that a concern
to work the land and make a living might eventually leave the

---

4. *Shemot* 15:15-16.
5. *Joshua* 2:10.
6. *Mechilta, Beshalach* 14:5; *Zohar, Shemot* 6a.
7. *Likkutei Torah*, beg. of *Shelach*.
8. *Devarim* 8:4. *Yalkut Shimoni* and *Rashi*, ad loc.

Israelites with progressively less time and energy for the service of G-d. They said, "It is a land which eats up its inhabitants," meaning that the land and its labor, and the preoccupation with the materialistic world, would "swallow up" and consume all their energies. Their opinion was that spirituality flourishes best in seclusion and withdrawal, in the protected peace of the wilderness where even the food was "from the heavens."

4. THE MISTAKE

And yet, the spies were wrong. The purpose of a life lived in Torah is not the elevation of the soul: It is the sanctification of the world.

The end to which every Mitzvah aims is to make a dwelling-place for G-d in the world—to bring G-d to the light within the world, not above it. A Mitzvah seeks to find G-d in the natural, not the supernatural. The miracles which sustained the Jews in the wilderness were not the apex of spiritual experience. They were only a preparation for the real task: Taking possession of the land of Israel and making it a holy land.

We can now see the rationale of the spies' argument. The miracles which they had witnessed did not prevent them saying of Canaan, "they are stronger than we." Precisely because the Israelites had been delivered, protected and sustained by miracles, they had been able to dedicate their whole existence to G-d. But in a land where every benefit had to be worked for, their spirituality might decline and be defeated. The miracles were not, in their eyes, a reason for being confident about the entry into the land. On the contrary, they were the reason for wishing to stay in the wilderness. And when as the Talmud says, they claimed that, as it were, "even the master of the house cannot remove his furniture," they meant: G-d Himself created the natural order (i.e., "His furniture"), and He decided (according to their misconception) not to dwell in the natural world. So long as miracles surrounded them, the Israelites could make themselves into vessels to receive His will. But land, labor, natural law—everything that faced them in the land of Israel—were not the vehicles of Divine revelation. G-d, they argued, is higher than the world. So let us, too, be higher than the world. As soon as we enter the land of Israel we leave this realm.

5. THE MIRACULOUS AND THE EVERYDAY

The spies had drawn a distinction between miracles and natural events, since the natural order is as it is only because it is G-d's will. But this was their error. For, the inner will of G-d is to be found in the sanctification of the natural world.

And this is why Joshua and Caleb did not comfort the people by talking of the miracles that had taken them this far and which would see them safely into their land.

For, in crossing the Jordan, they were to pass beyond a faith that lives in miracles, into a life that would sanctify time and place, and turn the finite familiar world into the home of G-d.

They said: "If the desire[9] of the L-rd is in us, He will bring us into the land . . . (then its people) are our bread, their defense is removed from over them, and the L-rd is with us, fear them not."

In other words, if it is G-d's will that we should enter the land, then we can remain close to Him there. Instead of being "a land that eats up its inhabitants" it will be "our bread." Instead of our being reduced to its level, it will be raised to ours.

6. CALEB'S ANSWER

In fact, the miracle concealed in nature is *more* miraculous than the supernatural.[10] The plagues, the division of the Red Sea, and all similar supernatural events show that G-d is not confined by nature but can break through its regularities. But a miracle which is clothed in nature shows that G-d is not bound at all, not even by the "confines" of supernatural law; but He

---

9. In Hebrew, *chafetz;* a word denoting the inner, or true ultimate will; as opposed to *ratzon.*
10. *Torah Or, Megillat Esther,* 100a.

can combine the natural with the supernatural. So the Mitzvah, the act which discovers G-d within the everyday shows that G-d is truly everywhere. He does not need the extraordinary to proclaim His presence. He is G-d even within the dimensions of the world. This is the real miracle, that the infinite can inhabit the finite, and that natural and supernatural can become one.

This is what the entry into the land of Israel signified.

And so Caleb's answer to the ten spies was, "Let us go up, let us indeed go up and inherit the land." In other words, let us "go up" twice over. We have ascended to the spirituality of the wilderness, we have risen above the concerns of the world. Let us now make a new and greater ascent, finding G-d within the world itself. And let us possess the land, not as someone who buys something from a stranger, but as someone who *inherits* something because of his oneness with its owner.[11]

7. THE WILDERNESS OF THE DAY

None of the Torah's narratives is simply a story. Every Jew experiences the two realms of the wilderness and the land of Israel, and knows the tensions between them. They are two periods in his life, and they are two parts of every day. He begins in the wilderness, in the morning seclusion of learning and prayer. And then he must emerge into the "land of Israel," the world of business, livelihood and labor.

It is then that he may feel stirring in him the doubts that plagued the spies. While he is learning and praying he feels himself wholly given over to the spiritual demands of Judaism. But in his work he can see little or no religious significance. Worse than that, he may feel that it is "a land that eats up its inhabitants"—that work so consumes him and invades his mind that even while he is praying or learning, the world of his everyday worries constantly intrudes and breaks his concentration.

---

11. Cf. *Baba Batra,* 65a; *Zevachim,* 4b. Responsa, *Tzafnat Paneach* I, ch. 118.

But he is making the spies' mistake, of placing G-d outside the world, of failing to respond to G-d's presence in every human transaction, of forgetting the imperative to "Know Him in *all* your ways." He must remember Joshua and Caleb's words that "if the desire of the L-rd is with us" that we take our Judaism into every facet of our involvement with the world,[12] then "they are our bread," and the world is assimilated into holiness.

There is also another wilderness. The desire of the spies to rest secure in G-d's miraculous protection was a wish for the intensity of religious experience. Ultimately it was self-centered, because their reluctance to accept the responsibility of changing the world was also an unwillingness to move beyond private satisfactions to helping others. In us, their argument has its counterpart. We are sometimes hesitant in helping others with their spiritual development because we feel it would adversely affect ourselves—we might have to compromise ourselves, or we might become condescending. But these are rationalizations of the same mistake. Spirituality is not self-contained, a private possession not to be shared with the world. Instead, its essence lies in a Jew reaching out beyond himself to his fellow Jew, to the world of his work, extending holiness to everything he touches, without the fear that he is placing his faith at risk, without the thought that this or any situation lies outside the domain of G-d.

(Source: Likkutei Sichot, Vol. IV pp. 1041-1047)

---

12. Cf. *Psalms* 37:23; *Hayom Yom*, 10 Tammuz.

פרשת קרח
KORACH

The Sidra of Korach concerns the revolt of Korach and his followers against the Priesthood of Aaron and his sons. But what exactly
was Korach's aim? On the one hand, he voiced protest against the
whole institution of priesthood or at least against its carrying any
special status. On the other, it is clear from the narrative that he was
seeking the High Priesthood for himself. Can we make sense of his
apparently contradictory aims? This is the central point of the Sicha's inquiry. And as a result of its analysis we can understand two
further difficulties: Why "Korach," the name of an inciter to dissent,
is eternalized by making it the name of one of the sections of the
Torah, and why this one Sidra contains two such seemingly opposite themes: Korach's revolt, and the conferring of the "twenty-four
Gifts of Priesthood" on Aaron.

1. THEMES AND OPPOSITIONS

Each of the 53 Sidrot of the Five Books of Moses has a
central theme: One that is carried through each of its verses,
from first to last, and which is suggested in the name it bears.[1]
This connecting motif is so strong, that the thematic link between the first and last verses of a Sidra is stronger than that
between the ending of one Sidra and the beginning of the next,
even though it may continue what appears to be the same narrative. In fact, the very existence of a break between two Sidrot
indicates that there is some *discontinuity* between them sometimes going so far as to point out an *opposition:* As we see in the
ending of Behaalotecha, where Miriam was punished for her
evil report against Moses; and the beginning of Shelach, where
the spies about to be sent to Israel saw the punishment and did
not take heed of it, ultimately to repeat the sin.[2]

---

1. Cf. supra, p. 10.
2. *Rashi, Bamidbar* 13:2.

252

On the face of it, this general rule seems hard to apply to the Sidra of Korach, which begins with the accusation of Korach and his followers against Aaron and the priesthood: And ends with G-d giving the "twenty-four Gifts of Priesthood." The initial accusation and the ultimate validation seem to stand as opposites to one another; and yet it is not merely that the latter is the *outcome* of the former. Rather, we must search for a way in which the "Gifts of Priesthood" are an *integral part* of the story of Korach. For the Sidra is called by his name—and this is where the core of the Sidra lies.

But the search is beset by this problem: The insurrection of Korach was an opposition to the priesthood, as it stood in the hands of Aaron; while the "twenty-four Gifts" were, as Rashi says, a way of "writing and sealing and recording in the court" the gift of priesthood to him.

2. THE NAME OF KORACH

There is an additional difficulty. How came the Sidra to be called Korach in the first place? For, on the verse[3] "The name of the wicked shall rot" the Talmud[4] comments, "Their names shall decay for we do not mention (the wicked) by name." If *we* should not mention the wicked by name in ordinary conversation, still less should a Sidra of the *Torah* be named after one of them, for this is a way of *perpetuating* a name.

And there is no saving grace in Korach, for though, as Rashi tells us, his sons repented, he himself did not. In the name itself there is no hint of righteousness: It means a bald spot,[5] and as the Midrash[6] explains, it has the connotation of *making divisions*—creating a bald spot between two factions where previously there had been unity.

---

3. *Proverbs* 10:7.
4. *Yoma*, 38b.
5. *Sanhedrin*, 109b.
6. Cf. *Yalkut Shimoni*, *Re'eh*, Remez 891.

Rambam writes[7] that the Torah "was given to make peace in the world." How then should a portion of it be called by a name that suggests divisiveness?

3. KORACH'S CLAIM

And finally, there is an apparent inconsistency in the very claim that Korach made. On the one hand it appears that he was set against the very institution of the priesthood, or at least its special status, for he said:[8] "For all the congregation is holy, and the L-rd dwells in their midst; and why therefore do you elevate yourselves above the congregation of the L-rd?" On the other hand, it was apparent that Korach and his followers sought the priesthood for themselves, as Moses explicitly says to them.[9]

One explanation is that they did not want the status of the priesthood to be abolished, merely that they did not want it confined to Aaron. They wanted *many* High Priests; they sought to be included in that rank. And yet it is clear from Rashi's commentary[10] that Korach sought the High Priesthood for himself alone: He thought that he alone would be vindicated in the trial that the accusers were to undergo. If he had this ambition, why then did he say, "Why do you elevate yourselves?"—for he had reason to wish to see the priesthood elevated.

4. THE FIRMAMENT WHICH DIVIDES THE WATERS

The opening words of our Sidra, "And Korach took," are translated in the Targum as "And Korach *divided,*" and in the book Noam Elimelech, Rabbi Elimelech of Liszensk compares Korach's dissension to the firmament which G-d created on the second day to divide between the higher and lower waters.

---

7. End of *Hilchot Chanukah.* Cf. *Gittin,* 59b; *Sifri,* 6:26.
8. *Bamidbar* 16:3.
9. Ibid., v. 10.
10. *Bamidbar* 16:7.

What is the analogy? One difference between the priests and the rest of the children of Israel was that the priests were withdrawn from the affairs of the world and entirely taken up with their holy office. Especially the High Priest (against whom Korach's accusation was primarily intended), of whom it is written[11] that "he shall not depart from the Sanctuary."

But despite this, he was not uninvolved with the rest of the people: On the contrary, he exercised his influence over them *all*, drawing them up to his own level of holiness. This was symbolized by the kindling of the seven branches of the Menorah.[12] Aaron's special attribute was "Great, or everlasting Love"—and he drew the people near to this service.

But Korach did not see this. He saw only the *separation* between priest and people. And viewed in this light, he saw that just as the priests had their special role, so too did the people, in enacting G-d's will in the *practical* world, which was, indeed, the whole purpose of the Torah. Seen as separate entities, the people had at least as much right to honor and elevation as the priests.

And this removes the inconsistency from his claim. He sought the priesthood, but as an office entirely remote from the people. Hence his accusation, "Why do you elevate yourselves?" In his eyes, the two groups, utterly distinct, each had their special status.

In this way Korach was like the firmament: His aim was to divide the people, like the waters, and sever the connection between the Sanctuary and the ordinary world.

5. DIVISION AND PEACE

On the second day of creation we find that G-d did not say: "And it was Good." The Rabbis explain[13] that this was because division (the firmament) was created on that day. It was not

---

11. *Vayikra* 21:12. Cf. *Rambam, Hilchot Klei Hamikdash,* 5:7; *Hilchot Bi'at Hamikdash,* 1:10.

12. Cf. supra, p. 235 ff.

13. *Bereishit Rabbah,* 4:6. Cf. *Zohar,* Part I, 46a.

until the third day that this judgment was pronounced and repeated, once for the creation of that day, and once for the firmament,[14] which was purified and its division healed.[15] Thus
we learn that in the Divine scheme, there has to be a division
between the things of heaven and those of earth, but that its
consummation is in their re-uniting. And just as on the third
day, so too in the third millennium Torah was given to bring
together heaven and earth, G-d descending and Israel ascending to union.[16]

The same applies to the children of Israel. Although there
are those who are totally involved in holy service and "do not
depart from the Sanctuary," and those whose service is in the
practical world ("In all your ways, know Him"[17]); the one must
not be separate from the other, but the former must lead the
latter, in the manner of Aaron, ever closer to G-d. This the
man of the world, the businessman etc., reaches through setting regular times for study of Torah. And this study should be
of such intense concentration, that he is, at that time, as one
who never departs from the Sanctuary!

And just as the work of the second day was consummated
on the third, so did G-d allow the division caused by Korach,
so that it would reach its fulfillment in the "twenty-four Gifts
of Priesthood." For the priesthood was established as an everlasting covenant in a way that could not have happened had
Korach not raised dissent about it previously. *This* is the connection between the beginning and the end of our Sidra. The
dissension, although it seems on the face of it to be opposed to
the covenant of priesthood, was in fact a precondition of it.

And this is why the name of Korach is perpetuated by
standing as the name of the Sidra. Even though Korach represents division and Torah represents peace, the peace and union
which Torah brings comes not merely in spite of, but *through*,

---

14. *Bereishit Rabbah*, Ibid. *Rashi, Bereishit* 1:7.
15. *Or Hatorah, Bereishit* 34a. Cf. *Zohar*, Ibid.
16. *Shemot Rabbah*, 12:3. *Tanchuma, Vaera*, 15.
17. *Proverbs* 3:6.

the medium of division: That though there is a heaven and an earth, worship and service bring them together until G-d Himself dwells in our midst.

(Source: Likkutei Sichot, Vol. VIII pp. 114-9)

פרשת חקת
CHUKAT

Chukat begins with an account of the Red Heifer, a strange practice
whose object was the purification of those who had become con-
taminated through contact with the dead. The heifer was burned,
and its ashes, mixed with water, sprinkled on those who had become defiled. But the paradox was that though it purified them, it
made impure all those who were involved in its preparation. Thus it
is called, in the Sidra's second verse, a *chukah* ("ordinance")—a
technical term meaning, "law for which no reason can be given."
Rashi gives this explanation for the word, but his comment has
some unusual features which the Sicha first points out, and then
explains, showing that it is intelligible only if we distinguish two
different kinds of *chukah*.

1. RASHI'S COMMENT ANALYZED

"And the L-rd spoke to Moses and Aaron, saying: This is
the ordinance (chukat) of the Torah which the L-rd has commanded. . . ."[1]

Rashi interprets the phrase, "this is the ordinance of the
Torah" thus:

"Because Satan and the nations of the world provoke Israel,
saying, 'what is the meaning of this commandment to you and
what is its reason?,' therefore it is described as an 'ordinance' it
is a decree about which you have no right to speculate."

But there are difficulties here:

(i) From the words of Rashi—"therefore it is described as
an 'ordinance'"—it is apparent that he intended not to explain
the meaning of the word "ordinance" itself—which he has already done previously on many occasions.[2] (And even though
he has not done so previously in the book of Bamidbar, it is not

---

1. *Bamidbar* 19:1-2.
2. E.g., *Bereishit* 26:5; *Shemot* 15:26; *Vayikra* 18:4.

as if he suspected that readers of his commentary would have forgotten his earlier explanation, because the word "ordinance" occurs earlier in Bamidbar[3] and passes without comment from Rashi.) Rather, Rashi wants to explain the fact that it appears to be *superfluous,* since the phrase "this is the law" would have been sufficient.

And if this is so, since the reader already knows the meaning of "ordinance," a brief explanation would have served. Why then does Rashi add, at length, the comments about Satan and the nations of the world, which he has already made several times previously?

(ii) Also, there are several differences between Rashi's answer here, and in earlier places, which require understanding.

In earlier comments the agent provocateur is the "evil inclination"; here it is "Satan."

In these earlier places, he is represented as "raising objections"[4] or "caviling"[5]; Here, as "provoking."

And in one earlier comment, one is said to be forbidden to "exempt oneself"[6] from the ordinances; here one is forbidden to "speculate about them."

(iii) If our earlier reasoning is correct, Rashi's comment applies only to the seeming superfluity of the word "ordinance." Why then should it bear the heading[7] "this is the ordinance of the law," as if Rashi intended to explain the whole phrase?

2. WITHIN REASON AND BEYOND

The explanation is as follows:

The wording of the phrase, "this is *the* ordinance of the law" suggests that the law of the Red Heifer is the *only* ordinance in the Torah. But surely there are *other* ordinances

---

3. E.g., *Bamidbar* 9:3,12,14; 15:15.
4. *Bereishit* 26:5; *Vayikra* 18:4.
5. *Shemot* 15:26.
6. *Vayikra*, Ibid.
7. *Rashi's* comments are prefaced only by the word or phrase in the text which he wishes to explicate.

(mentioned as such by Rashi), like the prohibition of eating the meat of pig or wearing clothes made of a mixture of wool and linen.[8] Therefore, we are forced to say that there is a *special class* of ordinance, of which the Red Heifer is the only example; that is, that there are two kinds of ordinance:

(i) those which could in *principle* be understood by human intelligence, but *details* of which are beyond comprehension;

(ii) those which are *entirely* beyond the scope of human understanding.

The phrase "this is *the* ordinance of the law" is thus intended to indicate that the law of the Red Heifer is alone in belonging to the second category.

Therefore when Rashi brings examples (in Vayikra[9]) of ordinances, he mentions the prohibitions of the meat of the pig and of clothes made of wool and linen mixture, and the waters of purification, but he does not include the Red Heifer, since that belongs to an entirely separate category.

The "waters of purification" (water mingled with the ashes of the Red Heifer) is something whose *principle* can be understood rationally. For, just as purification through immersion in a Mikvah is a notion which Rashi never classifies as an "ordinance," because it is quite reasonable that waters of the Mikvah have the power to cleanse spiritually; similarly, the "waters of purification" can have equal effect. Their only peculiarity lies in the *detail* that only a few drops of it suffice to purify, whereas the Mikvah requires total immersion.

Hence the waters belong to the first class of ordinances— decrees which are *partially* intelligible.

But the laws of the Red Heifer itself are entirely beyond understanding. It cannot be construed simply as a kind of burnt offering, since:

(i) no part of the Red Heifer was offered up at the altar;

---

8. Cf. e.g., *Rashi, Bereishit* 26:5.
9. Ibid.

(ii) all the actions involving the Red Heifer were to be done "outside the three camps";[10] whereas all the offerings were made specifically *within* them;

(iii) the Red Heifer is not even analogous to the goat of Azazel[11] which, (besides its preliminaries being conducted *within* the camp,) was something for which a partial explanation was given ("and the goat shall bear forth on it their iniquities unto a desolate land"[12]).

And it has the following exceptional features that the goat of Azazel did not:

(i) it was to be carried out by the Deputy High Priest;[13]

(ii) its blood was to be sprinkled seven times towards the front of the *Ohel Moed;*[14]

(iii) it was called a "sin offering" to show that it was similar to holy things.[15]

In short, the Red Heifer does not belong to the first category of ordinance for it cannot be even partially understood.

3. G-D AND MAN

In the light of this, we can understand why Rashi uses expressions here ("Satan" as opposed to "evil inclination": "Provokes" in place of "raising objections"; and "forbidden to speculate" instead of "forbidden to exempt oneself from them") which do not occur in his other explanations of the word "ordinance."

It is clear that G-d's intellect surpasses man's, so that if we are told by G-d that a given commandment cannot be humanly understood, there is no ground on which the evil inclination can argue from its unintelligibility to its non-Divine origin. For, why *should* finite man be able to comprehend infinite G-d?

---

10. Cf. *Rashi, Bamidbar* 19:3.
11. Cf. *Vayikra* ch. 16.
12. Ibid., v. 22.
13. Cf. *Rashi, Bamidbar* 19:3.
14. Ibid., v. 4.
15. *Rashi,* Ibid., v. 9.

But when a commandment is *partially* open to human understanding, the evil inclination and the nations of the world
do have (albeit fallacious) grounds for "arguing" or "raising
objections" that it is not Divine: For how could G-d command
something which on the one hand was accessible to human
reason and on the other hand was inaccessible to it? They
would therefore argue that they are not Divine, and not binding on the Jew.

But since the Red Heifer is *entirely* inaccessible to reason, it
cannot be "refuted" by the evil inclination or the nations of the
world. All they can do is to "provoke" the Jew by saying "what
meaning has this commandment for you, and what is its reason?" Admittedly you have to obey the word of G-d, but in
doing so you are doing something which to the human mind is
completely meaningless and irrational.

Thus Rashi uses the word "Satan" instead of the "evil inclination"—for the skeptical voice seeks here only to *trouble*[16] a
Jew at the moment of acting, not to *dissuade* him from it at all.

And thus he does not say, "it is forbidden to 'exempt
yourself' from the command" (for a case cannot be made out
for exemption); but, that "it is forbidden 'to speculate' about its
rationale," and instead perform it with joy as if one understood
it completely.

The reason is (as Rashi continues), that the Red Heifer is a
"decree" of G-d: That is, that *G-d Himself* is telling us not to be
perturbed by the absence of a rationale, and to do it simply *because G-d* so decrees. This is the only way that it can be prop-
erly fulfilled.

We can now understand why Rashi cites the *whole phrase*
"this is the ordinance of the law" as his heading: For it is this
phrase which makes it clear that *this* ordinance is different from
all others; and this is what underlines the nuances of Rashi's
explanation.

(Source: Likkutei Sichot, Vol. VIII pp. 123-7)

---

16. The word *satan* means to trouble, to make uncomfortable (cf. *Bamidbar* 22:22; Ibid.,
   v. 32; *I Kings* 11:14).

פרשת בלק

BALAK

Balak contains an episode where some Israelites have illicit relations with women of surrounding heathen tribes; and this is brought to a climax when Zimri sins openly with a Midianite woman in front of Moses and the people. Pinchas, a grandson of Aaron, though not himself a priest is seized with righteous anger and kills them both. For his zeal, G-d's punishment of the Israelites is stayed and Pinchas is granted the priesthood. The language of the narrative and the comments of the Talmud and Rashi make it clear that this was no ordinary sin; and Pinchas' act was of a special order of virtue. The Rebbe explores these themes, culminating in an inquiry into the philosophy of sin, punishment and reward.

1. THE ZEALOUSNESS OF PINCHAS

"And when Pinchas . . . saw it, he rose up from among the congregation, and took a spear in his hand."[1]

On this verse the Talmud[2] (cited in Rash's commentary) comments "He (Pinchas) saw the deed and remembered the law (about it). He said to Moses, 'I have received a tradition from you: That he who has sexual relations with a heathen, zealous people may attack him.'"

Even though this law is not stated explicitly in the Bible, it can nonetheless be inferred from it, namely from the episode of Pinchas stabbing Zimri.[3]

And thus we can understand why the Torah tells us, "and he (Pinchas) stabbed both of them, the man of Israel, and the woman in her stomach,"[4] on which Rashi comments, "He struck exactly at Zimri's male and her female parts so that eve-

---

1. *Bamidbar* 25:7.
2. *Sanhedrin,* 82a, also *Bamidbar Rabbah,* 20:25.
3. *Rambam, Hilchot Issurei Biah,* 12:4.
4. *Bamidbar* 25:8.

ryone could see that he had not killed them without just cause." For apparently the Torah need not have mentioned *where* Pinchas stabbed the woman; nor did Pinchas need to show the Israelites that he had just cause for his action: For the Talmud tells us that Zimri was openly defiant of Moses.

The reason is that the Torah is alluding to the *details* of the law about punishing one who has relations with a heathen woman: That the zealous may punish the offender only *at the time of his act,* and not subsequently.

But why this allusive manner? Why does the Torah not state the law explicitly and directly, instead of weaving it into a narrative?

The Talmud[5] tells us that "if someone comes to inquire about this particular law, we should not instruct him to act upon it," and this would be impossible if the law were mentioned explicitly in the written Torah. For, because of the very nature of the written Law, that which is written is a *continual* instruction and command. Indeed, the oblique way in which Torah informs us about this law itself suggests that "we should not instruct" the one who inquires about it.

2. THE LOCATION OF GUILT

There is a division of opinion amongst early legal commentators as to whether the law about one who sins with a heathen woman is a law about the offender, or about the zealous who are charged with inflicting punishment.

One side[6] holds that the offender, since he is not to be executed by the Beth Din, is not himself condemned to death; it is rather that the *zealous person* is commanded to kill him. And thus they maintain that had Zimri turned around and killed his assailant Pinchas, he would not be guilty of murder,[7] since he himself was not sentenced to death and yet Pinchas was seeking

---

5. *Sanhedrin,* Ibid.
6. *Ran, Sanhedrin,* Ibid.
7. *Sanhedrin,* 82b.

to kill him, so that his act would have been a justified case of self-defense.

But the Talmud states: "Who is there that G-d would pardon, and yet we should kill him?" From this it seems clear[8] that Zimri (and in general, he who sins with a heathen woman) was *himself* liable to death. And it is merely that this death-sentence differs from all others in that its execution is:

(i) entrusted to the zealots (and not to the Beth Din) and;

(ii) at the very time of the offense (and not, as otherwise, subsequent to it).

There is evidence that Rashi holds this second view, for his commentary says that Pinchas thrust through the offenders in their male and female parts "so that they (the Israelites should all see that he did not kill them *without just cause.*"

Now, Rashi seems to be telling us that this act of Pinchas was to demonstrate that he had killed them *at the moment of their sinning.* For, if he had not done so, he would have killed them *unlawfully.* But if so, why does not Rashi say simply "so that all should see that he killed them *according to the law*" instead of his indirect, weaker phrase, "not without just cause?"

The explanation is that on certain occasions a Beth Din must exact exemplary punishment, where the offense *in itself* does not merit it but where a "fence must be made around the Torah"[9] to prevent widespread abuse. And this was such a situation; where the Israelites en masse were beginning to stray into illicit relations with the Moabite women,[10] and where Pinchas would have been justified in punishing Zimri even *after* his act. But had this been Pinchas' reason, Zimri would have been killed "without just cause" (i.e., for the exemplary effect, rather than because of the intrinsic act). So that Rashi's phrase "not without just cause" is intended to convey that Pinchas was not merely acting within the law, but that Zimri himself merited death; not as an example, but for his own sin. This indicates

---

8. As is the opinion of *Ramban*, in *Sefer Hamitzvot, Shoresh* 3.

9. *Rambam, Hilchot Sanhedrin*, 24:4; *Sanhedrin*, 46a.

10. *Bamidbar* 25:1.

that Rashi is of the opinion that one who sins with a heathen woman is himself liable to death.

3. THE EXECUTION OF SENTENCE

But we still have the difficulty that if the man deserves death, why should the sentence be executed (i) by the zealous only, and (ii) at the time of his act?

And this is complicated by the fact that the Talmud holds that this sin also bears the punishment of *excision (karet);*[11] and his liability remains even *after* the act.

We are forced, therefore, to say that the sin has *two* aspects, one which deserves excision and remains *after* the act has been done; the other which lasts only *during* the act and which merits death at the hands of the zealous.

4. THE GRAVEST OF SINS

To understand this we must first consider what the Torah tells us about Pinchas: "Behold I give unto him My covenant of peace. And he and his seed after him shall have it; the covenant of priesthood, for ever; because he was zealous for his G-d."[12]

Now this presents two difficulties:

(i) It is apparent from the wording of the text ("because he was zealous for his G-d," "when he was zealous with my jealousy"[13]) that this sin (illicit relations with a heathen woman) is above all others relevant to G-d. As Rashi comments "he (Pinchas) displayed the anger that I (G-d) should have displayed." Why this of all sins?

(ii) Because of his virtue, Pinchas was certainly entitled to a great reward, but not, surely, that of the *priesthood,* which was allocated to Aaron and his sons as a *natural* quality, to be transmitted eternally, just as time had been allocated into day and night (as Rashi comments in a previous Sidra).[14] And, as Pin-

---

11. *Sanhedrin*, 82a, based on *Malachi* 2:11-12. *Rambam, Hilchot Issurei Biah*, 12:6.
12. *Bamidbar* 25:12-13.
13. Ibid., v. 11.
14. *Bamidbar* 17:5.

chas had not until that time been a priest,[15] how could he suddenly become one?

The explanation is that of all sins, forbidden sexual unions are the most grave. Sexual union involves, as it were, the whole essence of a man,[16] for from it a child may be born, with perhaps greater powers than his father.[17] For, although the revealed faculties of the father are not so great, the sexual union draws from his essence. And on this level, his powers are greater. So he can beget a child with superior faculties to his own.

So that an illicit union involves a transference of a man's very essence to the realm of the unlawful, unlike other transgressions which involve only certain of his capacities. And of these, union with a non-Jewish woman "involves a loss greater than all other sexual sins"[18] for it alone transgresses the boundary which G-d has set between Jews and all other peoples (a boundary also compared in the Midrash[19] to that between light and darkness). The Jew who sins within his people remains a Jew, and his son, though illegitimate, is still a Jew[18] and can rank higher than the High Priest in wisdom and the respect which attaches to it.[20] But he who sins with a non-Jewish woman begets offspring who are not Jewish, and all his powers and the *essence* of his soul are used for this.

It is even worse than this, in fact. For birth is a miraculous event; as the Talmud says,[21] "three partners produce a man: His mother, his father, and G-d who gives him his soul." Even as a *physical* process, birth is manifestly miraculous. And for this open disclosure of *G-d's* presence to be turned to sin is something in which we can understand the phrase, that Pinchas "was jealous *for his G-d*."

---

15. *Rashi, Bamidbar* 25:13.
16. Cf. *Reishit Chochmah, Shaar Hakedushah,* chs. 11:16.
17. Cf. *Shavuot,* 48a; *Chullin,* 49b, 63a.
18. *Rambam, Hilchot Issurei Biah,* 12:7.
19. *Bamidbar Rabbah,* 18. Cf. *Shemot Rabbah,* 36:1.
20. *Horiot,* 13a.
21. *Kiddushin,* 30b.

But how, if the division between the nations and Israel is one of G-d's laws of nature, is it *possible* for it to be transgressed? The answer is that man's free will makes him, as it were, like G-d in being able to choose his own path ("Behold man is become like one of us"[22]), even where it crosses the natural boundaries which G-d has set, just as G-d Himself is not bound by any natural law at all.

And, since reward is given "measure for measure," and Pinchas had atoned for this crossing of G-d's boundaries, so he was rewarded by the priesthood: He himself crossed the boundary that G-d had set between priest and people.

5. THE ENDURANCE OF GUILT

Now we can understand why guilt attaches to this forbidden union only at the time of the act. In all other sins, the Jew's sanctity remains, even though embedded in the realm of the forbidden. This is why it can be rectified by subsequent repentance. Even in illicit unions amongst Jews, the offspring, though irrevocably illegitimate, is still holy: A member of the Jewish people. So, until the repentance, the guilt remains (holiness is still trapped in forbidden domains). But union with a heathen woman severs the offender from his sanctity: So the guilt ceases with the act. Or to put it more precisely:

(i) as a forbidden act, involving a man's human capacities, it shares the lasting guilt of other sins, and bears the punishment of excision.

(ii) as the unique act of transferring the most Divine and essential power to unholiness, it carries the sentence of death, and its guilt lasts no longer than the act. This is why punishment for this aspect must be executed at that very moment, or not at all.

6. THE TASK AND REWARD OF THE ZEALOUS

Why though must death be at the hands of the zealous and not the Beth Din? The freedom of choice which man is given

---

22. *Rambam, Hilchot Teshuvah*, beg. of ch. 5. *Bereishit* 5:22.

through the Torah, is the choice between good and evil, life and death.[23] But not the power to *turn good into evil* or evil into good. This is something which *transcends* Torah and which a Jew has in his ability, by repentance, to turn (intentional) sins into merits; or conversely, as in the case of Zimri, to turn the most holy into the most profane by forbidden union.

The punishment must match the crime; and since Zimri's was a misuse of a power higher than Torah, it could not be punished by the representatives of Torah: The Beth Din; but had to be executed by the person whose attachment to G-d transcended Torah: The zealous Pinchas.

The Torah sets boundaries, good and evil, permitted and forbidden, Israel and the nations. But the Jew has resources in his soul to cross the boundaries, for good or for bad, and to rescue holiness from the lowest reaches of the profane.

(Source: Likkutei Sichot, Vol. VIII pp. 150-158)

---

23. *Devarim* 30:15.

פרשת פנחס

PINCHAS

The beginning of the Sidra describes G-d's reward to Pinchas for his zealousness in avenging Zimri's insolence in bringing a heathen woman into the camp of the Israelites. Rashi, in his commentary, seems to be troubled by an apparently unnecessary repetition of the genealogy of Pinchas, which states that he was the son of Elazar the son of Aaron the priest. This has already been stated only a few verses earlier, and Rashi concludes that its purpose here, in our Sidra, is not simply to inform us of Pinchas' ancestry, but to defend him from a criticism that the Israelites were urging against him, that he was the grandson of Jethro, who had once been an idol-worshipper, and that he had inherited some of Jethro's pagan inclinations. The details of Rashi's account, however, raise a number of difficulties, which are investigated in the Sicha. Its central theme is the concept of zealousness itself. Is religious zeal to be encouraged or criticized? Is it the result of pride and ostentation or genuine devotion? What should be our response when we suspect someone's motives for his religious behavior? The Sicha ends by confronting these difficult and yet vitally important questions.

1. THE COMPLAINT OF THE TRIBES

"And the L-rd spoke to Moses, saying: Pinchas, the son of Elazar, the son of Aaron the priest, has turned My wrath away."

Rashi, commenting on this genealogy, says: "Because the tribes spoke disparagingly of him, (saying) 'Have you seen this grandson of Puti the father of whose mother used to fatten calves for idolatrous sacrifices, and he dared to slay a prince of one of Israel's tribes!' Therefore, the Torah comes and connects his genealogy with Aaron." This malicious talk of the Israelites was based on the fact that Pinchas' father, Elazar, had married a daughter of Putiel, who is identified with Jethro, the father-in-law of Moses, who at one time had been an idol-worshipper.

270

Now what is there in the simple statement of Pinchas' ancestry to suggest to Rashi this elaborate explanation? The answer is that we had already been told, only a few verses previously,[1] who Pinchas' father and grandfather were. Since there is no unnecessary repetition in the Torah, there must be some further reason for restating it here. Therefore Rashi is forced to conclude that Pinchas was being criticized in terms of his ancestry (his descent from Jethro) and that the Torah intends to emphasize the *distinction* of his family tree (his descent from Aaron).

Nonetheless, there are still some features of Rashi's explanation that need understanding.

Granted, for example, that Pinchas was being criticized, how does Rashi infer that "the tribes" in general were a party to the complaint? Surely it is more likely that it was only the tribe of Simeon, whose prince, Zimri, Pinchas had killed. Indeed the other tribes had been severely distressed by Zimri's act of bringing a Midianite woman into the camp; as Rashi says,[2] "they all burst out weeping" at that moment. And as a result of Pinchas' zealousness, they all benefited, because "the pestilence was restrained from the children of Israel."[3] They had every reason to praise him. Why then does Rashi say they criticized him?

Secondly, their criticism was based on the fact that Jethro was his maternal grandfather. Now according to the Midrash[4] and to Rashi[5] himself Jethro's idolatry was such that "he left no idol unworshipped by him." The tribes therefore had this comprehensive indictment available to them. Why did they seize only on the fact that he had "fattened calves" for idolatrous sacrifice?

---

1. *Bamidbar* 25:7.
2. Ibid., v. 6.
3. Ibid., v. 8.
4. *Tanchuma, Yitro*, 7.
5. *Shemot* 18:11.

Thirdly, the Biblical verse connects Pinchas' lineage to "Elazar the son of Aaron the priest." But Rashi says only, "Torah comes and connects his genealogy with Aaron." Why does he omit mention of Aaron's priesthood, and of Elazar who was at that time High Priest of Israel?

Finally, the whole purpose of the tribes' disparaging remarks about Pinchas' ancestry is unclear. The object of their scorn was Pinchas, *himself*, for having killed Zimri for bringing a heathen woman into the camp. Now either they did not know the law that "he who has intercourse with a heathen woman, zealous people may attack him," in which case they should have accused Pinchas of murder; or, they thought that Pinchas did not come into the category of "zealous people," in which case they should have accused him of having ulterior motives for his act. The only alternative is that they knew both the law and the fact that Pinchas was zealous,[6] and if this were true, they should have had no grounds for complaint whatever. So, in any case, reference to Jethro, his maternal grandfather, seems quite irrelevant to the issue at hand.

2. THE MOTIVE OF THE ISRAELITES

The answer to these difficulties lies in the realization that the tribes, in disparaging Pinchas, were seeking to *defend the honor* of Israel and of Moses.

Zimri had brought the Midianite woman into the camp "before the eyes of Moses and before the eyes of all the congregation of the children of Israel."[2] And of all these people, only Pinchas had the zeal to rise and avenge this profanation of G-d. Certainly the rest of the Israelites knew the law as well as Pinchas, for it had been transmitted to "the whole people" together.[7] And without a doubt, Moses knew it, because Pinchas said to him, "I have received it as a tradition from you."[8] Pin-

---

6. Cf. supra, pp. 263-4.
7. Cf. *Rashi, Shemot* 34:32.
8. *Rashi, Bamidbar,* 25:7.

chas' solitary response had brought shame upon Israel and upon Moses.

This is why they tried to cast doubt on the purity of Pinchas' motives. What they did was to accuse him of a streak of cruelty, inherited from his grandfather Jethro, as contributing a share in his zealous act. This is why they seized on Jethro's practice of fattening calves for sacrifice, for it is the supreme cruelty to appear to be acting for someone's benefit—feeding him well—only for the sake of the ultimate slaughter.[9] The Israelites' defense was this: Why did only Pinchas rise and take vengeance into his hands. Because he was animated also by cruelty, not only by conscience. We were not so cruel. Therefore we hesitated.

And this is why Rashi includes all the tribes in the disparagement. Only the tribe of Simeon were concerned to defend Zimri's honor, but *all* the tribes were concerned to defend the honor of Moses and of the Jewish People.

3. THE MOTIVE OF PINCHAS

Now we can see the precise point of the Torah at this stage repeating the genealogy of Pinchas, that he was the "son of Elazar, the son of Aaron the priest." It is to show that in his act, Pinchas was not the "grandson of Jethro" but only the "grandson of Aaron": In other words that he was not driven at all by cruelty but only by a burning religious zeal. And Rashi tacitly points out to us that in this phrase, the crucial words are "the son of Aaron." The emphasis of the Torah is not simply that Pinchas was the son of Elazar, who was first the deputy High Priest, and then after Aaron's death the High Priest himself. Nor is it that Pinchas was the grandson of "Aaron *the priest.*" Rather, the emphasis is on Aaron's character *aside from his priesthood,* that he "pursued peace and caused love to descend between contending parties."[10] Where contention existed between the Israelites and G-d, Pinchas sought to replace it with

---

9. Cf. *Rashi, Behaalotecha* 11:22.
10. *Rashi, Bamidbar* 20:29.

love, as G-d says, "Pinchas . . . has turned My wrath away from the children of Israel."[11] This was the underlying nature of Pinchas' zealousness—a deep love of peace that he had inherited from Aaron, and a desire to remove the cause of the bitterness between G-d and His people.

4. ULTERIOR AND INTERIOR MOTIVES

In Rashi we find more than simply a literal commentary to the verses of the Torah. We find profound and general truths that have a bearing on our lives. From his understanding of this particular episode of Pinchas, we learn that when one sees a man engaged in a religious act, even though we seem to have overwhelming evidence that he is doing so for some ulterior motive, it is forbidden for us to belittle him.

Even if it is in fact true that he has ulterior motives, there is a categorical statement in the Talmud[12] that "a man should *always* be preoccupied with the Torah and the commandments, even if not for its own sake, for in the course of acting for some other end he will come to do it for its own sake." The true motive will eventually displace the false one.

Indeed, the Hebrew original of this statement reads, not "in the course of" but "in the midst of."[13] And the deep implication is that the right motive will be found "in the midst" of the wrong one: That although a Jew may formulate ulterior motives in his mind for doing G-d's will, subconsciously, in the true depths of his being, he seeks to keep to the Torah for its own sake alone.

Furthermore, the obligation of a Jew, when he sees another doing the right act for the wrong reason, is not to dissuade him from doing the act at all; but to help him towards a true understanding of its purpose and to bring him more quickly to the state where he does G-d's will for its own sake.

---

11. *Bamidbar* 25:11.
12. *Pesachim*, 50b. Cf. *Shulchan Aruch Harav, Hilchot Talmud Torah*, 4:3.
13. *"Mitoch."*

This is so even when there is in reality an ulterior motive. But in fact it is never given to us to know with certainty the motives of someone else. The tribes had powerful grounds for suspecting Pinchas' motives; but G-d who "sees into the heart,"[14] testified that they were wrong.

5. MODESTY AND PRIDE

Someone who follows the example of the tribes may fall into a deeper error, the error of self-deception. For when someone prevents someone else from doing something which in itself is good, merely because his motives were suspect, the first person's motives may also be suspect. He may reason thus: Since I am by nature modest and self-effacing, I cannot tolerate pride, and therefore when I see someone learning Torah with conspicuous passion, or performing the commandments beyond the requirements of the Torah, which appears ostentatious, I cannot pass it by in silence. But in fact, he is wrong and the person he criticizes is right. The tribes criticized Pinchas in their wish to exonerate themselves and Moses; but it is of Pinchas that G-d says "he was zealous with My jealousy." Indeed, there may be an element of pride in this very show of modesty. A true response to seeing someone learning with passion and fulfilling the commandments lavishly would be to be roused to a similar ardor oneself.[15] If instead one is critical, it is almost as if one could not bear the sight of someone more virtuous than oneself. Pirkei Avot says:[16] "Judge all men in the scale of merit." When one has a feeling towards another person which does not accord with this maxim, then it is a feeling whose source does not lie in holiness and truth.

6. THE REWARD OF THE ZEALOUS

The episode of Pinchas took place while a pestilence afflicted the Israelites. And, though he was not, like Moses, a

---

14. *I Samuel* 16:7.
15. *Baba Batra,* 21a: "Envy amongst scholars increases knowledge."
16. 1:6.

leader of his generation, nor was he even (as yet) a priest, nonetheless by his action the pestilence was stilled, and peace was restored between the Jews and G-d: "Behold I give him My covenant of peace."

Thus, even at a time of spiritual affliction, when one sees a Jew zealous in his service of G-d, even a Jew with no claims to leadership or distinction, one must not dissuade or discourage him. For he, like Pinchas, is the bringer of true peace between G-d and His people, the peace which is the opposite of separation and exile. He is the harbinger of the Messianic Age,[17] who "shall turn the heart of the fathers to the children, and the heart of the children to the fathers"[18] in the ultimate and everlasting peace.

(Source: Likkutei Sichot, Vol. VIII, pp. 160-170.)

---

17. "Pinchas is Elijah": *Targum Yonatan ben Uziel, Vo'era* 6:18; *Pirkei de Rabbi Eliezer,* ch. 47; *Zohar,* Part II, 190a; *Rashi, Baba Metzia,* 114b.
18. *Malachi* 3:24.

פרשת מטות

MATTOT

In the opening verses of our Sidra we encounter the laws of making and annulling a vow. And whereas a person cannot release himself from his pledges, in certain cases, others can do it for him. In particular, a father can release his daughter (if she has not reached the age of maturity) or a husband his wife, from their vows. There is a further intermediate case, which is something of a combination of these two; a girl who is as yet only betrothed, can be released from a pledge by the combined veto of her father and her husband-to-be. Indeed, their conjoint power is retroactive—it applies even to vows made before betrothal. The Rebbe develops the contrast between marriage and betrothal and applies it to the relationship between the Jew and G-d. And it asks the important question: How is it that betrothal confers even greater rights on a man than marriage itself?

1. MAKING AND UNMAKING A VOW

The Sidra of Mattot opens with an account of the laws of making a vow, and of having it annulled. There are three ways in which annulment can take place: (1) by a recognized sage (a *chacham*) who has the power retroactively to release a person from a pledge he has undertaken, (2) by the father of a girl who has made a vow while still under his guardianship; and (3) by a husband who can veto the wow of his wife. The powers of a father and a husband are not retroactive—i.e., they only annul the obligation to fulfill the vow from the present onwards.

In the times when the two distinct stages to a Jewish marriage, betrothal *(kiddushin)* and marriage proper *(nissuin)*, took place at two different times, there were two corresponding degrees of power of the husband over his wife's pledges. We would naturally assume that this power would be greater after marriage than during betrothal. But in one respect this is not so. For a man has the power—during betrothal but not after it—to annul the vows his wife made when she was single.[1]

How is it that betrothal grants the husband greater power over his wife's commitments than marriage itself?

One explanation is based on the fact that he does not have this right in himself but only in conjunction with the father of the girl.[2] Acting together, her father and her betrothed can annul her vows. So that the father, as it were, communicates his authority over the girl while she is single, to her husband to be. On the other hand, a husband has, in and by himself the right of veto and thus he borrows no powers from her father. His right therefore does not extend back to the period when she was single, and not as yet bound to him.

2. BETROTHAL AND MARRIAGE TO G-D

This fact of *halacha* has a bearing on our religious life. There are two ways a Jew can bind himself to G-d: In betrothal and in marriage.

When a man is betrothed to a girl, she becomes forbidden to any other man. Thus, when a Jew is "betrothed" to G-d he has taken a decisive commitment. He has decided to let nothing else waylay and capture his devotion. He has set himself aside from all but G-d's will. This in itself is a momentous act, but it is a negative one. He has not yet reached the spiritual equivalent of marriage, the state where he "shall cleave . . . and be one flesh"[3] with his partner. And as the fruit of marriage is children—children who reflect their parents so—the fruit of a total oneness with G-d is good deeds which express both the will of G-d and the self-effacement of man. "What are the offspring of the righteous? Their good deeds."[4]

---

1. *Nedarim,* 67a, b. *Shulchan Aruch, Yoreh Deah,* 234:5 and 35.
2. *Nedarim,* 66b.
3. *Bereishit* 2:24.
4. *Rashi, Bereishit,* 6:9. *Bereishit Rabbah,* 30:6.

3. THE SENSE OF INCOMPLETENESS

Although the state of spiritual "marriage" goes far beyond "betrothal," betrothal has its own unique virtue.

The man who has reached the level of marriage may fall prey to a certain kind of pride. He may feel that he has reached perfect righteousness, that he is now the "master of the house" with the right in *himself* to "annul vows." Unlike the betrothed man—he may reason—his power does not need the co-operation of the father.

That this is a fatal error can be seen from the case of Bar Kochba,[5] whose attitude proved to the Rabbis that he was not in fact entitled to the name Bar Kochba (literally, "the son of a star," a Messianic title derived from the verse, "There come a star out of Jacob"), but was instead Bar Koziba ("the son of lies").

The strength of betrothal lies in the fact that the betrothed knows that he has (halachic) powers only in conjunction with the father. He has no rights in himself. Spiritually, this means that he knows that all his capacities are dependent on G-d. And, acting together with Him, he can reach heights that he alone could not aspire to. He can arrive at the power of "annulment," namely, nullifying in himself and the world, the masks of illusion that hide G-d's presence from man. And this power is "retroactive," that is, beyond the normal limitations of time and space. Just as a vow binds, and an annulment breaks the bond, so he, with the help of G-d, releases the world from its bondage, from falsehood, finitude and the concealment of G-d.

4. THE STRENGTH OF CONJUNCTION

The implication is this: However far a man travels on his spiritual journey, even if he "marries" himself completely to G-d, he must never forget that by his own power he can achieve nothing. He must unite himself with what is higher

---

5. Cf. *Jerusalem Talmud, Taanit*, 4:5. *Gittin*, 57a; *Sanhedrin*, 93b.

than himself. There is no room in the religious life for complacency. However high he has risen, there is always something
higher to cling to and reach out towards. He is as yet incomplete, as yet only the betrothed. But together with G-d—the
father—it is within his power to annul—the bondage of the
world in a way that knows no limits.

(Source: Likkutei Sichot, Vol. II pp. 612-614)

פרשת מסעי

MASSEI

Our Sidra begins with an account of the 42 journeys by which the Israelites left Egypt and came to the borders of the Chosen Land. The opening verse, however, suggests that all of the journeys were an exodus from Egypt, whereas in fact only the first one was. To understand this, the Rebbe develops the theme that Egypt is not only a place but also a state of mind. Mitzrayim, the Hebrew word for Egypt, also means "confinement," and there is an obvious contrast with the land of Israel, which is called the "good and spacious land." The questions that confront us, therefore, are: What is "confinement" and "spaciousness" in the life of the Jew? And, what is the significance of the idea of a "journey."

1. ONE EXODUS OR MANY

"These are the journeys of the children of Israel by which they went forth out of the land of Egypt."

This verse raises a well-known difficulty. For only the *first* of the journeys mentioned in our Sidra—from Rameses to Succot—constituted "going forth out of the land of Egypt." The others were all made outside Egypt. Why, then, does the verse use the plural, "these are the journeys?"

Also, what is the significance of these 42 journeys in traveling from Egypt to the land of Israel, the "good and spacious land?" The word "spacious" is opposed to "confined" or "restricted." But as soon as the Jewish people had left Egypt, they had left their confinement. Why was it only after 42 journeys that they were said to have reached "spaciousness?"

These concepts of confinement and spaciousness have a spiritual sense: "Out of my confinement I called upon the L-rd. The L-rd answered me with enlargement." As a Jew moves towards his spiritual goal, he passes from the straits of inner conflict to the open spaces of serenity, from the narrow path

281

through secular distractions to the broad plain of unity with G-d. Every stage he reaches is spacious in relation to the level he has left, and restricted in relation to the level he is heading towards, until he reaches the final open space, the Messianic Age, with the crossing of the Jordan that marks the divide between journeying and arriving.

This is why all 42 journeys, not merely the first, were a "going forth out of the land of Egypt." For every journey that brought them nearer to the land of Israel and their destiny made the previous stopping point seem like a confinement, another Egypt. Each stage was a new exodus. They had already left the physical Egypt. But they still had to pass beyond the Egypt, the narrowness of the soul.

2. EGYPT AND THE INDIVIDUAL

The Torah is eternal. And it is clearly so where it concerns the exodus, about which the Jew is explicitly obliged "to see himself as if he had traveled out of Egypt that very day."[1] The 42 journeys therefore have a special perpetual significance.

There are many Egypts through which the individual has to pass. At one level it may be the confinement of the secular world, which seeks to hold him captive. At another, it may be the narrow scope of the human mind, as it filters his Judaism through the dark lens of rationalization. But even if he has traveled beyond these, and his faith is no longer confined to his understanding, he has always to strain towards new plateaus of expansiveness, compared to which his present state is a confinement.

3. THE RUNGS OF PRAYER

We can see this process exemplified in prayer. There is a difference between Torah and prayer,[2] for Torah is G-d's word to man, while prayer is the word of man to G-d. Prayer is Ja-

---

1. *Pesachim,* 116b. *Tanya,* Part I, ch. 47.
2. *Tanya,* Part III, ch. 10. *Torah Or,* lc. *Sefer Hamaamarim,* 5708, p. 80.

cob's ladder, "set on the earth and its top reaching to heaven."[3] It has many rungs. Each step upwards is a movement from the straits of the earth to the expanses of heaven.

The first rung is preparation. How can finite man stand before infinite G-d in prayer? How much less can he do so if he has sinned and betrayed his relationship to G-d? It is this sense of momentous awe, in which a man divests himself of the masks of self-sufficiency and pride, which is the preparation for prayer. And this setting oneself to pray—even before a word of prayer is spoken—is in itself an exodus, a liberation, from one's normal situation.

Then comes prayer itself, a series of ever-widening chambers of the spirit, to which the preparation is, in comparison, a narrow and humble entrance-hall.

From the outpourings of devotion in the "Psalms of Praise," through the expression of love in the *Shema*, we ascend to the final point of self-abandonment and openness to G-d in the *Amidah,* standing "like a servant before his master." At that moment we ourselves are nothing; G-d is everything; we are powerless to speak; we can say only, "O L-rd, open *Thou* my lips, and my mouth shall declare Thy praise."[4]

4. BEYOND PARADOX

The *Amidah* embodies a paradox. On the one hand we abandon our ego and become a mere mouthpiece for the words of G-d. On the other hand, it is a prayer of requests for the satisfaction of our spiritual and material needs. And yet surely it is just at this point of selflessness that we forget our needs and are unconcerned with our welfare.

These two aspects of the *Amidah* are indeed opposed. But it is only reason and logic that cannot tolerate the joining of two opposites. The *Amidah is* a level of spirituality beyond the reach of reason. The nearer we reach to G-d, the more all opposites

---

3. *Zohar*, Part I, 266b; Part III, 306b; *Tikkunei Zohar, Tikkun* 45.
4. *Psalms* 51:17. *Alshich,* ad loc. *Likkutei Torah, Shir Hashirim*, 2c. *Sefer Hamaamarim,* 5627, p. 436.

can be accommodated, all tensions dissolved. We say, "He who makes peace in His high places," for it is in the heights beyond reason that there is peace between contending parties, and compatibility amongst opposites. In this respect, the *Amidah* is a foretaste of the future world, when "all *flesh* shall see" the presence of G-d, when—in other words—the opposites of substance and spirit will be interfused.

5. THE JOURNEY

Even though the *Amidah* is the apex of the daily prayers, each day the Jew must begin again, preparing and praying; making yesterday's high point, today's point of departure. Although on his personal journey he has left the "Egypt" of transgression, he must cast off the successive layers of narrowness of soul, the ever-fainter traces of that original Egypt. Even if a man does no wrong, the Baal Shem Tov said that if he sees a fault in another person, this is a symptom that he has a trace of that same fault within himself.[5] Evil leaves its traces, and even these must be removed.

The religious life is not a matter of suddenly arriving, but of constantly journeying.

6. TWO MISTAKES

The journeys of the Israelites from Egypt serve as a warning against the two kinds of error into which a Jew can fall.

One is to believe that one has arrived. He may think: Having reached so far in my Judaism, I can rest content. But the truth is that the Jew was not created to stand still. There is always a new journey before him.

The other is to despair. He may feel: I know so little, I am capable of so little, that my religious efforts are in vain. But in truth, even a single journey is a liberation from some personal Egypt. (And the direction in which one is traveling matters more than how far one is along the way.)

Alongside personal despair, there may be historical despair,

---

5. Cf. *Sefer Hasichot, Summer,* 5700, p. 83. Supra, p. 7.

the feeling that never has an age been less conducive to Messianic hope. But the opposite is the truth. The Israelites, who in Egypt had reached the penultimate point, the forty-ninth gate, of impurity,[6] were still able to reach Israel, their destination. But for us, virtually all of the journey towards the Messianic destiny has already been traveled; the goal is near; and we live after Sinai and have the power of that revelation constantly with us; and we have the spiritual leaders of the generation to bind us to G-d and to help us in our upward climb.

7. THE THREE WEEKS

The Sidrot of Mattot and Massei are always read in the period of the three weeks between the 17th of Tammuz and the 9th of Av. They are set in this time of bitter confinement between the first breach in the walls of Jerusalem and the Temple's destruction.

The significance of their timing is that they convey to us, at the time when we most need reminding, the concept of "destroying in order to rebuild." Destruction may be for the sake of replacing a building with a better and stronger one. The Baal Shem Tov commented on the verse "It is the time of Jacob's trouble; but he shall be saved out of it" that salvation is not something that simply *follows* trouble: It is implicit in it. Here, too, we find the fusion of two opposites—destroying and rebuilding, affliction and salvation—that comes only when we leave the confinements of human reasoning and journey towards the all-encompassing expanses of faith. At this level, everything is drawn into our faith. We see G-d's goodness everywhere, even in the seeming catastrophe. Seen from the eyes of a son, punishment is an evil. In the eyes of his father, it is for his son's own good. Our goal is to see history through the eyes of G-d. And by so doing we are able to turn G-d's hidden mercy into open kindness, and change the darkness of exile into the light of the Time to Come.

(Source: Likkutei Sichot, Vol. II pp. 348-353)

---

6. *Zohar Chadash*, beg. *Yitro. Tikkunei Zohar, Tikkun* 32.

פרשת דברים

DEVARIM

The Sidra of Devarim is always read on the Shabbat before the 9th
of Av, the date on which both Temples fell. These tragedies are reflected in the choice of Haftorah for the surrounding weeks, those
before the 9th of Av expressing prophecies of rebuke for the sins
that were the spiritual cause of the destruction; those afterwards
conveying messages of comfort and solace. This week's Haftorah,
the famous "Vision" of Isaiah, gives its name to the day—*Shabbat
Chazon*, the "Shabbat of the Vision." Traditionally, this is read as a
powerful indictment of a rebellious people. But, true to the Chassidic tradition of seeing the Divine blessing even in the apparent
curse, Rabbi Levi Yitzchak of Berditchev, one of the early Chassidic
teachers, saw in it a distant "vision" of the Third Temple of Messianic times. The Rebbe traces the connection between this thought
and the content of the Sidra of Devarim, the opening of the
"repetition of the law" by Moses to the Israelites as they stand on
the threshold of their Promised Land.

1. THE SHABBAT OF THE VISION

There is a saying of Rabbi Levi Yitzchak of Berditchev[1] that
this Shabbat, Shabbat Chazon (when we read as the Haftorah,
the famous Vision *(Chazon)* of Isaiah), is a day when we are
presented with a vision of the future Third Temple, even
though we see it from a great distance.[2]

And this leads us to understand the connection between
the "vision" of the Haftorah, and the Sidra of Devarim, which
are always read together on the Shabbat before the 9th of Av.

For, with Devarim begins the "Second Torah"—Moses' re-
capitulation of the Torah. And the whole book of Devarim
differs from the other four books of the Chumash in being addressed to the generation who were about to enter the Holy

---

1. Cf. *Notes of Tzemach Tzedek on Eichah*, p. 45.
2. The word used for vision, *chazon*, indicates a vision from *a distance*.

Land.[3] They needed counsel and caveat in a way that the previous generations did not. For the people who had traveled in the wilderness possessed an immediate knowledge of the Divine[4]—they had seen G-d on Sinai. But the succeeding generation, already touched by their responsibilities in the physical world, lost that immediacy, they *heard* G-d but did not see Him. They were addressed in the words[5] "And now, Israel, *listen.* . . ."

And the difference between seeing and hearing is this:[6] someone who witnesses an event is unshakable in his testimony about it—he has seen it with his own eyes. But one who hears about an event may eventually entertain doubts. Hearing does not confer certainty.

That is why the generation who were to enter Israel, who heard but did not see G-d, had to be commanded about self-sacrifice and the like, a warning which would have been superfluous to the people of the wilderness.

In one way, then, the later generation lacked the spiritual immediacy of their forebears. But they were, nonetheless, to reach something unattained by their fathers, who were told:[7] "You have not, as yet, come to the rest and the inheritance which the L-rd your G-d has given to you." Shiloh and Jerusalem[8] were reached only by that later generation. For only by the descent into material concerns, the translation of G-d's will into practical action, could the fulfillment be reached of "the rest and the inheritance."

Devarim, in short, tells us of the paradox that through descent comes true uplifting: The highest achievements of the spirit are won in earthly and not heavenly realms.

And this is also the message of the "vision"—even though this Haftorah is read in the "Nine Days" of mourning for the

---

3. Cf. *Megillah,* 31b. *Likkutei Torah, Bamidbar,* 17c.
4. *Pesikta, Parshat Parah,* 14:9. *Likkutei Torah, Bamidbar,* 37b.
5. *Devarim* 4:1.
6. Cf. supra, pp. 106-7.
7. *Devarim* 12:9.
8. *Megillah,* 10a; *Zevachim,* 119a; *Jerusalem Talmud, Megillah,* end ch. 1. Cf. *Zohar,* Part II, 241a, 242a.

loss of the Temples, nonetheless through the resultant exile
will come the true redemption, the vision of which we glimpse
(in the words of the Berditchever) in the very moment of our
loss.

2. SADNESS AND REJOICING

The sense of mourning, of being "in the straits"[9] which
dominates our consciousness in the Nine Days when we recall
the destruction of the Temples, is broken by Shabbat, the day
on which joy must prevail.[10] Indeed, on the Shabbat before the
9th of Av we are bidden to rejoice even more than usual, to
remove any possibility that the melancholy of the surrounding
days should intrude into the Shabbat spirit.

But the injunction has a deeper meaning. Shabbat is a reflection of the World to Come; and that future redemption will
be so complete as to efface all traces of the exiled past. So on
this day there is no place for the evocations of exile.

But we go further on this Shabbat than to eliminate sad-
ness—we increase our joy.

For the future redemption will be more spiritually intense
than any previous one. If it merely restored the status quo, exile
would have been unnecessary. Each exile of the Jews has culminated in new levels of spirituality, for by being scattered,
they have been able to redeem and bring into G-d's service en-
vironments that would otherwise have been untouched by the
hand of Torah. And the end-point of this journey—the Time
to Come—will be a redemption without further exile, a completeness of spirituality that needs no new excursions.

So the Shabbat most connected with exile, the day of the
"vision," sees in its foretaste of the future, the consummation
of all exile and its transformation into undisturbed rejoicing.

---

9. *Lamentations* 1:3, alluding, say our Sages, to the Three Weeks between 17th of
   Tammuz and 9th of Av.
10. *Tosefot, Moed Katan*, 23b (quoting *Jerusalem Talmud, Berachot*, 2:7). Cf. *Jerusalem Talmud, Megillah*, 1:4. *Sifri, Behaalotecha* 10:10.

The Shulchan Aruch[11] tells us that on this day it is permitted to prepare a feast like that which Solomon made when he was made king: That the anticipation of the future kingdom might give us the strength to turn the sorrows of exile into the joys of redemption.

(Source: Likkutei Sichot, Vol. II pp. 357-359)

---

11. *Orach Chayim*, 552:10.

פרשת ואתחנן

VAETCHANAN

The 9th of Av is the date on which both Temples were destroyed.
Each year, on the subsequent Shabbat, we read as our Haftorah the
famous passage of consolation from Isaiah "Comfort ye, comfort ye
My people." The Midrash tells us that this is, literally, a two-fold
consolation for the loss of the two Temples. And yet, would not
one have been sufficient? For the First Temple saw a greater revelation of the Divine Presence than the Second, so that our grief and
our consolation for its loss encompasses our feelings for the Second
Temple. The Rebbe, however, argues that there was something
unique about the Second Temple, and that this has repercussions
for our daily religious life. At the heart of its analysis is the distinction between two different approaches to G-d: Through righteousness and through repentance.

1. ONE CONSOLATION OR TWO?

This week's Haftorah, the first of the "Seven Weeks of
Consolation" after the 9th of Av, begins with the words[1]
"Comfort ye, comfort ye My people."

The Midrash[2] explains that this apparent repetition refers
in fact to two consolations and two tragedies: The loss of the
First and Second Temples.

But this is not as simple as at first sight. The idea of consolation is that, when a calamity befalls a man, even though a second person may not be able to restore his loss, he still gives
comfort by his sympathy. And if the man has sustained not one
loss but two, then he can certainly be comforted twice over.

But in the case of the Temples, the consolation lies in the
fact that a Third Temple will be built to replace those that were

---

1. *Isaiah* 40:1.
2. *Yalkut, Isaiah, Remez* 445.

destroyed.[3] And since the First Temple was greater than the Second in the revelations it housed and the miracles it witnessed,[4] replacing it would, in itself, be replacing the Second Temple as well. The First contained all that was in the Second, and more. So it follows that the consolation for the loss of the First would in itself include consolation for the loss of the Second.

The answer is, that though the Second Temple was, in absolute terms, less exalted than the First, it still had certain unique virtues. Thus, the Talmud[5] interprets the verse, "Greater shall be the glory of the latter house than the former,"[6] to refer to the Second Temple, which was greater than the first in its size and duration.

This is why there will be two consolations, for the Third Temple will combine the virtues of both its predecessors.[7]

2. TABERNACLE AND TEMPLE

To understand what the unique virtue of the Second Temple was, we must first see the way in which a Temple as such went beyond the Tabernacle that accompanied the Israelites in the wilderness. Both were "dwelling-places" of G-d's presence. But the Temple was a permanent dwelling, the Tabernacle a temporary one.[8]

For, there are two elements in drawing down a high degree of holiness to this world:

(i) where the holiness is *apparent* in the physical, but it does not actually transform it. This is a manifestation of the power of the spirituality, in that it can even permeate so gross a being.

(ii) where the holiness actually *transforms* the physical; that the material becomes, as it were, a "vessel," or receptacle, to

---

3. *Radak* (Rabbi David Kimchi), *Isaiah*, Ibid.
4. *Yoma*, 21b.
5. *Baba Batra*, 3a.
6. *Haggai* 2:9.
7. Cf. *Zohar*, Part III, 221a.
8. Cf. *Shir Hashirim Rabbah*, 1:16. Cf. *Psalms* 132:14; *II Samuel* 7:6.

holiness. This is an even stronger revelation, whereby the "light" not merely affects, but intrinsically changes, the physical.

Similarly, the Tabernacle was holy: "And they shall make Me a Sanctuary and I will dwell in their midst." Its sanctity extended even to the curtains, the beams, and the ground on which it rested. But these were not the source of its holiness. The source was in the *revelation from Above,* the infinite light of G-d which shone within it. That is why, when the Tabernacle was moved, its previous resting-place ceased to be holy ground. For its holiness was not from itself: It lasted only as long as the Divine Presence rested there.

But the sanctity of the Temple was vested in the *physical materials* from which it was built. Even after its destruction, the ground on which it rested was, and still is, sacred.[9]

This is the inner meaning of the fact that the Temple was built by Solomon. For in his reign, "the moon reached its fullness," in the words of the Zohar.[10] The sun gives light; and moon reflects it. And in spiritual terms, G-d is the source of light, and the earth receives it. Whereas the Tabernacle had the sanctity of *G-d's* light, the holiness of the Temple lay in the *very material* of which it was constructed, in the things of the *earth* which were dedicated to G-d. It was as the "moon" which receiving G-d's light and reflecting it outwards to the whole world.

3. REFLECTED AND GENERATED LIGHT

But there is a difference between the moon as it is now, and as it will be in the World to Come.

Now it draws its radiance from the sun. But in the future world, "the light of the moon shall be as the light of the sun."[11] It will shine, not with reflected light, but with its own.

----

9. *Rambam, Hilchot Beit Habechirah,* end ch. 6.
10. Part I, 150a. Cf. *Shemot Rabbah,* 15:26.
11. *Isaiah* 30:26.

And this is paralleled by the difference between the two ways that the world and its beings are purified and transformed.

We may be changed by a light that comes from above, as a pupil learns from his teacher. He may come to understand what he has been taught, to the extent that, through *his own* efforts, he reaches the very essence of the subject. But still he is a reflection of his teacher. He is like the moon, shedding a light that came to him from elsewhere.

We may, on the other hand, be changed by a light from within. When a person, for example, returns to G-d after forsaking His will, he does not do so because of any revelation from Above. On the contrary, at the point of return, he is far from visions of G-d. He does so because of a prompting from *within*. For every Jew, in the true depths of his being, seeks to do G-d's will: It is merely that sometimes his inclinations get the better of him, and hide his real nature.[12] The essence of the Jew is that he is part of G-d. And the change that he brings to his life when he returns to G-d is from within, in the strictest sense. He penetrates the surface of his inclinations, and finds G-dliness at the core of his self. *"All flesh shall see . . . for the mouth of the L-rd has spoken."*[13] He reaches the word of G-d through his flesh itself, through seeing the real nature of his existence. Such a person is like the moon of the World to Come. The light he casts is from the fire that burns within him.

4. THE WORD, THE COMMAND, THE RETURN

There are therefore three stages: Receiving light from elsewhere, reflecting it, and generating light from within.

They are mirrored by three facets of Judaism: Torah, the commandments (Mitzvot) and the act of return (Teshuvah).

---

12. *Rambam, Hilchot Gerushin,* end ch. 2.
13. *Isaiah* 40:5.

Torah is the word of G-d, the light from Above. Even though, when we learn Torah, we become united with it,[14] Torah is always the giver of light and we are always the recipients. In our learning we add nothing to it, we merely strive to uncover what was already there.

But through the Mitzvot, we both receive and give light. By wearing *tefillin* or *tzitzit* we turn parchment and wool into holy objects. By abdicating our egos in favor of G-d's will, we refine the world: "The Mitzvot were only given so that, by them, all creatures should be purified."[15] Whereas the Torah exists eternally in itself, the Mitzvot need the partnership of man. The Torah, although it speaks of the physical world, does not enter into it. But the commandments require physical acts and objects, and they change the fabric of the world. The Torah is like the "light of day"[16] which illuminates but does not change that upon which it shines.[17] But the commandments are like the "light of a lamp"[16] in which wick and oil are turned into flame.

Nonetheless, the Mitzvot are still a reflected light. They need, first, the word of G-d who commands them. But the *ba'al teshuvah*—the person who returns to G-d—has shut himself off from the word of G-d, and returns because of a flame *within* himself that refuses to be separated from its source.

By the Mitzvot a Jew sanctifies only what is permitted to him.[18] But by Teshuvah he sanctifies his whole past life, lived in the realm of forbidden acts.[19] His past sins become his merits. And this is the unique virtue of the act of return: It sanctifies not only a part, but the whole of experience.

---

14. *Tanya*, Part I, ch. 5.
15. *Bereishit Rabbah*, beg. ch. 44.
16. *Proverbs* 6:23: "For a Mitzvah is a candle, and Torah is light."
17. *Torah Or*, 87b.
18. Cf. *Shabbat*, 28b.
19. *Yoma*, 86b. Cf. *Derech Mitzvotecha*, 191a.

5. THE SECOND TEMPLE

We are now able to understand the unique significance of the Second Temple.

During the period of the First Temple, the Jewish people were in general at the level of "righteousness," living a life of obedience to G-d's commandments. The light it gave to the world was a *reflection* of the will of G-d.

But the Second Temple belonged to a time of repentance and return. The world was being sanctified from *within,* through *Israel's* own spiritual resources. Thus it is significant that its building was ordered by Cyrus,[20] the king of Persia, a non-Jew.

This is why we needed two consolations, "Comfort ye, comfort ye My people." For the two Temples each had its own distinctive virtue. The revelations of G-d's presence which belonged to the First were greater, but those of the Second were more inward. They issued from the very texture of the physical world. Thus the Talmud[5] says that the greatness of the Second Temple lay in its size (space) and its duration (time). For it drew its sanctity from man's own efforts to purify his finite world, not from G-d as He is above space and time.

The consolation will be the Third Temple, in which the light from above and the light from within will combine.

6. WHAT CAN BE LOST, AND WHAT CANNOT

All inner meanings of the Torah have their reflection in Halacha (Jewish law).

We can see that the land of Israel had a greater sanctity during the First Temple than during the Second. For—to take one example—when Rosh Hashanah fell on Shabbat, the Shofar was blown throughout the land in the First Temple times, but in the Temple alone in the time of the Second.[21]

---

20. *Ezra* 1:1. Cf. Ibid., 6:4. *Rosh Hashanah*, 4a.
21. *Rosh Hashanah*, 29b (*Likkutei Torah, Rosh Hashanah*, 57c).

On the other hand, the land lost some of its sanctity with the destruction of the First Temple, but none with the loss of the Second.[9]

The laws attaching to the land of Israel show that the First Temple conferred a more intense holiness; the Second, a more permanent one.

This can be compared to the two sets of tablets on which Moses received the Ten Commandments. The first set was the more miraculous: But they were broken. The second were not. So too the First Temple conferred greater holiness on Israel, yet when it was destroyed that sanctity was removed. But the holiness of the land in the time of the Second Temple persists for all time.

By reading this week's Haftorah, "Comfort ye, comfort ye My people," we remember not only what was lost, but what survives. The generation of righteousness may belong to the past and the future. But the generation of return is a present possibility. It is the enduring heritage of the Second Temple. And by turning possibility into fact we bring close the time of the Third Temple—the twofold and final consolation.

(Source: Likkutei Sichot, Vol. IX pp. 61-70)

פרשת עקב

EKEV

Last week and this, we read the first two Haftorot of "consolation," two powerful passages from Isaiah which present a vision of hope and solace to Israel in the dark times of the loss of the Temple. A Midrashic source, however, tells us that there is a difference between them. The first is G-d's call to the prophets to comfort the people. But Israel seeks more. It seeks comfort from G-d Himself. And this is what the second Haftorah represents. The Sicha relates this distinction to the difference between the *Sidrot* of Vaetchanan and Ekev, in particular between the first and second paragraphs of the *Shema* which they respectively contain. The underlying theme is the difference between two kinds of revelation, that which comes from outside a person, and that which comes from within. The significance for our time is clear: What form must our spiritual life take when visions of G-d no longer break in on us, when the face of G-d is hidden, and we must discover Him from within?

1. CONSOLATION: THE PROPHETS AND G-D

This week's Haftorah, the second of the "Seven Weeks of Consolation," for the destruction of the Temples, is the passage from Isaiah[1] beginning, "But Zion said, the L-rd hath forsaken me, and the L-rd hath forgotten me." The Midrash[2] tells us that this is a continuation of the theme of the previous Haftorah, "Comfort ye, comfort ye My people."[3] In that first message of comfort, G-d instructs the *prophets* to console Israel. To this, Israel's response is, "The *L-rd* hath forsaken me." They seek, in other words, not the voice of the prophets but a consolation that comes directly from G-d.

Each year these Haftorot are read, respectively, with the Sidrot of Vaetchanan and Ekev. It follows that if the Haftorot are connected by this common theme, so too are the Sidrot.

---

1. 49:1 ff.
2. Quoted in *Avudraham, Sefer Haparshyot Vehaftorot.*
3. *Isaiah* 40:1.

297

Vaetchanan must contain some reference to the consolation of the prophets, and Ekev, to Israel's demand for the solace that stems from G-d Himself.

2. THE SHEMA

The two Sidrot differ considerably in their content, so that this contrast of emphasis is not immediately apparent. But there is one obvious link, namely that the first paragraph of the Shema is to be found in Vaetchanan and the second in Ekev. These two passages are clearly related; they have many ideas in common; but they also diverge at a number of points. And it is here that we will find an echo of the contrast between the two Haftorot and the two kinds of consolation.

3. CONTRASTS

Amongst the differences between the first and second paragraphs of the Shema are the following:

(i) In the first, we are commanded (individually) to "love the L-rd your G-d with all your heart and with all your soul and with all your might." But in the second, we are addressed (collectively) only with the phrase "with all your heart and with all your soul." The "might" is missing.

(ii) In the first paragraph, we are told first "And you shall teach them diligently to your children, and talk of them . . ." and then, "And you shall bind them for a sign upon your hand . . ." But in the second, the order is reversed. First "You shall bind them" and only then, "You shall teach them to your children." The commandments follow the study of the Torah in the first paragraph but precede it in the second.

(iii) The first paragraph contains only commandments. But the second also mentions the rewards ("That your days may be multiplied . . .") and the punishments ("The anger of the L-rd be kindled against you . . .") which attend them.

4. UNDERLYING DIFFERENCES

An underlying difference between the two passages is, as Rashi[4] points out, that the first (written throughout in the singular) is addressed to the *individual* Jew, while the second (which uses the plural) is directed to Israel as a *community.*

This applies to the general command of the love of G-d. In addition, the specific commands of *tefillin* and *mezuzah,* which occur in both paragraphs, also convey something new when stated a second time. In Rashi's words,[5] the extra significance is that "Even after you have been exiled, make yourselves distinctive by means of My commands: Lay *tefillin,* attach *mezuzot,* so that these shall not be new (unfamiliar) to you when you return."

Lastly, there is a nuance which distinguishes the two commands of spreading the knowledge of Torah. "And you shall teach them *diligently*"—the version in the first paragraph—refers to the obligation of a teacher to his disciples.[6] "And you shall teach them"—the reading in the second paragraph—refers to the relation of a father to his children.[7]

5. ABOVE AND WITHIN

All these distinctions stem from a single point of difference: Vaetchanan concerns the revelation and deliverance that come from *Above,* from G-d's grace. Thus it begins with Moses' supplication to G-d for His grace, that he be allowed to enter the Promised Land. For Moses was G-d's emissary through whom came the supernatural events of the exodus and those in the wilderness. Had he been permitted to lead the Israelites across the Jordan, the conquest of the land, too, would have been a supernatural event instead of a slow succession of military victories.

---

4. *Devarim* 11:13 (and *Sifri,* ad loc.).
5. Ibid., v. 18.
6. *Rashi,* Ibid. 6:7.
7. *Sifri, Rashi.* Ibid., v. 19. Cf. *Kiddushin,* 29b.

But the Sidra of Ekev concerns *man's* situation, and the
revelation he draws down upon himself by his own acts. So it
begins with an account of what *he* can achieve, and how: "And
it shall come to pass, because you hearken to these judgments. . . ." Even its name, *Ekev* ("because"), also has the connotation in Hebrew of a "heel"—the lowliest and least sensitive
of man's limbs, and an apt symbolism of his physical nature,
which by hearkening to G-d's word he can transform.

This contrast is also reflected in the choice of verbs in the
opening of the two Sidrot. In Vaetchanan, Moses pleads that he
might *"see* the good land."[8] But in Ekev, G-d says "because you
hearken to (literally: 'hear') these judgments." "Seeing" describes the vision of the supernatural that G-d confers in moments of grace. "Hearing" refers to the more distant, less lucid
perception of the spiritual, to which man can aspire by his own
efforts.

6. Seeing and Hearing

Seeing something is clearer and more forceful than hearing
about it.[9] Nonetheless, this force and clarity are due to *what* is
seen rather than to the person who sees it. It is the object
which is clearly defined; and the man who sees it may still be
unaffected by it. But if he has made the effort to hear about
something, he has already aroused his feelings and made himself sensitive to what he is about to hear. It can then enter the
inwardness of his soul.

This is true, too, of the difference between Vaetchanan and
Ekev. Although the "vision" which Moses sought from G-d
was a greater revelation than the "hearkening" which the Israelites could achieve by themselves, it was less inward—it would
have come to man from outside instead of mounting within
him.

The effect on the world would have been different, also.
Through G-d, via Moses, the nations who opposed Israel

<hr/>

8. *Devarim* 3:25.
9. Cf. *Rosh Hashanah*, 26a; supra, p. 106-7.

would have had their hostility utterly removed: "All the inhabitants of Canaan are melted away. Terror and dread fall
upon them."[10] But through Israel's own faithfulness a greater
and more inward transformation would take place: "You shall
be blessed above all peoples,"[11] meaning that even Israel's adversaries would bless and praise her.

7. THE PARTIAL AND THE WHOLE

Another difference between the two senses in this: Seeing
is only one of man's faculties. But hearing touches them all—
his intellect, in striving to understand G-d's command, his will,
in choosing to obey, and his practical faculties in translating his
intentions into deeds.

Jewish law reflects this. For if someone is guilty of causing
a person to become blind, he must compensate him for the loss
of his eyes. But if he is responsible for his deafness, he must
pay him the whole value of his life, as if he had robbed him of
all his faculties.[12]

8. THE TWO REVELATIONS AND THE SHEMA

Now we can trace all the many differences between the
two paragraphs of the Shema to their source.

The first belongs to the Sidra of Vaetchanan, which concerns the revelation from Above, as symbolized by the sense of
sight.

The second is from Ekev, which concerns the revelation
from within, which is like "hearing."

Thus the first is addressed to the individual, the "one," for
it speaks of the revelation from G-d, the "One," which awakens
the oneness of man. This vision of infinity makes man restless
to cast off his earthly constraints, and this is why it adds "with
all your might." But the second paragraph, relating as it does to
man within his human situation, speaks in the plural, to the

---

10. *Shemot* 15:15-16.
11. *Devarim* 7:14.
12. *Baba Kama*, 85b. *Shulchan Aruch, Choshen Mishpat*, ch. 420:17 and 25.

community, for it is addressed to man in his diversity and in the plurality of his powers. The love of G-d which man achieves by himself is settled and serene ("with all your heart and all your soul"). It does not share that violent desire to rise beyond the world which the words "with all your might" signify.

The first paragraph, as a consequence, sets the study of Torah (the word of G-d) before the command of *tefillin* and *mezuzah* (the act of man). But the second, starting from man and working towards G-d, reverses the order.

The first paragraph also omits any reference to reward and punishment. For in the face of a vision of G-d, man needs no other inducement to do His will. But when he sets out to work towards G-d from his own situation, he needs at the outset some motive (reward and punishment) that he can understand in purely human terms.

9. FAITH IN EXILE

Despite this concession to human frailty, it is here, in the second paragraph, that we find a reference to keeping the commandments "even after you have been exiled." For the first paragraph represents a state of mind where exile might take away the will to obey, might even remove the whole force of the Divine command. If the desire to do G-d's will rests on the vision of His presence, then once it is hidden by the dark clouds of exile, the desire too goes into hiding. But when it comes from within man himself, it remains, even in exile, in its strength.

And just as this revelation from within persists whether there is light or darkness in the face that G-d sets towards the world, so it is to be communicated not only to those who have seen the light, the "disciples," but to everyone; the "children."

10. THE TRUE CONSOLATION

Lastly, we can see the link between the two kinds of revelation represented by Vaetchanan and Ekev, and the two kinds of consolation embodied in their Haftorot.

The revelation that comes from outside of man lacks the ultimate dimension of inwardness. That is why the Haftorah of Vaetchanan, "Comfort ye, comfort ye My people," describes an indirect consolation, one that comes via the prophets.

But the Haftorah of Ekev is set in the human attempt to struggle towards G-d from within. Its opening words dramatically convey this situation at its darkest: "But Zion said, the L-rd hath forsaken me, and the L-rd hath forgotten me." And yet this is a measure of its inwardness, that the consolations of a prophet are not enough. And so, the Midrash tells us, G-d accedes to Israel's request. He admits, "O thou afflicted, tossed with tempest, are not comforted."[13] And He proclaims "I, even I, am He that comforts you"—with the true, the final and the imminent consolation, the coming of the Messianic Age.

(Source: Likkutei Sichot, Vol. IX pp. 79-85)

---

13. The opening words of the Haftorot of the following two Sidrot: Re'eh and Shoftim. Cf. *Avudraham* quoted above in note 2.

פרשת ראה
RE'EH

The following Sicha illustrates in a striking way an important truth
about the nature of Chassidic thought. Chassidut is not simply one
amongst many of the branches of Jewish thinking. It is not separate
from or merely supplementary to the "revealed" facet of Torah—
halachic or legal reasoning. Instead, it lies at the heart of the other
branches of Torah, shedding light on them all. In this way, pursuing an apparently minor halachic problem, we may travel deeper
and deeper until we arrive, unexpectedly, and yet inevitably, at a
fundamental Chassidic truth. In this case the problem concerns the
law of a city led into idolatry—one of the subjects of the Sidra of
Re'eh. One difficulty that confronts us immediately is the way in
which even innocent people seem to be involved in the collective
guilt and punishment of the city. The other is that Rambam rules
that if the city repents of its sin, this collective guilt is averted. And
yet there is a principle in Judaism that repentance cannot save a man
from human judgment, only from Divine retribution. Rambam's
ruling is the only exception to this principle. What grounds did he
have for making it? In working towards an answer we find ourselves
led ultimately to an inward truth about the Jewish soul, its unity
and its spiritual power.

1. THE IDOLATROUS CITY

The Sidra of Re'eh contains the laws which were to apply
in the Holy Land to a city tainted with idolatry:

"If you shall hear in one of your cities, which the L-rd your
G-d has given you to abide there, saying: Certain men, worth-
less persons, are gone out from among you and have drawn
away the inhabitants of their city, saying, 'Let us go and serve
other gods which you have not known.' Then you shall inquire
and make search and ask diligently, and behold, if it be truth
and the thing certain. . . . You shall surely smite the inhabitants
of that city with the edge of the sword, destroying it utterly,
and all that is in it and its cattle with the edge of the sword.

And you shall gather all its spoil into the midst of its broad place and shall burn the city and all its spoil with fire unto the L-rd your G-d, and it shall be a heap forever; it shall not be built again."[1]

This Sidra is always read on the Shabbat when we bless the coming month of Elul, or on the New Moon itself.

Elul, the month of Divine mercy and forgiveness, is dominated by the idea of *teshuvah*,[2] "returning" to G-d and away from sin. Thus we find in Re'eh an unprecedented statement of the power and scope of *teshuvah.*

As a general rule, the act of repenting and "returning" to G-d affects only Divine justice, not the rulings of a human court. The principle is stated in the Talmud:[3] "Those who were liable to *karet* (death by the hand of heaven) . . . if they repent, the Heavenly Tribunal pardons them. But those who have become liable to death by the sentence of a (human) court . . . even if they should repent, the Earthly Tribunal can not pardon them." The same applies to lesser punishments: Repentance does not affect the sentence of a human court. The reason is that *teshuvah* is a change of *heart*[4] and so it lies outside the consideration of human judges who can deal only with visible, objective fact.[5]

Nonetheless, in the ruling of Rambam,[6] the punishments to which a city led into idolatry is liable—the smiting of its inhabitants, the burning of its spoil—are averted if the people repent of their collective sin. This is a unique instance of repentance affecting the ruling of a human court.

Rambam's ruling has been explained by one of his commentators, the Kesef Mishneh, in this way: To become liable for the death sentence an individual must be *warned* that the act

---

1. *Devarim* 13:13-17.
2. Cf. e.g., *Tur, Orach Chayim,* ch. 581.
3. *Makkot,* 13b.
4. *Tanya,* Part I, ch. 29.
5. Cf. *Noda Biyehudah, Orach Chayim, Mahadura Kama,* ch. 35.
6. *Hilchot Akum,* 4:6.

he is about to commit is a capital offense. But in the case of an idolatrous city, the warning about its conduct is collective, addressed to the people as a whole. Therefore the normal requirement of *individual* caution is not present, and therefore, repentance averts the punishment.

However this explanation seems to miss the central point. What prevents repentance from affecting a human court's verdicts has nothing to do with warning, but with the fact that men cannot see into men's hearts to know whether an expression of repentance is sincere or not. Why should this principle not apply in the present case, the idolatrous city? Why should repentance be effective in just this instance? Besides, Rambam's point is that in this case the people concerned *were* liable to punishment, and only afterwards won their *pardon* by repentance.

2. COLLECTIVE AND INDIVIDUAL RESPONSIBILITY

The Rogotchover Rav[7] explains Rambam's statement in a different way. According to him, Rambam does not maintain that repentance brings universal pardon; but that it changes collective guilt into individual guilt. The law of an idolatrous city involves *collective* liability. Even the innocent members of idol-serving families, even the property of the righteous men who live in the town, come under its penalties.[8] But if the inhabitants repent of their deeds, they become judged as *individuals*. No one who is personally innocent suffers. But the idol-worshippers are punished, and repentance does not alter their sentence.

But, again, this leaves the central difficulty unsolved. Repentance is something that happens after the act. It follows therefore that between the act and the repentance there is a period when the collective liability of the inhabitants is in force. How can a redirection of the heart, something that no human

---

7. *Tzofnat Paaneach, Vayera*, p. 74.
8. *Rambam*, Ibid., 4:6-7.

judge can assess, have the retroactive effect of mitigating a liability or softening a verdict?

3. THE DESTRUCTION OF SODOM

What is the Scriptural basis for Rambam's ruling? The Rogotchover Rav suggests that it lies in the destruction of Sodom,
the city which had been led into idolatry. Before sending His
punishment G-d says, "I will go down now and see if they have
done according to the cry of it."[9] This cannot mean straight-
forwardly that an omniscient G-d needed to establish what He
had heard by hearsay. Instead it has been taken to mean that
G-d would see whether they had repented, and, in the reading
of the Targum,[10] "If they have repented I will not punish
them."

This is certainly an instance of an idolatrous city given the
chance to gain pardon by repentance. But one fact which prevents it from being the precedent on which Rambam bases his
views is that it happened before Sinai, before the Giving of the
Torah. And there is a general principle that "we do not derive
laws on the basis of events before the Giving of the Torah."[11]
Also, Sodom was punished by the *Heavenly Tribunal.*

4. A GROUP AND A COMMUNITY

There is one further difficulty in understanding the position of an idolatrous city.

There is more than one kind of death sentence in Jewish
law, and there is a rule that if a man is liable to death in two
different ways for two separate crimes, he is condemned to the
more severe or painful of the two.[12]

But in the case of the idolatrous city, they are liable to the
collective sentence of a relatively painless death; whereas each

---

9. *Bereishit* 18:21.
10. *Onkelos*, ad loc.
11. *Jerusalem Talmud, Moed Katan,* 3:5. (Quoted in *Tosefot, Moed Katan,* 20a.)
12. *Sanhedrin,* 81b; *Rambam, Hilchot Sanhedrin,* 14:4.

as an individual idolater would be liable to a more severe punishment (stoning). Yet the more lenient one prevails.[13]

The problem can be put more forcefully. Until the majority of the town worships idols, the collective sin does not apply. Each idolater is guilty only of his personal wrongdoing, and hence liable to a severe death sentence. But when that last person who turns a minority into a majority commits the sin, he brings the whole town into the category of an idolatrous city, and hence to a more lenient punishment. How can this one extra act of the sinner have the effect of softening the liability which already applied to the others?

We are forced to conclude that this point—where the majority of the town becomes idol-worshippers—creates a whole new entity, a collectivity, a community of sin. It ceases to be, legally, a group comprised of *individuals,* and becomes instead one unity. So it is not that their individual liability is *lessened* at this point, but that it *ceases to apply,* and a new situation is created, where all are judged as one.

This is why the punishment for an idolatrous city is so extensive, applying even to innocent members of idol-worshipping families (unless they fled to another city), and to the property of the righteous minority. For although *individually* they may be blameless, they are nonetheless a part of the whole, the community which is judged as if it were a single entity.

And this is why Rambam is able to take as his precedent the case of Sodom, even though it occurred before Sinai. For what he wishes to derive is not a *legal* point but a *conceptual* one, namely, the difference between a group of individuals and a community. Even though this distinction has legal consequences, it is not in itself a point of law, and it may therefore be learned from events which preceded Sinai.[14]

Finally, we can see how repentance—on the interpretation of the Rogotchover Rav—has the power to annul collective responsibility and leave only individual guilt to be punished.

---

13. *Sanhedrin,* 111b; *Rambam, Hilchot Akum,* 4:1-2.
14. Cf. *Encyclopaedia Talmudit,* on the concept "Ein Lemedin Mikodem Mattan Torah."

For *teshuvah* has indeed no power to affect the sentence of a human court. But we are not concerned here with a matter of law but of fact, namely, do the idolaters form a unity or are they to be treated as separate individuals? And this—which is not a question of *how* the law is to be applied but of *which* law is to be applied—can be affected by repentance. Repentance does not alter the punishment so much as change the facts of the case.

5. THE UNITY OF THE JEWISH SOUL

Yet we have not yet solved our problem, only shifted its emphasis. Human judges can deal only with what they know, not with the feelings of other men's hearts. If repentance alters the facts of the case how can judges establish what are the facts, how can they distinguish real from insincere *teshuvah*?

We need to go deeper and understand the *inner* meaning of the principle that a human court can not pardon on the grounds that a guilty person has repented.

The inner reason is, that what is handed over to human jurisdiction are actions whose wrongness is independent of the heart. Therefore, subsequent remorse cannot set them right. But the wrong done by an idolatrous city is different. It is *essentially* related to the inner feelings of the idolaters; and so, it is something that a change of heart can effect.

The explanation is this:

The Jewish people are capable of a special kind of unity, an essential oneness, because their souls have their source in G-d who is the ultimate Unity. And even though this is a spiritual unity, it creates in addition a physical unity: "Who is like Your people Israel, *one nation* on the earth? It is this unity which finds its expression in the law of an idolatrous city where the oneness of the community creates a collective liability so strong as to implicate even the property of the city. But this seems strange. Idolatry is the very opposite of G-d's will and unity. It wraps the soul in darkness and division. How, then, can it manifest such a oneness?

But there is no paradox. It is precisely because the Jewish soul is a part of G-d that its freewill has no limits; that a Jew can move so far from his true nature as to serve idols and deny his faith.[15] Even in this gravest of transgressions the special character of his soul and its power of oneness is manifest.

In all other wrongs that a Jew may commit and be judged by a court of fellow-Jews, there are two distinct harms that he must remedy: The wrong he has inflicted on his soul, and the damage he has caused to the world. Repentance sets right the first; punishment, the second. The two are separate and the one cannot alter the need for the other.

But the whole nature of the idolatrous town is its collective involvement which implicates even innocent inhabitants, even inanimate property. This unity is a *spiritual* unity; the wrong is a spiritual wrong; and the remedy is a spiritual one—repentance. Punishment is a remedy for harm done to the world. But the "world" of the idolatrous town—neighbors, cattle, property—is entirely assimilated to the oneness of the souls of its inhabitants. It has become totally subordinate to the spirituality, even in transgression. And this is why here and only here, in a township that has ceased to be a group of individuals and become a community, that repentance even heals with regard to the jurisdiction of man.

(Source: Likkutei Sichot, Vol. IX pp. 106-114)

---

15. Cf. *Likkutei Torah, Emor,* 38b, *Tanya,* Part I, end of ch. 18. *Rambam, Hilchot Teshuvah,* beg. ch. 5.

פרשת שופטים

SHOFTIM

In our Sidra we read of the cities of refuge, to which a man who had killed accidentally could flee, find sanctuary and atone. The month of Elul, in which this Sidra is always read, is, in time, what the cities of refuge were in space. It is a month of sanctuary and repentance, a protected time in which a man can turn from the shortcomings of his past and dedicate himself to a new and sanctified future. The Rebbe analyzes an important feature of the cities; they were only to be found in the land of Israel, even though the judges and officers who executed Torah law were to be appointed wherever Jews live. Why does the law extend everywhere, while refuge belongs to the Holy Land? And what does this imply for the month of Elul, our place of spiritual refuge in the calendar of the Jewish year?

1. THE JUDGES AND THE REFUGE

The month of Elul, in a well-known Chassidic comparison, is like a city of refuge.

The Sifri[1] interprets the opening verse of our Sidra, "You shall set judges and officers in all your gates" to apply to "all your dwelling-places," even those outside Israel. It then continues: One might think that cities of refuge were also to exist outside the land of Israel. Therefore the Torah uses the restrictive term *"these* are the cities of refuge" to indicate that they were to be provided only within Israel.

Nonetheless, the Sifri says[2] that someone who committed accidental homicide outside the land of Israel and who fled to one of the cities of refuge would be granted sanctuary there. It was the cities themselves, not the people they protected, that were confined to the land of Israel.

---

1. Quoted in *Rambam, Sefer Hamitzvot*, Positive Command 176.
2. *Bamidbar* 35:13.

311

The fact that the Sifri initiates a comparison between the "judges and officers" and the cities of refuge, indicates that they have a relationship to one another. It is this: The judges who applied the law and the officers who executed the sentences, did not aim at retribution, but at the refinement of the guilty. And the aim of the cities of refuge was to impose on the fugitive an atoning[3] exile—atonement in the sense of a remorse which effaces[4] the crime until he regains his original closeness to G-d's will. We might then have thought that if this safeguard, this place of atonement, was available in the holy environment of the land of Israel, it would be all the more necessary outside its borders where it was easier to fall into wrongdoing. And yet only judges and officers were to be provided beyond the land of Israel's borders—only the agents of the law, not its refuge.

2. PAST AND FUTURE

There are two phases in *teshuvah,* or repentance. There is *remorse* over what has been done, and *commitment* to act differently in the future.[5] These are inextricably connected. For the only test of sincere remorse is the subsequent commitment to a better way of life. To be contrite about the past without changing one's behavior is a hollow gesture.

This is why refuge was found only in Israel. For a man could not atone while clinging to the environment which led him to sin. He might feel remorse. But he would not have taken the decisive step away from his past. For this, he had to escape to the land of Israel, i.e., to holiness. There, on its sanctified earth, his commitment to a better future could have substance.

Judges, however, could be appointed outside the land of Israel. For it is written in Pirkei Avot,[6] "Do not judge your fel-

---

3. *Makkot*, 10b.
4. *Tanya*, Part III, ch. 1.
5. *Rambam, Hilchot Teshuvah*, 2:2. *Tanya*, Ibid.
6. 2:4.

low-man until you come to his place." A court which sits in the land of Israel cannot know the trials and temptations which exist outside, or the difficulties of being loyal to one's faith in a place of exile. The land of Israel is a land where "the eyes of the L-rd your G-d are always upon it, from the beginning of the year to the end of the year."[7] It is a land of Divine grace. One cannot judge a man by its standards if that man lives outside its protection. So judges had to be drawn from the same environment as their defendants. They had not only to know what he had done; they had to experience for themselves the environment which brought him to it.

The Mitteler Rebbe (the second Chabad Rebbe) was once giving private audiences, when he interrupted for some time before continuing. It transpired that a man who had had an audience wanted the Rebbe's help in setting right a particularly degrading act he had done. The Rebbe explained that one must discover some analogous quality in oneself—on however refined a level—before one can help someone to remedy his sin. His interruption of the audiences had been to attempt to find in himself this point from which he could identify with the sinner.[8]

It was this principle that lay behind G-d's command to Moses when the Israelites had made the golden calf: "Go, get thee down, for thy people have dealt corruptly."[9] For at that moment, Moses was inhabiting the spiritual heights of Mt. Sinai, neither eating nor drinking, divorced from the world. The Israelites were degraded through their sin. But by saying *"thy people"* G-d created a bond between Moses and the people, on the basis of which Moses was able to plead on their behalf.

3. THE REFUGE AND THE SIN

Although all the cities of refuge were to be in the land of Israel, they were not all in the same territory. There were the

---

7. *Devarim* 11:12.
8. Cf. *Sefer Hamaamarim Kuntreisim*, p. 712.
9. *Shemot* 32:7.

three in the land of Israel proper—the Holy Land. Three were in trans-Jordan, where "manslaughter was common."[10] And, in the Time to Come "the L-rd your G-d will enlarge your borders"[11] three more will be provided, in the newly occupied land.

This means that every level of spirituality has its own refuge, from the relatively lawless trans-Jordan to the Holy Land, and even in the Time to Come. And this is true spiritually as well as geographically. At every stage of a man's religious life there is the possibility of some shortcoming for which there must be refuge and atonement. Even if he never disobeys G-d's will, he may still not have done all within his power to draw close to G-d. This is the task of the month of Elul. It is a time of self-examination when each person must ask himself whether what he has achieved was *all* he could have achieved.[12] And if not, he must repent, and strive towards a more fulfilled future. Businessman and scholar, he who has lived in the world and he who has spent his days under the canopy of the Torah—both must make Elul a time of self-reckoning and refuge.

It is the way of the Western world to make Elul—the month of high summer—a time for vacation from study. The opposite should be the case. It is above all the time for self-examination, a time to change one's life. And the place for this is the city of refuge, in the Holy Land, which means for us, in a place of Torah. Each Jew should set aside Elul, or at least from the 18th onwards (the last 12 days, a day for each month of the year[13]), or at any rate the days when *Selichot* are said, and make his refuge in a place of Torah. A refuge is a place to which one flees: That is, where one lays aside one's past and makes a new home. Elul is the burial of the past for the sake of a better future. And it is the necessary preparation for the blessings of

---

10. *Makkot*, 9b.
11. *Devarim* 19:8. *Jerusalem Talmud, Makkot*, 2:6.
12. *Ketubot*, 67a, 104a; *Sotah*, 13b.
13. Cf. *Chai Elul, 5703* p. 42.

Rosh Hashanah, the promise of plenty and fulfillment in the year to come.

(Source: Likkutei Sichot, Vol. II pp. 380-384)

פרשת כי תצא

Ki Tetze

Among the laws detailed in our Sidra is a section about divorce. The Rebbe analyzes the concept of divorce, both as it applies between man and wife and between man and G-d. It pursues certain paradoxes in the Talmudic tractate on divorce (Gittin) and in the very name given in Jewish law to the document which finalizes the separation. The paradoxes share the tendency to hint that though divorce is, outwardly, a separation, this is not its true nature. Chassidic thought, with its emphasis on discovering the essence of G-d and man, must pursue this problem to its core: Since the essence of the universe is G-d's unity, can separation ever be real and ultimate?

1. THE SCROLL OF DIVORCEMENT

Our Sidra mentions the subject of divorce,[1] and it calls the document which effects the separation, a "scroll of divorcement" *(sefer keritut)*. This name embodies two opposites. "Divorcement" conveys the idea of separation. Indeed it is taken legally to imply[2] that the document must be unconditional in its terms, leaving no ties between the man and his former wife. The term "scroll" however implies that it should conform to certain rules of a scroll of the Law, *a Sefer Torah;* that it should, for example, be written on ruled lines and its length should be greater than its width.[3] The *Sefer Torah* is itself a symbol of unity. In Rambam's words, "The whole Torah was given to make peace in the world."[4] The divorce scroll must, in addition, be written on a single sheet—another token of "oneness."[5]

---

1. *Devarim* 24:1, onwards.
2. *Gittin*, 84b.
3. *Tur, Shulchan Aruch, Even HaEzer*, ch. 125.
4. End of *Hilchot Chanukah*.
5. *Gittin*, 20b.

The same contrast is implicit in the custom that the document should be written in twelve lines "corresponding to the twelve lines which separate the first four books of the Torah from one another"[6] in a *Sefer Torah*. Again we have the idea of separation, and again the comparison with the Torah, the word of the One G-d and the bringer of unity to the world.

2. MARRIAGE AND DIVORCE

The paradox of divorce is also apparent in the close connection between divorce and marriage in Jewish law.

Marriage is, of course, the idea of unity and togetherness: "Therefore shall a man . . . cleave to his wife and they shall become one flesh."[7] And yet the Jewish laws of marriage—the three ways in which it may be contracted—are derived from the very passage in our Sidra which deals with divorce.[8] And on the other hand, the tractate of the Talmud devoted to divorce (Gittin) concludes with an admonition *against* it: "The School of Shammai say, a man may not divorce his wife unless he has found her guilty of unchastity."[9] Even the School of Hillel, who accord greater leeway to the husband, do so only in the case of a second marriage. And the Talmud concludes, "If a man divorces his first wife, even the altar sheds tears."[10]

The same opposition to divorce is to be found, in an oblique way, in the opening of the tractate Gittin as well. It begins, "The bearer of a scroll of divorce from (a husband in) a foreign country (i.e., outside the land of Israel) is required to declare, "In my presence it was written and in my presence it was signed."[11]

This is a strikingly unusual opening. The more expected approach would be to start with such basic rules as, when may

---

6. *Tosefot*, beg. of *Gittin*.
7. *Bereishit* 2:24.
8. Cf. *Kiddushin*, 2a, 4b, 5a.
9. *Gittin*, 90a.
10. Ibid., 90b.
11. *Gittin*, 2a.

a divorce be granted (with which, as we saw, the tractate *ends),* how it is to be drawn up, how delivered and so on. Instead we find as our opening law, a particular case rather than a general rule. Moreover, it concerns a side-issue: It does not concern divorce itself but the rule of sending a divorce by a messenger. And it is, further, an *unusual* case, where a divorce-document is being brought from abroad.

The explanation is that when Rabbi Judah Hanasi compiled the Mishnah he chose this particular passage to open the laws of divorce, to make a point about the very nature of divorce it- self. "The bearer of a divorce from a foreign country . . ." tells us that divorce has its origins in the "foreign country" of the spirit. Without that, there would be no separation between husband and wife. Rabbi Judah Hanasi was hinting, with this opening sentence, at the unnaturalness of divorce. And after detailing all its laws, he reminds us with the closing paragraph (of the Mishnah of Gittin) that still "A man may *not* divorce his wife, unless. . . ."

3. ISRAEL AND G-D

All this has its wider spiritual significance. The marriage of man and woman is the metaphor for the relationship between G-d and Israel.[12] At Sinai the bond between them was forged. We use the same word to describe G-d's commandments and the marriage vow: "Who has *consecrated* us with His com- mandments," and "Behold you are *consecrated* to me by this ring, according to the Law of Moses and of Israel."[13]

Subsequently, in exile, Israel experienced the counterpart of divorce from G-d. The Talmud[14] tells us the story that the prophets asked the community of Israel to repent and return to G-d. They replied, "If a husband divorces his wife, has the one a claim on the other?" This reply, that since G-d had divorced

---

12. In fact, the whole book of *Shir Hashirim* is based upon this concept.
13. *Tanya,* Part I, ch. 46 (p. 65b).
14. *Sanhedrin,* 105a.

Israel by sending them into exile, He had no further claim on their loyalty, the Talmud calls a "victorious answer."

But how could it be victorious? The Talmud itself concludes otherwise, by quoting Isaiah: "Thus saith the L-rd where is the scroll of your mother's divorcement, whom I have sent away?"[15] And indeed, how could there be a divorce between G-d and Israel? The law is that divorce is finalized only when the scroll has been handed over, leaving the husband's possession and becoming the property of the wife. But nothing can leave G-d's possession. The universe is His.

The answer lies in the beginning of the tractate, that divorce has its source in the "foreign country" of the spirit. For G-d inhabits the "foreign country," the realm beyond our comprehension. And sometimes, in our eyes, He seems distant. It is then that the possibility of separation takes root in our minds, separation between man and G-d (and between husband and wife).

Yet in reality it is not so. For when G-d said, "I will surely hide My face"[16] he conveyed the truth that even when His face is hidden we can still discover the "I," the Essence. The divorce between G-d and Israel is an appearance. The reality is a bond that is never broken.

4. In a Foreign Country

The apparent departure of G-d to a "foreign country" is a result of Israel's own departure. For all events in the realm of the spirit are a consequence of what we do in this world.

A "foreign country" means, in the context of the Talmud, a place distant from the land of Israel, and from which there are certain difficulties of passage to the land of Israel—a sea-crossing or something similar.[17]

---

15. *Isaiah* 50:1.
16. *Devarim* 31:18.
17. The Hebrew term, "Medinat Hayam," means, "a land over the sea."

To translate this into spiritual terms: The land of Israel, the land of Divine grace, represents the desire and will of G-d.[18] And when a man is far from that will, and there are obstacles between him and it, (his mind and heart cannot cross the sea of separation) then he is in a "foreign country." This is the point at which G-d, too, moves away. For when man travels away from G-d, G-d moves far from man.

5. THE MESSENGER

Perhaps we might then imagine, that if G-d can hide His face and can travel to a "foreign country" out of man's reach, He can cast off His people with the finality of divorce, G-d forbid.

But against this the Mishnah tells us, "the bearer of a divorce from a foreign country must declare, 'In my presence it was written and in my presence it was signed.'" In other words the bearer must testify that he is not himself the husband, only his messenger.

In historical and spiritual terms, this means that the foreign powers who have defeated Israel and sent her into exile, are themselves ultimately aware that they are only G-d's messengers, that they have no final sovereignty over Israel, that Israel remains still, and always G-d's own people. Consequently, the divorce document has never really left the "husband's" possession, and is not a true divorce.

6. THE HOLY WEDDING

We have found two facts about the relationship between G-d and Israel: That outwardly Israel is divorced by G-d, and that inwardly, their bond is never shaken. To understand this further, we must explain the nature of the marriage between them.

In Jewish marriage, although it is the husband who consecrates his wife to him, and not the other way round,[19] it can

---

18. Cf. *Malachi* 3:12. *Bereishit Rabbah*, 5:8.
19. *Kiddushin*, 5b.

only be with the woman's knowledge and consent.[20] On Sinai, at the holy wedding of G-d and nation, G-d revealed His love for Israel to arouse their love for Him,[21] a love which expressed itself in their famous words of commitment, "We will do and we will hear." Even though this love was initiated by G-d, it took root in their souls, until it became the crucial fact of their existence. So much so that as Rambam has written (in his Hilchot Gerushin),[22] every Jew "wishes to do every commandment and to keep himself far from transgression" and he sins only when this essential desire is hidden by some compelling inclination. The love of the Jew for G-d is constant. It may be momentarily eclipsed, but it still burns even in concealment. So, as it were, is the love of G-d for Israel. The shadow of exile may eclipse that love, but it does not extinguish it.

Thus exile is not divorce. It is the hiding of love. This is why when exile is ended and love reveals itself again, G-d and Israel will not need a new Sinai, a second wedding. For the first was never ended.

7. LOVE OUTWARD AND INWARD

There is another and deeper point. It is not merely that the exile of Israel from G-d is only an appearance, not a reality. In addition, exile reveals an even *deeper* love between them. Before the separation, it would have been possible to suppose that G-d's love was conditional—it depended on Israel's obedience to His will. But in exile, G-d's grief ("even the altar sheds tears") expresses a love without conditions, a love which belongs to the essence of both G-d and the Jew.

Thus the tractate Gittin ends with the words, "She is your companion and the wife of your covenant," to show that in the last analysis the apparent divorce of Israel from G-d only serves to reveal that she is unchangeably the "wife of His covenant."

---

20. Ibid., 2b.
21. *Torah Or*, 98d.
22. End of ch. 2.

8. THE MEANING OF EXILE

Now we see the significance of the fact that though a *Sefer Torah* may be written on several pieces of parchment sewn together, a divorce must be on a single sheet.

For exile, that apparent divorce, shows an even greater unity between G-d and man than did the Giving of the Torah.

Sinai was witness to a revealed love. But revelation is prone to the changes of time. In exile, what remains is the essential love, which though it may sometimes be hidden, is always constant and alive.

This is why the passage on divorce in the Sidra of Ki Tetze is always read in the Seven Weeks of Consolation after the 9th of Av.

It is to show that the apparent forsaking of Israel by G-d is not real. That, instead, it takes us to a more inward and lasting covenant of love. And—as the Talmud follows its tractate on divorce (Gittin) by the one on marriage (Kiddushin)—so our spiritual exile will be followed by a revealed expression of the essential love between Israel and G-d.

(Source: Likkutei Sichot, Vol. IX pp. 143-151)

פרשת כי תבא

KI TAVO

Our Sidra contains a description of the ceremony of offering the first-fruits of the land of Israel, and gives the prayer that was to be recited by each person as he made his offering. One peculiarity of this prayer, is the way it singles out two miracles in particular— Jacob's deliverance from Laban and the Exodus from Egypt. Why were these and only these to be mentioned? The Rebbe concludes that they had a special relevance to the ceremony of the first-fruits, and it analyses the significance of this offering and its counterpart in our own time.

1. TWO MIRACLES

Our Sidra begins with the procedure to be followed when bringing the first-fruits to the Sanctuary as an expression of thanksgiving to G-d:

"And you shall speak and say before the L-rd your G-d: 'An Aramite destroyed my father, and he went down into Egypt and sojourned there, few in number . . . And the L-rd brought us out of Egypt with a mighty hand . . . And he has brought us into this place and has given us this land, a land flowing with milk and honey. And now behold I have brought the first-fruit of the land which You, O L-rd, have given me. . . .'"[1]

The phrase "an Aramite destroyed my father" is taken (by Rashi and others[2]) to refer to Laban's intention to destroy Jacob and hence the whole Jewish nation. Thus the bringing of the first-fruits was accompanied by his acknowledgment of G-d's deliverance in saving the nation from destruction, once at the hands of Laban and again by the Egyptians, and of His grace in bringing them to a land "flowing with milk and honey."

---

1. *Devarim* 26:5-10.
2. Cf. *Targum Yonatan*, ad loc.

But if the intention of this prayer was to mention G-d's kindness, why were only these two instances cited? There were many other saving miracles—the division of the Red Sea, the battle with the Amalekites, the Manna and the Well in the wilderness, the wars with Sichon and Og, etc.

Perhaps we might argue that only Laban and the Egyptians threatened the *total* extermination of Israel, and so the deliverance from these two adversaries was more fundamental than from any of the other miracles.

But even on this reasoning, there would still be a serious omission: The delivery of Jacob and his children from his brother Esau. Had Esau acted as Jacob feared ("lest he come and smite me, the mother with the children"[3]) there would equally have been nothing left of the Jewish people.

What is also strange is that Rashi does not raise this question. For the omission presents a difficulty in the literal understanding of the text, and it is the burden of Rashi's commentary to deal with all problems at this level. And from Rashi's silence on the point, we can conclude that there is in fact no problem—that we, by our reasoning or by taking into consideration Rashi's previous remarks, can understand why Jacob's deliverance from Esau was inappropriate to the prayer said over the first-fruits.

2. REAL AND POTENTIAL DANGER

Perhaps the explanation is that Esau did not constitute a real danger. For when he met Jacob, after their years of estrangement, he did him no harm. The threat he posed lay in Jacob's mind, in his anxiety and apprehension.

Laban, it is true, also did no harm to Jacob. But his intention to do so was accounted by G-d as if he had actually done what he planned. Rashi, in explaining why the Torah says of Laban "an Aramite destroyed my father" instead of "an Aramite sought to destroy . . ." says, "Because he intended to do it, G-d

---

3. *Bereishit* 32:12.

accounted it to him as though he had actually done it, for as far as the nations of the world are concerned, the Holy One, Blessed be He, reckons intentions as deeds." This also explains the emphasis of the verse of the fact that Laban was an Aramite. On the other hand, Esau was a Jew, albeit an apostate.[4] As a result, his intention to harm Jacob was considered as a possible rather than an actual danger, and Jacob's deliverance on this occasion does not merit special mention in our prayer of thanksgiving.

Yet we are still left with a dilemma. Either it is right that we should mention deliverance only from a situation of *real* danger in which case we should include only the deliverance from Egypt (where the Jewish nation was afflicted and oppressed). For in the last analysis, Laban did no actual harm to Jacob. And if G-d counted his intention as if it had been realized, this only applies to *Laban's punishment,* and has no bearing on the situation of Jacob. Or, on the other hand, we should mention all the kindnesses of G-d, even if they only took the form of deliverance from *possible* danger; in which case we should include the episode of Esau in our prayer.

We are forced to conclude, then, that the two saving miracles against Laban and the Egyptians (and only they) have a special connection with the command to offer up the first-fruits of the Land.

3. A PLACE OF SETTLEMENT

The offering of the fruits became obligatory on the Israelites only after they had entered the Land, conquered, allocated and settled it.[5]

From this we can see that the commandment was not simply a thanksgiving for G-d's *gift* of the Land, but primarily for having *settled* in it as a permanent home. It was only then that they could rejoice in it with an easy mind; only then that they brought the first-fruits.

4. *Kiddushin,* 18a.
5. Cf. *Rashi, Devarim* 26:1.

The fruit expressed gratitude for the "land flowing with milk and honey" and for the chance of inhabiting it permanently "to eat from its fruits and be satiated with its goodness."

It was therefore to emphasize *this* point that two examples were chosen where our ancestors were living in a place of permanent settlement and where—from that seeming security—enemies arose to destroy them and were defeated by G-d. These two cases point firmly to the gift of a permanent land ("And He has brought us into *this place*") from which there arises only goodness and sustenance.

It was precisely these two examples, Laban and Egypt, where the miracle took place where those ancestors had made a settled home. Jacob stayed in Syria 20 years, and the Israelites lived in Egypt for 210 years. And the wording of the prayer, "An Aramite destroyed my father, and he went into Egypt." Emphasizes at the outset how it was that from the very places of settlement the threat of destruction arose. On the other hand, Esau confronted Jacob when he was traveling, and the other miracles that were sent to the Israelites came when they were journeying out of Egypt or wandering in the wilderness. They have no relation to that special feeling of gratitude that the Israelites expressed on coming to a settlement in a land that was theirs that overflowed with goodness.

4. THE OFFERING AND THE PRAYER

What is the Chassidic analysis of the offering of first-fruits?

It is explained in *Or Hatorah*[6] that the fruit of a tree is akin to the soul as it is enclothed in the body, and that offering up the first-fruit is an act whose significance is the binding of the incarnate soul with its source in G-d. It is written in Hosea, "I saw your fathers as the first-fruit of the fig-tree."[7] So too is the "father" of the soul—its heavenly source—like a first-fruit. This binding of the soul to its source has two parts: The raising

---

6. *Parshat Ki Tavo*, p. 1040 ff.
7. *Hosea* 9:10.

of the earthbound (the offering of the fruit) and the drawing down of the heavenly (the accompanying prayer).

Thus the prayer suggests the idea of the drawing down of the holy. Jacob's journey to Laban was a descent (from the spirituality of Beersheba to the corruption of Haran[8]) and so too was the Israelites' journey to Egypt. And it was these two descents which precipitated the two great acts of grace and deliverance which saved the Jewish people from destruction.

The significance of this extends to the life of every Jew. It is not enough for the Jew to rest content with his own spiritual *ascent*, the elevation of his soul in closeness to G-d. He must also strive to *draw spirituality down* into the world and into every part of his involvement with it—the world of his work and his social life—until not only do they not distract him from his pursuit of G-d, but they become a full part of it. These are his first-fruits, and by dedicating them to sanctity he is fulfilling the purpose for which the world was created—to be made by man into a dwelling-place for G-d.

(Source: Likkutei Sichot, Vol. XIV pp. 93-98)

---

8. Cf. *Torah Or. Likkutei Sichot*, Vol. I, 60.

פרשת נצבים

NITZAVIM

Nitzavim is the Sidra invariably read before Rosh Hashanah, and it begins with Moses' address to the Jewish people, "You are standing today, all of you, before the L-rd your G-d. . . ." This invocation is both general and specific. It mentions the individual classes of Jew, from the "heads (of) your tribes" to the "drawer of your water." And it gathers them all into the collective phrase, "all of you." The following Sicha is drawn from two Rosh Hashanah letters by the Rebbe. The first half concerns the relation of the individual to the community, and asks whether the Torah, in seeking the unity of the Jewish people, demands the sacrifice of individuality. The second half concerns those Jews who still live in areas of political oppression, where they are prevented from living out their faith, and asks: What can we learn from their example?

1. THE INDIVIDUAL AND THE COMMUNITY

The Sidra of *Nitzavim* is always read on the Shabbat before Rosh Hashanah, and constitutes a preparation for it.

The Torah addresses itself to every Jew in these words, "You are standing today, all of you, before the L-rd your G-d: Your heads, your tribes, your elders, your officers, even all the men of Israel . . . from the hewer of your wood to the drawer of your water."[1]

This is in itself something of a contradiction. The verse begins by speaking to Israel as a unity—"You are standing . . . all of you"—without making any distinctions. But immediately afterwards, it proceeds to detail the different classes of Jew separately. Why, in any case, did it need to do so, when the phrase "all of you" already encompasses them all?

It did so in order to make a fundamental point:[2] that on the one hand, there must be unity amongst Jews; and, at the same

---

1. Devarim 29:9.
2. Cf. *Likkutei Torah*, beg. of *Nitzavim*.

time, each has his unique contribution to make, his own individual mission.

But, if there have to be distinctions amongst Jews, especially ones as extreme as that between "your heads" and "the drawer of your water," how can there be true unity amongst them?

The verse supplies its own answer: "You are standing today, all of you *before the L-rd your G-d.*" It is as Jews stand before G-d in the full recognition that He is the author of their powers[3] and the ground of their being, that they are one.

This can be seen by a simple example. When men form a group of community for a specific purpose; economic, intellectual or whatever, they share their money or labor or ideas towards a given end and for a specified time. Outside this partnership they remain separate individuals, each with his own private world.

The community of Israel is not like this. For it is a partnership "before the L-rd your G-d" and its purpose is "that you should enter into the covenant of the L-rd your G-d, and into His oath. . . ." This encompasses the *whole* man[4]—not just his labor or his ideas—each according to his capacity. And it is a partnership in perpetuity, as eternal as the Torah. This is true unity.

Moreover, in the efforts of each Jew playing his *unique* part in the covenant, is implicit the work of the whole community. The unity of Israel is created not by every Jew being the same, but by his being himself in fulfilling directives of "the L-rd your G-d." Israel is one before G-d when, and only when, each Jew fulfills the mission which is his alone.

2. THE HOUR AND THE TASK

There is a clear message in this, and one that needs emphasis in our time, concerning the "heads (of)[5] your tribes," the

---

3. Cf. *Tur* and *Shulchan Aruch, Orach Chayim*, ch. 5.
4. "...all of you" in the sense of "the whole of you," i.e., all of your being.
5. *Rashi*, ad loc.

spiritual leaders of the Jewish world, from the heads of communities to the heads of families.

Should the objection be raised that at the present time and in our given circumstances, it is hard for a Jew to keep his Judaism intact, without compromise, throughout the year, the Torah itself answers, "You are standing today." This is not a command or a prediction or a promise. It is stated as a *fact*. The fact is that every Jew stands before G-d, who is his life and his strength. The duty is to bring this fact into the open, from the potential to the actual.

And with the assurance implicit in these words, each Jew, and all Jews, come to the coronation, as it were, of G-d on Rosh Hashanah, the acceptance of His sovereignty and the proclamation of His kingship over Israel, and over all the world.

3. PROMISE OR FACT

It is their first duty, especially in this period of the Days of Awe, to spread the light of Torah and the commandments to all who come within their sphere of influence. They must make their inspiration felt in the tenor of everyday life, in practical deed. And to those groups who are, at the moment, far from contact with Judaism, they have a duty to create in them a feeling for return to the roots of their identity, and for beginning to live as *complete* Jews, with *complete* Judaism, for the *complete* year.

Sadly, this, the best opportunity of the year, is often missed, and the time spent instead in talking about world problems, which for all their importance are not within the sphere of influence of the speaker or his listeners, who are not at all likely to help solve them. It is particularly sad that, instead of using these moments of Jewish spiritual awakening to reinforce the Jewish community in its all-inclusive and eternal covenant with G-d and to strengthen individual Jews in their personal missions of G-d Himself, the time and energy is set aside for world problems, political discussion and other matters inappropriate to the occasion.

4. THE FOOT THAT LEADS THE HEAD

There is another point implicit in the verse, "You are standing today. . . ." Although it distinguishes the various kinds of Jew from the "head" to the "foot" of the communal body, it must be remembered—as the Alter Rebbe pointed out[6]—that the "foot" sometimes plays the role of the "head." For, to follow the metaphor, although the head contains the brain which directs the whole body, it is the feet which take the body (including the head) from place to place. So spiritually it can sometimes be the "drawer of your water" who serves as the example for the "heads (of) your tribes."

The characteristic of the head is that it is the seat of the mind, the intellect. The foot, however, responds to the brain's instruction; its feature is, as it were, obedience, immediate fulfillment of an imperative. How then can the "drawer of your water"—the simple Jew with his obedient, unmeditated faith—be an example to the intellectual leaders of the community? He may be gifted with neither the chance nor the capacity for studying Torah; the victim of the constraints of nature or circumstance. What does he have that can serve as the model for those who are more fortunately placed?

And this raises in turn a further question. It is G-d Himself who has given the instruction and the imperative to each individual Jew as to how he should conduct his daily life. How then can it be that certain Jews do not have the opportunity to live as G-d wishes them to? For He is the Master of the Universe. And yet there are situations in which Jews, despite their desire, despite even their self-sacrifice, are barred from living a Jewish life in its proper fullness. A person can sacrifice himself by jumping off a roof to the ground. He cannot do so by jumping from the ground to the roof. It may be beyond his

---

6. *Likkutei Torah*, beg. of *Nitzavim*.

powers to raise himself from his enforced depths. How can such oppression be tolerated by G-d?

5. THE ACT AND THE DESIRE

The answer, in brief, is this. It is true that the deed is more important than the sentiment. The intention is not enough without the act. But still, feelings and intentions are significant. And when it happens that a Jew *cannot* act as he wishes, even by the greatest self-sacrifice, this creates in him a profound sense of grief and loss, a feeling so deep as to touch the very essence of his soul. And this leads him to a deep attachment to G-d, His Torah and His commandments, such that without this grief his Judaism could never have meant so much to him. In such a situation, not only is he without blame for failing to fulfill G-d's will, but he is rewarded for his desires even though they did not become deeds. And, more importantly, his spiritual life achieves a depth of perfection to which he in more fortunate circumstances, could perhaps not aspire. Furthermore, when by the grace of G-d he is able to leave that situation for one which grants him religious freedom, his performance of the *Mitzvot* takes on an unprecedented fervor and intensity.

It is thus that such a "drawer of your water" becomes a model for the "head," and for all Jews, so that those who have been spared the "iron furnace" of affliction can learn and draw inspiration from him.

6. REAL AND IMAGINARY IMPOSSIBILITY

But there is an important point which must be made clear. The temptations by which we allow ourselves to be led astray are sometimes very subtle. And the strongest of these is self-deception and self-love. One of its commoner strategies is when we convince ourselves that we *cannot* perform a Mitzvah. We would like to—we tell ourselves—but circumstances prevent us. We shift the burden of responsibility from ourselves to factors beyond our control.

"Man is close to himself" and it is difficult for him to see himself objectively. He must therefore remember that in the seemingly impossible, there may be more of what he wants to see than what is there, objectively, to be seen. To understand the real nature of his situation he must turn to someone else, someone who is above self-deception and will not be tempted to say only what he wants to hear; someone above all, whose whole outlook is that of the Torah, for Torah is "Torat Emet" (a Torah of truth), and truth brooks no compromise. Only he can distinguish for one the constraints which are genuine from those which one has erected for himself as an escape from responsibility.

This is the time of the year—the Ten Days of Teshuvah—when the Jew "returns" to his essential self[7] when the masks of self-deception are broken. And this essential self—that he is a veritable part of G-d above[8]—expresses itself in all details of his daily life, in thought, speech and deed.

(Source: Letters, end of 5731, beg. of 5732)

---

7. Cf. *Rambam, Hilchot Gerushin*, end of ch. 2.
8. *Tanya*, Part I, ch. 2.

עשרת ימי תשובה
THE TEN DAYS OF TESHUVAH

The following Sicha is about the difficulties of translation itself.
The act of translation assumes that for every word in one language,
equivalents can be found in another. But this may be untrue, especially when we are dealing with ideas that are central and unique to
Judaism. We may then fall into the error of equating a Jewish idea
with one drawn from another culture when the two are in fact dis-
similar, even opposite. This is the case with the three words constantly on our minds during the Ten Days of Teshuvah. In English
they are repentance, prayer and charity. How far these differ from
their Jewish counterparts—*teshuvah, tefillah* and *tzedakah*—the Rebbe
emphatically explains.

1. THE SERVICE OF THE TEN DAYS

We express the hope that on Rosh Hashanah G-d blessed
us with a "good and sweet year" to come, a year made fruitful
by children, health and sustenance.

But there is no limit to goodness and blessing. Thus, during the Ten Days of Teshuvah we have the opportunity
through our service, to cause G-d to grant us yet greater benefits from His "full and expansive hand."

What is this service? It is, as we say in our prayers,
"repentance, prayer and charity" which avert evil and bring the
good. But the words "repentance, prayer and charity" are mis-
leading. By thus translating the Hebrew terms *teshuvah, tefillah*
and *tzedakah,* we are led into a false comparison of these three
elements of the religious life as they exist in Judaism and outside it.

In fact, there are crucial differences. *Teshuvah* is not repentance. *Tefillah is* not prayer. And *tzedakah is* not charity.

2. TESHUVAH AND REPENTANCE

"Repentance" in Hebrew is not *teshuvah* but *charatah*. Not only are these two terms not synonymous. They are opposites.

Charatah implies remorse or a feeling of guilt about the past and an intention to behave in a completely new way in the future. The person decides to become "a new man." But *teshuvah* means "returning" to the old, to one's original nature. Underlying the concept of *teshuvah* is the fact that the Jew is, in essence, good. Desires or temptations may deflect him temporarily from being himself, being true to his essence. But the bad that he does is not part of, nor does it affect, his real nature. *Teshuvah* is a return to the self. While repentance involves dismissing the past and starting anew, *teshuvah* means going back to one's roots in G-d and exposing them as one's true character.

For this reason, while the righteous have no need to repent, and the wicked may be unable to, both may do *teshuvah*.[1] The righteous, though they have never sinned, have constantly to strive to return to their innermost. And the wicked, however distant they are from G-d, can always return, for *teshuvah* does not involve creating anything new, only rediscovering the good that was always within them.

3. TEFILLAH AND PRAYER

"Prayer" in Hebrew is not *tefillah* but *bakashah*. And again these terms are opposites. *Bakashah* means to pray, request, beseech. But *tefillah* means, to attach oneself.[2]

In *bakashah* the person asks G-d to provide him, from above, with what he lacks. Therefore when he is not in need of anything, or feels no desire for a gift from above, *bakashah* becomes redundant.

But in *tefillah* the person seeks to attach himself to G-d. It is a movement from below, from man, reaching towards G-d.

---

1. Cf. *Kuntres Bikkur Chicago*, p. 23.
2. Cf. *Rashi, Bereishit* 30:8; *Or Hatorah, Vayechi*, 380a.

And this is something appropriate to everyone and at every time.

The Jewish soul has a bond with G-d. But it also inhabits a body, whose preoccupation with the material world may attenuate that bond. So it has constantly to be strengthened and renewed. This is the function of *tefillah*. And it is necessary for every Jew. For while there may be those who do not lack anything and thus have nothing to request of G-d, there is no-one who does not need to attach himself to the source of all life.

4. TZEDAKAH AND CHARITY

The Hebrew for "charity" is not *tzedakah* but *chessed*. And again these two words have opposite meanings.

Chessed, charity, implies that the recipient has no right to the gift and that the donor is under no obligation to give it. He gives it gratuitously, from the goodness of his heart. His act is a virtue rather than a duty.

On the other hand *tzedakah* means righteousness or justice. The implication is that the donor gives because it is his duty. For, firstly, everything in the world belongs ultimately to G-d. A man's possessions are not his by right. Rather, they are entrusted to him by G-d, and one of the conditions of that trust is that he should give to those who are in need. Secondly, a man has a duty to act towards others as he asks G-d to act towards him. And as we ask G-d for His blessings though He owes us nothing and is under no obligation, so we are bound in justice to give to those who ask us, even though we are in no way in their debt. In this way we are rewarded: Measure for measure. Because we give freely, G-d gives freely to us.

This applies in particular to the *tzedakah* which is given to support the institutions of Torah learning. For everyone who is educated in these institutions is a future foundation of a house in Israel, and a future guide to the coming generation. This will be the product of his *tzedakah*—and his act is the measure of his reward.

5. THREE PATHS

These are the three paths which lead to a year "written and sealed" for good.

By returning to one's innermost self *(teshuvah), by* attaching oneself to G-d *(tefillah)* and by distributing one's possessions with righteousness *(tzedakah),* one turns the promise of Rosh Hashanah into the abundant fulfillment of Yom Kippur: A year of sweetness and plenty.

(Source: Likkutei Sichot, Vol. II pp. 409-411)

פרשת וילך
VAYELECH

The Sidra of Vayelech is usually read on the Shabbat after Rosh Hashanah. And the Rebbe establishes the connection between its content and its place in the calendar. The Sidra describes how Moses, having finished putting the Torah into writing, handed it to the Levites to be placed in the Ark in the Holy of Holies. Rosh Hashanah and Yom Kippur are, in another dimension, the Holy of Holies of the Jewish year. The Sicha therefore searches out the meaning of the Holy of Holies and its relation to the world outside. Are the holy and the profane two distinct and separate realms? Is sanctity confined to special places and appointed times?

1. THE ARK, THE TABLETS AND THE TORAH

In *Vayelech,* Moses commands the Levites with these words: "Take this book of the Law, and put it by the side of the Ark of the Covenant of the L-rd your G-d. . . ."[1]

The Talmud[2] records two conflicting interpretations of the phrase "by the side of the Ark." One maintains that the Sefer Torah was placed *inside* the Ark, together with the tablets on which the Ten Commandments were engraved. The other holds that it was placed outside, on a ledge which projected from the side of the Ark. Both agree, however, that it was within the area of the Holy of Holies. Thus the Holy of Holies contained both the *written* Sefer Torah and the *engraved* tablets.

We can see that the tablets were appropriate to the Holy of Holies, because both were miraculously in space and at the same time beyond it. The Ark had physical dimensions. It was 2 1/2 cubits in length, and 1 1/2 cubits in height and breadth. And yet it occupied no space. For it is recorded that the Holy of Holies was 20 cubits wide, and yet that the Ark had a free

---

1. *Devarim* 31:26.
2. *Baba Batra,* 14a, quoted by *Rashi, Devarim,* Ibid.

space of ten cubits on either side. The Talmud[3] resolves the contradiction by saying, "We have it as a tradition that the place of the Ark . . . is not within measured space."

Similarly the letters of the tablets, although they were letters that could be read and measured, they had no substance apart from the stone. In particular, the (final) *mem* and *samech* were preserved by a miracle.[4] They are closed letters, so the stone which they surrounded was joined to nothing, but was kept in place by G-d. The letters, in other words, were in space but not of it.

But what was the relation of the Sefer Torah to the Holy of Holies? Its letters were *written*. They were ink on parchment. There was nothing miraculous about them.

2. THE HOLY OF HOLIES AND THE WORLD

The Holy of Holies contained in space and time what was above space and time. But its ultimate purpose was that this miracle should spread its light outwards, to the Priests' Court, the Court of the Israelites, the Women's Court, the Temple Mount and beyond, to all the nations of the world, to make them all aware that the Infinite may be found in the finite, that G-d dwells within the world.

Therefore, the Sefer Torah was housed in the Holy of Holies, as an intermediary between this inner sanctum and the world. For the Ark and the tablets represented complete effacement in the presence of G-d. They occupied no space: They were something become nothing. But the letters of the Torah were tangible, written in ink on parchment. Thus the Torah is the medium through which the light of G-d reaches the world which lives in time and space.

3. ROSH HASHANAH AND THE YEAR

In Chassidic thought, Rosh Hashanah has a particular spiritual characteristic. Throughout the rest of the year, we

---

3. *Yoma*, 21a.
4. *Shabbat*, 104a; *Megillah*, 2b.

serve G-d mainly within the limits of our reason, and even the self-sacrifices we make relate to our understanding of the needs of the hour. But on Rosh Hashanah we reach a state of self-effacement which is totally beyond reason. We are not pursuing a rational objective: We are responding to a revelation from a source beyond our understanding.

This state, though it belongs to Rosh Hashanah, must not be confined to it. Throughout the rest of the year, while we live and behave within our rational framework, we must carry with us that inspiration of something higher than that which reason can grasp. It is like the Holy of Holies and the letters of the tablets: Though they had their location in space, they gave light to the whole world. And though Rosh Hashanah has its location in time, it illuminates the whole year.

4. THE PREPARATION

But for this to happen there must be a preparation. And the clue lies in the opening sentence of the Sidra we always read before Rosh Hashanah, *Nitzavim:* "*You* are standing this day, all of you, before the L-rd your G-d: Your heads, your tribes, your elders and your officers . . . from the hewer of your wood to the drawer of your water." Every Jew must attach himself to the community. Even the "heads (of) your tribes" must not stand aloof from the "drawer of your water." Jewish unity demands no less than "all of you."

The Jew who breaks through social distinctions to become one with the whole community, breaks through the distinctions of time as well. He brings the spirit of Rosh Hashanah into the rest of the calendar, and spreads its blessings throughout the year.

(Source: Likkutei Sichot, Vol. II pp. 407-8)

פרשת האזינו

HA-AZINU

The Sidra of Ha-azinu begins with Moses' great oration, "Give ear, ye heavens . . . and let the earth hear." The Midrash, with its usual sensitivity to the nuances of language, notes that Moses seems to be talking in terms of intimacy towards the heavens, and of distance towards the earth. There is an almost exactly opposite verse in Isaiah, "Hear, O heavens, and give ear, O earth," in which Isaiah expresses closeness to earth and distance from heaven. Which path is the Jew to follow? Is he to strive towards heaven and keep himself aloof from worldly events? Or is he, like Isaiah, to find his spiritual home in the things of the earth? And what bearing does this dilemma have on the time in which the Sidra is usually read, the Ten Days of Repentance, and the days immediately following Yom Kippur, the supreme moments of self-examination in the Jewish year?

1. WORDS OF CLOSENESS AND DISTANCE

The Midrash[1] tells us that Moses was "close to heaven" and "far from the earth," and this is why he said, "Give ear, ye heavens, and I will speak; and let the earth hear the words of my mouth." "Give ear" speaks in the tone of closeness, "let the earth hear" bears the accent of distance.

In the same way, the Midrash says that Isaiah was "far from the heavens . . . and close to the earth," for he said, in exact opposition to Moses, "Hear O heavens, and give ear, O earth."[2]

But this opposition is a surprising one. "Torah" means "teaching," and all its words are words of instruction for every Jew.[3] When Moses said, "Give ear, ye heavens . . . and let the earth hear" the implication was that every Jew should strive to be close to heaven, and to liberate himself from the constraints

---

1. *Sifri*, beginning of *Ha-azinu*. Cf. *Zohar*, *Ha-azinu*, 286b.
2. *Isaiah* 1:2.
3. *Zohar*, Part III, 53b.

341

of earth. If Isaiah, the greatest of the prophets,[4] could not reach
this, how then can the Torah demand it of every Jew? And, if
closeness to heaven is, in fact, within the reach of every Jew
through the inspiration of Moses which is "within" every Jew,[5]
why had Isaiah failed to reach this level?

The matter is all the more strange since—as the Midrash[6]
says—Isaiah's words were spoken as a continuation of Moses'
address. Speaking as he was under the direct inspiration of
Moses, it should have been all the easier for Isaiah to rise to his
heights.

We are forced to conclude, then, that Isaiah was not outlin-
ing a lower level, but an even higher one, than that of which
Moses had spoken. It was in this sense that he was continuing
where Moses left off. Reaching upwards to Moses' heights,
"close to heaven," he was able to strain to a yet greater
achievement, of being "close to earth." And since Isaiah's
words, too, are part of the Torah, they form a universal message to the Jew.

We must also realize that, since every teaching of the Torah
has a special relevance to the time of the year when it is read,[7]
these words of Moses and their continuation in Isaiah are of
particular significance to the time between Rosh Hashanah and
Succot, during which they are always read.

2. DAYS OF WEEPING

Rabbi Yitzchak Luria, the Ari, said,[8] "Whoever does not
shed tears during the Ten Days of Repentance—his soul is imperfect." The simple meaning of this is that during these days
G-d is close to every Jew[9] with, in the Chassidic phrase,[10] "the
closeness of the luminary to the spark."

---

4. *Yalkut, Isaiah, Remez* 385.
5. *Tanya*, Part I, ch. 42.
6. *Sifri; Yalkut, Ha-azinu, Remez* 942.
7. Cf. *Shaloh*, beg. *Vayeshev. Or Hatorah*, beg. *Nitzavim*.
8. *Pri Etz Chaim, Shaar Hashofar*, ch. 5.
9. *Rosh Hashanah*, 18a (explaining *Isaiah* 56:6). *Rambam, Hilchot Teshuvah*, 2:6.
10. *Derech Chayim*, 13d; 21b; 91a.

If, even in such a time of grace, a Jew is not moved to the tears of repentance, there is an imperfection in his soul. Nothing wakes it to return to its source. It has moved far indeed from its destiny.

But the Ari suggests, by saying *"Whoever* does not shed tears," that this applies to every Jew, even to the perfectly righteous. And yet repentance, certainly when accompanied by tears, is about sin, transgression, wrongdoing, of which the righteous man is innocent. How can we expect that *he* repent, and so much so that there must be some imperfection in *his* soul if he is not moved to penitential tears?

We could understand the Ari's remark if it referred to the "benoni," the Jew who has never sinned, even in thought, but who has not yet removed the desire to do wrong, even though it is kept in continual suppression.[11] For in him there is always the *possibility* of sin, and this alone is enough for tears in these supreme days of self-examination.

But the completely righteous, whose nature is unstirred by even the trace of misguided desire, would seem to have no need, no cause for tears.

Humility may lead him to them. Even the great Rabban Jochanan ben Zakkai wept and said, "When there are two ways before me, one leading to Paradise, and the other to Gehinnom, and I do not know by which I shall be taken, shall I not weep?"[12] In their fervor, the righteous may mistakenly think themselves unworthy. But why should the Ari suggest not that they *can* sometimes weep, but that they *should?* For self-knowledge is a virtue, and it is no duty to think oneself worse than one is.

3. TEARS OF JOY AND BITTERNESS

The Alter Rebbe explained[13] that the tears of which the Ari spoke were not tears of bitterness and self-recrimination, but

---

11. *Tanya*, Part I, chs. 12, 13, etc.
12. *Berachot*, 28b.
13. *Likkutei Torah, Tetze* 37d.

tears like those which Rabbi Akiva shed when he penetrated the secret mysteries of the Torah[14]—tears of intense joy.

But these cannot be the only tears which the righteous shed, or it would transpire that the Ari using one word to denote two opposites—the joyous tears of the righteous and the bitter tears of other Jews. The first would express a closeness to G-d, the second a sense of distance.

4. THE SPIRIT SHALL RETURN

The explanation is that *teshuvah* is not merely repentance, something which comes only where there was sin. It means the *return* of the soul to its source.[15] "And the spirit shall return to G-d who gave it."[16]

Even the righteous man who serves G-d with love and fear and the totality of his being has not yet reached that stage of complete closeness to Him, which the soul experienced before birth.[17] Earthly existence creates a distance between the soul and G-d which not even righteousness can wholly bridge, and this is the grief of the righteous and the source of his tears. He senses, even in the highest human life, a descent of the soul from its heavenly enthronement. His tears, like those of the ordinary Jew, are born of a consciousness of distance from G-d.

5. TEARS OF EFFACEMENT

But even this answer will not suffice. For the righteous would then be grieving over the inevitable: The fact that bodily existence sets a distance between G-d and the soul. This is a fact that man cannot change. And what man cannot alter, he cannot blame himself for.

If the righteous man were thinking about his own spiritual satisfaction he might feel embittered that birth was a loss to the

14. *Midrash Haneelam, Vayera,* 98b.
15. *Likkutei Torah,* beg. *Ha-azinu.*
16. *Ecclesiastes* 12:7.
17. *Tanya,* Part I, ch. 37.

soul. He might, without feeling guilty, feel aggrieved. But the righteous do not think of themselves. They think instead of the Divine will,[18] which is that their soul should live within the world's narrow boundaries. Why, then, should they weep over their situation?

Perhaps it might be that the righteous weep because they have not (yet) fulfilled their mission. For the descent of the soul is not an end in itself; it is a means to a yet greater ascent, a complete self-effacement as the soul recognizes its nothingness and the all-embracing reality of G-d. And since the righteous man has some reality in his own eyes,[19] he is not yet at his journey's end. He still has cause for tears.

And yet, if even the greatest man cannot reach this stage, how can we say he ought to? We cannot demand the impossible.

The truth is that the Jew is a part of G-d. He can rise above the ordinary spiritual possibilities of the world. And he sheds tears at his human limitations, because *this is the way to overcome them.*

"From my confinement I called upon the L-rd: The L-rd answered me with enlargement."[20] It is the sense that after all the achievements of a righteous life one is still in a "confinement," that brings about the "enlargement" which is the loss of man's self-consciousness and his assimilation into the Divine.

6. ONENESS WITH G-D WITHIN THE WORLD

This is the significance of the Ten Days of Teshuvah, the time when G-d is at His closest to man, although *teshuvah* is always important.[21] For these days not only accord it special favor; they elevate it to a new degree. It becomes more than repentance for sin; it becomes the returning of the soul to G-d,

---

18. Ibid., ch. 10.
19. Ibid., ch. 35.
20. *Psalms* 118:5.
21. *Rambam, Hilchot Teshuvah,* 2:6.

the end of spiritual alienation. This sudden possibility allows
man to see his human limitations as no longer inevitable. They
can be transcended. And therefore they can be wept over—by
every Jew.

When man achieves this self-transcendence, he has made a
break-through which is possible *only* to the soul in its earthly
existence. He has become one with the Infinite in the very
midst of the finite. He thus reveals that the soul's union with
G-d has no limitations whatsoever, for he has reached union
with G-d without forsaking the world. "From my confinement
I called upon the L-rd," and within this body, this narrow
world, "the L-rd answered me with enlargement."

7. THE SHOFAR

This explains the meaning of the *shofar* blown on Rosh
Hashanah. Through the *shofar* (whose physical shape indicates
"confinement" at one end and "enlargement" at the other) we
evoke the kingship of G-d. And as the Talmud[22] reports, that
G-d says, "Recite before Me on Rosh Hashanah verses of
kingship, remembrance and the *shofar*. Kingship—so that you
may make Me king over you . . . and through what? Through
the *shofar*."

The statement is puzzling, because the natural order would
be first to proclaim G-d as our king, and *then* to obey His decrees.[23] How can we evoke G-d's desire to be our king through
performing one of His decrees, which assumes that He is already our King?

The explanation lies in our prayer before the *Shofar* is
blown: "From my confinement I called upon the L-rd. . . ."
Our "confinement" is not simply our sins, but our very existence as beings-in-ourselves, as people who feel that we are
separate from G-d, and as long as this is true, we have not admitted G-d as our king. But when we stand in this
"confinement" and yet "call upon the L-rd" we reach the very

22.*Rosh Hashanah*, 16a, 34b.
23.Cf. *Mechilta* and *Yalkut Shimoni*, *Yitro* 20:3.

Essence of G-dliness, and bring G-d's "enlargement" into the heart of human life. This is the making of G-d's kingship. He is king within the world, not above it.

8. THE CONFINES OF THE WORLD AND ITS ENLARGEMENT

The relation between the Sidra of Ha-azinu—of Moses' call and Isaiah's completion of it—and the Ten Days of Teshuvah (as well as the four days following Yom Kippur[24]), is now clear.

Throughout the year our religious life is concerned with things of the "earth," the study of the Torah and the practical performance of the commandments. Even the "duties of the heart" belong to our human personality, our intellect, our temperament.

But during the Ten Days, "the spirit shall return to G-d who gave it." Every Jew must become aware of the "confinement" which the world represents: Aware to the point of tears. He must "call upon the L-rd," with a thrust and desire to become one with G-d.

A man is where his will is.[25] And by this very act of shedding tears over his "confinement," he takes himself beyond it. He becomes "close to heaven" and "far from earth." His overpowering desire is to be "close to heaven": And that is where he is.

G-d's response is to "answer me with enlargement," that is with His presence within the earth, which reveals the *true* Essence of G-d, as above. The Infinite enters his human habitation. And then he finds G-d "close to the earth" and "far from heaven."

9. THE LESSON OF ISAIAH

This is true throughout a Jew's life.

---

24. Cf. Preface of the Lubavitcher Rebbe to *Kuntres 97*, in *Sefer Hamaamarim*, 5709.

25. Cf. *Likkutei Sichot*, Vol. VI, p. 24, note 29.

"Heaven" is the Torah, the word of G-d. "Earth" is the commandments, the actions of man.[26] Through learning Torah a Jew draws close to G-d.[27] Through the commandments, he draws G-d into the world.[28]

At first, he must be "close to heaven." Though he must keep the commandments, his heart must be in the study of Torah.

But this is only the first stage. He must come in time to know that "not learning but doing is the essential thing,"[29] for the real task of man is to change the world, to make it G-d's dwelling.[28]

It needed Isaiah to give us this second stage. For the Torah was received by Moses. But to Isaiah fell the prophecy of the future redemption,[30] the time when the world will be G-d's dwelling-place, when "every form shall know that You have formed it."[31] When the form of the world will be fused with the Infinity of G-d.

(Source. Likkutei Sichot, Vol. IX pp. 204-214)

26. *Torah Or*, beg. *Bereishit*; *Likkutei Torah, Ha-azinu*, 74b.
27. *Tanya*, Part I, ch. 23. Cf. Ibid., ch. 5.
28. Ibid., ch. 37.
29. *Pirkei Avot*, 1:17.
30. Cf. *Baba Batra*, 14b.
31. Rosh Hashanah and Yom Kippur prayers.

פרשת וזאת הברכה
Vezot Haberachah

On Simchat Torah, the day of Rejoicing with the Torah, we complete our yearly reading of the Torah and begin the cycle again. What is the connection between the day itself and the Sidra we read on it, Vezot Haberachah? And why do we celebrate the Torah on this day instead of on Shavuot when it was first given? In the Sicha that follows, one point must be made clear to avoid confusion. Shemini Atzeret—the eighth day of Succot and a festival in its own right—and Simchat Torah, the day following, were originally a single festival. Outside the land of Israel, however, where we celebrate two festive days instead of one, they are separated. But they are in essence a single religious event, and they are treated as such in the Sicha.

1. SHEMINI ATZERET—THE DAY AND THE READING

Basing himself on the Talmud,[1] Rambam writes[2] that on every festival we read a passage from the Torah relating to that day, for "Moses instituted for Israel that they read on every festival its appropriate section." He continues by specifying the readings for the individual festivals, and says, "On the last day (of Succot) we read the section beginning *Kol Habechor,* 'All the firstling males . . . ,' and on the next day we read the Sidra Vezot Haberachah, 'And this is the blessing. . . .'"

Thus the reason that we read Vezot Haberachah on the second day of Shemini Atzeret is not merely, as has been suggested, to end the cycle of the year's festivals with Moses' concluding blessing to Israel.[3] Nor is it to couple the celebration of the festival with that of completing the annual reading of the

---

1. *Megillah,* 31a.
2. *Hilchot Tefillah,* 13:8.
3. *Ran,* Talmud, *Megillah,* Ibid.

349

Torah.[4] Nor again is it to join Moses' blessing with the blessing that Solomon pronounced over the people on Shemini Atzeret.[5] These are all reasons, but they are incidental. The main one is, as Rambam implies, that the Sidra of Vezot Haberachah directly concerns the festival itself.

But what is the connection between them?

2. THE UNIQUE NATION

In the Talmud[6] we find an explanation of the symbolism of the sacrifices made on Succot and Shemini Atzeret. "To what do the seventy bullocks (that were offered during Succot) correspond? To the seventy nations. To what does the single bullock (of Shemini Atzeret) correspond? To the single (i.e., unique) nation (Israel)."

Shemini Atzeret is therefore the day when Israel's uniqueness is revealed.

This is its connection with Vezot Haberachah. For Moses begins his blessing with the words, "The L-rd came from Sinai, and rose from Seir unto them; He shined forth from Mt. Paran." Rashi explains the reference to Seir and Paran in this way: "He first addresses Himself to the sons of Esau (the inhabitants of Seir) that they should accept the Torah, but they refused. Then He went and addressed Himself to the sons of Ishmael (who lived in Paran) that they should accept it, and they too refused." The descendants of Esau and Ishmael here stand for the whole non-Jewish world, and the meaning of Moses' words is therefore that the whole world[7] had the opportunity of accepting G-d's law at the time of Sinai, but only Israel, "the unique nation"—took it upon themselves.[8]

Yet, although this emphasis of Israel's uniqueness links Vezot Haberachah with Shemini Atzeret, it surely connects it

---

4. *Machzor Vitri*, 385.
5. Ibid.; *Avudraham*.
6. *Sukkah*, 55b.
7. *Avodah Zarah*, 2b.
8. Cf. *Likkutei Sichot*, Vol. IV, p. 1309.

more strongly with another festival, Shavuot, the "season of the Giving of our Torah." For Moses was referring to the events which surrounded Mt. Sinai, and these took place on Shavuot.

3. THE BREAKING OF THE TABLETS

The explanation lies in the last words of the Sidra, with which the Five Books of Moses close: "There has not since risen a prophet in Israel like Moses . . . in all the mighty hand, and in all the great terror, which Moses wrought in the sight of all Israel."

Rashi is prompted by the question, what precisely was the act referring to in the phrase "which Moses wrought in the sight of all Israel?" He says it was the moment when "his heart inspired him to shatter the tablets (of the Ten Commandments) before their eyes."

But why should this act have been counted amongst Moses' virtues? It was, on the face of it, connected with an episode of Divine displeasure. Indeed Rashi writes elsewhere[9] that "the death of the righteous is as grievous before the Holy One blessed be He as the day on which the tablets were broken." Rashi himself answers this question, by saying that when Moses broke the tablets, "the Holy One blessed be He agreed with Moses' opinion" and congratulated him.

But this does not solve our difficulty. The Talmud[10] tells us what was Moses' reasoning. He argued, *a fortiori,* "If, about the Passover sacrifice, which is only one of the 613 precepts, the Torah says,[11] 'no alien shall eat thereof,' here is the whole Torah, and the Israelites are apostates—how much more so." In other words, Moses was defending the honor of the Torah in not wanting to transmit it to "apostates," but he was, at the same time, stressing the *unworthiness* of Israel. How then can Vezot Haberachah—Moses' blessing to Israel—end with their dispraise? Indeed, the Sidra's ending would contradict its be-

9. *Devarim* 10:7.
10. *Shabbat,* 87a, quoted in *Rashi, Shemot* 32:19.
11. *Shemot* 12:43.

ginning, for it opens by stating Israel's uniqueness in accepting the Torah, and ends by suggesting their unworthiness to do so. It is stranger still that the final words of the Torah, whose whole purpose was to be addressed to and accepted by Israel, should concern the shattering of the tablets on which its laws were inscribed.

4. THE SECOND TABLETS AND THE PATH OF RETURN

We are forced instead to say that G-d congratulated Moses for the breaking of the tablets, because his act was in honor not only of the Torah but also of Israel.

Here we must remember that G-d did not congratulate Moses immediately. He waited until forty days had passed, until He gave the command, "Hew thee two tablets of stone like the first which you broke."[12] And Rashi does not give his interpretation that G-d's words were a congratulation until Vezot Haberachah, on Moses' death, forty years later. This in itself suggests that the full virtue of Moses' act was not apparent until the end of his life.

The explanation is this. The Talmud[13] tells us that "the Israelites only made the golden calf to place a good argument in the mouth of those who return and repent." G-d allowed the Israelites to be tempted into making the calf only for the sake of their ultimate repentance, which was an unprecedented type of repentance: One which would bring them to an even higher level of spirituality than they had achieved before the sin.[14]

Thus the breaking of the first tablets because of the sin of the golden calf prepared the way for the second tablets which were greater than the first[15]—the perennial reminder of the power of repentance not merely to efface the sins of the past, but to bring man to new spiritual heights.

---

12. Ibid. 34:1; *Devarim* 10:2.
13. *Avodah Zarah*, 4b. *Rashi*, ad loc.
14. Cf. *Rambam, Hilchot Teshuvah*, 7:4.
15. *Shemot Rabbah*, ch. 46.

This, too, was Moses' ultimate intention in refusing to give the Torah to "apostates." He did not wish simply to defend the Torah's honor, but rather to awaken in *Israel* a desire to return to G-d. He was like a father who drives his errant son from his house, not to cast him off, but to create a longing to return.[16] This is why Moses broke the tablets "in the sight of all Israel."[17] He was making a public gesture, directed towards the Israelites; something they would witness and by it be changed for good.

This is why the fast of the 17th of Tammuz, the day when the tablets were broken,[18] will be transformed in the Time to Come into a day of gladness and rejoicing.[19] At the present we see only the immediate consequences of the golden calf, the sufferings of exile, several of whose major tragedies also occurred on the 17th of Tammuz. Therefore we fast. But when Israel's return to G-d is complete, it will be seen to have begun on the day when the tablets were shattered, and it will be a day of rejoicing.

But only when the second tablets had been commanded— the sign of the power of repentance—did G-d congratulate Moses. And this congratulation was not made *explicit* until the end of Moses' life, when he was granted a vision of the "final day" and saw "all that would happen to Israel in the future until the resurrection of the dead."[20] For it was then that he saw the final triumph of repentance, the Messianic fulfillment of what he had begun at Sinai.

5. THE REJOICING WITH THE TORAH

This, then, is the connection between Vezot Haberachah and Shemini Atzeret.

On the face of it, we should celebrate Simchat Torah Rejoicing with the Torah, on Shavuot when the Ten Command-

---

16. Cf. *Or Hatorah, Vaera*, p. 123.
17. Cf. *Devarim* 9:17.
18. *Mishnah, Taanit*, 26a.
19. *Zechariah* 8:19.
20 *Sifri* and *Rashi, Devarim* 34:2.

ments were first given. But our greatest rejoicing belongs to the *second* tablets, which were given on Yom Kippur. And Shemini Atzeret is the end of the festive cycle which begins with Yom Kippur.[21]

However, we must also remember that the opening words of Moses' blessing, "The L-rd came from Sinai . . ." refer to the *first* occasion of the Giving of the Torah, so that this too must have relevance to Simchat Torah.

6. THE RIGHTEOUS AND THE REPENTANT

The difference between the first tablets and the second is like that between the righteous and the repentant. When the first were given, Israel was still righteous; by the time of the second, they had sinned and repented.

The righteous are men whose virtue consists of the fact that they live according to the Torah. But repentance reaches even *higher* than Torah.[22] It rests on the bond between G-d and man which survives even when man transgresses G-d's law. Thus at the time of the first tablets, Israel received a revelation from the Torah. But at the time of the second, they themselves gave revelation to the Torah. They had reached beyond it, to the essential union between G-d and Israel.

This is the relation of Vezot Haberachah to Simchat Torah: The Sidra begins with the first tablets, when Israel rejoiced in the Torah. And it ends with the second tablets, when the Torah itself rejoiced in Israel. Similarly, Simchat Torah means "rejoicing with the Torah," and also means "rejoicing of the Torah."[23]

7. THE DAY AND THE YEAR

The Festivals were not instituted as self-contained events, days of light and joy. Our task is to bring what we feel on these

---

21. *Or Hatorah, Shemini Atzeret*, p. 1779 ff.
22. Cf. *Likkutei Torah*, Acharei, 26c; *Derech Mitzvotecha, Mitzvat Vidui Uteshuvah*.
23. *Sefer Hamaamarim* 5699, pp. 68 and 72. Cf. *Zohar*, Part III, 256b.

days to the whole of the year. They form a sanctuary in time, whose light is to spread to every corner of the calendar.

But when confronted with this mission, the Jew may feel intimidated by its enormity. How can the secular world, from which G-d is so heavily hidden, be made receptive to its opposite, the light of holiness?

Here the Sidra gives us the precedent and the strength. For even that seeming calamity, the breaking of the tablets, was potentially the beginning of the path of return to G-d, the opening of a new and higher access to the heights of the spirit. This is why, as soon as we have read the phrase about the tablets, "in the sight of all Israel," we begin again with the Torah's opening words, "In the beginning, G-d created. . . ." For by the G-dly powers within him, the powers he discovers by returning to G-d, the Jew can stand in the darkest confines of a secular order and create a new world. He can be architect and builder of a world in which "every creature knows its Creator, and where every dominion recognizes the sovereignty of G-d."[24]

(Source: Likkutei Sichot, Vol. IX pp. 237-243)

---

24. Rosh Hashanah prayer.

INDEX
OF SCRIPTURAL
AND RABBINIC
QUOTATIONS

SCRIPTURE

Bereishit	Page
1:1	101
1:2	5
1:3	1
1:4	3
2:24	278, 317
5:22	268
7:8	6
9:22	9
9:23	6
9:26-27	7
11:32	40
15:5	31
15:15	39
17:5	42
18:12	22
18:19	41, 89
18:21	307
20	28
21:6	34
23:1	21
23:2	30
23:3	30
23:21	45
25:19	28
26:5	39
27:28	43
28:5	36
28:12	49
29:25	40
30:4	38
30:43	86
31:42	86
32:12	324
32:29	42, 44
33:18	86
34:7	40
37:2	49
37:5-9	48
41:1-7	48
41:32	48
47:2	11
47:12	66

	Page
49:1	71
49:2	72
49:10	78
50:20	68

Shemot	
2:2	84
2:11	87
2:13	87
3:12	82, 203
3:16	170
4:6-7	100
4:13	77
4:31	95
6:20	38
7:17	92
7:19-25	100
8:18	92
9:14	92
9:31-32	92
11:4	91
12:21	170
12:22	92
12:43	351
13:8	171
14:21	100
14:26	99
14:27	97
15:15-16	247, 301
18:11	271
19:1	203
19:11	11
19:20	106, 232
20:1	103
20:15	104, 107
21:1	112
23:15	203
24:1	232
25:7	11
25:8	120
27:1 ff.	124
30:1 ff.	124
32:7	313
31:16	177

359

32:19...75
34:1 352
35:22...122
38:26-27 121
40:34...149

Vayikra
6:6 159
8:33 174
9:23-24 162
12:2 180
13:8 186
13:46..187
16:6 195
16:22..261
18:18.......................................37, 39
19:25..197
21:7 107
21:12..255
23:15..202
23:16..178
23:17..203
25:10..209
25:20-21 212
26:3 ....127, 196, 216
26:4 ....127, 196

Bamidbar
1:1 203
1:3 223
1:51 109
5:12 236
5:28 239
8:2 242
11:5 51
11:12 90
16:3 254
16:7 254
16:10..254
17:5 266
19:1-2...258
22:22..262
22:32..262
24:14..71

24:17 72
25:1 265
25:6 271
25:7-8 ....263, 271
25:11 ....266, 274
25:12-13...266
35:13 311

Devarim
3:25 300
4:1 287
4:30 71
6:5 205
6:20 113
7:14 301
8:4 247
8:17 169
9:17 353
10:2 352
10:7 351
11:12 313
11:13 299
11:15 218
11:18, 19 299
12:9 287
13:13-17...305
14:1 94
15:18 132
16:1 169
19:8 314
21:1-9...26
23:11 8
24:1 ff..316
25:17-18...161
26:1 325
26:5-10...323
28:10 58
29:9 328
29:9-10..90
30:15 269
31:18 ....130, 319
31:26 338
33:14 145
34:2 353

Joshua
2:10 247
2:11 59

I Samuel
16:7 275

II Samuel
7:6 291
14:14.. 47

I Kings
6:4 244
8:51 80
11:14.. 262
18:21.. 135
18:39.. 135

Isaiah
1:2 341
2:2 71
8:2 109
30:26.. 292
40:1 .... 290, 291, 297
40:5 .... 80, 293
41:8 86
42:8 239
44:1 45
44:6 83
45:18... 194
49:14.............................. 240, 297
50:1 319
51:12.. 297
54:11.. 297
54:12.. 152
56:6 343
58:13.. 160
60:19... 5
60:21............................... 47, 101

Jeremiah
2:2 225
2:13 138
4:22 206

23:20 71
44:18 137

Ezekiel
16:6 95
20:32-33......................... 188, 189

Hosea
9:10 326

Micah
7:15 .... 96, 178

Haggai
2:9 .... 14, 291

Zechariah
8:19 353
13:2 79

Malachi
1:2-3 94
2:11-12 266
3:12 320
3:22 .... 78, 87
3:24 276

Psalms
35:10 163
37:18 21
37:23 251
51:5 156
51:17 283
80:2 66
84:8 25
109:22 46
118:5 345
128:2 143
132:14 291
139:12 .... 134, 190

Proverbs
3:6 256
6:23 .... 57, 294

8:30-31 182
10:7 253
10:12 7
14:4 .... 155, 205
16:7 45
17:6 33
20:27 242

Job
31:2 47
32:7 220
41:3 146

Esther
2:17, 19, 21-23 130
3:7 127
3:8 133
4:1, 3, 8, 11, 16 131
9:24, 26 129

Song of Songs
1:4 204
8:6 157

Lamentations
1:3 288

Ecclesiastes
12:7 .... 52, 344

Ezra
1:1 295
6:4 295

I Chronicles
29:2 ff. 233

TARGUMIM
Targum Onkelos
Bereishit 18:21 307

Targum Yonatan Ben Uziel
Bereishit 32:39 44
Shemot 6:18 276

Shemot 12:13 92
Devarim 26:5 323

Targum Sheni to Esther
Beg. 61
4:1 131

MIDRASHIM
Bereishit Rabbah
1:1 .... 2, 101
3:3 78
3:6 1
4:6 .... 255, 256
5:5 .... 97, 98
5:8 320
14:7 78
23:1 21
30:6 .... 89, 278
39:2 12
40 13
40:2 12
44:1 294
46:2 87
56:7 .... 85, 152
58:5 26
61:1 86
65:16 43

Shemot Rabbah
2:4 77
3:15 218
9:10 100
12:3 .... 88, 231, 256
15:26 292
21:1 116
21:6 97
28:6 103
29 end 82, 232
36:1 267
46 352
47:1 217

Vayikra Rabbah
2:3 218

12:1 181
12:2 145
12:3 250
20:8, 9 191
22:1 217
27:2 146
29:11 85
31:7 244
34:7 238
36:4 61

Bamidbar Rabbah
1:2 246
2:11 224
2:23 191
4 233
10:2 73
18 267
19:6 220
20:25 263

Devarim Rabbah
1:10 83

Shir Hashirim Rabbah
1:3 18
1:9 199
1:16 291
4:12 13

Kohelet Rabbah
beg. ch. 2 80
11:8 175
end ch. 11 80

Mechilta on Shemot
12:6 95
13:21 246
14:5 247
14:31 95
18:11 96
18:13 .... 142, 144
18:19 218
20:3 346

21:1 116

Sifra (Torat Kohanim)
Shemini 192
beg. Acharei 191
Vayikra 24:2 242

Sifri on Bamidbar
6:26 254
10:10 288
10:34 246
11:5 51

Sifri on Devarim
6:5 33
6:7 299
11:13, 19 299
11:22 73
16:18 305
32:1 ff 341, 342
34:2 353

Tanchuma
Lech Lecha 5 12
Toledot 1 28
Toledot 4 29
Vayigash 12 86
Vaera 15 256
Beshalach 3 246
Yitro 7 271
Yitro 11 103
Mishpatim 21:1 116
Ki Tissa 9 224
Pekudei 3 82
Acharei 6 191
Nasso 13 233
Nasso 16 192
Nasso 16 200

Tanchuma (Buber)
Bereishit 3 61

Pesikta DeRav Kahana
Parshat Shekalim 224, 287

Pirkei De Rabbi Eliezer
ch. 24.. 43
ch. 29....................................... 92, 95
ch. 41.. 104
ch. 47.. 276

Tana Deve Eliyahu Rabbah
ch. 9... 238
ch. 25... 157

Yalkut Shimoni
729... 246
850... 247
891... 253
Psalms 25:1 .... 4, 82
Psalms 80:2 66
Esther, 5.................................... 132

Otiot De Rabbi Akiva
Letter Beth................................. 61

Lekach Tov
Shemot 4:13............................... 77

Yalkut Reuveni
Shemot 14:27............................ 93

ZOHAR
Part I
27b 53
28a 14
46a.................................... 255, 256
52b 79, 147
91a 103
104b 148
135a 29
150a 292
224a 17
234b 73
253a 77
266b 283

Part II
6a.. 247

35b 92
170b 93
128a 51
190a 276
193b 79
195a 142
198b 97
239a 156
241a 287
242a 287

Part III
26b 156
28b 2
29a 145
7a 218
20a 226
39a 154
53b 30, 50, 85, 195, 226, 341
73a............................... 113, 226
93b 226
117b 203
221a................................. 237, 291
221b 238
232a 218
245a 211
256b 354
265a 218
283a 58
286b 341
306b 283

Zohar Chadash
85a.. 4
beg. of Yitro 84, 285

Tikkunei Zohar
13 148
21 145
32 285
45 283
69 152

THE TALMUD

JERUSALEM TALMUD
Berachot 2:7 288
Peah 2:4 217
Sheviit 1:2 210
Shekalim 1:1 119
Yoma 4:6 159
Taanit 4:5 .... 75, 279
Megillah 1:4 288
Megillah end ch. 1 287
Moed Katan 3:5 307
Chagigah 2:3 231
Gittin 4:3 210
Sanhedrin 1:1 83
Makkot 2:6 314
Avodah Zarah 2:7 113

BYBALONIAN TALMUD
Berachot
4a 91
6a 58
8a 143
9b 53
13a 42
13b 81
20a 121
28b 343
32a 74
54a 158, 205
61b 107

Kilayim
9:8 30

Shabbat
10a 207
10b 177
21a 242
21b 49, 55
22a 55
28b 56, 294
30a 233
33a 86

67a 53
87a 351
88a 227
88b 206
89a 78, 232
104a 339
105b 117
112b 31
119a 145
146a 79, 147
156a 31

Eruvin
19a 20, 68
53a 43
54a 163
54b 112
100b 114

Pesachim
3a 6, 85
49b 107
50b 274
56a 71
62b 184
68b 182
116b 207, 282

Yoma
2a 195
21a 339
21b 161, 291
24b 242
28b 79, 86
38b 253
53b 195
69b 138
76b 157
86b 69, 294

Sukkah
27b 126
45b 219
47a 64

55b 64, 350

Rosh Hashanah
4a..295
16a..346
16b 26
18a.. 195, 342
26a.. 105, 300
29b 295
34b 346

Taanit
26a..353
26b 222

Megillah
2b 339
6b 53, 134
7b 130
10a..287
13a..130
17a..128
26b 177
29b 10
31a.. 10, 349
31b 287

Chagigah
5b 143
12a.. 1
14b 194
26 124
27a..20, 68

Yevamot
22a..38
63b 194
109b 201

Ketubot
62b 107
67a..314
104a..314

Nedarim
25a.. 136
32a.. 18
66b 278
67a-b 278

Nazir
23b 29

Sotah
3a.. 236
4b 194
12a.. 3
13a.. 84
13b 314
14a.. 203
15b 239
26a.. 240
35a.. 245
36a.. 90
40b 10

Gittin
2a.. 317
20b 316
36a.. 210
36b 214
50b 177
57a.. 279
59b 254
84b 316
88b 112
90a, b.. 317

Kiddushin
2a.. 317
2b 321
4b 317
5a.. 317
5b 320
18a.. 325
29b 299
30b 267
35a.. 58, 59

36a 238
41a 12
82a 79

Baba Kama
65a 45
85b 301
93a 26

Baba Metzia
31a 7
46a 125
87a 28
114b 276

Baba Batra
3a 291
14a 338
14b 10, 348
21a 275
25b 125
65a 250
75a 152
156a 177
167b 10

Sanhedrin
24a 211
27b 140
31a 1
38a 181
46a 265
55b 156
56b 40
81b 307
82a 263, 264, 266
82b 264
90a 47
93b 279
97a 75
97b 219
104a 27
105a 238, 318
106b 218

109b 253
111b 308

Makkot
9b 314
10b 312
13b 305
24b 109

Shavuot
15a 150
39a 140
48a 267

Avodah Zarah
2b 350
3a 177
4b 352
19a 182

BIBLE COMMENTARIES

RASHI
Bereishit
1:1 .... 5, 61
1:7 256
6:9 .... 31, 89, 278
9:5 40
10:8 43
15:5 31
17:1 18
18:19 89
25:19 28
25:23 64
26:5 .... 258, 259, 260
27:1 86
27:15 43
28:9 40
29:25 41
30:8 335
31:50 37
32:5 37
32:7-12 39

32:29 43

Shemot
11:4 91
12:6 95
12:22 92
15:26 .... 258, 259
18:9 96
19:12 103
21:1 112
24:3 40
30:16 223
32:7 74
32:19 351
34:32 272

Vayikra
1:1 104
9:23 162
10:3 192
18:4 .... 258, 259

Bamidbar
7:1 233
8:2 242
9:3, 12, 14 259
11:5 51
11:22 273
13:2 252
14:16 246
15:15 259
15:39 73
19:2 .... 115, 217
19:3, 4, 9 261
20:29 273
24:17 72
25:7 272
25:13 267
26:5 253
29:18 64

Devarim
1:5 90
5:16 40

6:7 299
8:4 247
10:7 351
11:13, 18-19 299
26:1 325
29:9 330
31:26 338
34:2 353

Psalms
80:2 66

RAMBAN
Bereishit
1:1 61
12:6 13
26:5 37

Shemot
36:8 150

OTHER COMMENTARIES
Alshich, Lech Lecha 11
Alshich, Psalms 51:17 283
Baal Haturim, Bereishit 49:10 . 78
Baal Haturim, Shemot 14:27 ... 97
Chizkuni, Metzora 187
Divrei Shalom, Bo 128
Ibn Ezra, Esther 3:7 129
Kli Yakar, Vayikra 8:33 174
Radak, Isaiah 40:1 291
Seforno, Metzora 187

COMMENTARIES ON TALMUD

Rashi
Pesachim 62b 184
Yoma 22b 107
Gittin 36a 210
Baba Metzia 114b 276
Avodah Zarah 4b 352
　19a 182
Chullin 49a 107

Tosefot
Megillah 31b 222
Moed Katan 20a..................... 307
    23b 288
Gittin 2a 317
Arachin 33a 210

Ran
Megillah 31a 349
Sanhedrin 82a 264

Rabbenu Yonah
Berachot 2a 138

Maharsha
Yoma 69b 138
Sanhedrin 97a 83

LEGAL CODES
Ramban
Sefer Hamitzvot, Shoresh 3 ... 265
Rambam
Sefer Hamitzvot....................... 311

Rambam
Mishnah Torah
Hil. Deot............... 24, 50, 83, 157
Hil. Talmud Torah............. 29, 48
Hil. Akum.........86, 136, 145, 305,
                              306, 308
Hil. Teshuvah.......... 29, 189, 268,
          310, 312, 343, 346, 352
Hil. Kriat Shema..................... 121
Hil. Tefillah 349
Seder Teffilot......................... 186
Hil. Lulav............................... 115
Hil. Shekalim......................... 119
Hil. Taanit 132
Hil. Chanukah................ 254, 316
Hil. Gerushin 63, 69, 73,
                    224, 293, 321, 333
Hil. Sotah.............................. 240
Hil. Isurei Biah 263, 266, 267

Hil. Shemittah
    Veyovel 210, 212, 243
Hil. Beit Habechirah 292
Hil. Bi'at Hamikdash 56, 242, 255
Hil. Klei Hamikdash 255
Hil. Tumat Tzaraat 188
Hil. Sanhedrin 265, 307
Hil. Aivel 87
Hil. Melachim 17, 78-79, 233, 235

TUR/SHULCHAN ARUCH
Orach Chaim
ch. 2 56
ch. 5 329
ch. 61 81
ch. 70 121
ch. 156 133
ch. 231 157
ch. 343 156
ch. 428 186
ch. 552 289
ch. 581 305
ch. 603 138
ch. 670 58
ch. 694 120

Yoreh Deah
ch. 234 278

Even Haezer
Remo ch. 120:3........................ 10
ch. 125 316

Choshen Mishpat
ch. 49:3 10
ch. 420:17, 25.......................... 301

SHULCHAN ARUCH HARAV
Orach Chaim
ch. 60:4 .... 79, 161
ch. 98 192
ch. 306 144

Hilchot Talmud Torah:
47, 73, 122, 188, 192, 194, 201,
217, 274

OTHER WORKS

Avudraham 297, 303, 350
Kuzari.................................. 238
Machzor Vitri 350
Melo Haroim.......................... 150
Meor Eynayim (by R. Menachem
    Nachum of Tchernobil).......... 7
Noam Elimelech (by R.
    Elimelech of Lizhensk)........ 254
Noda Beyehudah................... 305
Or Torah (by the Maggid of
    Mezeritch) 98
Parashat Derachim 38
Pri Etz Chaim................. 130, 342
Rambam: 13 Principles of
    Faith................................ 76
Rashba (Responsa).......... 162, 238
Reshit Chochmah................... 267
Riva's Commentary
    Sefer Hayashar................. 26
Sefer Habahir.......................... 182
Shnei Luchot
    Habrit....................... 222, 342
Siddur R. Saadiah Gaon 186
Taamei Hamitzvot
    of the Arizal 212
Tzofnat Paneach 250, 306
Yad Malachi 14
Yedei Mosheh on Bereishit
    Rabbah 98

CHABAD WORKS

R. SCHNEUR ZALMAN OF LIADI
(THE ALTER REBBE)

TANYA
Part I
Introduction............................ 211

ch. 1 46
ch. 2 .... 47, 52, 183, 333
ch. 4 .... 88, 183
ch. 5 .... 193, 230, 294, 348
ch. 7 156
ch. 10 345
chs. 12, 13 etc. 343
ch. 13 64
ch. 14 46
ch. 17 156
ch. 18 310
ch. 19 137
ch. 23 .... 228, 348
ch. 24 ....182, 184, 237
ch. 25 .... 20, 224
ch. 27 155
ch. 29 .... 182, 305
ch. 31 .... 204, 225
ch. 32 .... 188, 241
ch. 35 345
ch. 36 ....3, 79, 80, 178, 192
ch. 37 . 80, 163, 200, 205, 344, 348
ch. 39 ....29, 47, 188
ch. 41 .... 29, 74
ch. 42 .... 78, 342
ch. 43 29
ch. 46 318
ch. 47 .... 207, 282
ch. 50 192

Part II
ch. 1 .... 2, 4, 5, 235
ch. 6 34

Part III
ch. 1 312
ch. 10 282

Part IV
4 .... 83, 240
23 33
25 44
28 26
29 .... 58, 193

31 238

Part V
David Zemirot 182
Ulehavin Peratei 217

Torah Or
  34, 51, 56, 57, 63, 81, 84, 93, 113,
  130, 133, 249, 282, 294, 321, 327,
                                      348
Likkutei Torah
   42, 45, 51, 52, 57, 62, 63, 80, 84,
   113, 133, 140, 143, 145, 150, 152,
   155, 159, 177, 184, 198, 212, 217,
   218, 220, 226, 242, 247, 283, 287,
   295, 310, 328, 331, 343, 344, 348,
                                      354

Siddur 56

R. DOV BER
(THE MITTELER REBBE)
Biurei Hazohar 49, 61, 69, 211
Shaarei Orah 150
Shaar HaEmunah 80
Pokeiach Ivrim 156
Derech Chaim 342

R. MENACHEM MENDEL (THE
TZEMACH TZEDEK)
Or Hatorah: 25, 29, 49, 61, 94,
   256, 286, 326, 335, 342, 353, 354
Derech Mitzvotecha: 136, 140,
      162, 212, 220, 234, 294, 354

R. SHMUEL (MAHARASH)
Sefer Hamaamarim 5627 283

R. SHALOM DOVBER (RASHAB)
Kuntres Uma'ayon ... 64, 138, 196
Maamar Ner Chanukah 5643 .. 56
Maamar Acharei Mot 5649 192

R. JOSEPH ISAAC SCHNEERSOHN
Sefer Hamaamarim
   Kuntresim 51, 144, 313
Sefer Hamaamarim 5699 354
Sefer Hamaamarim 5708 282
Sefer Hamaamarim 5709 347
Sefer Hamaamarim 5710 .... 47, 52
Sefer Hamaamarim Yiddish 41,
                                   198-9
Kuntres Bikur Chicago 335
Kuntres Chai Elul 5703 314
Maamar Ner Chanukah 5704 .. 56
Maamar Vayehi Bayom
   Hashemini 5704 162
Maamar Kiymay Tzetcha
   5708 178
Maamar Bati Legani 5710 156,
                                190, 236
Sefer Hasichot 5700 284
Likutei Diburim 32, 50, 51

RABBI M. M. SCHNEERSON
Acharei Mot 5722 192
Hayom Yom .. 16, 50, 98, 160, 251
Mayim Rabim 5717 .... 136, 145

LIKKUTEI SICHOT
Vol. I pp. 183-187 .... 135 ff.
Vol. I pp. 187-192 .... 141 ff.
Vol. I p. 60 327
Vol. I pp. 205-208 .... 153 ff.
Vol. I pp. 217-219 .... 159 ff.
Vol. I p. 239 186
Vol. I pp. 265-270 .... 202 ff.
Vol. II pp. 301-303 .... 227 ff.
Vol. II pp. 311-314 .... 236 ff.
Vol. II pp. 314-318 .... 241 ff.
Vol. II pp. 348-353 .... 281 ff.
Vol. II pp. 357-359 .... 286 ff.
Vol. II pp. 380-384 .... 311 ff.
Vol. II pp. 407-8 .... 338 ff.
Vol. II pp. 409-411 .... 334 ff.
Vol. II pp. 612-614 .... 277 ff.
Vol. III pp. 780-7 .... 28 ff.

Vol. III pp. 795-9 ....42 ff.

Vol. III pp. 805-10 ....48 ff.

Vol. III pp. 819-822 ....60 ff.

Vol. III p 832...........................61

Vol. III pp. 854-62 ....84 ff.

Vol. III pp. 864-8, 872 ....91 ff.

Vol. III pp. 895-901 ....112 ff.

Vol. III pp. 910-912 ....124 ff.

Vol. III pp. 933-936 ....148 ff.

Vol. III pp. 973-977 ....174 ff.

Vol. III pp. 987-993 ....191 ff.

Vol. III pp. 1012-1015 ....216 ff.

Vol. IV pp. 1041-1047.........245 ff.

Vol. IV p. 1095.......................232

Vol. IV p. 1309.......................350

Vol. V pp. 57-67...................10 ff.

Vol. V pp. 86-91...................16 ff.

Vol. V pp. 92-104.................21 ff.

Vol. V pp. 141-8...................36 ff.

Vol. V pp. 223-7...................55 ff.

Vol. V pp. 239-50 ....66 ff.

Vol. VI p. 24...........................347

Vol. VI pp. 86-94 ....97 ff.

Vol. VI pp. 119-129 ....103 ff.

Vol. VI pp. 189-195 ....128 ff.

Vol. VII pp. 74-79...............180 ff.

Vol. VII pp. 100-104...........186 ff.

Vol. VII pp. 134-138...........197 ff.

Vol. VII pp. 170-174...........209 ff.

Vol. VIII pp. 1-7 ....222 ff.

Vol. VIII pp. 21-8 ....231 ff.

Vol. VIII pp. 114-9 ....252 ff.

Vol. VIII pp. 123-7 ....258 ff.

Vol. VIII pp. 150-158 ....263 ff.

Vol. VIII pp. 160-170 ....270 ff.

Vol. IX pp. 61-70.................290 ff.

Vol. IX pp. 72 ff. 213

Vol. IX pp. 79-85.................297 ff.

Vol. IX pp. 106-114.............304 ff.

Vol. IX pp. 143-151.............316 ff.

Vol. IX pp. 204-214.............341 ff.

Vol. IX pp. 237-243.............349 ff.

Vol. X pp. 7-12 ....1 ff.

Vol. X pp. 24-29 ....6 ff.

Vol. X pp. 167-172 ....71 ff.

Vol. XI pp. 8-13.....................77 ff.

Vol. XI pp. 109-122.............119 ff.

Vol. XIV pp. 93-98 ....323 ff.

IGROT KODESH

Vol. 7 pp. 205-206 ....165 ff.

Vol. 18 pp. 318-319 ....166 ff.

Vol. 20 pp. 204-205 ....167 ff.

Vol. 23 pp. 361-365 ....169 ff.

Vol. 15 pp. 33-37 ....171 ff.

 formatting; formatting

GENERAL
INDEX

Aaron, 191 (death of his sons); 223; 226 (elevated the people from below to above); 241 (drew fellow-creatures near to Torah); 253 ff., 258, 270.

Abimelech, 32.

Abin, R., 67.

Abnegation—see *Nullification*.

Abraham, 11 ff., 16, 28 ff., 42; 86 (expresses love).

Acceptance of the Yoke of Heaven—see *Kabbalat Ol*.

Acher (Elisha ben Abuya), 194.

Action, 69 (significance of outward action); 88 (led to by emotion); 94 (action is needed to reveal even G-d's unconditional love); 114, 121 (prayer, study and action); 184, 287, 301; 332 (and yearning, which transcends action, when Jew is oppressed).

Adam, 185 (dual meaning).

Adanim (sockets of Sanctuary), 119 ff.

Adar, 151.

Adultery, 236 (prototype of all sin).

After-life, 27 (righteous who die before their time can complete their work in after-life); 34 ff. See also *World to Come*.

Aggadah, 73 (communicates the inwardness of G-d).

Akiva, 104 ff., 194 (entered the Grove of mystical teaching in peace and came out in peace); 197, 344.

Altar, 124 (of gold and of copper); 155 (offering of sacrifice on altar); 159; 317, 321 (sheds tears if a man divorces his first wife).

Alter Rebbe—see *Schneur Zalman of Liadi, R.*

Amalek, 161 (symbol of coldness in religious life); 324.

Amidah, 207 (extinction of self-consciousness); 283 (two contrary aspects of the Amidah); 284 (foretaste of the World to Come).

Angels, 44 (divine emanations).

Animal Kingdom, 63.

Animal Soul, 45 (refined by effort in Divine Service); 51 (orientation towards self and separateness); 64 (wants blessings without effort); 126 (the sacrifice on the inner altar); 154 (sanctification of the animal soul is the aim of the sacrifices in the Sanctuary); 155 (through quelling one's animal nature one reaches a transcendent level of G-d); 205 (transfers its passionate intensity to the life of holiness). See also *G-dly Soul, Soul*.

Annulment, of—279 (of vows, of illusion that hides G-d from man).

Apostate, 325 (Esau); 351 ff.

Architect, 2, 4.

Arizal, 342 ff.

Ark of the Covenant, 338, 339 (occupied no space).

Assimilation, 172, 204 (of Israelites in Egypt).

Astrology, 31, 91, 136, 170.

Atzilut, 198.

Av—see *Ninth of Av.*

Avodah—see *Divine Service.*

Awakening (from sleep), 4 (a new creation).

"Awakening from above" and "From below," 150 ff. (in construction of the sanctuary); 159 (in relation to the fire on the altar). See also *Revelation.*

Azazel, 261.

Baal Shem Tov—see *Yisrael Baal Shem Tov, R.*

Baal Teshuvah, 107 (path of); 294 (sanctifies his past life); 354 (compared with righteous man). See also *Repentance.*

Balaam, 71.

Balak, 71.

Bar Kochba, 279.

Beauty, 12, 22 ff. (of Sarah); 90.

Beersheba, 327 (symbolizes spirituality).

Ben Azai, 194.

Ben Zoma, 194.

Benoni ("lntermediate Man"), 46; 343 (does not sin, even in thought, but has not yet removed the *desire* to do wrong).

Bentzion (servant of Rebbe Maharash q.v.), 50.

Berditchev, 286 ff.

Beruriah (wife of R. Meir), 163.

Beth Din, 264 ff., See also *Judge, Law Court.*

Betrothal, 277, 278, (to G-d).

Bikkurim—see *First fruits.*

Birth, 183; 267 (miraculous event).

Birthday, 16.

Bittul, 207 (*bittul ha-yesh* and *bittul bi-metziut*); 212 (same, expressed by seventh year and Jubilee respectively). See also *Nullification.*

Body and Soul, 30, 32 (only body has been sent into exile); 35 (in the World to Come the body will give life to the soul); 52 (co-ordination of body by brain; body should not conceal light of soul); 57 (as body clothes the soul, so act of Mitzvah clothes Divine light).

Boethusians, 202.

Brain, 52.

Breaking of the Tablets, 351, 352 (paved the way for the second tablets which were greater); 353 (when Israel's return to G-d is complete it will be seen to have begun on day of breaking of the tablets).

Brit Milah—see *Circumcision.*

Businessman, 43 (does business for the sake of heaven); 256 (during Torah study a businessman should be as one who never departs from the Sanctuary); 314. See also *Work.*

Caleb, 246 ff.

Campaign (Tefillin), 59.

Census, 222 ff.

Chabad, 244. See also *Chassidut.*

Chametz—see *Leaven.*

Change and Changelessness, 25, 63.

Chanukah, 55 (Chanukah lights compared with Mezuzah); 57 (Chanukah lights illuminate and purify the realm of alienation from G-d; Chanukah lights and Torah); 58 (Chanukah lights and Tefillin; giving extra charity on Chanukah); 59 (Chanukah suitable time for Tefillin campaign); 64 (Chanukah lights express increase, hence sanctity); 129.

Chariot, 228 (expression of *Nullification*).

Charity, 58 (extra charity given on Chanukah); 58 (material and spiritual charity); 163 (includes all commandments, needs inner warmth); 336 (distinction between *Chesed* and *Tzedakah*).

Chassidut, 33, 42, 45, 136, 143, 231, 235 (teaches one to see G-d in the world); 247, 295 (all inner teachings of Torah are reflected in Halacha; 304, 311, 326, 339, 342.

Chesed—see *Charity.*

Chesed, Gevurah, Tiferet, 243. See also *Emotion.*

Child, 36 (begins to study Torah at five years old); 121.

Chukim—see *Statutes.*

Chumash (Pentateuch), 10, 286. See also *Sefer Torah, Torah.*

Circumcision, 16 ff., 38, 92, 95 (union between Jew and G-d beyond the rational); 175 (can be performed on Sabbath); 228.

Cities of refuge, 311 ff.

Civilization, 169.

Coldness, 161 (in religious life).

"Collective Soul," 61.

Command, 152 (the command itself is a promise of achievement).

Commandments—see *Mitzvot, Ten Commandments.*

Commitment, 219 (does not rule out the pursuit of understanding); 321 (of Israel to G-d at Sinai).

Community—see *Individual and Community.*

Concealment, 44 (of G-d—to be broken through by Jew); 51 world of concealment compared to a field in which all is separate); 53; 81 (of G-d in the world); 96, 130.

Conflict, 62 (ultimately has no reality); 166 (transcending the inner conflict between what is physical and what is Divine).

Consolation, 290 (purpose of consolation); 295 (the Third Temple); 296, 303, Israel seeks consolation from G-d rather than from Prophets).

Constancy, 163 ff. (need for constancy in attachment to Torah). See also *Change* and *Changelessness.*

Contemplation, 205 (on nature of G-d).

Convert, 38 (like new born child); 107.

Creation, 1 ff., 4 (continuous, Torah is the blueprint of creation); 98 (was on condition all created objects obeyed the will of righteous men); 181 ff. (creation of man after the animals); 255.

Cunning, 43 (in relation to dealing with the materiality of the world).

Cynics, 28, 32.

Cyrus, 295.

Dance, 46.

Darkness, 3, 5, 189 (transformation into light); 285 (darkness of Exile transformed into light of Time to Come).

David, King, 72, 231, 233.

Day of Atonement—see *Yom Kippur.*

Days of Awe, 330.

Death Sentence, 305, 307.

Deceit, 41 (considered a sin before the Giving of the Torah).

Delight, 115 (in carrying out a Mitzvah); 125.

Descent in order to rise, 287.

Despair, 5, 284 (personal, and historical despair).

Destruction, 285 (in order to build).

Devarim, Book of (Deuteronomy), 286 ff. (differs from other four books of *Chumash*).

Disagreement, 211 (disagreement among sages due to different aspects of spirituality); 253.

Diversity, 228 (diversity of world, reveals oneness of G-d); 328 ff. (of Jewish people).

Divided Loyalties, 172.

Divine blessings, 64; 127.

Divine light, 57 (clothed by action of Mitzvot as body clothes the soul; different levels of); 208 (from beyond the world); 248 (within the world, not above it); 292 (shining from G-d to world); 293 (three aspects, corresponding to Torah, Commandments, Repentance); 302; 339 (reaches finite world).

Divine Name, 34, 44, 87, 129, 133 (absent from the *Megillah);* 155.

Divine Presence, 72, 75; 120 (in heart of every Jew); 149 ff. (in Sanctuary); 161 (did not immediately descend in Sanctuary); 163 (condition for dwelling in man); 207; 218 (spoke through Moses); 240 (revealed in soul of individ-

ual); 256 ff.; 279 (hidden
from man by illusion).

Divine Providence, 7, 14, 133,
231, 246.

Divine Service, 29 (different
modes of); 45 (strenuous effort to refine one's physical-
ity); 51 ff. (symbolized by details of Joseph's dreams); 125
(service in the soul mirrors
the Temple service); 149
(elicits a Divine response);
156 (enthusiasm in Divine
Service); 213 (contrast between "simple" and "faithful"
servant); 232 (aim to turn
world into a "vessel" receptive
of G-d); 248 (aim is sanctification of the world, rather
than elevation of the soul);
278 ("betrothal" to G-d); 288;
295 (man's effort to purify finite world imparted sanctity
to second Temple); 302
(motive at outset is reward
and punishment); 327 (aim to
draw spirituality into world of
work and social life); 340
(Divine Service within and
beyond reason).

Divine Soul—see *G-dly Soul.*

Divine Sparks—see *Holy
Sparks.*

Divine Will, 101 (embodied in
nature); 115; 116 ("Thou
shall not steal" should be
obeyed not simply as Reason,
but as Divine Will); 120
(submission to); 287
(translated into practical ac-

tion); 294; 345 (the righteous
are not concerned for their
own spiritual satisfaction, but
for the fulfillment of Divine
Will).

Divorce, 316, 322 (divorce
document paradoxically suggests unity).

Doeg, 218 (signifies superficial
study).

Dov Ber of Mezeritch, R.—see
Maggid of Mezeritch.

Dov Ber Schneuri, R.—*Mitteler
Rebbe* (1773-1827), 313.

Doubt, 116.

Dreams, 48 ff., 60 ff. (of Joseph
and of Pharaoh).

Dualism, 170.

**Dwelling place for G-d in
lower world**, 3; 81 (through
Torah and Mitzvot); 101; 151
(the Sanctuary); 192, 200,
248, 327, 347.

Earth, 126 (symbol of human-
ity); 341 (earth and Heaven);
347 (man finds G-d "close to
the earth").

Eating, 43 (for the sake of
Heaven).

Ecstasy, 104 (at Giving of Torah); 192 ff.

Education, 39 (in case of Abraham); 94, 299, 336. See also
*Study, Teacher and Pupil, To-
rah.*

Egypt, 11 (spiritual descent); 13
(exile); 77. 166 (liberation
from Egypt every day); 169
(idolatry led to enslavement

of the weak minority); 281, 282, 323, 326. See also *Exodus*.

Eight, 81 (symbolizes seven heavens and earth), 162; 175 (symbol of holiness).

Elazar, son of Aaron, 270 ff.

Elazar Ben Azariah, R., 109.

"Elevation," 14 (of world); 80 (in Messianic Age). See also *Purification*.

Eliezer Ben Hyrcanos, R., 124, 126.

Elijah, 135.

Elimelech of Lizhensk, R., 254.

Elisha Ben Abuya, —see *Acher*.

Elokim (Name of G-d), 34, 44 ff., 87 (plurality and finitude).

Elul, 305, 311, 314.

Emanation—see *Atzilut, Spirituality*.

Emotion, 87 (expressed by Forefathers); 88 (leads to faith and action); 115, 125, 160, 219.

End, 13 (implicit in beginning).

End of Days, 71 ff. See also *Messiah, Messianic Age, World to Come*.

"Engraving," 218 (union with Torah).

Environment, 24 (relationship with); 96, 312.

Esau, 43 ff., 86, 94, 324, 325 (a Jew, albeit an apostate); 350 (refused the Torah).

Esther, 130 (signifies concealment).

Esther, Book of—see *Megillah*.

Evil inclination, 58 (bound into service of G-d through Tefillin); 83; 117 (begins cunningly); 138; 197 (taken into consideration by Torah); 204, 205 (love G-d with evil inclination); 261 ff.

Excision, 266.

Exile, 13; 14 (an integral part of spiritual progress); 32 ("only our bodies have gone into exile not our souls"); 80 (service in exile purifies the world and brings the Messiah); 133; 238; 288 (each exile has brought new levels of spirituality); 299, 302; 312 (cities of refuge); 313; 318 (apparent divorce from G-d); 321 (hiding of love, which reveals a deeper love); 353.

Exodus, 166 (every day); 178 (the Exodus will only be completed through the future redemption); 203; 207 (every day); 223; 281 ff. (a repeated process); 323.

Faith, 76 (in coming of Messiah); 88, 95, 116; 126 (spark of faith); 135, 167; 220 (begins where understanding ends; levels of); 246.

Fall, 79 (for the sake of ascent).

Famine, 11 ff., 67.

Fast day, 131, 353. See also *Ninth of Av, Seventeenth of Tammuz, Yom Kippur*.

Father, 13; 39 (relationship of Terach to Abraham); 89, 277 ff., 299; 353. See also *Forefathers*.

Fear of G-d, 29 (lower and higher fear); 86, 344.

Fellow, 7, 41, (fellow Jew who knows nothing of his religious heritage); 138.

Festivals, 349, (Scriptural readings on); 354 (festive cycle); 355 (their light to spread through the whole year). See also *Pesach, Shavuot,* etc.

"Fifth Son," 171 ff. (the son who is not aware of the Seder).

Fire, 158 (within the Jew, merging with the fire of heaven); 160 (need for outward fire of love for G-d).

Firmament, 254.

First fruits, 323; 326 (Chassidic explanation).

Flood, 40.

Folly, 236 ff.

Forefathers, 13, 18 ("works of the fathers are a sign for the children"); 37 (kept Torah before it was given); 41, 49; 80 (their service brought about the Giving of the Torah); 86 (embodied emotion, learned Torah); 157 ("when will my acts be like theirs?"); 170, 232.

Foreign Country, 319 (of the spirit); 320 (contrasting with Land of Israel).

Four Sons, 171.

Freedom, 45 (from sin); 165; 166 (from limitations); 212 ff. (expressed in Jubilee year).

Free will, 136, 268; 310 (has no limits).

Fruit Tree, 197 ff. (spiritual significance of years of growth); 326.

Gamliel, Rabban, 109.

Gan Eden and *Gehinom*, 343.

Garments, 193 (Mitzvot are garments for word of G-d).

Gemarra, 33 (distinction from Midrash).

Gematria (numerical equivalence of words), 2 ("light" and "secret" are numerically equivalent).

Genealogy, 270.

Ger—see *Convert.*

Gift, 177 (distinction from reward; Divine gift).

Ginnai, River, 98 (split by R. Pinchas ben Yair).

Giving of Torah—see *Sinai.*

G-d, 44 (G-d is concealed—and the service of the Jew is to break down this concealment); 49 (a man who has one G-d has nothing to fear); 58 (alienation from); 69 (G-d present even in actions done from ulterior motives); 80 (revelation at Sinai); 93 (executed the Tenth plague); 94 (His unconditional love for Israel); 99 (can "uncreate" something retroactively); 106 (revealed at Sinai); 110

(beginning of worship is to strive to make G-dliness real for oneself); 133 (beyond all Names); 150 (relationship with man: three stages); 160 (permanent link with individual); 199 (praises of G-d induce Him to "inhabit" the world); 232 (His "descent" towards world); 249 (can combine the natural with the supernatural); 261 (infinite and beyond understanding); 278; 279 (man together with G-d has power to annul the bondage of the world); 283 (the nearer to G-d, the more all opposites can be accommodated); 285 (our goal is to see history through eyes of G-d); 292; 293 (to find G-dliness at the core of oneself); 297; 303 (consoles Israel); 307 (omniscience of); 318 (relationship with Israel compared with marriage); 330 (acceptance of G-d's sovereignty on Rosh Hashanah); 344 (grief at distance from G-d); 345, 346 (kingship of); 347 (man finds G-d "close to the earth"); 354 (bond with G-d survives even when man transgresses the law). See also *Divine Blessings, Divine Light,* etc.

G-dly Soul, 46 (two levels); 183, 185, 200, 239, 309; 333 (essential self of Jew); 355 (by returning to G-d the Jew awakens the G-dly power within him). See also *Israel, Jew, Oneness, Soul, Unity.*

Golden Calf, 79 ff., 142, 145, 152; 161 (prevented immediate revelation of Divine Presence in the Sanctuary); 223; 313; 352 (was only for sake of ultimate repentance).

Good deeds, 278 (fruit of oneness with G-d). See also *Mitzvot.*

"Grove" (of mystical secrets of Torah), 194.

Haftorah, 135, 286, 290, 296; 297 (relationship with Sidra).

Hagadah, 171 (Four sons and "fifth son").

Halacha, 8, 45; 295 (halacha reflects esoteric teachings); 301 (halacha reflects distinction between "seeing and hearing").

Haran, 327 (symbolizes corruption).

Harmony, 52, 53.

Heart, 73 (can be at odds with the innermost will of the soul); 238 (symbol for Jewish people); 347 (even duties of the heart can be considered of a finite nature).

Heathen Woman, 263 ff., 272.

Heaven, 62 ff., 142, 341; 347 (man's desire to be "close to heaven").

Hebrew Language, 180.

Heel, 46, 88; 300 (symbol of lowly physical nature which can be transformed).

High Priest, 107, 261, 267.

Hillel, 241, 317.

Holiness, 51 (only through effort); 63 (eternal and ascending in perfection, unlike unholinesss); 51 (core of holiness within every Jew); 175 (degrees of); 234; 251 (should permeate life); 291 (two elements in drawing holiness to this world); 355 (should permeate the secular world).

Holy of Holies, 109 (fox emerging from); 191; 338 (contained written Sefer Torah and Engraved tablets).

Holy sparks, 44; 57 (those embedded in forbidden realm are released by study of Torah); 342.

Homicide, 116, 311, 314.

Honesty, 114 (could be learned from the ant).

Hosea, 326.

Humility, 126, 343.

Husband, 277 ff. See also *Marriage, Wife.*

Idolatry, 108, 117, 135 ff., 145; 169 (deification of forces of nature and of man; in Egypt idolatry led to enslavement of the weak minority); 170 ff. (modern forms of idolatry); 188 (does not deny G-d, but His uniqueness); 224, 270 ff., 304 ff. (city led into idolatry).

Illusion, 279 (hides G-d's presence from man).

Immanence and transcendence, 34, 87 ff.

Immediacy, 287.

Immigrants, 172 (thought assimilation was the solution).

Incompleteness, 280 (incompleteness preferable to complacency).

Individual and Community, 139, 299, 301-2, 306 (collective and individual guilt and responsibility); 308, 310; 329 (unique contribution of each individual, permanent and impermanent communities); 331; 333 (organic unity within community); 340 (need to break through social distinctions).

Infinity, 162, 250; 339 (dwells in the finite world).

Inheritance, 250 (of Land of Israel); 287.

Intellect, 90, 115, 125; 160 (must be accompanied by fire of love); 282 (narrow limitations of). See also *Knowledge.*

Inwardness, 300 (result of personal effort); 303.

Isaac, 28 (looked like Abraham); 86 (expresses attribute of fear).

Isaiah, 152, 238, 286, 341; 347 ff. (contrast with Moses).

Ishmael, 350 (refused Torah).

Ishmael, R., 104 ff.

Israel, 42 (and Jacob, two stages in service of G-d); 45; 46 *(Li-*

Rosh); 88; 309, 317 *(unity of entire nation)*; 350 ff. *(uniqueness of Israel revealed on Shemini Atzeret)*; 353 (when Israel's return to G-d is complete, it will be seen to have begun on the day when the tablets were broken); 354 (at giving of the second tablets, Israel reached beyond Torah to their eternal union with G-d). See also *Jew.*

Israel, Land of, 245 (Canaan); 248 (the task: to take possession and make it a Holy Land); 250 (signifies the daily world); 287, 295; 299 (had Moses led the Israelites in conquest of the Land this would have been a supernatural event); 301 (transformation of nations inhabiting Land); 304, 311 ff., 313 (Land of Divine grace); 319, 323, 325.

Iyar, 203; 207 (spiritual aspect); 223, 229.

Jacob, 37; 42 (and Israel, two stages in service of G-d); 43 ff.; 46 *(Yud-Ekev)*; 61, 63, 69 (compared with Joseph); 71 (wished to reveal the end of days); 86 (expresses mercy); 88 *(ekev)*; 170; 282 (Jacob's ladder signifies prayer); 323.

Japheth, 6, 9.

Jeremiah, 136.

Jeremiah, R., 211.

Jericho, 247.

Jerusalem, 11, 201; 285 (breach in walls of); 287.

Jerusalem Talmud—see *Talmud.*

Jethro, 270 ff.

Jew, 7 (is an end in himself); 31 (can transcend natural law); 32 (only the body has gone into exile); 41 (Jew who knows nothing of his religious heritage); 45, 47 (service to break through concealment of G-d); 50 (simultaneously involved in material and spiritual worlds); 50 (lives to obey G-d); 52 (collective body); 61 (source of challenges to him are in himself rather than in the world; he creates the state of the world he inhabits); 63 (has a single mission); 73 (can desire what the Torah forbids—but in his true inwardness never seeks to separate himself from G-d's Will); 75 (has power to reach in a single bound the final revelation); 85; 90 (highest and lowest should work together); 110; 135 (called "believer"); 140 (all interlinked); 144 (labor of); 166 (has capacity to transform himself from one extreme to the other); 188 (every Jew will ultimately repent); 192 (at point of spiritual ecstasy must turn again towards physical existence); 218 (his whole being must be Torah);

239 (no Jew so distant from G-d that he cannot return); 267 (boundary of Jew from other nations); 269 (has power to cross boundaries set by Torah); 274 (subconsciously seeks to keep Torah for its own sake); 284 (was not created to stand still); 293 (every Jew, in his true depths seeks to do G-d's Will); 299; 301-2 (as individual, and as community); 309 (unity of all Jews); 321 (every Jew wishes to keep every commandment); 329 (each Jew has his own unique contribution); 330 ff.; 332 (power of simple Jew in time of oppression); 345 (the ordinary Jew is a part of G-d); 355 (through the G-dly power within him the Jew can create a new world). See also *G-dly Soul, Israel, Soul.*

Jewish History, 14; 63 (its apparent fluctuations are permeated by a single will); 109 (at darkest moment, R. Akiva saw only the good); 135, 178; 213 (three epochs of); 284 (historical despair); 285 (our goal is to see history through eyes of G-d); 320.

Jochanan, R., 22.

Jochanan Ben Zakkai, R., 343.

Jordan, 249, 299; 314 (trans-Jordan).

Joseph, 48 ff. (his dreams); 61 (a "collective soul"); 63 ff. (his

dreams belong to realm of holiness); 66 (sustained his brothers, and in a similar manner G-d gives blessing to His people); 69 (translated spiritual reality into material terms).

Joshua, 247 ff.

Journey, 281 (42 stages of Israelites' journey through wilderness).

Joy, 47 (a soldier goes with a song of joy); 288; 344 (tears of joy through studying secrets of Torah).

Jubilee, 209, 212 (expresses complete abnegation and freedom).

Judah, 78.

Judah Hanasi, R., 318 (ethical significance in his arrangement of the Mishnah).

Judge, 105, 305, 309, 312. See also *Law Court.*

Kabbalat Ol, (Acceptance of the Yoke), 88; 120 (expressed by sockets of Sanctuary); 212 (service of seventh year).

Kavvana—see *Motive.*

Kesef Mishnah (commentary on the Rambam), 305.

Keter (crown), 198.

Kiddush, 230.

Kindness, 94.

King, Kingship, 2, 233; 346, 346 (of G-d on Rosh Hashanah); 355 (the Jew can create a new world in which the kingship of G-d is recognized).

Kli Yakar (commentary), 174.
Knowledge, 86 (embodied by Moses); 88 (by itself, leads to detachment). See also *Emotion*.
Korach, 252 ff.

Laban, 323.
Lamp, 294 (image for commandments).
"Last in action, first in thought," 184.
Law—see *Halacha, Mitzvot, Torah*.
Law Court, 112, 114; 117 (Jewish and non-Jewish); 305 ff. (its rulings not affected by Repentance, except in case of idolatrous city); 307 (Heavenly tribunal); 312.
Leaven, 204 (symbolizes inclination to pride).
Lecha Dodi, 184.
Left hand, 56 (relates to disunity).
Legal document, 10.
Leper, 186 ff.; 190 ("the Leper" a suitable name for Sidra in light of approaching Messianic Age).
Levites, 154 (songs and praises); 243, 338.
Levi Yitzchak of Berditchev, R., 286, 288.
Light, 1 ff. (creation of). See also *Divine Light*.
Limitation, 162 (of man, unless something Divine intervenes); 168 (freedom from limitation through Torah and Mitzvot); 345 (way to overcome human limitation is by grief at one's confinement); 346 (human limitation is not inevitable).
Love, 29 (expressed by Abraham); 86; 126 (love of G-d is the fire on the inner altar); 157 ff. (love reshapes animal force into Divine love); 173 (love of one's fellow, of G-d, of Torah); 194 (of G-d); 205 (with *both* inclinations); 223 (of G-d to Jew, expressed by census); 241, 298; 321 (hiding of love in Exile, reveals a deeper love); 344. See also *Self Love*.
Lubavitcher Rebbe—see *Schneur Zalman, R.; Dov Ber Schneuri, R.; Menachem Mendel, R.; Shmuel, R.; Shalom DovBer, R.; Yosef Yitzchak, R.*
Luminary, 342 (closeness of luminary to spark).
Luria, R. Yitzchak (d. 1572), 342 ff.

Maggid of Mezeritch, R. Dov Ber (d. 1772), 98, 160.
Maharash, Fourth Lubavitcher Rebbe, R. Shmuel (1834-1882), 50.
Maimonides—see *Rambam*.
Man, 1 (created last); 4 (microcosm of world); 34 (has imminent and transcendent aspects); 181 (his place in Creation); 185 (dual meaning in name Adam).

Manna, 246, 324.

Marah, 228.

Marriage, 36 ff. (prohibition of marrying one's sister); 191 ff., 237 (between Jewish people and G-d); 267, 277, 317; 318 (metaphor for relationship of G-d and Israel); 321 (only with woman's consent). See also *Procreation, Wedding.*

Martyrdom, 107. See also *Self-sacrifice.*

Materiality, 2, 138, 144; 248 (fear that materiality swallows up spiritual force); 287 (only by descent into materiality could fulfillment be reached); 291 (vessel for holiness).

Megillah, 128 ff.; 133 (Divine Name absent from).

Melancholy, 240 (sinner should not fall prey to melancholy).

Memory, 165 (a spiritual achievement); 166 (reawakens the Divine benevolence of the past).

Menachem, R., 67 ff.

Menachem Mendel of Lubavitch, R., *Tzemach Tzedek* (1789-1866), 16, 19, 45 ff.

Menorah, 242 (symbol of Jewish soul); 255.

Messiah, 14, 59; 75 (the fact we feel our time is unworthy of redemption is proof of the nearness of the Messiah); 76 (faith in Messiah will itself bring the redemption); 77 (connection with Moses); 79 (descendant of David, steeped in Torah); 80 (will teach Torah to all Israel; Messiah is brought by service in exile which purifies the world); 96, 173, 215, 224, 279.

Messianic Age, 80 (world will be purified); 90 (brought by uniting "higher" and "lower"); 134; 152 (unity of man and G-d); 175 (harp of eight strings); 176 (not a sudden break in the history of Jewish consciousness); 190 (its imminence affects name of Sidra); 235, 240, 276, 282, 285; 353 (seen by Moses at end of his life).

Mezeritcher Maggid, 98, 160.

Mezuzah, 55 (compared with Chanukah lights); 56 (includes all Mitzvot); 146, 299, 302.

Microcosm, 4; 82 (man is microcosm of world).

Midian, 271 ff.

Midnight, 94 (revealed the all transcending face of G-d).

Midrash, 33 (intermediary between revealed and inward aspects of Torah); 66, 77, 97, 104, 142, 290, 297, 303, 311, 341. See also *Index of Scriptural and Rabbinic Quotations.*

Mikvah, 260.

Mind—see *Intellect.*

Miracles, 31; 100 (two types of miracles); 104 (at Giving of Torah); 246; 248 (not apex of spiritual experience); 249 (a miracle concealed in nature is greater than the supernatural); 291, 299, 324, 338; 339 *(mem* and *samech* on Tablets).

Miriam, 247, 252.

Mirror, 7 (one's perception of others reflects oneself).

Mishkan—see *Sanctuary*.

Mishnah, 124; 318 ff. (ethical significance in its order).

Mitteler Rebbe, R. Dov Ber Schneuri (1773-1827), 313.

Mitzvah Campaign, 59.

Mitzvot (commandments), 18 (of Patriarchs and subsequently); 56; 57 (mitzvot bring spiritual life to the world; act of mitzvot clothes the Divine Light as body clothes the soul); 69 (inner essence, or outer action); 79 (of Adam, of Noah and of Patriarchs); 107 (two aspects); 113 (three kinds: judgments, testimonies, statutes); 115 (should involve every facet of man); 118 (means "connection" with G-d); 122 (women exempt from positive command connected with a specific time); 149 (the preparation for mitzvot is also holy); 168 (bring freedom from limitations); 193 (garments for work of G-d); 197 (practical purpose of); 216 (statutes, testimonies and judgments); 228 (preceded Sinai but were transformed by Sinai); 248 (make dwelling place for G-d in the world); 294 (through mitzvot we both receive and give light; the mitzvot purify existence); 318 (analogy of blessing on mitzvot with marriage formula); 332 under oppression, the Jew yearns to keep mitzvot); 333; 347 ("earthly" quality); 348 (contrasted with Torah; mitzvot draw G-d into the world).

Modeh Ani, 123, 207.

Modesty, 12; 113 (could be learned from cat).

Money, 139.

Moon—See *Sun and Moon*.

Moses, 77 ff. (connection with Messiah); 84 (his questions to G-d); 86 (embodied knowledge); 90 (translated the Torah); 91; 97 (splitting the sea); 100 (his hand smitten with leprosy); 141, 170; 218 (Divine Presence spoke through his throat); 220 (the reason behind the Red Heifer was revealed to him); 223; 226 (as communicator of revelation, a channel from above to below); 232, 245, 258, 263, 296, 299 (had he led Israelites in conquest of the Land this would have been a supernatural event); 313, 338, 341; 347 (contrast with Isaiah); 349 (instituted appropriate Torah readings on festivals); 351 ff. (broke tablets, seeking to elevate Israel); 353

(on his last day saw vision of future).

Motive, 68-69 (distinction between motive and action); 114.

Mysticism, 194.

"Naaseh Venishmah," 321.

Nachmanides, 37.

Nadab and Abihu, 191 ff.

Name, 10 ff. (of person, of Sidra); 42 (of Abraham and of Jacob); 129 (a sign of essential character of a thing); 180 (Hebrew name has meaning); 186; 186 ff. (of Sidra, changing through the generations); 253. See also *Divine Name*.

Nations of the world, 32; 40 (after the Flood restrained themselves from unchastity); 64, 258 ff., 301 (transformation of); 320; 325 (their intentions considered as deeds); 350 (had opportunity to accept Torah at Sinai). See also *Noachide Laws*.

Nature, 31 (Jew can transcend nature) 33; 248 ff.

Nimrod, 43.

Nine days, 287 ff.

Ninth of Av, 246, 285, 286, 290, 322.

Nissan, 203; 207 (spiritual aspect); 223, 225, 229.

Noachide Laws, 17, 38 ff., 79, 228.

Nomadic Life, 168 (mistrusted in agricultural Egypt).

Non-Jew, 114 (non-Jewish law); 295 (ordered building of Second Temple). See also *Nations of the World*, *Noachide Laws*.

Nullification, 53 (of will); 82; 106 (nullification of world at Giving of the Torah); 194; 206 (of self at Giving of Torah); 207 *(bittul ha-yesh* and *bittul bi-metziut)*; 212 ff. (same, represented by Seventh Year and the Jubilee respectively); 218 (nullification of self, in case of Moses and of R. Shimon ben Yochai); 228 (of self, through *Mitzvot)*; 283 (of self, in Amidah prayer); 294 (through self nullification, we refine the world); 340 (of self, on Rosh Hashanah, transcending Reason); 345 (of self, through grief at the limitations of one's achievement).

Omer, 178 (preparation for Giving of Torah and for the Messianic revelation); 202; 205 (of animal food); 226, 229.

Oneness, 78 (service with quality of oneness will bring Messiah); 81 (of G-d; explanation of *echad)*; 83; 147 (of assembly of Israelites, and of G-d); 229 (of G-d, perceived through the multiplicity of the world); 240 (to attach significance to things independently of G-d is a denial of G-d's oneness);

256; 278 (fruit of oneness with G-d is good deeds); 309; 310 (manifest even in deepest transgression); 316 (symbolized by Sefer Torah and, paradoxically, by the divorce document); 347 (yearning of man for oneness with G-d).

Oppression, 32 (only our bodies in servitude, not our souls); 96, 224; 332 (yearning of oppressed Jew to fulfill the commandments).

Paradise and Gehinom, 343.

Paradox, 2, 6; 32 (of freedom of soul whole body is enslaved); 283 (of the Amidah prayer); 287 (that through descent comes true uplifting); 317.

Pardes, 194. See also *Pashat, Remez, etc.*

Parents, 40 (respect for); 136.

Pascal lamb, 92; 95 (act of self-sacrifice); 170, 351.

Passover—see *Pesach.*

Past, 156 (sins of past); 165.

Patriarchs—see *Forefathers.*

Peace, 256 ff. (comes through the medium of division); 276.

Pentateuch—see *Chumash.*

Pentecost—see *Shavuot.*

Perfection, 7 (of oneself, and of others); 18 (of Abraham); 21 ff., 25, 26, 41; 62 (progression from lower to higher forms of perfection in Joseph's dreams); 78; 110.

Persecution—see *Oppression.*

Persia, 295.

Pesach, 165 ff., 178, 202 ff., 206 ff., 225, 229.

Peshat, Remez etc. (levels of Torah interpretation); 124.

Pesukei Dezimrah—see *Psalms of Praise.*

Pharaoh, 49 (his dreams); 60 ff., 91, 94, 166.

Pinchas, 263 ff., 270 ff.

Pinchas ben Yair, R., 98.

Pirkei Avot—See *Index of Scriptural and Rabbinic Quotations.*

Plagues, 91 ff.; 100 (the river returned from blood to water without a second miracle); 246.

Prayer, 18 (morning prayer instituted by Abraham), 82 (diffuses G-dly spirit through one's being); 121; 163 (not a fixed mechanical task); 282; 283 (rungs of the ladder of prayer); 335 (distinction between *Bakashah* and *Tefillah*). See *Amidah, Psalms of Praise.*

Pride, 279; 283 (divestment of pride before prayer).

Priests, 107; 154 (their "silent service" in the Temple); 187 ff., 191 ff.; 244 (not only the priests spread the light of Torah); 253 ff., 266, 272 ff.

Private Domain, 147 (domain of the Unity of G-d). See also *Public Domain.*

Procreation, 194 ff.

Progress, 14 (spiritual progress of world); 26 (of righteous);

62; 220 (from level to level, even in faith).

Prophets, prophecy, 20 (prophetic awareness of G-d); 71 ff. (prophetic power of Jacob); 297; 303 (Israel seeks consolation from G-d, rather than from prophets); 318.

Psalms of Praise, 207; 283 (a rung of prayer).

Psychoanalyst, 139.

Public Domain, 55 (suggests multiplicity and disunity).

Purification, 260; 294 (through Mitzvot existence is purified).

Purim, 120, 128 ff.; 151 (expresses going beyond rationality).

Purity and Impurity, 125 (of vessels of Sanctuary, and of thought).

Purpose, 3 (manifested explicitly and implicitly).

Putiel, 270.

Rambam (Maimonides), 78, 83, 136, 145, 186, 243, 254, 306 ff., 316, 321, 350.

Ramban (Nachmanides), 37.

Ramses, 281.

Rashab, Fifth Lubavitcher Rebbe, R. Shalom DovBer (1860-1920), 16 ff., 19.

Rashi, 21, 36, 39, 72, 89, 101, 105, 110 (addresses his commentary to the "five year old"); 142, 186, 197, 210, 217, 222, 253; 258 ff. (methodology of); 263, 270; 274 (more than a literal com-

mentary); 299, 323; 324 (silence in his commentary indicates there is no problem in the Scriptural text); 350.

Rava, 157.

Reason, 95 (laws beyond reason); 113 (compels certain laws, while others are beyond reason); 116 ("thou shalt not steal" should be obeyed not only as reason but as G-d's Will); 117 (limitation of reason); 151 (going beyond reason, and expressing this in ordinary life); 282 (limitations of reason); 284 (beyond reason opposites are compatible); 340 (service within realm of reason and beyond).

Rebecca, 43.

Redemption, 14, 15; 240 (personal redemption is a preface to collective redemption); 288; 288 (redemption without further Exile); 348 (future redemption). See also *Messiah, Messianic Age, World to Come.*

Red Heifer, 220 (the reason behind it revealed to Moses); 259 ff., 260 ff.

Red Sea, 97 ff., 246, 324.

Refuge, cities of, 311 ff.

Repentance, 52, 69, 107, 131, 137; 140 (takes one higher than before the sin); 188; 189 (turns willful sins into merits); 224 ("nothing stands before repentance"); 269 (transcends Torah); 293

(prompted from within, rather than from Above); 294 (sanctifies the whole of experience); 306 (power of); 307; 309 (changes the facts of the case); 310; 312 (remorse effaces the crime; two phases in repentance: remorse and commitment); 335 (distinction between *Charatah* and *Teshuvah*); 343 (tears of); 344 (means return to source); 352 (brings one to a higher level of spirituality than before the sin); 354 (reaches higher than Torah); 355 (awakens G-dly power within Jew).

Repentant—see *Baal Teshuvah.*

Revelation, 16 (of G-d to Abraham, and to us); 130, 149 (in the Sanctuary); 151 (of G-d within the human sphere); 285, 287; 291 (in Temple); 292 (revelation from Above in Sanctuary); 299 (from Above); 300 (revelation evoked by man's own acts); 340; 354. See also *Sinai.*

Reward and punishment, 6, 20, 27; 34 (reward is the good deed itself); 67 (reward in World to Come is revelation of our acts in this world); 138; 302 (motive at outset of Divine Service); 310 (punishment is a remedy for harm done to the world); 312 (punishment aims not at retribution, but at refinement of guilty).

Righteous Man *(Tzaddik,* **Righteousness)**, 16; 19 (at the deepest level of the soul there is no distinction between the righteous man and the ordinary man); 21; 26 (the righteous go from strength to strength); 27 (the righteous who die before their time can complete their work in the after life); 46 (completely righteous); 61 (foundation of the world); 89; 98 (power over nature); 107 ff., 278; 295 (Jews at level of righteous during epoch of First Temple); 335 (righteous can repent); 343 (righteous should also weep in repentance); 344 (righteous man grieves at his distance from G-d); 345 (righteous man concerned for G-d's Will, rather than his own spiritual satisfaction); 351; 354 (compared with repentant).

Rogotchover Rav, R. Joseph Rozin (1858-1936), 306 ff.

Rosh Hashanah, 295, 315, 328; 330 (acceptance of G-d's sovereignty); 334, 337; 340 (expresses self-effacement beyond reason; illuminates the whole year); 342; 346 (the Shofar; kingship of G-d).

Russia, 49.

Saadiah Gaon, (892-942), 186.

Sacrifice, 153 (must be of yourself); 154 (the aim of sacrifice is to sanctify the Animal Soul); 155, 156; 225 (achieves the "revelation that comes from below").

Sage, 11, 277. See also *Judge, Righteous Man.*

Sanctuary, 119; 120 (sanctuary of the soul); 123 (personal sanctuary, recreated day by day); 125, 141; 149 (built by created being, eliciting a Divine response); 150 (stages in its construction); 151 (a dwelling place in the lower world); 154 (within each Jew); 159; 161 (Divine Presence did not immediately descend in Sanctuary due to sin of Golden Calf); 223, 225; 234 (distinction from Temple); 242, 255, 291; 292 (distinction from Temple); 323.

Sarah, 12 ff., 21 ff.

Satan, 258 ff.

Saul, 233.

Schneersohn—see *Shalom DovBer, R.; Yosef Yitzchak, R.*

Schneur Zalman of Liadi, R., *Alter Rebbe* (1745-1813), 113, 182, 188, 218, 219, 331, 343.

Secular World, 13 (transformed by Abraham); 32 (rulers of); 282 (a confining force); 355 (to be made receptive to holiness).

Seder Service, 171.

Seeing and hearing, 105 ff. (intermingling of the senses at the Giving of the Torah); 287, 300 ff. ("seeing" from Above, "hearing" from man himself).

Sefer Torah, 316 (symbol of unity); 338; 339 (medium whereby Divine radiance reaches finite world). See also *Torah.*

Self-abnegation—see *Nullification.*

Self-deception, 275, 332 ff.

Self-examination, 155 (like examining sacrifice for a blemish); 314 (in Elul); 343 (in the Ten Days of Repentance).

Self Knowledge, 343 (there is no duty to think oneself worse than one is).

Self love, 7; 332. See also *Animal Soul.*

Self-sacrifice, 95 (is beyond reason. Expressed in sacrifice of Pascal lamb in Egypt); 107 (R. Akiva's yearning for); 137, 224; 331 ff. (of oppressed Jew); 340 (can be within reason).

Selichot, 314.

Seven, 85 (seventh is precious); 162 (seven days express measure of earthly time); 174; 175 (the created order; the harp of seven strings); 212 (significance of seventh year); 243.

Seven Noachide Laws, 17, 38 ff., 79, 228.

Seventeenth of Tammuz, 285; 353 (will be a day of rejoicing in the Time to Come).

"Seventy Princes," 44.

"Seven weeks of consolation," 290, 297, 322.

Severity, 94.

Shaatnez, 30, 260.

Shabbat, 44 (difference between Shabbat and weekday meals); 47, 141, 157; 160 (a state of mind; contemplation and understanding); 175; 177 (the Sanctuary within the week, and the glimpse of the World to Come); 181, 207, 221 ff.; 286 (*Shabbat Chazon*); 288 (rejoicing on Shabbat before 9th of Av).

Shabbat Chazon, 286 ff.

Shalom DovBer, R., Fifth Lubavitcher Rebbe (1860-1920), 16 ff., 19.

Shammai, 317.

Shavuot, 178, 203, 206, 222, 227 ff., 351.

Shekalim, 119 ff. (for Sanctuary).

Shem, 6, 9.

Shema, 81; 81 (explanation of *Echad*); 207, 283; 298 ff. (differences between first and second paragraphs).

Shemini Atzeret, 349; 350 (day when uniqueness of Israel is revealed); 354 (concludes festive cycle beginning with Yom Kippur).

Shemittah (seventh year), 210 ff.

Shepherd, 89.

Shiloh, 78, 287.

Shimon ben Yochai, R., 218.

Shmuel, R., Fourth Lubavitcher Rebbe (1834-1882), 50.

Shofar, 295, 346.

Shulchan Aruch, 110, 289.

Sichon and Og, 324.

Sidra, 148 (each Sidra has an individual point of meaning); 180, 186; 189 (name of Sidra changed through the generations); 222 (connection with time of year); 252 (each Sidra has central theme); 297 ff. (relationship with Haftorah).

Simchat Torah, 353 ff.

Simeon (tribe of), 271 ff.

Simlai, R., 181; 183 ff. (his character in relation to his teaching).

Sin, sinner, 20 ("even the sinners of Israel are full of Mitzvot"); 24; 47 (the power to remain free from sin); 68, 131; 139 (drawing others into one's sin); 156 (the sin remaining in one's memory—or being effaced, and replaced by enthusiasm); 189 (transformed into merit); 237 (is irrational); 284 (a personal "Egypt"); 294 (through repentance, sins become merits); 308; 310 (in deepest transgression the power of oneness is manifest); 313 (for a Rebbe to help someone remedy his sin, he must find an analogous quality in himself); 343 (the possibility of sin a cause for weeping).

Sinai, 18 (before Sinai good deeds had only temporary effect on the world); 79 (at Sinai the "spirit of impurity" left the Jews); 80 (revelation of G-d's essence); 87; 90 (a two-way process); 103 ff. (intermingling of senses at Sinai); 118 (recreating Sinai when carrying out a Mitzvah); 140, 142, 167, 178, 206 ff., 217, 227; 228 (Sinai changed the nature of a Mitzvah); 230 (Sinai represents fusion of two opposites); 231 (at Sinai there was an annullment of the decree separating heaven and earth); 232, 285, 287; 307 (events prior to Sinai are not a basis for deriving law); 313; 318 (Sinai forged a bond between G-d and Israel); 322, 350; 353 (Messianic fulfillment began at Sinai).

Sivan, 203, 207 (spiritual aspect); 227, 230.

Slander, 188.

Social life, 327 (should be filled with spirituality). See also *Individual and Community*.

Social laws, 116.

Social status, 139.

Sockets (of the Sanctuary), 119.

Sodom, 307.

Soldier, 47 (confronts danger, but goes with song of joy).

Solomon, 206, 233, 289, 292, 350.

Sorrow, 289 (transformed into joy).

Soul, 11 (moving towards the essence of the soul); 19 (at the deepest level of the soul there is no distinction between the righteous and the ordinary); 25 (a life inspired by the essence of the soul); 30, 32, 52, 57; 61 (collective soul); 70 (revealing essence of soul); 73 (innermost soul never assents to a sin), 103 (all Jewish souls at Sinai); 113; 117 (inwardness of soul should be involved when carrying out Mitzvah); 120 (the Sanctuary of the soul); 125 (faculties of); 126 (the soul is void of all Will except that of G-d); 223; 242 ff. (seven kinds of soul symbolized by lamps of Menorah); 248 (the elevation of the soul is not the aim, rather the sanctification of the world); 326 (connecting the soul with its Divine source); 336 (the soul is strengthened by prayer).

Speech, 6 (purity of); 73 (three kinds of speech); 115; 283 (powerless to speak, for G-d is everything).

Spice box, 12.

Spies, 245 ff., 252.

Spiritual dimensions, 198.

Spirituality, 11 (spiritual journey of Abraham); 12, 14

(exile an integral part of spiritual progress); 33; 107 ff. (different stages of spiritual path); 198 (five spiritual dimensions); 251 (should not be self-centered); 314 (each level of spirituality has its own "refuge"); 327; 345 (the righteous are not concerned for their own spiritual satisfaction, but for the Divine Will); 352 (through repentance, a higher level of spirituality achieved than before the sin).

Spiritual leaders, 52; 285 (of generation); 330 (from heads of communities to heads of families).

Spring, 170 (climax of Egyptian cultic activities); 171 (represents epoch of modern technological achievement).

Statutes (*Chukim*), 216 (beyond understanding); 218 (signify engraving, words of Torah on one's soul); 258 ff.

Stealing, 116 ("thou shalt not steal" should be obeyed not only as reason but as G-d's Will).

Stringency, 39 (self-imposed).

Study, 121 (study, prayer and action); 163; 182 (stages in study); 200 (study alone insufficient); 218 (must be "engraved" in the Jew); 347 ("earthly" quality of Torah study). See also *Torah*.

Submission, 51 (expressed by bowing of sheaves in dream of Joseph). See also *Kabbalat Ol*.

Succot, 64 (seventy bullocks sacrificed represent the seventy nations); 281 (place name); 342; 350 (seventy bullocks sacrificed).

Sun and Moon, 48 ff., 145; 292 ("moon reached its fullness" in time of Solomon; future radiance of moon like that of sun in World to Come).

Suppression and Sublimation, 205 (of force of Animal Soul); 343 (suppression of desire to sin in Benoni).

Survival, 172 (depends on fidelity to Jewish tradition).

Syria, 326.

Tabernacles—see *Succot*.

Tablets—see *Ten Commandments*.

Talmud, 13, 113, 209, 211, (different levels of spirituality of Babylonian and Jerusalem Talmuds). See also *Index of Scriptural and Rabbinic Quotations*.

Tammuz—see *Seventeenth of Tammuz*.

Tanya, 182.

Targum, 254, 307.

Teacher and Pupil, 112, 233, 293, 299.

Tefillah—see *Amidah, Prayer, Psalms of Praise*.

Tefillin, 58 (binds Evil Inclination in service of G-d, and reveals G-dliness to all the peoples of the earth); 59 (Tefillin
campaign); 114, 157, 294,
299, 302.

Temple, 14, 59, 119; 125
(within each Jew); 210
(Second Temple); 213 ff.
(distinction between epochs
of First and Second Temple);
215 (Third Temple); 233
(apex of ascent of Jewish people towards G-d); 234
(distinction from Sanctuary);
242 ff.; 285 (destruction of
Temple); 286 (Third Tem-
ple); 288 (destruction of
Temple); 291 (Third Temple
will combine virtues of both
previous Temples); 292 (site
of Second Temple still sacred
after destruction); 295 (First
Temple represents righteousness, Second Temple—re-
pentance, Third Temple—
combination of both); 296
(Second Temple superior to
First); 339. See also *Sanctuary*.

Ten Commandments, 103 ff.,
116 ff. (should be obeyed as
Divine Will, not simply as
reason; 142; 296 (superiority
of second set of Tablets); 338;
351 ff. (breaking of the tablets); 354 (second tablets
given on Yom Kippur). See
also *Sinai*.

Ten Days of Repentance, 333
ff.; 342 (G-d close to every
Jew).

Teshuvah—see *Repentance*.

Tetragrammaton, 87, 155.

Thought, 125, 143 (remains
with Torah, while the hands
work); 184.

Three, 228 (three fold Torah,
people, etc.; significance of).

Three weeks, 285.

Time, 25 (a life inspired by the
essence of the soul is beyond
time); 27 (sanctification of
time by our actions); 91; 99
(time a human conception);
151 (within time, we must
not be bound by time; the
meeting of timelessness with
time); 162 (eighth day beyond
human time); 208 (beyond
time); 224 (the relation between G-d and the Jewish
soul is beyond time).

Tisha B'Av, 246, 285, 286, 290,
322.

Tithes, 18 (instituted by Isaac).

Torah, 2 ff. (architect's plan of
world); 8 (use of language);
10; 30 (different interpretations of Torah are linked); 33
(revealed and esoteric levels);
36 (studied by child); 37 (kept
by forefathers before it was
given); 57 (called "light," relates to Chanukah lights;
study of Torah releases Holy
sparks embedded in the forbidden); 58 (compared to Tefillin; 72 (contains no redun-

dant passages); 73 (inwardness of Torah); 78 (gives redemptive strength to the
Messiah and to Israel); 81
(makes world a dwelling place
for G-d); 86 (Divine Knowledge); 86 (learned by Forefathers); 88 (in itself, could lead
to detachment); 90 (translated
by Moses); 113 (different interpretations of Torah are
linked); 120 (every detail
eternally relevant); 124 (Infinite, in time and meaning;
four levels of interpretation);
127 (the only Jewish reality);
139; 148 (division into
Sidras); 163 (Torah study
should penetrate every facet
of being); 167 (law of life);
175 (in Messianic Age); 182
(stages of study); 194
(mystical teachings of); 197
(takes into consideration the
evil inclination); 217 (differences between Written
and Oral Torah); 226
(through Torah, Israel becomes unified with G-d); 228
(threefold); 230 (unity of opposites); 241 (not to compromise Torah); 254 (given to
make peace in the world); 256
ff. (brings together Heaven
and Earth); 282, 286; 294
(represents Divine light from
above; contrast with Mitzvot
and Repentance); 295 (all inner teachings of Torah are
reflected in Halacha); 298;

299 (taught from teacher to
disciples, and from father to
children); 302; 316 (given to
make peace in the world); 336
(Torah education); 341
(means "teaching"); 344
(mysteries of); 348 (contrasted with Mitzvot); 349
(passages from Torah read on
each festival); 351 ff. (honor
of Torah); 354 (repentance
reaches higher than Torah).
See also *Sefer Torah, Sinai,
Study.*

Tosefot, 210 ff.

Translation, 90 (Moses' translation of the Torah); 334
(inadequacy of translation).

Tree, 197, 326.

Tree of Knowledge, 78-79.

Trials, 12 (of Abraham); 61 (of
every Jew).

Tribes (twelve), 38.

Truth, 83 (is Oneness; explanation of *emet).*

Twelve Tribes, 38.

Tzaddik—see *Righteous Man.*

Tzemach Tzedek, Third
Lubavitcher Rebbe, **R.** Menachem Mendel (1789-1866),
16 ff., 45 ff.

Tzitzit (fringes), 146, 157, 294.

Understanding, 213 ff., 219
(accompanied by commit-
ment); 260 (laws beyond understanding). See also *Intellect,
Knowledge.*

Unity, 9; 74 (of sons of Jacob, in
order to receive Divine reve-

lation); 146 (of assembly of Israelites); 150 (of man and G-d); 170; 226 (through Torah, Israel becomes unified with G-d); 228 (two kinds of unity); 230; 316 (symbolized by Sefer Torah); 329 (unity of Israel is not achieved by every Jew being the same); 340; 354 (unity between G-d and Israel is source of Israel's spiritual power). See also *Oneness*.

Vacation, 314.
Vegetable Kingdom, 63.
Vision, 286 ff., 300 ff.
Vow, 277; 279 (annulment of).

Wedding, 41, 222, 237 ff.; 321 (of G-d and Israel). See also *Marriage*.
"We will do and we will hear," 321.
Wilderness, 250 (signifies spirituality and seclusion); 287, 291.
Will, 53 (nullification of); 63 ("a man is where his will is"); 98 (of righteous man); 125, 213; 302 (will to obey G-d survives Exile); 347 ("a man is where his will is"). See also *Divine Will*.
Wisdom, 83 (manifest in one's eating and drinking).
Women, 122.
Work, 2 ff., 51, 64, 65, 142 ff.; 327 (should be filled with spirituality). See also *Businessman*.

World, 4; 18 (transformed permanently through Torah); 43 (transformed to holiness by Jacob); 44; 50 (two "worlds" of Jew); 51 (material world must contribute to spiritual); 61 (conceals its spiritual source; created for sake of Israel); 78; 80 (purified by service in Exile); 81 (Hebrew name for world implies concealment of G-d); 106 (nullified before G-d); 111 (two paths: bringing G-d into the world, or raising world to G-d); 139 (Western world); 280 (man together with G-d has the power to annul the bondage of the world); 294 (world purified through Mitzvot); 295 (man's effort to purify world imparted sanctity to Second Temple); 310 (punishment is a remedy for harm done to the world); 327 (the aim is to draw spirituality into every aspect of the world); 348 (real task of man is to change the world, to make it G-d's dwelling); 355 (the Jew, through the G-dly power within him, can create a new world).
World to Come, 4, 23, 31; 35 (then the body will give life to the soul); 49, 67; 69 (comparison with This World); 139, 190; 284 (*Amidah* prayer a foretaste of); 288 (reflected in Sabbath);

292 (radiance of moon will be as that of sun); 353 (17th day of Tammuz will be a day of rejoicing).

Yisroel Baal Shem Tov, R. (1698-1760), 7, 51, 98, 128, 198 ff., 231; 234; 284 (taught that seeing faults in others indicates a trace of that fault in oneself); 285 (taught that salvation is implicit in trouble).

Yitzchak Luria, R. (d. 1572), 342 ff.

Yom Kippur, 142, 145, 193, 337, 347; 354 (day of giving of second tablets; begins festive cycle).

Yomim Noraim (Days of Awe), 330.

Yosef Yitzchak Schneersohn, R., sixth Lubavitcher Rebbe (1880-1950), 16, 32, 45, 47, 49, 117, 126, 156, 178, 236.

Zealots, 264 ff., 275.
Zecharia, 109.
Zimri, 263 ff., 271 ff.
Zodiac, 170. See also *Astrology*.
Zohar, 32 ff., 58, 73, 142, 237, 292. See also *Index of Scriptural and Rabbinic Quotations.*

ॐ • ॐ

הוצאת ספרים

קרני הוד תורה

קהת

ליובאוויטש